From Life

JULIA MARGARET CAMERON
& Victorian Photography

VICTORIA OLSEN

First published 2003 by PALGRAVE MACMILLAN™
175 Fifth Avenue, New York, N.Y. 10010 and
Houndmills, Basingstoke, Hampshire, England RG21 6XS.
Companies and representatives throughout the world.

PALGRAVE MACMILLAN is the global academic imprint of the
Palgrave Macmillan division of St. Martin's Press, LLC and of
Palgrave Macmillan Ltd. Macmillan® is a registered trademark
in the United States, United Kingdom and other countries.
Palgrave is a registered trademark in the European Union and
other countries.

ISBN 1-4039-6019-4

Library of Congress Cataloguing-in-Publication Data available
from
the Library of Congress.

First published in 2003 by Aurum Press Ltd.

First PALGRAVE MACMILLAN edition: October 2003.

10 9 8 7 6 5 4 3 2 1

Printed in the United States of America.

For Naomi and Amanda

CONTENTS

ACKNOWLEDGMENTS

I was very fortunate to have been working on this biography while the first complete catalogue raisonné of Cameron's photographs was being assembled and produced by the J. Paul Getty Museum and the National Museum of Photography, Film, and Television in England under the leadership of Julian Cox and Colin Ford. This ambitious and pathbreaking work will set the study and appreciation of Cameron's work on an entirely new footing, as scholars and readers are able to see the whole range of her production for the first time. Although the catalogue was not yet published when I finished my manuscript, I was the beneficiary of much valuable information that the contributors unearthed and I was privileged to read some of the text prior to its publication. Their book also allowed me to focus my own efforts on Cameron's life and world with the confidence that anyone wanting greater detail about her work would have a comprehensive source available.

My first and greatest debt, then, is to Julian Cox, whose knowledge of Cameron and her work was an inspiration and an invaluable resource for me. He was also the very model of a generous scholar and colleague. He shared his own work freely and he read mine carefully. He made this book not only better, but possible.

I have also been greatly and generously helped by the formidable research skills of John Beaumont, an "amateur" only in Cameron's sense. Joanne Lukitsh found time just before I went to press to review my manuscript and suggest important revisions. Her own work on Cameron has been a very important source for mine. Among the many other scholars who have offered me insights or assistance through this project a few stand out, including Brian Hinton and the scholars at the Institute for Research on Women and Gender at Stanford University in 1997–2000. Helmut Gernsheim, Brian Hill, Mike Weaver, and Amanda Hopkinson paved the way for all the work being done today, including my own.

Among the many archivists, librarians, and curators who have contributed to parts of this book, I would like to thank Chloe Barnes and Andrew Russell at the National Art Library in the Victoria & Albert Museum; Stuart Bligh and Helen Orme of the Centre for Kentish Studies, Kent County archives; Joanna Corden at the Royal Society, London; Robin Darwall-Smith of University College, Oxford; Emma Dennis at the Watts Gallery, Guildford; Wim deWit at the Getty Research Institute, Los Angeles;

Christine Dowland at the Isle of Wight County archives; Joy Eldridge, Elizabeth Inglis, and Dorothy Sheridan at the University of Sussex libraries; Robin Francis at the National Portrait Gallery, London; Elizabeth Fuller at the Rosenbach Library; Sue Gates at the Tennyson Research Centre; P. Hatfield at Eton College Library; Victoria Hesford and Linda Matthews at the Robert W. Woodruff Library at Emory University; Mary McNaughton at Scripps College; Leslie Morris at the Houghton Library, Harvard University; Emma Robinson at the University of London Library; Jim Wayre at the Canterbury Cathedral archives; Mrs. Ann Wheeler at the Charterhouse School; and Helen Samuels, my own archivist-at-large.

For help with picture research and permissions I would like to thank Colin Ford; Jacklyn Burns at the J. Paul Getty Museum; Linda Briscoe Myers at the Harry Ransom Humanities Research Center at the University of Texas at Austin; Caroline Nutley at the Art Institute of Chicago; Ron Smith and the staff at Dimbola Lodge, Freshwater; Sarah Sykes at the Science and Society Picture Library in London; Marilyn Ward at the Royal Botanic Garden at Kew; and most of all, Violet Hamilton at the Wilson Centre for Photography, who generously shared both her photographs and her contacts with me. Meir Berk, Harriet Einsiedel, and Michael Mattis provided art from their own collections and graciously permitted its publication. Photographer Margrit Olsen documented Cameron's house on the Isle of Wight for me.

For financial support I would like to thank the Harry Ransom Humanities Research Center for awarding me an Andrew Mellon visiting fellowship and the Institute for Research on Women and Gender at Stanford University for awarding me a Marilyn Yalom grant. Irene Skolnick and Arabella Stein were enthusiastic and sensitive agents for the book and I am thankful that they found it such attentive and scrupulous editors in Kristi Long and Michael Flamini at Palgrave and Karen Ings at Aurum Press.

During the long years of working on this book I relied on the advice and support of many, including Regenia Gagnier, Barbara Gelpi, Gerhard Joseph, Fred Kaplan, Merloyd Lawrence, Rob Polhemus, Joyce Seltzer, Jack Hall, and the members of his National Endowment for the Humanities summer seminar on literary biography in 1996. I have been lucky in my early readers too, especially Stephen Espie, Earle Olsen, Josh Seiden, and my reading group: Christina Boufis, Laura Mann, Lisa Nakamura, Christina Olsen, and Susie Wise. At different stages, each offered invaluable encouragement and feedback. The people who enabled me to spend my time writing and researching have more than earned their acknowledgment, especially Roberta Espie Barry, Robert Barry, and Henry and Sara Seiden, who (among other things) provided an ideal writer's colony, complete with childcare. Other friends and friends of friends who kindly stepped in and steered me when I needed steer-

Acknowledgments

ing include Steven Amsterdam, Abigail Asher, and David Rakoff.

Finally, my deepest thanks to Josh, Naomi, and Amanda, who gave me reasons to write the book in the first place and then helped me do so.

Any errors and all opinions are, of course, my own.

LIST OF ILLUSTRATIONS

Julia Margaret Cameron, *Annie, My First Success*, January 1864. 18 × 14.3 cm. Albumen print. Courtesy of the J. Paul Getty Museum, Los Angeles.

Julia Margaret Cameron, *Charles Hay Cameron*, 1864. 29.1 × 22.3 cm. Albumen print. Courtesy of the J. Paul Getty Museum, Los Angeles.

Henry Herschel Hay Cameron, *Julia Margaret Cameron*, 1874. 25.6 × 21.6 cm. Albumen print. Courtesy of the J. Paul Getty Museum, Los Angeles.

Julia Margaret Cameron, *The Double Star*, April 1864, 25.4 × 20 cm. Albumen print. Courtesy of the J. Paul Getty Museum, Los Angeles.

Julia Margaret Cameron, *Paul and Virginia*, 1864. Albumen print. 26.6 × 21.1 cm. Courtesy of the J. Paul Getty Museum, Los Angeles.

Unknown photographer, *Julia Margaret Cameron with her two youngest sons, Charlie and Henry Herschel Hay*, c. 1858. Courtesy of the Wilson Centre for Photography, London.

Unknown photographer, *Julia Margaret Cameron and her daughter Julia Hay Cameron in a garden*, c. 1858. Courtesy of the collection of Meir Berk.

Henry Herschel Hay Cameron, *Portrait of Julia Margaret Cameron by G. F. Watts (1852)*, 1890. 23.5 × 18.9 cm. Platinum print. Courtesy of the J. Paul Getty Museum, Los Angeles.

Daniel Maclise, illustration for *Leonora* by Gottfried Bürger, translated by Julia Margaret Cameron, London: Longman, Green, and Longmans, 1847.

Julia Margaret Cameron, *The Whisper of the Muse/Portrait of G. F. Watts*, April 1865, 26.1 × 21.5 cm. Albumen print. Courtesy of the J. Paul Getty Museum, Los Angeles.

Julia Margaret Cameron, *Angel of the Nativity*, 1872, 32.7 × 24.3 cm. Albumen print. Courtesy of the J. Paul Getty Museum, Los Angeles.

J.-F. Garneray, Pattle family portrait, 1818. Private collection.

Unknown photographer, Dimbola Lodge, *c.* 1871. Reproduced with the permission of the Julia Margaret Cameron Trust, Dimbola Lodge, Freshwater Bay.

Oscar Rejlander, *Mrs. Cameron Receiving the Post*, 1863. Collection of Michael Mattis and Judith Hochberg.

Julia Margaret Cameron, *Hardinge Hay Cameron*, May 1864, 24.9 × 19.5 cm. Albumen print. Courtesy of the J. Paul Getty Museum, Los Angeles.

Julia Margaret Cameron, *Pray God Bring Father Safely Home*, 1872/1910. 37.7 × 29.5 cm. Gelatin silver print. Courtesy of the J. Paul Getty Museum, Los Angeles.

Julia Margaret Cameron, *Alfred Tennyson*, May 1865. 25.6 × 21 cm. Albumen print. Courtesy of the J. Paul Getty Museum, Los Angeles.

Julia Margaret Cameron, *Sir Henry Taylor (A Rembrandt)*, 1866, 10½ × 7⅞ in. Albumen print. Courtesy of the J. Paul Getty Museum, Los Angeles.

Julia Margaret Cameron, *Grace Thro' Love*, 1865, 24.8 × 19.6 cm. Albumen print. Courtesy of the J. Paul Getty Museum, Los Angeles.

Julia Margaret Cameron, *Prayer and Praise*, 1865, 28.1 × 22.7 cm. Albumen print. Courtesy of the J. Paul Getty Museum, Los Angeles.

Julia Margaret Cameron, *The Shunamite Woman and her dead Son*, 1865, 27.1 × 21.4 cm. Albumen print. Courtesy of the J. Paul Getty Museum, Los Angeles.

Julia Margaret Cameron, *Ellen Terry at Age Sixteen*, 1864/1875, 24.1 cm. diameter. Carbon print. Courtesy of the J. Paul Getty Museum, Los Angeles.

Julia Margaret Cameron, *Thomas Carlyle*, 1867, 36.4 × 25.8 cm. Albumen print. Courtesy of the J. Paul Getty Museum, Los Angeles.

Julia Margaret Cameron, *J. F W. Herschel*, April 1867. 35.5 × 27.4 cm. Albumen print. Courtesy of the J. Paul Getty Museum, Los Angeles.

Julia Margaret Cameron, *Romeo and Juliet*, 1867. Reproduced with the permission of the Julia Margaret Cameron Trust, Dimbola Lodge, Freshwater Bay.

Julia Margaret Cameron, *The Bride (Annie Chinery)*, November 1869. Collection of Michael Mattis and Judith Hochberg.

Julia Margaret Cameron, *Anne Isabella Thackeray (Lady Ritchie)*, *c.*1867, 31.8 × 23.5 cm. Courtesy of the Gernsheim Collection, Harry Ransom Humanities Research Center, University of Texas at Austin.

Julia Margaret Cameron, *Ewen Wrottesley Hay Cameron*, 1865, 25.5 × 20 cm. Albumen print. Courtesy of the J. Paul Getty Museum, Los Angeles.

Julia Margaret Cameron, *Henry Herschel Hay Cameron*, about 1870, 34.2 x 25.5 cm. Albumen print. Courtesy of the J. Paul Getty Museum, Los Angeles."

Julia Margaret Cameron, *My Son Eugene of the R.A.*, 1867. Courtesy of the Science and Society Picture Library, London.

Julia Margaret Cameron, *Charlie Hay Cameron*, October 28, 1867, 24.5 × 19.1 cm. Albumen print. Courtesy of the J. Paul Getty Museum, Los Angeles.

Julia Margaret Cameron, *Mrs. Herbert Duckworth*, April 1867, 34.2 × 26.2 cm. Albumen print. Courtesy of the J. Paul Getty Museum, Los Angeles.

Julia Margaret Cameron, *King Arthur*, 1874, 36 × 28.5 cm. Albumen print. Courtesy of the J. Paul Getty Museum, Los Angeles.

Julia Margaret Cameron, *Vivien and Merlin*, September 1874, 31 × 21.6 cm. Albumen print. Courtesy of the J. Paul Getty Museum, Los Angeles.

Julia Margaret Cameron, *'So Like a Shatter'd Column Lay the King'*, 1875, 35 × 27.5 cm. Albumen print. Courtesy of the J. Paul Getty Museum, Los Angeles.

Julia Margaret Cameron, *Déjatch Alámayou*, 1868. Courtesy of the Wilson Centre for Photography, London.

Julia Margaret Cameron, *Marianne North*, 1876. Courtesy of the Director and the Board of Trustees of the Royal Botanic Gardens, Kew.

Julia Margaret Cameron, *Cingalese Girl*, 1875–78, 25.3 × 18.9 cm. Albumen print. Courtesy of the J. Paul Getty Museum, Los Angeles.

Julia Margaret Cameron, British, 1815–79, Ceylon (two natives, one with vase over head), *c.* 1875, albumen print from wet collodion negative, 27.5 × 22.8 cm., Harriott A. Fox Fund, 1970.843, image © The Art Institute of Chicago.

Julia Margaret Cameron, British, 1815–79, Ceylon (unidentified girl with drape over head), *c.* 1875, albumen print from wet collodion negative, 25.5 × 19.3 cm., Harriott A. Fox Fund, 1970.841, image © The Art Institute of Chicago.

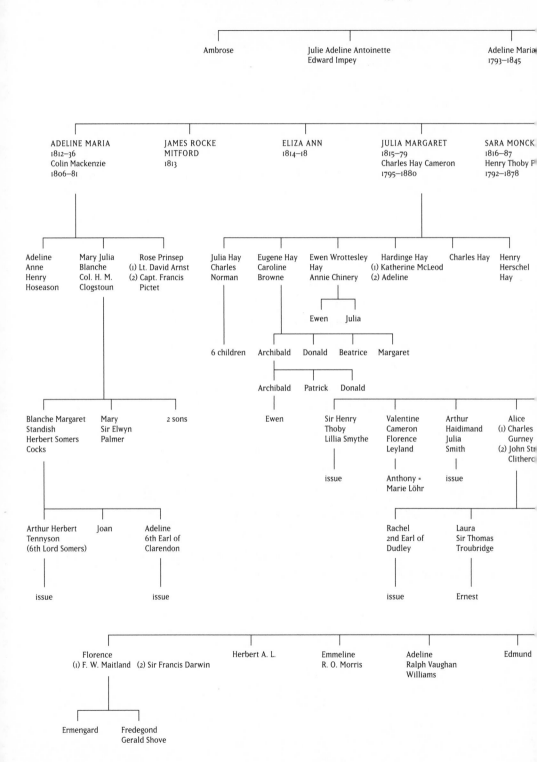

Ambrose Pierre Antoine
Chevalier de L'Étang
1757–1840

Ambrose

Julie Adeline Antoinette
Edward Impey

Adeline Maria
1793–1845

ADELINE MARIA
1812–36
Colin Mackenzie
1806–81

JAMES ROCKE
MITFORD
1813

ELIZA ANN
1814–18

JULIA MARGARET
1815–79
Charles Hay Cameron
1795–1880

SARA MONCK
1816–87
Henry Thoby P
1792–1878

Adeline
Anne
Henry
Hoseason

Mary Julia
Blanche
Col. H. M.
Clogstoun

Rose Prinsep
(1) Lt. David Arnst
(2) Capt. Francis
Pictet

Julia Hay
Charles
Norman

Eugene Hay
Caroline
Browne

Ewen Wrottesley
Hay
Annie Chinery

Hardinge Hay
(1) Katherine McLeod
(2) Adeline

Charles Hay

Henry
Herschel
Hay

Ewen   Julia

6 children   Archibald   Donald   Beatrice   Margaret

Archibald   Patrick   Donald

Blanche Margaret
Standish
Herbert Somers
Cocks

Mary
Sir Elwyn
Palmer

2 sons

Ewen

Sir Henry
Thoby
Lillia Smythe

Valentine
Cameron
Florence
Leyland

Arthur
Haidimand
Julia
Smith

Alice
(1) Charles
Gurney
(2) John Str
Clitherc

issue

Anthony ⹀
Marie Löhr

issue

Arthur Herbert
Tennyson
(6th Lord Somers)

Joan

Adeline
6th Earl of
Clarendon

Rachel
2nd Earl of
Dudley

Laura
Sir Thomas
Troubridge

issue

issue

issue

Ernest

Florence
(1) F. W. Maitland   (2) Sir Francis Darwin

Herbert A. L.

Emmeline
R. O. Morris

Adeline
Ralph Vaughan
Williams

Edmund

Ermengard

Fredegond
Gerald Shove

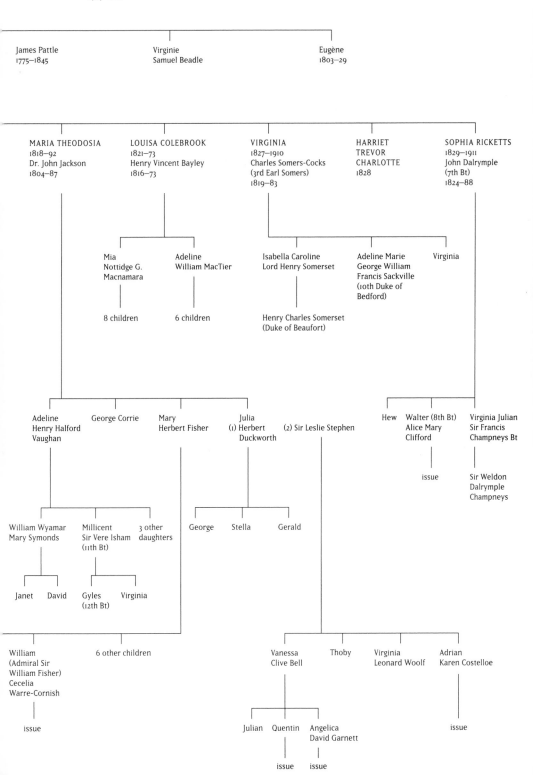

Thérèse Josephe Blin
de Grincourt
1767–1866

James Pattle
1775–1845

Virginie
Samuel Beadle

Eugène
1803–29

MARIA THEODOSIA
1818–92
Dr. John Jackson
1804–87

LOUISA COLEBROOK
1821–73
Henry Vincent Bayley
1816–73

VIRGINIA
1827–1910
Charles Somers-Cocks
(3rd Earl Somers)
1819–83

HARRIET
TREVOR
CHARLOTTE
1828

SOPHIA RICKETTS
1829–1911
John Dalrymple
(7th Bt)
1824–88

Mia
Nottidge G.
Macnamara

Adeline
William MacTier

Isabella Caroline
Lord Henry Somerset

Adeline Marie
George William
Francis Sackville
(10th Duke of
Bedford)

Virginia

8 children

6 children

Henry Charles Somerset
(Duke of Beaufort)

Adeline
Henry Halford
Vaughan

George Corrie

Mary
Herbert Fisher

Julia
(1) Herbert
Duckworth

(2) Sir Leslie Stephen

Hew

Walter (8th Bt)
Alice Mary
Clifford

Virginia Julian
Sir Francis
Champneys Bt

issue

Sir Weldon
Dalrymple
Champneys

William Wyamar
Mary Symonds

Millicent
Sir Vere Isham
(11th Bt)

3 other
daughters

George

Stella

Gerald

Janet

David

Gyles
(12th Bt)

Virginia

William
(Admiral Sir
William Fisher)
Cecelia
Warre-Cornish

6 other children

Vanessa
Clive Bell

Thoby

Virginia
Leonard Woolf

Adrian
Karen Costelloe

issue

Julian

Quentin

Angelica
David Garnett

issue

issue

issue

Orlando in Los Angeles

It was now November. After November, comes December. Then January, February, March, and April. After April comes May. June, July, August follow. Next is September. Then October, and so, behold, here we are back at November again, with a whole year accomplished.

This method of writing biography, though it has its merits, is a little bare, perhaps, and the reader, if we go on with it, may complain that he could recite the calendar for himself and so save his pocket whatever sum the publisher may think proper to charge for this book . . .

– Virginia Woolf, *Orlando* (1928)

T O READ Julia Margaret Cameron's letters one must go to Los Angeles, so one windy day several years ago I took a car to a plane to a shuttle van to a tall office building in Santa Monica and got in a shiny mirrored elevator and pressed a button. In *Orlando*, her fictional biography of a Renaissance-man-turned-Edwardian-woman, Virginia Woolf writes that modern inventions require a renewal of one's faith in magic. Orlando rides the elevator of a department store and muses: "In the eighteenth century, we knew how everything was done; but here I rise through the air; I listen to voices from America; I see men flying – but how it's done I can't even begin to wonder."[1] For Woolf, the transformation to modernity occurred in the nineteenth century, when Orlando turned from male to female, when revolutionary technologies like the telegraph and electricity were invented, and when her Great Aunt Julia took up the new and unexplored art and science of photography. With its ability to fix images in time and place, photography was itself one of those magical Victorian inventions. Miraculously, it confirmed the presence of an absent loved one, just as it now implacably brings the past into the present.

The first letters of Cameron's that I read were incongruously, ridiculously located above a bank in an office building. Yet inside that modern wrapping paper were the

1

letters themselves: tiny envelopes scratched by fountain pens and sealed with wax, delightfully addressed to "Mrs. Cameron, Garden Reach, Calcutta." Those letters and many family papers were carefully preserved by her son Hardinge Hay Cameron, who had a successful career in the colonial civil service like his father. Hardinge carried his mother's letters, his parents' marriage settlement contract, and his official correspondence from Ceylon (now Sri Lanka) to England and back again many times, and they have been labeled in his neat handwriting and bundled with string into little packets.

It is a function of the Victorian age of mechanical reproduction, and the medium of photography, that Cameron's images are easily available in countless books and postcards, as well as museum collections all over the world. Her handwriting can be seen on many prints in some variation of her familiar credit line: "From Life, Copyright Julia Margaret Cameron." But her letters – the relatively few that survive – are uncollected, unedited, and often uncatalogued. To read them I had to e-mail scholars, type letters to librarians, and fly to special collections. I have no way of knowing if I found them all, but I doubt I did.[2] Once found, the letters must be deciphered. Dates – and sometimes whole pages – may be missing. Cameron's large, sprawling hand – often squeezing only a few words per line to each small square of paper – must be transcribed onto my laptop. I must guess what conversations preceded the letter and how her correspondent may have replied. And I must try to immerse myself in Cameron's profoundly different culture – to conjure up her breathing body writing those letters and taking those photographs – even when I emerge blinking and dizzy after a day in the library onto the streets of Los Angeles or Austin, Texas.

The world had changed dramatically during Cameron's lifetime. Her grandparents were French aristocrats in the service of Marie Antoinette; her children would be civil servants in the embattled British Empire. Railways, steamships, and the Suez Canal were shrinking the distances Cameron once traveled. Cameron had entered an international, aristocratic culture, whose members dominated politics and the professions, lived off their rent rolls, and bought their art and literature by commission and subscription. The England she left had extended voting privileges twice, demoted the House of Lords, and taken over the administration of India from the private British East India Company. Women had been granted legal rights to their own children and property, though they were still denied the vote. Victorian science had mapped the heavens and traced the evolution of the species. The Church of England had survived attacks from within and without, but it was losing many of its exclusive privileges. Church and civil service reform, the development of public education, and the rapid growth of industry and trade meant that power was less and less exclusive to landowners.

Consumer culture had arrived, with its cheap paperback novels, mass-produced celebrity portraits, and ready-made fashions. By the 1870s, authors were less likely to know their readers, and more likely to publish under their own names. Artists were knighted and art lovers now crowded into public museums. Actors, musicians, and ballet dancers all mingled in the best society. Photographs had migrated from the scientist's laboratory to the amateur's studio, the bourgeois parlor, and the shop window.

This is the story of photography's struggle to become an art form and one determined middle-aged woman's struggle to become an artist. Like Orlando, Cameron transformed herself. She lived the first half of her life as a stereotypical nineteenth-century daughter, wife, and mother. She gave parties, collected money for charities, and raised six children. Then one day in 1864 she reinvented herself as a photographer and put all her formidable energy into pursuing models, money, and acclaim. She was surrounded by geniuses and related to great beauties, and she started photographing many of them. Her move from private to public life, from amateur to professional, from the domestic sphere to the art world reflects the transformations of her times. Despite her famous eccentricities and her singular talent, her life and work illuminate the most rarefied parts of Victorian culture and society. She lived within a charmed circle at the center of Victorian culture, and it is in part her own work that keeps that Victorian past before our eyes.

In a sense, Cameron's story begins when her great-niece Virginia Woolf began writing it down. Before then, Cameron's work had been the subject of revived interest among turn-of-the-century art photographers, but her life had been mostly the object of family legends as anecdotes about her passed from generation to generation. Then, in 1926, Woolf collaborated with Roger Fry to publish a selection of Cameron's photographs for the Hogarth Press. Woolf wrote the biographical essay, which drew on family stories and Victorian memoirs to celebrate Cameron's accomplishments and eccentricities, while Fry wrote a modernist re-evaluation of her work. Fry's critique of Cameron's work set the standard for the twentieth-century reception of her photographs: he admired the portraits and dismissed the allegorical photographs as mawkishly sentimental.[3] Although recent feminist criticism[4] has questioned the gendered division of her work into masterpieces (usually the portraits of men) and failures (especially the narrative tableaux of women and children), this long-held critical view is still influential today.

If Fry framed Cameron's photographs for modern viewers, Woolf traced her life for modern readers. In addition to working with Fry on *Victorian Photographs of Famous Men and Fair Women*, she wrote *Freshwater*, a play about Cameron, in 1923. It was revised and performed privately in 1935 with the leading members of the Bloomsbury group acting all the parts. It was a perfect homage: the intensely gifted Bloomsbury clan pretending to be their own Victorian forerunners, the elite circle of artists, authors, beauties, and celebrities who passed through the Tennyson and Cameron homes on Freshwater Bay on the Isle of Wight. Both circles were held together by sisters – the five Pattle sisters and the two Stephen sisters – who forged the links between the private bonds of family and the public world of culture. Woolf's comic and mythic exaggerations of Cameron's life make the family stories into public performances.

It seems almost a shame to look backwards past Woolf's early-twentieth-century view of Cameron toward the Victorian "reality." But the real history behind Cameron's extraordinary work is not just the semi-fictional stories of eccentric privilege; it is also the story of Victorian culture itself, and the development of mass media. Cameron was well situated for her new career – domestically, socially, and even historically: she learned to take photographs at the very moment when the public learned to view them. Photography was still a wide-open field at mid-century. By describing her work as "recording faithfully the greatness of the inner as well as the features of the outer man,"[5] Cameron points to the paradox of her art, and that of all artistic photography: the push and pull between the artist's vision and the camera's viewfinder, between the internal essence and the external reality. The Victorians were already sensitive to these paradoxes, but they hadn't yet made up their minds about them.

As Cameron knew, the study of the human – the body, the soul, the individual – could be a powerful antidote to the rapid changes and disorienting technologies of the nineteenth century. As she wrote to one friend in 1869,

> Yes – the history of the human face is a book we don't tire of, if we can get its grand truths, & learn them by heart. The life has so much to do with the individual character of each face influencing form as well as expression so much – + it is so refreshing to meet one who has not had enthusiasm trodden out but in whose soul love + reverence + trust survive the dust of this 19th Century life of hurry + worry, crush + crowd –[6]

Cameron always insisted on photography's status as an art that could express the inner "greatness," the "grand truths." In some ways, the confusion surrounding photography's status helped Cameron's career, but it also sabotaged her critical reception at the time. Critics and photographers either admired Cameron's obvious efforts to draw on Renaissance portraiture or they reviled her technical abilities. Many felt that her work was not soft-focus but out of focus, due to her supposed ineptitude with a camera. They condemned her for exhibiting photographs with spots and smears on them: one successful contemporary coolly pointed out that "it is not the mission of photography to produce smudges."[7] Her colleagues argued that photography was a mechanical process in which technical perfection should super-sede any artistic intentions.

Before the 1850s, few people had ever seen a photograph, and it wasn't until the 1860s, when Cameron took up her camera, that photographs were widely available to the working classes. The Victorian journalist Henry Mayhew included an astonishing interview with a street photographer in his 1861 classic *London Labour and the London Poor*. The street photographer was able to get away with all kinds of fraud because people didn't know what to expect of a photograph. When portraits turned out badly, he charged extra for "brightening solutions" or "American Air-Preserver" papers, or he would promise them the likenesses would "come out" in a few hours. He charged them a penny to have their warts painfully removed by a photographic acid, two pence to be mesmerized by the camera, and a shilling to dye their hair and whiskers with nitrate of silver (though it stained their skin too). But the best scam was when he and his partner didn't have enough time or light to take a photograph at all . . . and they offered their sitter someone else's likeness.

When a young woman complained that "this isn't me; it's got a widow's cap, and I was never married in all my life!," the photographers persuaded her that "this ain't a cap, it's the shadow of the hair." Another woman saw her picture and cried out, "Bless me! there's a child: I haven't ne'er a child!" She was told, "It's the way you sat; and what occasioned it was a child passing through the yard." Only once did the scam fail: when they offered an elderly woman a photograph of a sailor as her portrait.

> But she put on her spectacles, and she looked at it up and down, . . . and she cries, 'Why this is a man! here's the whiskers.' I left and Jim tried to humbug her, for I was bursting with laughing. Jim said, 'It's you, ma'am; and a very excellent likeness, I assure you.' But she kept saying, 'Nonsense, I ain't a man,' and wouldn't have it.[8]

The canny photographer concluded, "People don't know their own faces. Half of 'em have never looked in a glass half a dozen times in their life, and directly they see a pair of eyes and a nose, they fancy they are their own."

People had to learn to see photographs, just as they had learned to read the popular triple-decker novel. They had to learn how to interpret the shades of gray, the shadows, the lights, the miniature features. Cameron understood that. She emphasized faces, lit them dramatically, and made her photographs as large as possible. Photography was perhaps the first technological mystery in a century full of them. Cameron mastered it, and her work helped make those Victorian "famous men and fair women" recognizable today.

PART ONE

Pattledom

CHAPTER I

The Empire's Children

A squat middle-aged woman bustles around a small, rickety shed with quick, decisive motions. Her name is Julia Margaret Cameron, and she is related to Victorian aristocrats and empire builders, though one wouldn't know it to look at her now. Holding a large plate of glass in one hand, she struggles to lift a heavy can with the other hand in order to pour collodion evenly over the glass surface. This chemical solution makes the glass negative sensitive to light, and Cameron places the wet glass plate carefully into a wooden frame in her camera. "No dust, no cracks, no hairs this time, please!" she mutters to herself. The photograph must now be taken before the collodion dries.

Her photography studio has been converted from a chicken coop into a glasshouse: the walls and floors are of thin wood but the ceiling is all glass skylight, to let in as much as possible of the dim English sun over the Isle of Wight. It is January 1864 and bitterly cold. The windows are open to let out the suffocating odor of chemicals, and an icy wind blows in from the Solent nearby. Despite the piles of Indian shawls she has swathed herself in, Cameron's hands are turning blue and stiff, making it hard to adjust the curtains so that the light falls on the model's face just so. The child-model too is shivering, and Cameron sharply reprimands her to be still. "A little cold is nothing – and you must be still or you'll ruin poor Mrs. Cameron's picture!" The child buttons her sweater higher, and Cameron brushes the shaggy brown hair from her face. She stares at the child, then moves the girl's chin so that the light bisects her face in a vertical line above the row of buttons.

Just nine years old, Annie already knows she must obey this short, imperious woman. She is good friends with the great poet, who strides about in a flapping black coat and wide-brimmed hat. So when Mrs. Cameron drew her away from the other children playing outside with the promise of sweetmeats if she could stay very still . . . she felt she had no choice, and it might, after all, be fun. It had been fun at first, before the cold and the dreary boredom set in.

The bulky camera on a tripod takes up most of the room, and Cameron disappears beneath its black curtain. "Stay, Annie, stay! For Mrs. Cameron's sake, don't move a hair! The chemicals are dear, and my poor strength is fading. You mustn't waste them!" were the muffled words from beneath the curtain. Cameron screws her lens into focus and opens the aperture, exposing the wet glass plate for one . . . two . . . three minutes . . . . Annie wonders where the candy might be hidden. There are no shelves or cabinets in the bare room, just bottles and cans of foul-smelling stuff and piles of curtains and drapes. For three minutes the two people barely breathe while the light works its magic.

Cameron rushes into motion again, taking the glass plate from its wooden frame in the camera and racing from the shed. Annie observes quietly; she has not yet been given permission to move. In her darkroom, formerly a coalhouse, Cameron mixes and pours more chemicals over the glass. Her hands are black with stains; her sons fear she will be poisoned if the chemicals get into her blood. Cameron turns to several jugs of water that she has carried in from the well outside and washes the negative several times. Finally, she places it in another wooden frame that presses the glass negative against specially treated paper.

Leaving this frame in the sun to print out an image, Cameron returns to the child. "My dear, you are an angel from above! I do believe this one took – after all those blotched and blurry efforts! You will be immortalized in Art, child! Bless you, sweet sunny-haired little Annie! – let me find something for you. Hmmm . . . candles, feathers, no, let me look . . ." She dashes out of the shed again, pulling the child by the hand. "Mary, Henry, what have we for this delightful child? She has quite made my picture! My first success!" While the household looks on in amusement, Cameron runs around the big rambling house piling Annie's arms full of odd knick-knacks – a colorful glass paperweight, a tin of Indian curry, a lace doily embroidered by one of Cameron's nieces, a well-thumbed edition of Mary Howitt's Girlhoods of Shakespeare's Heroines. *Annie is satisfied with the peppermint stick, and later Cameron formally presents the perfected photograph to her father* [see figure].

T HE FIRST KNOWN PORTRAIT of the English Victorian photographer Julia Margaret Cameron is actually a French Romantic painting [see figure]. Painted in around 1818 by Jean-François Garneray, a student of the neoclassicist Jacques-Louis David, the painting shows an elegant bourgeois family. The mother reclines graciously on a bench, while her four eldest girls lean against her. As the third eldest, Julia Margaret is probably the small child at the far left of the canvas, with her arms full of flowers. The females are all dressed alike, in Regency gowns with puffed sleeves and flounces around the hems. Flowers are everywhere: large bouquets frame the family group and blossoms seem to spill out onto the girls' arms and laps. The composition centers on the female group of mother and daughters, emphasized by the pale masses of their dresses and the poses and flowers that unite them as they lean into each other. The father, on the other hand, stands behind the bench in dark clothes, facing in the opposite direction. One would never know from this portrait that the family had lived in French and English colonies in India for generations. Julia Margaret's parents, Adeline de l'Etang and James Pattle, were born and married in the Indian colonies, though each of them was educated at least partly in Europe, as was the custom among colonial families. Together they founded a clan that would be determinedly English by the end of the century, and that would pride itself on its birthright of beauty and privilege. The beauty was already apparent in this early portrait.

The painting as a whole achieves a balance through the contrast between the feminine and masculine figures, between the pale and the dark, the seated and the standing. James Pattle seems a little ghostly in the portrait: the contours of his frame seem to bleed into the background and his form seems less finished than those of the women. There is in fact a family tradition that James wasn't present for the sitting at all, but painted in from a miniature: Garneray is never known to have painted in India and James Pattle does not seem to have visited Europe at that time.[1] Ironically, the painting anticipates the marvels of retouching that photography will accomplish later in the century: though photography seems unable to represent a sitter who wasn't present, in fact printing from mulitiple negatives enabled combination prints even by mid-century. It seems likely that James's position in the Garneray painting is literally that of the absent father – living, but somehow superfluous to the girls and women who dominated the household. Educated by a grandmother who lived apart from her husband, surrounded by six sisters to whom she was extremely close, and later a founding mother of a clan that included generations of independent women, Julia Margaret began life as she meant to go on, forging her own identity and finding support from the women around her.

The Garneray portrait is pure Romanticism, from the studied informality of the family group to James Pattle's Byronic sideburns. The daughters are miniature versions of their mother, which reveals the culture's assumptions about the shared traits of bourgeois women and children: helplessness, vulnerability, and innocence. The portrait is an apt reminder of the world Cameron entered, where even an Anglo-Indian[2] family like the Pattles looked to the European bourgeoisie for their standards of behavior and appearance.[3] There is no sign of India in this representation of the family. It is interesting, then, to contrast this first portrait of Julia Margaret with the last: a portrait of the photographer taken by her son in 1874 [see figure]. By that time, Julia Margaret was a well-established professional, a fifty-nine-year-old woman with grown children, an English matron. The portrait shows her swathed in Indian shawls, a substantial figure who fills the frame. Her hair is graying and uncurled. Her hands are capable and almost rough around the knuckles. Her expression is firm – not cold, certainly, but not warm and yielding either. Like most of Julia Margaret's own work, the portrait emerges from a deep black background, without any details to reveal time or place except for the Indian shawls. While the 1874 portrait doesn't literally represent her as a professional photographer, it couldn't be further from the portrait of elegant maternity that Garneray painted of Julia Margaret's mother decades before. This portrait reveals a woman who had stood her ground against the photographic establishment for the past ten years and hectored the celebrities of her age to sit still for her. Cameron had changed, of course, but so had her times.

Julia Margaret Cameron was born Julia Margaret Pattle on June 11, 1815, seven days before the Battle of Waterloo that ended the devastating Napoleonic Wars between England and France. With England's victory, the eighteenth century was officially over – the wheel of fortune that had brought down the *ancien régime* in France, had crippled the French Revolution, and had brought Napoleon to power was taking another fateful turn, and now it was England that was on the rise. Though Queen Victoria was not yet born, the Victorian age can be said to have begun; by century's end, the queen would be Empress of India and ruler over the first truly global empire. Industrialization in England was well under way, transforming the class structure and shifting the traditional base of power from land to capital. Inspired by the revolutions in France and America, Romanticism was in full bloom in England and France: many Europeans were questioning established traditions of the eighteenth century, from child-rearing practices to religious worship. The Romantics looked at nature with fresh eyes and saw beauty, the sublime, or even God. In 1815 Samuel Coleridge, Mary and Percy Shelley, and Jane Austen were all in the middle of their careers. It was a good year to be born English.

But Julia Margaret was not born on William Blake's green and pleasant isle. And the outcome of the Napoleonic wars must have been much on the minds of her parents as they awaited the birth of their third child. James Pattle and Adeline de l'Etang lived in Calcutta, then the capital of the British government in India. James was an eccentric Englishman and a high-ranking employee of the British East India Company, a private, for-profit institution that governed the British colony and dominated trade in India from the late seventeenth century until the mid-nineteenth century. Adeline was a beautiful daughter of French émigrés. She had been born and raised in the French colony of Pondicherry, south of Madras on the eastern coast of India.

The Pattles had a stolid history of serving the British East India Company as clerks and judges for generations. James had been born in 1775 in Bengal in northeastern India, where the British were consolidating their hold on the subcontinent against the rival trading companies of the French, Dutch, Danish, and Portuguese. India's position in the middle of the trade routes between Asia and Europe had attracted European colonists since the Renaissance. The decline of the Moghul empire in the eighteenth century meant that new territories were ripe for development and lucrative concessions could be wrested by force or treaty from native rulers.

The European wars of the eighteenth century spilled over into skirmishes on their colonial turfs. The French and English had both established outposts along the Hooghly River in Bengal and along the eastern coast of India in Pondicherry and Madras respectively. The decades of strife between them over the American colonies and later the Napoleonic Wars led to regular squabbling in both regions. The French captured Madras in the mid-eighteenth century and the English returned the favor by capturing Pondicherry several times in later years. Julia Margaret's English, French, and Indian heritages reflected both the fluid composition of colonial cultures and also the impact of international events on a specific family.

This is especially true of Julia Margaret's French lineage through her mother, Adeline de l'Etang. Adeline's father, the Chevalier Antoine de l'Etang, came from a long-established noble family. At age thirteen he had been made a page to the young Marie Antoinette at the court of Versailles and later a member of King Louis XVI's Garde du Corps. Family rumor held that the Chevalier had been perhaps too intimate with the young queen, and that she had given him a gift of a miniature of herself that was buried with him at his death. It is at least certain that he was suddenly exiled from Versailles to serve in a cavalry regiment in Pondicherry some time in the 1780s.[4] Thus he was luckily not in France when the Revolution broke out and the king and queen were executed: his association with the unpopular queen would have certainly endangered his life.

In 1788 the Chevalier married Thérèse Josephe Blin de Grincourt, whose family had already been in Pondicherry for generations. Her grandfather was probably a French-Swiss Calvinist named Abraham Guerre who came to Pondicherry as the director of its new hospital. In the eighteenth century relations between the colonized and the colonists were less formal and constrained than they would become during the heyday of the British Raj in the nineteenth century. The French colonies in particular were known for their easy acceptance of mixed-race marriages and illegitimate or biracial children. Abraham Guerre settled in Pondicherry and married Maria Brunet, whose mother was a high-caste Bengali.[5] Abraham and Maria's granddaughter, Thérèse Blin de Grincourt, married the Chevalier and became Julia Margaret's grandmother. This mixed racial heritage may have been perfectly acceptable in eighteenth-century

Pondicherry, where Maria Brunet's Bengali and French parents were officially married by civil ceremony, but it may not have been quite the thing in nineteenth-century Calcutta, although mixed-race liaisons were quite common and openly spoken about there too.[6] In fact, gossip did circulate about the family's mixed heritage: even as late as the 1840s an English visitor to Calcutta snickered about Pattle being a variation of "Patel," a common Indian surname.[7] Ironically, Pattle really was an English name and the Bengali ancestry was on the de l'Etang side. Nonetheless this Bengali background did not feature among the many family stories that were told and retold to the following generations.

The de l'Etangs did not stay long in Pondicherry, which was often under attack from the English at Madras. The Chevalier seems to have been briefly a prisoner of the English during a siege of Pondicherry in 1793, the year his daughter Adeline was born. He must have seen the way the wind was favoring the English, because he spent the rest of his long career in India in the service of the British East India Company. He had a way with horses, and held various jobs training horses, running a riding school, and providing veterinary services for the Company. He rose to be in charge of the Company's stud farm at Ghazipur, an important English colony northwest of Calcutta. The de l'Etangs raised their three daughters there, and all three went on to marry Englishmen. Within two generations the family was "English," although, more specifically, they were part of an elite class of British civil servants who lived like aristocrats in a colonized land. Julia Margaret seems to have always considered herself English, but she probably did not set foot in England itself until she was a young woman. She grew up speaking English, French, and Hindi, which was used to talk to servants even in the Bengali region of India. She later learned German well enough to publish translations from that language.

The Pattle family was very comfortable, if not wealthy by colonial standards. A civil servant in the British East India Company, called John Company by insiders, could live very well. The Pattles lived in a large house in the affluent Garden Reach suburb of Calcutta. The Company had established a trading post among the villages on the banks of the Hooghly River in the Ganges valley region of West Bengal in the late seventeenth century. It built Fort William to defend and expand its territories and kept its own army there until the British government took over the management of India in the middle of the nineteenth century. Within a few decades, the community had grown into the city now known as Calcutta, which sits on the banks of the Hooghly River about 90 miles upstream from the delta of rivers opening onto the Bay of Bengal. In 1772 Calcutta became the capital of British India and the center of the Company's business.

The British developed the city on a Western model, with streets laid out in grids and government buildings designed in the neoclassical style of columns and domes.

The banks of the Hooghly were lined with the mansions of British colonial governors, cricket fields, and parade grounds for military pageants. The British dominated the city center, where they lived and worked among an international European community of traders from Portugal, the Netherlands, and the Mediterranean. The heterogeneous communities of Bengalis, Punjabis, Jains, and Asian immigrants lived on the outskirts of the city in humbler homes set on winding, crowded streets. In the mid-eighteenth century Calcutta was a bawdy frontier town, filled with young men on the make. Early deaths in the colony were as likely to be from drink as from disease. But by 1820, the city had grown up to be a cosmopolitan center of business and culture. It had a population of 180,000 people, although, then as now, it struggled to serve its numbers. The city is set among the marshes and swamps of the river valley, and the hot, wet climate encouraged diseases like malaria. Polluted water and sewage caused epidemics of cholera, and the summer monsoon months left the poorest people homeless in the torrential rains.

The Company's main business was exporting Indian goods such as indigo, salt, spices, and textile wares like silk and muslin. These were luxury goods that were in increasing demand back home, as the middle classes multiplied with the beginning of industrialization in England. Until 1813, the Company had a monopoly on all trade in its ever-growing territories, though private trading by employees was a popular means of making a fortune. More and more, however, the Company also eagerly pursued the opium trade with China. A first shipment of opium from India to China in 1773 was so successful that by 1858, 20 per cent of the Company's revenues derived from the opium industry.[8] The profits drew competition (and later outrage), and for this and other reasons the British government abolished the Company's monopoly on trade in 1813 and slowly lessened its authority over the next few decades. In 1854 the British Parliament took over the Company's territories, and in 1858 India was officially named a colony with its own government-appointed Viceroy.

But when Julia Margaret was born in 1815, the Company was still near the height of its powers, and her father was at the height of his Company career. In exchange for a life far from the comforts of home, the Company offered its loyal employees many perks: a close community of fellow British people, a comfortable lifestyle with plentiful servants, long vacations for home leave to England, and the prospect of making a fortune in the private trades that many employees engaged in on the side. Many a nabob returned to England fabulously wealthy after building a fortune with the Company in India. William Makepeace Thackeray, like Julia Margaret a Company child, satirically traced the habits and social lives of these self-made men in his novels. In early-nineteenth-century India, the British East India Company was considered master of all it surveyed – rich, immensely powerful in influence and military might, and extending its commercial territory every day. In England, it was considered a refuge for younger sons and social misfits who had no clear standing in the rigid hierarchy of the British class system. It offered steady salaries and the chance for advancement in a well-developed society that had closer ties to England than the Anglophone communities in the United States, Canada, or Australia. Britons might emigrate to the new United States or be forcibly transported to Australia, but those moves were usually permanent. The English in India, however, almost always returned to England: living in India was part of a job, which ended at retirement, even if it left individuals wholly changed.

Within this heterogeneous group of expatriates in Calcutta, James Pattle had a reputation as being particularly eccentric, which his daughter Julia Margaret would later share. Virginia Woolf, who loved a rowdy tale, relished the chance to tell this one about her great-grandfather:

> [He] was a gentleman of marked, but doubtful reputation, who after living a riotous life and earning the title of 'the biggest liar in India', finally drank himself to death and was consigned to a cask of rum to await shipment to England. The cask was stood outside the widow's bedroom door. In the middle of the night she heard a violent explosion, rushed out, and found her husband, having burst the lid off his coffin, bolt upright menacing her in death as he had menaced her in life. 'The shock of it sent her off her head then and there, poor thing, and she died raving.' . . . After 'Jim Blazes' had been nailed down again and shipped off, the sailors drank the liquor in which the body was preserved, 'and, by Jove, the rum ran out and got alight and set the ship on fire! And while they were trying to extinguish the flames she ran on a rock, blew up, and drifted ashore just below the Hooghly. And what do you think the soldiers said? "That Pattle had been such a scamp that the devil wouldn't let him go out of India"'[9]

This story is not entirely true. The ship bearing James Pattle's body to England for burial did wreck off the coast of India, and Adeline Pattle did die shortly after his death, but not in that dramatic manner. Tantalizingly, in this passage Woolf hints at more than she tells when she describes her great-grandfather's corpse "menacing" her great-grandmother "as he had menaced her in life." Woolf's source was a friend, the composer Ethel Smyth, whose father knew James Pattle in Calcutta and claimed he behaved very badly to his wife, who forgave him again and again.[10]

Julia Margaret was Adeline and James Pattle's third daughter. Their first child, a girl named after her mother, had been born in 1812. Between 1812 and 1829, Adeline bore ten children, of whom seven girls survived to adulthood. After Adeline came James, the only boy, who died before his first birthday, and Eliza, who lived for only four years. Julia Margaret came next in 1815, followed quickly by Sara and Maria in 1816 and 1818. Adeline had a brief break from childbearing before having Louisa in 1821 and then Virginia, Harriet, and Sophia in quick succession in 1827, 1828, and 1829. Harriet did not survive her first year. Both the size and the infant fatalities of the family were typical of the time. The distribution of the children mirrored Adeline Pattle's trips to and from Europe. For example, she was in Europe without her husband from 1818–20 and 1822–25, which enabled her to visit her older children and also have a respite from pregnancies.[11]

The children were all given English names, perhaps to strengthen their tenuous connection to what was for them a fatherland amid the competing cultural influences of colonial life. The names of the seven surviving girls – Adeline, Julia, Sara, Maria, Louisa, Virginia, and Sophia – would recur again and again throughout the family tree over the next few generations. The elder Adeline must have made an indelible impression upon her children; every generation of the family had at least one Adeline until the end of the century. There was an especially strong tradition of naming daughters after their mother's sisters. Adeline herself anglicized her sisters' names, Julie and Virginie, for two of her daughters. Julia Margaret's goddaughter and niece Julia Jackson continued the tradition, and Julia Jackson's own daughter Virginia Woolf was christened Adeline Virginia Stephen, after other maternal aunts and great-aunts. There is a strong family history of close bonds between sisters: Julia Margaret and her sisters were so close-knit that Thackeray coined the term "Pattledom"[12] to describe them; Virginia and Vanessa Stephen formed the core of the Bloomsbury group fifty years later.

The Pattle girls had an unconventional upbringing, even by colonial standards. It was the custom of British families in India to send their children back to the mother country for their early life and education. The climate of India was thought to be unhealthy for small children, and it was considered a parent's clear duty to send them away. This seems more reasonable when one remembers that perhaps as many as a third of the European population in Calcutta succumbed to early deaths from malaria or cholera. Those early years in England or Europe also developed ties that would maintain a strong national identity in the face of a life usually spent abroad. James Pattle, for example, came from a family that had been in the East India Company for generations. He had been born in India and he would die there. The only part of his life spent in England was probably his education, for most young men of the civil service were sent to England to learn writing, accounting, and a smattering of Latin before joining the Company. Despite living only briefly in England, he clearly identified himself and his family as English.

So it was not surprising that when the time came, the Pattles too decided to send their daughters abroad for their educations, but they were unusual in choosing

France instead of England. Adeline Pattle's mother, Thérèse de l'Etang, had moved back to France some time early in 1813. She lived first in Paris and then settled in her husband's family home at 1 Place St. Louis in Versailles, though her husband, the Chevalier, remained in India until his death in 1840. At some time between ages three and six each Pattle daughter was sent out to France to live with her grandmother to begin her education as a young lady. Adeline Pattle must have spent a good part of her life in voyages between France and India, ferrying her daughters back and forth between their two homes. They shuttled between Paris, Versailles, and Calcutta in the 1810s and 1820s, but in 1830 the Pattle parents settled temporarily in London for a few years.[13]

Rudyard Kipling, who also grew up in India of British parents in the civil service, wrote at century's end about the brutal experience of being torn from parents, servants, and the warm familiarity of India itself when he too was sent to England at age five. In the short story *Baa, Baa Black Sheep* he describes the child Punch's uncomprehending confusion when his parents brought him to a strange house in a cold land and then said goodbye. The parents too were miserable, with the poor mamma pleading, "Don't forget us!" as she left. William Makepeace Thackeray, Julia Margaret's exact contemporary in Calcutta, felt similarly traumatized by his relocation to England at that age. Years later he poignantly described the parting: "A ghaut, or riverstair at Calcutta; and a day when, down those steps, to a boat which was in waiting, came two children, whose mothers remained on shore." The young Thackeray peppered his letters home with precocious drawings of monkeys and of his former Indian servants. When he was reunited with his mother after a three-year separation, he was so overcome with emotion that he could not speak to her.[14] The fact that these separations were standard colonial practice did not make them any easier to withstand. Later, when Julia Margaret herself was a colonial matron, she too sent her children to England for their health and education. A few of her surviving letters make it clear how difficult that separation was for everyone.

No accounts of Julia Margaret's unusual childhood in Calcutta and Versailles have survived. The Versailles of the *ancien régime* was the center of the French court, dominated by the *château* that was designed as a showpiece for the Sun King, Louis XIV. Situated near Paris, it had been home to the twenty thousand people attached to the royal court, as well as the merchants, servants, and craftsmen who cared for them. It also housed an important military garrison. It was at Versailles that Marie Antoinette played at being a peasant in her custom-built hamlet. The French Revolution of 1789 sent most of the French nobility into exile, but Versailles remained a political hub throughout the tumultuous years afterwards. After Napoleon's defeat at Waterloo, the new constitutional monarchy granted amnesty to the exiles and they gradually returned to France, though many had lost property and privileges.

It seems that Julia Margaret and her sisters were largely self-taught and unsupervised in Versailles and that they followed their own fervent enthusiasms. One oft-repeated story is that they would wander through the countryside around Versailles by themselves, stopping to pray whenever they felt overcome by the sublimity of nature.[15] Julia Margaret had a lifelong admiration for nature and landscape, though it was demonstrated more in her letters than in her photographs. She was also a devout Christian, though she was friends with many of the Victorian age's most famous (or notorious) non-believers, from Charles Darwin to Thomas Carlyle. Her faith was based in the Anglican Church, the established Protestant Church of England, to which her father must have belonged. Her French mother and grandparents may have been Catholic, though at least one of her maternal forebears was Protestant. It is unclear if any religious divide affected her upbringing, especially since so much of her education occurred in France. Certainly the Catholic fascination with representations of the Virgin Mary must have been a profound influence on her later work: her obsessive studies of Madonna and child were unusual in nineteenth-century English art.

Religious training would have been an important part of most nineteenth-century girls' education. In addition to attending Sunday services, observant Christians were expected to read the Bible every day and to participate in daily family prayers. Julia Margaret had an ardent and emotional nature and in later life she wrote her own prayers for special occasions such as the birth of her first child. The inclination to worship was strong in her, and she later described her photographs too as "the embodiment of a prayer."[16] Smart Victorian girls were often drawn to religion as the only acceptable outlet for serious study or strong feelings. George Eliot, for example, had a religious "conversion" during her adolescence, even though she lost her faith later in adulthood. During her flirtation with piety, she read deeply in theology and lived according to strict notions of duty. Duty, of course, was an ever-present imperative for middle-class Victorians, and women were especially vulnerable to its claims. Like her heroines Dorothea Brooke and Maggie Tulliver, Eliot struggled to escape the oppressive claims of duty while respecting their social and ethical importance. It was a conflict that defined most Victorian women's lives, and Julia Margaret too would eventually be forced to decide between the claims of duty to her art and her family.

Besides religion, the Pattle girls' education included the social skills required of upper-middle-class hostesses. They learned to dance, play the piano, and sing. Julia Margaret enjoyed music all her life and studied piano whenever she could afford to hire a music master. The Pattles learned to converse intelligently and decorously in English, French, and German. They learned the etiquette of rank and class, how to run a large household of servants, and how to host a party. Like most Victorian girls, their book learning was probably haphazard, depending as it did on their own initiative and the indulgence of their elders. Julia Margaret was well read in Shakespeare, the Bible, and the literature of her day – especially what we now call Romantic poetry and drama. She had a lifelong love of theater and for generations her family regularly performed amateur theatricals for their own entertainment. From these dramas she learned to "stage" her sitters for the long exposures of Victorian photography, and she also learned to manipulate props and mood for dramatic effect.

The Pattle girls were probably taught drawing and certainly learned to appreciate art in the museums of Europe. Both Julia Margaret and her sister Sara were closely associated with painters for most of their lives. Sara's son, Valentine Prinsep, became a well-regarded Victorian painter in his own right and a member of the Royal Academy and the Holland Park circle of artists. Little is known about the girls' early artistic education, and, surprisingly, no evidence has survived to show that Julia Margaret ever drew or painted – not one sketch in the margins of a letter, not one watercolor mentioned in passing. This is especially odd during an era when upper-middle-class young women were expected to exhibit artistic skill in acceptable genres like watercolors, needlework, and sketching in order to be considered accomplished. The Pattle girls all went on to demonstrate great taste and style in their homes and dress. They each admired art and valued it highly. But none except Julia Margaret seems to have exhibited any interest in making art herself, and even Julia Margaret showed no clear signs of the visual genius that would make her name until she was forty-eight years old.

Romanticism dominated European culture during the years of Julia Margaret's youth. Her education may indeed have been influenced by the philosophies of Jean-Jacques Rousseau, who argued in the eighteenth century for the innate goodness of human nature against the corrupting influence of civilization. Rousseau's confidence in human goodness also promoted the idealization of landscape and everything "natural" in a society soon exhausted by the excesses of the *ancien régime* and then the French Revolution. He advocated an educational system that encouraged children to play and to teach themselves as much as possible. Radically, he believed that children would grow up to be moral adults if society intervened as little as possible. Julia Margaret's rather unstructured upbringing may have reflected Rousseau's influence in France.

Rousseau inspired many authors to create novels and poems illustrating his ideas, and one of the most popular in turn-of-the-century France was a novel called *Paul et Virginie* by J. H. Bernardin de St. Pierre, a friend of Rousseau's. First published in 1789, it was translated into many languages, and went through sixty English editions during the nineteenth century. In 1864 Cameron produced a photograph illustrating a scene from the novel, but it is likely that she first read the book during her child-hood in France. It is a story that would have reverberated for her in many different ways, and it may illuminate some of her own later artistic obsessions with children and innocence.

The novel describes a natural paradise, where good people could take refuge from evil forces and live in true peace. In the eighteenth and nineteenth centuries such stories always have colonial overtones: where else would highly "civilized" Europeans locate paradise than in the still-unspoilt lands across the seas, where they believed people were scarce and nature was bountiful? In this instance the story takes place on Mauritius, an island off the coast of Africa in the Indian Ocean that was a French colony at the time. Two pious and good young Frenchwomen sud-denly find themselves alone in the colony and despairing of supporting themselves and their babies. With the help of two native servants they farm the land and raise their children, Paul and Virginia, with little contact from the outside world. The two children grow up almost as twins, sleeping together, bathing together, and even nurs-ing interchangeably from the maternal breasts. The women have suffered from class and gender inequalities, but they reflect that "their more fortunate children, far from the cruel prejudices of Europe, those prejudices which poison the most precious sources of our happiness, would enjoy at once the pleasures of love, and the bless-ings of equality."[17] Bernardin de St. Pierre calls them children of nature and compares them to Adam and Eve.

This Edenic relationship cannot last, of course, and the domestic bliss is shattered when an aristocratic relative summons Virginia to France to complete her education. Duty calls, and Virginia obeys. The separation transforms the pair from brother and sister to lovers, and both pine romantically while they are apart. When Virginia finally manages to escape her rich relative and return home, her boat is shipwrecked within sight of the coast of Mauritius. While Paul watches in horror from the beach, sailors plead with Virginia to take off her heavy clothes so they can rescue her, but modest Virginia refuses and disappears into the waves. The rest of the once-happy family group dies of grief soon afterwards.

One can imagine that the young Julia Margaret would have been drawn to this story of an Edenic childhood in a colonial land and would have related to Virginia's abrupt separation from parents and her entry into aristocratic French society. She had relatives named Virginia and it was likely that she and her family stopped at ports in Mauritius on their trips between India and France, via the Cape of Good Hope. Cameron's mother, Adeline de l'Etang, may have attended a well-known French school for ladies at the turn of the century that was run by Madame Campan, to whom Bernardin de St. Pierre dedicated one of his literary works.[18] Perhaps most importantly, *Paul and Virginia* dramatizes a world without fathers, which Julia

Margaret may also have identified with. Perhaps James Pattle was as ghostly a presence in Julia Margaret's life as he was in their 1818 family portrait. At the very least he must have been often absent in Calcutta. If so, then Julia Margaret may have read the novel as both a celebration of an idealized women-centered world as well as a cautionary tale about the tragic end of such a manless society.[19] Thus *Paul and Virginia* may have been an influential book in Cameron's early reading and maybe even a reflection of the Romantic ideologies that informed her education.

Bernardin de St. Pierre's text emphasizes the idyllic unity of the child pair even after they have grown to be adults. Cameron's later photographs of children also emphasize an infantile unity between pairs. In photographs like *The Double Star*, Cameron places two children in very close proximity and fills the large glass plate with their almost-interlocking heads [see figure]. The filmy cloud around them frames them in a halo or an amniotic web that insists they are both single and double. Surprisingly, Cameron's Madonna and child photographs seem less enchanted with the transcendent bond between mother and child than these photographs: the sibling bond between young children may trump even maternal or divine love in Cameron's symbolism. Portraits of mothers and children seem framed by the pain of an inevitable separation to come; portraits of siblings seem to hold no threat of any parting. This would be in keeping with the emotional realities of Julia Margaret's early life.

The photograph that Cameron later takes of *Paul and Virginia* in 1864 shares this symbolism of duality blending into unity. The passage she chooses to illustrate is one where the narrator discovers Virginia caught in a sudden rainstorm:

> As I hastened towards her in order to help her on, I perceived that she held Paul by the arm, who was almost entirely enveloped in the same canopy [of her petticoat], and both were laughing heartily at being sheltered together under an umbrella of their own invention. Those two charming faces, placed within the petticoat, swelled by the wind, recalled to my mind the children of Leda, enclosed within the same shell.[20]

Cameron's photograph [see figure] does away with the petticoat and simply positions two rather weary-looking children under an umbrella. The children are alike in their draped garments, tousled hair, and general size and appearance, but they are clearly distinguished too – the girl Virginia, for example, stares boldly at the camera. The clothing that half covers them again differentiates them by blocking the bodies into contrasting halves of light and dark fabric, but it also gives Cameron an occasion for an early triumph in photographic bravura. The complicated folds of Virginia's clothes are a marvel of form and texture that demonstrate Cameron's often confusing use of focus. By focusing her lens on them, Cameron has clearly decided that the intricate drapery – so reminiscent of the Elgin Marbles from the Parthenon that Cameron studied to great advantage – was more important and interesting to her than the faces of the two children.

Like Bernardin de St. Pierre, Cameron wants to reveal Paul and Virginia's dyadic relationship – their innocent interdependence as two beings who are separate yet bound together. The umbrella serves the same function as it does in the text: as an emblem of the single bond that draws the two together. In Cameron's composition the drooping umbrella, perhaps too heavy for the children to hold up, frames the pair. That Cameron was careful and conscious about the formal elements of this composition is also revealed by her unusual use of retouching in this image. Paul's right foot, on the lower left side of the image, is visibly scratched over to make it less conspicuous in the foreground.[21] Cameron was exacting about form and rather loose about technique: it didn't seem to bother her that her retouching of the negative resulted in a messy blotch on the print. She also liked to introduce "real" artifacts into her fictional tableaux, as if to provide an extra guarantee for the verisimilitude of the scene.[22]

However, as a "romantic" work of art, Cameron's *Paul and Virginia* seems implausible. Like the umbrella, the children are insistently real. The caption may read "Paul and Virginia," but it is not surprising to learn that these children are in fact Freddy Gould and Lizzie Keown, young neighbors of Cameron's on the Isle of Wight in the 1860s. These two often modeled for Cameron, and indeed they look tired, bored, even a little sulky. They don't really look like children of Paradise. This tension between the inescapable reality of Cameron's models, props, and locations and the fictional narratives that they are supposed to embody is a constant in Cameron's work. Her photographs have been searched for many influences, but Romanticism is not one of them. Yet besides the influence of the occasional Romantic subject, like *Paul and Virginia*, the influence of Romantic ideologies on Cameron's life seems impossible to ignore. Her ardent approach to art, nature, and beauty, her unconventional upbringing, her force of personality even – all surely draw some of their power from the Romantic ideas that were circulating during her youth.

Mrs. Pattle continued to ferry her daughters back and forth between Europe and India for two decades. She was not in good health herself, and took extended stays in France and England to convalesce. On one such trip in 1830, while the fifteen-year-old Julia Margaret was probably staying with her grandmother at Versailles, Mr. and Mrs. Pattle took their eldest daughter Adeline and their two youngest, Virginia and Sophia, on the long trip from Calcutta to England. Mr. Pattle stopped off in Cape Town, perhaps burdened by the same ill health that would plague the family over the next decade. Mrs. Pattle left her husband and Adeline in Cape Town and continued on to England, but eighteen-year-old Adeline had already formed an attachment to a young Scotsman on board who was on sick leave from the British East India

Company army. Adeline was sweet-tempered and a little childlike. Colin Mackenzie was ambitious and ardent. After renewing their acquaintance in 1831, they were married in May 1832 in England, where Mrs. Pattle was staying at the time, probably for her health. The newlyweds soon embarked for India and Colin returned to his post in Madras in October.

In a memoir of Colin that was published much later, Adeline was described as "of a most affectionate, unselfish disposition and sweet temper; not pretty, but with fine eyes, a beautiful fair skin, and much of her mother's grace . . . ."[23] Except for the lack of prettiness, the description seems apt. Like her sisters, Adeline seems to have been haphazardly educated, with her spiritual instruction being left to some occasional lessons from an aunt (presumably one of her mother's well-married sisters, Julie Impey or Virginie Beadle). She was rather idle and prone to novel-reading. Her husband, at least, often urged her to exercise her mind more. She may not have shared in her sisters' imperious wills, though, for she was considered humble and lacking in confidence.

The rest of the family continued to shuttle between France and England: staying either in Versailles with Madame de l'Etang, in a Paris apartment, or in lodgings on Upper Montagu Street in London, which they took for at least the summer of 1831. The years between 1830 and 1833 seem to have been James Pattle's only extended home leave. In 1833 Parliament ended the British East India Company's monopoly on trade, and as a member of the Board of Revenue James Pattle was needed back in Calcutta to help manage the change. He left London and took eighteen-year-old Julia Margaret back to Calcutta with him in November, leaving the rest of the family to follow.[24] Her childhood was over and her "French finishing" complete; it was time to look for a husband.

By the time the youngest Pattle girls, Virginia and Sophia, were of school age, their older sisters were already married and settled in England, so the little girls were sent there instead. Only Adeline, Julia, Maria, and Sara were educated in France with their grandmother. Adeline died relatively young in India, but Julia, Maria, and Sara all married in Calcutta, raised their children, then retired to England. They formed a core group of sisters whose lives and families remained closely intertwined. The youngest sisters, Virginia and Sophia, traveled in slightly different circles through their marriages into the aristocracy. Louisa Bayley remained most in the shadows. Although Cameron's life and work dramatically confirm how important her sisters were to her, there are surprisingly few documents to provide details of this. Only one letter from Cameron to a sister has survived, and none of the sisters seem to have left behind letters to Julia Margaret or any memoirs or diaries. Many of Cameron's photographic albums were given to her sisters, and yet only one portrait of any of them by Cameron has survived, despite their legendary intimacy and beauty.[25] The story of their relationships, unfortunately, is based on the observations, memory, and gossip of others.

Like many Victorians, and especially colonials, Julia Margaret's life was defined by great distances and separations from loved ones. Her upbringing in France may have brought her close to her grandmother and sisters, but it created a distance from her father and mother, her aunts and her uncles. That distance mattered: Julia Margaret was arguably never as close to anyone as she was to the sisters with whom she spent most of her childhood. And she spent the rest of her life trying to manage the separations that inevitably occurred between herself and her husband, her sisters, her dearest friends, and her children. She sent her own children away to England, and her anxieties followed them around the world. She wrote letter after letter begging friends to visit, promising visits of her own, hoping for proximity and intimacy in a centrifugal life that flung those she loved to the far corners of the vast British Empire. Her friends traveled back and forth between India and England. Her husband took trips to his estates in Ceylon that would separate them for most of a year. Her sons joined the army and the civil service and roamed the globe. Julia Margaret's separation from her parents in India was merely the first in a lifetime of separations.

Photographs are famously useful for transcending distances between people and alleviating the strains of separation. Photographs make the absent present, and that may have held a powerful psychic appeal for Julia Margaret. She first took up photography as her children left home, and she eventually left England, and her photographic career, to be reunited with her family in Ceylon. She gave important photographic albums of her work and other family portraits to her sisters Maria and Virginia. Art historian Joanne Lukitsh notes that "photographs in one album were not unique to that album, but could be viewed by another sister in another location, thus serving the desire for communication and intimacy across distances demonstrated in the Pattle sisters' voluminous correspondence."[26] Becoming a photographer, photographing children and relatives, circulating her work among family and friends – these may have been strategies for dealing with the inevitable distances and separations of a Victorian colonial life.

The other legacy of Julia Margaret's childhood was a lifelong sense of the importance of the French strand within the multinational mix of her cultural inheritances. The French-Indian Madame de l'Etang was much loved by her granddaughters and she lived long enough to see her great-granddaughter married. It was she, not her daughter Adeline Pattle, who was the family matriarch. She instilled an aristocratic sense of entitlement and hauteur that the Pattle girls called upon at will. Pattle might sound like the name of a Dickens character, but these young women carried themselves like queens and expected to be obeyed. They were almost all beautiful and witty, and they inherited generations of self-assurance from the de l'Etangs. They were also bossy and practical. Being English and French and living in India meant that they were foreign everywhere they went, and they felt their difference as specialness.

One hundred years after Julia Margaret and her sisters romped around Versailles, picking up whatever learning was readily available in novels and conversation, their descendant Virginia Woolf wrote a novel in which she described the afterimage of this European heritage. In *To the Lighthouse* Woolf wrote an impressionistic portrait of her mother, Julia Jackson Stephen, godchild and favorite model of Julia Margaret. In the novel, as in her biographical portrait of her great-aunt, Woolf continues to braid together myth and fact, transposing her maternal French lineage into an Italian one, and frankly commenting on the mythic import of this family legacy:

> Had she not in her veins the blood of that very noble, if slightly mythical, Italian house, whose daughters, scattered about English drawing-rooms in the nineteenth century, had lisped so charmingly, had stormed so wildly, and all her wit and her bearing and her temper came from them, and not from the sluggish English, or the cold Scotch . . .[27]

Those years in France were enormously important to Cameron, and to the family's sense of itself. Rootless and refined, the Pattle sisters clung to their Frenchness even as they centered their lives between the two poles of England and India. They were not snobs as such. They loved beauty and art and good conversation, and later in life they would all pursue those things even across class boundaries. But they rejected the commercialism of their English community in India and they simply endured the stink of "trade" associated with the British East India Company; their hearts had been trained in Versailles. For the rest of her life, England and France, money and art, the real and the ideal would struggle for dominance in Julia Margaret's life.

CHAPTER 2

Double Stars

T HE LAST STAGES of the long sea journey from Europe to Calcutta are the most dangerous. The Hooghly River meets the Bay of Bengal in a delta of shifting sands and treacherous currents, called the sandbanks. Many ships have been wrecked there. Early in the nineteenth century most boats anchored and watched the currents while awaiting a native pilot to guide them through the passage and up the river to the city. The boat would then wind through green forests and stately mansions before docking at a grand ghat, with a triumphal arch announcing one's arrival. The river was always busy: people bathing and washing clothes, water buffalo cooling off, men rowing out to unload cargo from ships. When Thomas Babington Macaulay arrived in Calcutta to take up his appointment on the Council of India, he was surprised by the beauty of the green banks and the ugliness of the "black and turbid" waters. He wrote home that "the boiling coffee-coloured river swept several naked corpses along close to our ship. This ghastly sight would once have shocked me very much. But in India death and everything connected with it become familiar subjects of contemplation."[1] For newcomers, the first encounter with the vivid colors, smells, and bustling activity of Calcutta could be overwhelming. For a young woman like Julia Margaret, returning "home" after years of schooling, it was more like a reunion with the sights and smells and sounds of her earliest life.

The Calcutta that Julia Margaret returned to in 1833 was not exactly the one she had left some fifteen years earlier. The city was still growing rapidly and the East India Company was solidifying its hold on the region. James Pattle still held his lucrative post on the Company's Board of Revenue, but others were not faring as well as before. The unexpected failures of several prominent Calcutta banks between 1830 and 1834 ruined many wealthy families, though it seems to have had little effect on the Pattles. Upon his return, James Pattle got involved in a scheme to open the first ice house in Calcutta. When the first shipment of ice arrived from the United States, the city declared a half-day's holiday and everyone took time off work to enjoy cold drinks.[2]

The young William Makepeace Thackeray was one of those who lost his inheritance in the collapse of the Bank of Bengal, and he had consequently begun writing for a living. Enjoying a bohemian life in Paris, he often socialized with Mrs. Pattle and her daughters when they were in town. In October 1833, for example, he wrote to his mother: "I dine to day with the Pattles & shall meet pretty Theodosia – I wish she had L11325 in the 3 per Cts – I would not hesitate above two minutes in popping that question wh. was to decide the happiness of my future life –."[3] The sum he mentioned was the exact amount that he had lost in the bank failures. Thackeray biographers have long speculated over this reference to a "Theodosia" Pattle, since none of the sisters was so named. It seems likely that it was Thackeray's pet name for one of the girls, whom he had practically grown up with. Since Adeline was already married, only eighteen-year-old Julia Margaret or seventeen-year-old Sara could have been present and marriageable. But it is also possible that Thackeray was making a joke about the younger Maria, Louisa, Virginia, or Sophia Pattle, all under fifteen at the time. Later in his life, Thackeray was charmed by the grown Virginia. Mrs. Pattle seems to have taken Thackeray seriously as a suitor, writing him a letter suggesting a match. Thackeray replied with the news of his financial losses and that seems to have put an end to the idea.[4]

Thackeray's letter is the only suggestion that the Pattles may have been affected by the recent financial crises, which had occurred just as they would be expecting to produce large dowries for the eldest of their six daughters. Perhaps Thackeray knew that the girls would not have large dowries, or perhaps he just assumed that the Pattles were brought down along with everyone else. Since the remark was probably facetious to begin with, it is hard to speculate. James Pattle's will, probated after his death in 1845, left money only to his two youngest girls, explaining that the eldest had already been well provided for by an inheritance from their uncle, who had died the year Julia Margaret was born. It may have been that this generous bequest provided for the dowries of Adeline, Sara, Maria, Louisa, and Julia Margaret, all of whom were married between 1832 and 1838.

After Adeline, Julia Margaret would have been expected to marry next. As in other colonies, Anglo-Indian society was overpopulated with men employed by the armies, the missions, and John Company itself. Marriageable women were at a premium, and boatloads of English hopefuls would arrive on flimsy pretexts, looking for husbands. Residents mockingly called them "the Fishing Fleet," and jeered at those who went back to England unwed as the "Returned Empties." But the Pattle girls, with their prestigious connections and substantial dowries, would know that they could pick and choose among many suitors. And then there was their beauty . . .

In her biographical sketch of her great-aunt, Virginia Woolf asserted that the family drew its eccentricity from its English patrimony (James Pattle) and its beauty and style from its French mothers and grandmothers (Adeline de l'Etang). Certainly three generations of women in the family were considered remarkably lovely. The dark, heavy-lidded eyes, oval faces, and thick chestnut hair that the de l'Etang, Pattle, Jackson, and Stephen women inherited impressed eighteenth-century civil servants in India and Edwardian socialites alike. Beauty was part of the family story before either Julia Margaret or Virginia was born.[5] In this respect they were especially lucky, for, as one scholar has put it, beauty would become "the emblem of a poignant national dream in the 1860s," as industrialization covered England in soot.[6]

Later, when Julia Margaret took up photography, beauty became her professional mission, or even obsession: she famously wrote, "I longed to arrest all beauty that came before me, and at length the longing has been satisfied."[7] The romantic, almost desperate, language was no exaggeration. She accosted beautiful women on the sidewalk and asked them to sit for her. Less well known is her equal fascination with male beauty: she chose a gardener in Ceylon for the beauty of his back. She once took a guest upstairs to view her sleeping husband and announced, "Behold the most beautiful old man on earth!"[8] The pursuit of beauty must have had emotional resonance for her, coming from this family heritage, but it is also possible that her stated obsession with beauty was a convenient and acceptable mask for professional ambition. For a woman to take up photography was audacious; for a woman to devote herself to appearances was much less so. Julia Margaret might have found the pursuit of beauty to be useful and convenient as well as pleasurable. Beauty may be a random, passing gift of the gods, but photography put Julia Margaret in control of it: she chose the models, posed and arrayed them, framed the composition, and displayed her vision to the world.

Beauty did seem to unite and bind the sisters together, much as the family's sense of its aristocratic French heritage and English eccentricity did. They were "the beautiful Pattle girls" by nearly all accounts: their celebrity began there and then the stories started. Quentin Bell, their descendant and one of Woolf's biographers, noted that their beauty was in the grave, monumental style. They could strike poses and they looked lovely draped in shawls. Indeed, John Ruskin once described two of the Pattles as "two, certainly, of the most beautiful women in a grand sense–(Elgin marbles with dark eyes)–that you could find in modern life . . . ."[9] Clearly, the sisters had different personalities and ambitions, but they left few accounts of themselves besides the gossip itself: English society later nicknamed Virginia, Sara, and Julia Margaret "Beauty, Dash, and Talent" respectively. Maria was described by Bell, her great-grandson, as devoted to her family and obsessed with illness. She was

> as good as gold; but there is not one original thought, very little common-sense and not the slightest dexterity in the use of language in all her hundreds and hundreds of letters . . . . [Her letters] display the dull side of the Pattles; their silliness, their gush, their cloying sweetness, their continual demands for affection and with it a mawkish vein . . .[10]

To be fair, Bell was looking at Maria for evidence of Virginia Woolf's gifts; the Pattles were never known for their eloquence. They were women of the world and their talents were best expressed in their artful relationships with other people.

It was perhaps the third sister, Sara, who would best illustrate the Pattles' social genius when she established her London salon in the 1850s. In the spring of 1835 she married Henry Thoby Prinsep, another scion of a leading Calcutta family. Known as Thoby by everyone, Prinsep was the fourth son of John Prinsep, who had come out to Calcutta in its early days and made a fortune in private trade in indigo. It was the British who introduced printing onto Indian cotton in the eighteenth century, and indigo was a leading dye in the new textile industry in England and India. After a childhood and education in England, Thoby followed in his brothers' and father's footsteps, coming out to Calcutta at age sixteen to serve as a clerk in the British East India Company. He rose quickly through the ranks, in part through a well-received book he wrote on the military and political history of the British administration in India during the decade that he worked for the colonial governor. He was a big man, tall and wide, but his size hid a generous and childlike heart. He knew something about everything, G. F. Watts would later claim, and he liked to talk.[11] By 1820, he was Persian Secretary to the government in Calcutta and he was becoming a rich and powerful man in the civil service. In 1835, when he married Sara Pattle, fresh from France, he was named an acting member of the governing Council of India. In later years he worked closely alongside his brother-in-law Charles Hay Cameron. Thoby was twenty-three years older than Sara, but they were well suited. Vivacious and gregarious, Sara was as much a social creature as Thoby, and they made each of their homes a gathering place for lively conversations and informal entertaining.

It was Maria, the fourth sister, who married next. Early in 1837 she married Dr. John Jackson, then an assistant surgeon in the Indian Medical Service. He too was some fourteen years older than his new wife and solidly respectable, if not as well connected as Thoby. He was promoted to surgeon in 1847, shortly after the couple's youngest daughter, Julia, was born. In 1855 he published *Forms of Tetanus in India*. He was generally regarded as a popular and esteemed practitioner. Dr. Jackson does not seem to have joined in Maria's family's social whirl; he spent substantial periods of time apart from them while he finished his practice in India and his wife and daughters settled in England. As their great-grandson Quentin Bell noted, Maria's health was supposed to be delicate, and this was given as the reason for her extended residence in England without her husband. Perhaps their separation was necessary, but Julia Margaret made it a point of pride to battle her own ill health and remain in India for ten years by her husband's side. Maria eventually outlived Julia Margaret by thirteen years.

Adeline, the eldest sister, is sometimes supposed to have been the closest to Julia Margaret (though some critics – and Cameron herself – often name others for that honor) but her married life in Madras must have made it difficult for her family to see much of her in Calcutta in the early 1830s. In July 1835, however, Adeline brought her daughters to Calcutta to stay with her family while her husband Colin was assigned to Malaysia. She was expecting another child that fall. In contrast to Sara and Thoby's worldliness, Colin and Adeline grew more and more religious. By 1835, the young couple seem to have had some kind of religious awakening – the letters between them are dominated by spiritual questions. Later in his life, Colin was known in the Company army for his efforts to convert nonbelievers to Christianity.[12] The woman who early in her marriage was reprimanded for her frivolity and who appeared to have had little religious training was now advising her observant husband on spiritual matters. Adeline reported to Colin that her father found her much improved since she married, adding

> This gave me great pleasure. I cannot tell you how truly thankful I am to the Almighty for having blessed me with so pure and high-minded a man as your-self. I am very careful not to indulge in any scandal to which you have so decided an objection.

The reference to scandal may be an oblique acknowledgment of the colorful stories that always seemed to surround the Pattles. Besides the rumors of hard drinking and domestic troubles, James Pattle would later be involved in disputes with the British East India Company and a civil lawsuit.[13]

Separated from his family and frustrated in his attempts to advance his career, Colin grew depressed in Malaysia, sending despondent letters to Adeline in Calcutta. She urged him to be optimistic and advised taking Communion, which she had just done for the first time since her marriage. The sisters were all raised within the Anglican Church of their father, the established Church of England, but there was a broad range of observance within its bounds. It is possible that Julia Margaret's faith also became deeper or more serious in those years of young adulthood when she was living back in Calcutta with her pious sister. At least it would explain the fact that the Pattle sisters did not seem to have any religious background that would predict Julia Margaret's later strong faith.

If Julia Margaret and Adeline did have some kind of religious conversion in the early 1830s, they were certainly not alone. England was going through a popular reli-gious revival as different Protestant groups fought for control over the political and spiritual life of the nation. Evangelical and nonconformist Christians, who tended to emphasize the emotional and individual experience of faith, were gaining political power as the middle classes grew and gained in influence. In the 1830s they set about disassembling some of the entrenched political rights of the Anglican Church, which favored the traditions and rituals of religion over individual beliefs. As a state religion, the Anglican Church held enormous power through its ownership of land, its patronage for clerical jobs, and its exclusive rights to university positions and political offices. Until 1828 one had to be a member of the Church of England to hold public office in England, and until the 1870s one had to swear allegiance to the Anglican Church in order to hold a university position. But these privileges were gradually eroded over the course of the nineteenth century.

Alarmed by the attack on their long-held rights, some Anglicans fought back with a renewed insistence on the Church's supreme authority. Led by Edward Pusey, John Keble, and John Henry Newman, the "Tractarians," named for the pamphlets they started publishing in the 1830s, upheld the independence of the Church from state interference. Also known as the Oxford Movement, after their stronghold in the University, these clergymen revived the religious debates that had divided the nation when King Henry VIII established the Church of England and placed it under state control. In a sense, they wanted to undo Henry VIII's schism with the Catholic Church, and in Newman's case that eventually resulted in his conversion to Catholicism. The Tractarians had a rigidly hierarchical view of religion: texts determined doctrine; traditions and ritual demonstrated faith; the Church was infallible; and bishops mattered more than laymen. Julia Margaret later had many friends among the Tractarians, though her own faith incorporated elements of both the Tractarian love of history and biblical tradition as well as the evangelical insistence on personal religious feeling. Mike Weaver, who has examined Cameron's religious beliefs in more detail than any other scholar, asserts that she was probably a Tractarian herself.[14]

In January 1836 Colin returned to his family in Calcutta to find Adeline unwell. Since the birth of her baby in October, she had been suffering from a liver complaint and the medical course of bleeding only seemed to have worsened her condition. By April, it was clear that she and her daughters would have to leave Calcutta to convalesce in Europe, and Colin sailed with them down the Hooghly as far as the sandbanks to say goodbye on April 14. Adeline appeared to revive on board and pleaded with Colin not to leave her, but his last words were: "It is God's will." She died on board ship in May, on their fourth wedding anniversary, at age twenty-four; Colin, who had been sending heartfelt entreaties about her spiritual health and her care of the children, received the news in October.[15]

It was during this painful period in Julia Margaret's life that she came under criticism from one British observer of the Calcutta scene: Isabella Fane, daughter of the Commander-in-Chief of India. Isabella's is also the only early source to suggest that, like their father, the Pattle sisters themselves provoked gossip. Isabella arrived in

Calcutta with her father early in 1836. Despite being herself illegitimate (due to her mother's inability to dissolve a former marriage), she was a stickler for propriety and she took an instant dislike to Sara, then pregnant with her first child. Thoby fell ill and left town to convalesce, and Isabella was horrified at how Sara flirted and socialized in his absence. Her account, which may be biased by jealousy or ill temper, also provides the only evidence of Julia Margaret having a romance before her meeting with Charles Hay. In February Isabella wrote to a friend:

> Nasty Mrs Thoby [Prinsep] was of our party, and did not behave with what I should call propriety. She has a sister, a Miss Pattle, a little, ugly, underbred-looking thing; but she has the reputation of being very clever, which is better than beauty. She is courted by one Captain Smyth, an A.D.C. [aide de camp] of Sir C. Metcalfe's. These two doves sat behind me at the play, and the tiresome creatures did nothing but coo the whole time. I wished them at Jericho . . .[16]

By June, Isabella's opinion of Sara had improved and she grudgingly acknowledged her good nature. A reputation for amiability and a suggestion of laxness followed Sara to her salon in Little Holland House over a decade later. In August Sara gave birth to her first child, a healthy boy named Henry after his father, and Isabella reported on this in another letter:

> [Sara Prinsep] has an unmarried sister nursing her, who has been living with her of late. Because, I believe, she is so disgusted with her father, Jemmy Blaze, she is very unhappy at home. This creature, Miss Julia by name, sets up for a *bas-bleu* [blue-stocking] and the notes she writes in answer to our common-place enquiries are worth reading. She says in one, after enquiring about my father, 'many in this house will make offerings at the shrine of Aesculapius upon his recovery'!! She makes me so sick, and she is so ugly and conceited withal.[17]

This brief observation confirms the impression given by Woolf's sources that James Pattle made trouble at home. Likewise, Isabella's description of Julia Margaret's note, while mean-spirited, is borne out by her later prose-writing style. She was fond of high diction and grand phrases, though her writing had more charm than this implies. Julia Margaret's reputation for cleverness and her knowledge of classical literature also demonstrate that her intellectual interests were developed early in life.

Shortly after the birth of Sara's child, Julia Margaret must have suffered a physical breakdown, something that often occurred later in her life whenever she was anxious and unhappy. Her father was making home life difficult, her eldest sister had died, and she had perhaps lost a suitor. All of the Pattles seem to have been prone to collapses and Julia Margaret's health was never robust, despite her indomitable energy.

She suffered from bronchial attacks for most of her life, as did many of her friends and family. She was also plagued by dizziness and fainting spells, which she (and her doctors) attributed to overexertion. Many of the British in India repaired to the more temperate climate of Cape Town for rest and recovery when their health broke down. Julia Margaret arrived on October 3 on the SS *Cornwall*.[18]

The voyage to Cape Town by ship could be arduous: cabins leaked and heavy seas drove people from their rooms to the wet open decks; the pitch and roll of the boat made everyone seasick and sometimes made standing nearly impossible; the noise of crew, winds, and creaking wood and ropes was relentless. During one such voyage, Sir John Herschel noted in his journal that "To live on board ship is equivalent to living in a perpetual earthquake on land with the prospect of being drowned instead of crushed as a catastrophe."[19] Shipwrecks were indeed common. The sight of Table Mountain rising from the South African plains was a long-looked-for treat among weary voyagers. Cape Town had thrived because it was located on a bay with access to fresh water and a wide flat ground before the mountains rose up to the north and east, but it was swept by heavy winds that made winter travel perilous. While Napoleon was imprisoned on St. Helena, off the southwestern coast of Africa, Cape Town and other nearby ports flourished from the feeding, clothing, and housing of his jailers. St. Helena remained an important stop on the route between Cape Town and England, and many British travelers, including a five-year-old William Thackeray, went ashore to get a glimpse of the dethroned emperor.

Cape Town had earlier been claimed by the Dutch, but the English grew convinced of its strategic importance on the route to India and occupied the area in 1806. The sea route around the Cape of Good Hope furnished Europe with raw materials and luxury goods from Asia and India; in exchange, missionaries, colonists, and manufactured goods traveled east. In 1814 Cape Colony officially became part of the British Empire, but its European population was sparse. When Julia Margaret resided there, the population hovered around 20,000 people. Even in the 1830s the colony still looked Dutch: townhouses with high stoops dominated the center and thatched and gabled farmhouses punctuated the surrounding countryside. The area was picturesque, despite the inconveniences of dirt roads that raised clouds of dust on windy days. Vineyards and gardens abounded. Table Mountain made a majestic backdrop. It was wreathed in clouds and fog which rolled down the slopes as a white mist that was likened to Niagara Falls. Locals called the clouds the Table Cloth, and the mists the Cape Doctor, for it was believed that the mountain vapors chased away disease and kept the climate healthful.

The Dutch had used the port for the slave trade, but an alliance of liberals and evangelical Christians in Britain finally succeeded in abolishing slavery in the colonies in 1834. The colony was just beginning a difficult transition when Sir John

Herschel and Cameron met there. The Dutch settlers depended on their slaves, imported mostly from Malaysia, and the emancipation left many established Dutch families impoverished and embittered. They resented the British and they resented their former slaves, whom they now had to pay. Christian Europeans, Muslim Malaysians, native Africans of various ethnicities and regions, and many others of mixed backgrounds lived together uneasily within a thinly populated area.[20]

Sir John Herschel had arrived in Cape Town in 1834, two years before Julia Margaret. His father, William Herschel, had been a musician and amateur astronomer who made his name by discovering the planet Uranus. This historical feat – it was the first discovery of a planet since classical antiquity – was achieved through the new powers of the telescope. When William became interested in astronomy, he taught himself how to grind lenses and polish mirrors of immense size to serve as reflectors and refractors in powerful telescopes. He was the only person at the time who knew how to build these telescopes, and their use revolutionized astronomy. He began systematically "sweeping" the heavens – cataloguing everything he could see as he carefully moved his telescope across the skies above England. He published the first catalogue of double stars and inaugurated the field of stellar astronomy. William became Astronomer Royal and made a fortune selling his telescopes to observatories around the world. John inherited the fortune, the telescopes, and his father's scientific genius. He had had an eccentric upbringing as the only child in a house devoted to late-night star-sweeping, but the family was a close one. John's Aunt Caroline lived with the family and was an accomplished astronomer in her own right.

John first distinguished himself in mathematics at Cambridge, where he was Senior Wrangler, or first in his class. He could have had an academic career, and he tried one briefly, but after several false starts and many professional publications in different scientific disciplines, he decided to devote himself to the life of an amateur scientist. He pursued his experiments and observations wherever they led him – from optics to geology, from physics to chemistry. But as his father aged, John turned increasingly to astronomy and vowed to spend a part of his life confirming and extending his father's work. His own growing reputation and his father's fame gave him entrées into every scientific community in Europe, and he became lifelong friends with Charles Babbage, a pioneer of early computing, among others. In the 1820s he set out to complete William's catalogue of all the double stars in the universe with his father's telescopes and a colleague, James South. As Herschel ruefully noted in a letter to a friend, he might as well work on double stars since he was the only one who could see them. Herschel and South's first published catalogue, showing the precise location and measurements of these distant stars, won them a royal medal. But in order to finish the work, Herschel needed to take his powerful telescope to the southern hemisphere to map its lesser-known skies.

Double stars, seen from the earth as a pair of tiny pinpoints of light, were fascinating because of the questions they posed. Were they stars at all, or some sort of luminous gas? Were they in fact two stars in close proximity to each other, or were they distant stars that only appeared close when seen from the earth? Did they share an orbit? If so, this was important evidence that Newton's laws of gravity applied outside the Earth's solar system. John Herschel's work eventually confirmed that they were stars and they did orbit each other. He was one of the first to use both mathematics and observation to calculate their orbits, but to confirm his equations he needed a lot of data. Thus began his complete catalogue of double stars, his major contribution to astronomy, which took him to the Cape of Good Hope in 1834.

When Herschel left England late in 1833, he had already been knighted for his scientific achievements, though he had never held a paid scientific position. The Cape expedition entailed moving his growing family and two huge telescopes halfway across the world. In Cape Town the Herschels settled in a large farmhouse called Feldhausen, at the foot of Table Mountain. Herschel was devoted to his large family and his marriage was happy and companionable. He was a quiet, amiable man with a reputation among scientists for his generosity and his ability to mediate and avoid rivalries. He cultivated a wide group of loyal friends from different spheres. The novelist Maria Edgeworth, another lifelong friend, once wrote of him that "refined he is highly in sentiment and conversation and sensitive far far too much for health or happiness – mimosa sensitiveness that shrinks from every touch not merely of blame, but even from the very intimacy he most wishes to have."[21] It was hard to get to know him, she continued, but with those in his intimate circle he could be relaxed and sociable. All of her life Julia Margaret pursued friendships with moody, private people by simply ignoring their sensitivities and disarming them with her buoyant good nature. Herschel was one of her earliest conquests.

The renown of Herschel's name and the wonder with which the nineteenth-century world awaited new optical inventions like the telescope and photography facilitated the famous "moon hoax." In August 1835 an American journalist named Richard Adams Locke published a series of articles purporting to be reprinted from the *Edinburgh Journal of Science* (which was actually defunct). The articles were entitled "Great Astronomical Discoveries lately made by Sir John Herschel at the Cape of Good Hope" and they described in convincing detail "lunar observations" recently made by Herschel. The author pretended to have firsthand testimony from a Dr. Andrew Grant, a supposed colleague of the Herschels, which revealed John Herschel's discovery of life on the moon. Published in *The New York Sun*, the articles were a sensation: everyone talked about the new discoveries and the newspaper's circulation rose dramatically over the few days that the series ran. Recent developments in astronomy had outstripped general knowledge, and many were taken in by the hoax. Communications between New York and South Africa were so slow that the hoax was over long before Herschel heard the news and could deny the absurd reports.

To be fair, the article went to some trouble to make the science seem plausible. It described in detail the making of a powerful new telescope, the scientific obstacles that had to be surmounted, and even fictional conversations with real scientists like Sir David Brewster. Besides astronomy, the descriptions of the moon's surface drew on all the developing sub-specialties of Victorian science: zoology, botany, geology, geography, meteorology, and even the emerging social science of comparative anthropology. It was only with the fanciful descriptions of the plants, animals, and people of the moon that even an uninformed reader might have become suspicious. The moon turned out to be a fairy-tale version of our own planet: with dark-red flowers "precisely similar" to our rose-poppies, with "firs, unequivocal firs," and varieties of bison, goats, deer, beaver, and "good large sheep, which would not have disgraced the farms of Leicestershire . . . ." It was mostly a miniaturized Earth, with smaller animals, people, and topography than ours, but it had some fanciful touches: mountains of amethyst crystal, unicorns, and man-made temples of sapphire. Indeed, Locke wrote that "it was more like a creation of an oriental fancy than a distant variety of nature brought by the powers of science to ocular demonstration."[22]

The Oriental allusion is significant because the account is sprinkled with comforting references to both the familiarity of Western geography and the beguiling otherness that was most associated with explorations of other "frontiers" in Africa and Asia. Not surprisingly, the article exhibited other Western preoccupations: the people of the moon turned out to be of three races, of the species "Vespertilio-homo," or man-bat, because they were all winged. The fictional Herschel discovered them in ascending order: first, a short humanoid creature with a "yellowish" face and dark curly hair who was compared to an orangoutan but clearly "rational;" next, people of "a larger stature . . ., less dark in color, and in every respect an improved variety of the species," who "seemed to be eminently happy, and even polite;" and finally,

> the very superior species of Vespertilio-homo. In stature they did not excel those last described, but they were of infinitely greater personal beauty, and appeared in our eyes scarcely less lovely than the general representations of angels by the more imaginative schools of painters.[23]

Locke's moon hoax inspired another footnote in the history of literature and art: it had a tremendous impact on a young American writer named Edgar Allan Poe. A few weeks before Locke's moon hoax appeared in *The New York Sun*, Poe had published a short story entitled *The Unparalleled Adventure of One Hans Pfaall*, in which a Dutchman flies to the moon in a balloon. In subsequent book editions he took pains to distance himself from the moon hoax, appending a long note after the story that severely critiqued Locke's knowledge of astronomy and science. "That the public were misled," he declared, "even for an instant, merely proves the gross ignorance which is so generally prevalent upon subjects of an astronomical nature."[24] Poe was serious about science and took pains to make sure that his new brand of science fiction was as "real" as possible, yet he was also clearly ambivalent about the success of the moon hoax because ten years later he tried to duplicate it. In the 1840s he published another article, later described as a story and entitled *The Balloon-Hoax*, about a transatlantic balloon crossing in the very same *New York Sun* that had published Locke. Rumor has it, however, that when the issue got to the newstands Poe walked the sidewalks proclaiming that the story was only fiction.

The moon hoax had a long afterlife, due in part to the slow path of news throughout the English-speaking world. In September 1836 Lady Herschel was still writing to her aunt, Caroline Herschel, asking if she had heard of the

> clever piece of imagination in an American Newspaper . . . . The whole description is so well clenched with minute details of workmanship & names of individuals boldly referred to, that the New Yorkists were not to be blamed for actually believing it as they did for forty eight hours – It is only a great pity that it is not true, but if grandsons stride on as grandfathers have done, as wonderful things may yet be accomplished . . .[25]

In January 1837 Herschel was still complaining about the letters he received from all over Europe about "that ridiculous hoax."[26]

Julia Margaret arrived in Cape Town and befriended Herschel just as the moon hoax was winding down. She had connections to Cape Town that may have served her well: Colin Mackenzie had met Herschel the year before and Herschel also corresponded with James Prinsep, an amateur scientist in Calcutta and one of Thoby's brothers. Since Herschel was a renowned figure and the community at Cape Town was small, people armed with letters of introduction would stop to visit him on their regular journeys around the Cape. It was apparently a mutual friend, Lady Catharine Bell, who invited Julia Margaret to come to lunch and meet Herschel one Sunday afternoon after church.[27] Julia Margaret often described later in life how despondent and unwell she felt at that time, and the friendship with the Herschels meant the more to her for coming at such a low tide.[28]

Julia Margaret would soon have met every other British person in the community, including Charles Hay Cameron [see figure], then a lawyer in the East India civil service, and Edward Ryan, Chief Justice of Bengal. Ryan knew Charles Hay from Eton and

Calcutta and Herschel from Cambridge. He had also worked with James Pattle on the Board of Revenue, so there were many opportunities for Cameron, Herschel, Ryan, and Julia Margaret to develop their friendships within the small group of English visitors at the Cape.[29] Cameron and Ryan were in Cape Town to recover their health as well. Charles Hay was twenty years older than Julia Margaret and a rising legal scholar in Calcutta. He had just finished working with Thomas Babington Macaulay to reform the laws of India when his health broke down and he retreated to Cape Town to convalesce. In fact, he and Julia Margaret may have met first in Calcutta, as they had both been in residence there during the previous year. Like Julia Margaret, Charles Hay was the grandchild of aristocrats: his mother was Lady Margaret Hay, daughter of the Earl of Erroll of Castle Slains in Aberdeenshire, Scotland. Also like Julia Margaret, Charles Hay's aristocratic forebears had been on the losing side of a revolution: the Camerons came from a long line of Scottish Jacobites, supporters of the exiled Catholic King James after the restoration of the Protestant monarchy to the throne of England. Charles Hay's great-great-grandfather, Lord Lochiel, lost his title for that bit of treason, and his great-grandfather, Archibald Cameron, returned unrepentant from exile and was hanged and quartered at the Tower in London in 1753. Archibald had the misfortune to be the last man executed as a Jacobite. The family retained its upper-class status despite this run of bad luck, and Charles Hay's father became a colonial governor of the Bahamas. Both Julia Margaret and Charles Hay were members of families that probably converted from Catholicism to Protestantism only a generation or two earlier.

Charles Hay was forty-one years old when he met Julia Margaret. There has been speculation that he was married before, but no trace of any first wife has survived. He did, however, father an illegitimate son named Charles Henry Cameron in 1826 and a daughter named Ellen around 1830. Charles Hay gave the son over to his friend John Cowell to raise and kept in touch with them enough to recommend the boy to Haileybury, the East India Company's training school, in 1843.[30] Charles Henry and Ellen reappeared at regular intervals in the Camerons' lives. Many years later, when Charles Hay and Julia Margaret had borne another son, named Charlie Hay after his father, they made plans to send him out to meet his elder half-brother in Bombay. Julia Margaret clearly knew of and accepted these children in some manner: there are references to her writing letters to them and meeting them, which shows a remarkable open-mindedness for her time. Illegitimate children could have been a considerable problem for Cameron in the 1820s while he was establishing his career, and his actions seem to have been ambivalent: he made sure the children were cared for, and felt enough responsibility to acknowledge them with his own name, but perhaps it was shame that held him back from giving this son the aristocratic middle name, Hay, that his children with Julia Margaret all later bore.[31]

Cameron had prestigious connections besides his aristocratic cousin, the Earl of Erroll. He was an early member of the radical Political Economy Club, which included such important Victorian intellectuals and politicians as James Mill, David Ricardo, Thomas Malthus, and Charles Hay's friends George Warde Norman and George Grote. The latter had recommended him as the first professor of moral and political philosophy at the newly established University College in London. The College was to be England's first secular university, but some of the trustees balked at appointing a free-thinking atheist to a chair of moral philosophy, so Cameron lost the appointment.[32] Soon afterward, however, he was named as a special commissioner appointed by the Colonial Office to inquire into the laws and administration of Ceylon. He spent the year of 1830–31 in Ceylon, and in 1832 he and William Colebrooke submitted their report, which has been praised for its enlightened concern for the status of the native Sinhalese and Tamils under British rule and for its proposal that the British administration in Ceylon abolish all legal distinctions between colonized and colonizers. Cameron and Colebrooke have also been criticized for the imposition of English as the language of the courts and for their suppression of local and traditional systems of justice.[33] Their recommendations were largely carried out and became the basis for the Ceylonese legal system until the island became independent as Sri Lanka in 1948. Both Colebrooke and Cameron were utilitarians by training: Cameron was a disciple of Jeremy Bentham, the legal philosopher who founded utilitarianism and inspired the Political Economy Club.[34] Utilitarians held to two main goals: to promote rationalism in law and society and to foster the famous "greatest happiness for the greatest number." The Ceylon commission gave Cameron an opportunity to further both utilitarian goals, and it was a fitting start for his later legal reforms in India. It also inspired a lifelong love of the island, where he soon became the largest single landowner.[35]

Before he left England again, Charles Hay published a philosophical *Essay On the Sublime and the Beautiful*. It was a treatise with close ties to the Enlightenment tradition, dividing the subject into classes and subdivisions and emphasizing sensation and reflection as the sources of knowledge. He acknowledged that there are "certain qualities of the human figure which naturally excite that very powerful emotion, the desire of sexual intercourse." Men, he implied, responded reflexively and passively to the stimuli of physical beauty, which forced them into "unwilling admiration and reluctant homage" unless the response was tempered by "sublime or beautiful feelings."[36] This was a part of his main argument: "that sublimity and beauty (though men think they perceive them by the eye) are qualities of mental feelings."[37]

Although details about Julia Margaret's stay in Cape Town are scarce, she and Charles Hay were both there from February until October 1837. Herschel mentions calling on Charles Hay on April 5 in his diary and then mentions writing a note to Miss Pattle on April 7. It was a wet and stormy spring that year, with changeable weather that Herschel recorded meticulously in his diaries. On October 21 Julia Margaret dined with the Herschels, perhaps to say goodbye. She reported later that she had already boarded her ship home when she got the news of the birth of their sixth child later that week.[38] By then she was engaged. Over the course of that year in Cape Town, Julia Margaret and Charles Hay had fallen in love and decided to marry. They were well suited in status and connections. Cameron was exactly the sort of established Calcutta professional that Julia Margaret's sisters had already married. By temperament they were different but compatible: Julia Margaret was affectionate, impulsive, assertive; Charles Hay was reserved, good-natured, indulgent. They were both bookish and they shared a wry sense of humor.

There was only one problem: Charles Hay did not share her religious faith. He was a member of the Church of England, by birth and duty, but like most utilitarians, he found no rational basis for an emotional investment in more than the basic forms of religious observance. This was troubling to Julia Margaret, especially early in their relationship. She campaigned hard for his conversion, in her prayers and surely in his presence. On November 29 Julia Margaret gave her fiancé a book entitled *Evidence of Christianity* while on board ship together on their way back to Calcutta. She inscribed the inside cover:

> Julia Margaret to Charles Hay Cameron with her fervent and heartfelt wishes and most affecte. and unceasing prayers that their Heavenly Father in mercy may hear their joint supplication and thus answer the longings of her soul and make Jesus Christ their common Saviour God and Redeemer.[39]

The book was written by a clergyman for people who lacked an inner belief in Christianity and searched for external evidence of its truth. The author, John Bird Sumner, conceded that Christianity could not be defended merely because it already had many believers or because it was useful for people to believe in it. Instead, Sumner examined the innovations of Christian doctrine and looked closely at its language: he wrote sections on words like "grace," "righteousness," "flesh," and "faith" itself, all of which, he argued, were redefined in the New Testament.

In her photographic work Julia Margaret would also pay close attention to the multi-layered and contradictory meanings of words and names from the Bible in titling her images. One of her earliest series of images, entitled *Fruits of the Spirit*, was a systematic study of women posing allegorically as "grace," "faith," and other virtues from the Epistle to the Galatians. Like Sumner, Julia Margaret looked to sacred texts for evidence to support her faith. In a letter to her young children in 1845 she reminded them of the precepts of the Sermon on the Mount "which are so divine that they *could*

---

only have come from God and they are the most convincing *evidence* of his (God the Son) having lived upon Earth."[40] Sumner concluded that the sheer variety of evidence for Christianity was persuasive, and that it was best to approach faith with a humble, accepting disposition.[41] It was probably this disposition that eluded Charles Hay.

In February 1838 the couple married in Calcutta, despite their religious differences, but Julia Margaret refused to give up on her mission. In July, when she was carrying their first child, she wrote another heartfelt prayer for her unborn daughter that was testimony to both the deep love she had for her husband and the deep anxiety she felt for his spiritual state. After pleading for God's mercy and love for the child, especially if her life were taken in childbirth, she asks God's protection for her husband:

> Thou alone dost know how fondly dear This my husband is to me, how great is his tenderness, how true is his love. Thou knowest that I have only been too prone to make him my earthly Idol and thus have feared to offend Thee – Thou knowest also that his constant tenderness has sweetened every hour of my life & that my only grief has been that his faith is not yet fixed on the Saviour, the Rock of Ages in whom I trust & to whom I make my prayer. Thine eye canst see what no human eye has beheld & my secret sorrow is not hidden from Thee. If it be then Thy will that I should die in Childbirth my last prayer is that Thou shouldst grant me in death the blessing I have so earnestly desired in life and enlighten his mind so as to enable him to see more clearly & to believe more fully spiritual things . . .[42]

Julia Margaret's plea to survive childbirth was granted many times over, but her ultimate wish for Charles Hay never was. They spent over forty years happily married despite this profound difference. Charles Hay survived her, and at his deathbed in his beloved Ceylon the local minister asked if he could come and officiate. Charles Hay replied with his usual amiability: if it would be any comfort to him, let him come.[43] He must have answered Julia Margaret in much the same spirit of easy patience and indomitable stubbornness when she brought up questions of religion.

Although the rational skepticism of utilitarian philosophy disrupted Charles Hay's religious faith, scientific study did not disturb that of Herschel. Herschel's work on distant double stars, like his father's, was the first scientific evidence that there were other galaxies in the universe besides our own. Although astronomy's major challenge to religion had come centuries before, in the days of Galileo and Copernicus, the heavenly science was again pointing, if ever so discreetly, toward the notion that the Earth was neither the center of the universe nor even a particularly large and important part of it. Although his upbringing had been religious in a perfunctory way,

Herschel became more devout after his marriage to Margaret Stewart, the daughter of a clergyman. He, like many of his scientific peers in the early part of the century, saw science and religion as completely compatible. In his 1830 *Preliminary Discourse on Natural Philosophy* he wrote explicitly

> Nothing . . . can be more unfounded than the objection [that science] leads [its cultivators] to doubt the immortality of the soul, and to scoff at revealed religion. Its natural effect, we may confidently assert, on every well cultivated mind, is and must be the direct contrary.[44]

Decades later, this faith would stand in Herschel's way when he came to evaluate Charles Darwin's theories of evolution.

In fact, while Herschel was studying the southern skies, the young Charles Darwin was already touring the world on the HMS *Beagle*, collecting specimens and data for his later books. Darwin and the *Beagle* made a port of call at Cape Town in 1836 on their way home, and Darwin made sure to meet the renowned Herschel while he was there. As a student Darwin had already read and admired Herschel's *Preliminary Discourse*, which asserted that natural laws governed the universe and that God in his omniscience had foreseen and foreplanned how nature could change without any further intervention. This was a theory of science and religion that drew on William Paley's popular *Natural Theology*, which made the "argument by design" that the world was so beautiful and purposeful that there must be a God to design and maintain it. Herschel and friends like Babbage, who wrote *The Ninth Bridgewater Treatise* in 1837 to defend his views on this subject, scorned those who believed that God constantly tinkered with his creation. But they also recoiled from the cold indifference of a "watchmaker" God who set the universe ticking and then simply watched it wind down. Rather, Babbage argued, God's power and knowledge was such that he could set the universe in motion and preordain changes that would come later, by natural law.[45]

Darwin visited Herschel at Feldhausen on June 3, 1836 and found him "exceedingly good natured" but with "rather awful" manners. Herschel was known to be very modest and genial but his shyness did make him awkward in society. The two men spoke of Charles Lyell's new theories of continental drift, and Herschel may have confided in Darwin that he had recently written to Lyell urging him to confront that "mystery of mysteries" – the development of new species.[46] Already speculating intently on this subject, Darwin was encouraged. He soon returned to London, where Herschel's letter to Lyell had been passed around and much discussed in scientific circles. Scientists of all disciplines were now leaning towards theories of slow, incremental changes rather than abrupt or "miraculous" interventions in nature. That is, "evolutionary," or gradualist, theories were already favored over "revolutionary" theories that viewed events like catastrophes as the major agents of change. As Herschel wrote in his letter to Lyell:

> Time! Time! Time! – we must not impugn the Scripture Chronology, but we must interpret it in accordance with whatever shall appear on fair enquiry to be the truth for there cannot be two truths. And really there is scope enough: for the lives of the Patriarchs may as reasonably be extended to 5000 or 50000 years apiece as the days of Creation to as many thousand millions of years.[47]

The world was almost ready for Darwin. When *The Origin of Species* was finally published in 1859, Herschel called natural selection the "law of higgledy-piggledy,"[48] but nonetheless he had been an early inspiration to its author. Cameron would photograph both men in 1867 and 1868, when she was immersed in producing heroic portraits of England's great geniuses. Despite their differences, the two men were buried side by side in Westminster Abbey in the shadow of the memorial to Sir Isaac Newton.

The careers of both Darwin and Herschel were also testimony to the success, and even dominance, of the amateur science tradition in England. Both men held few, if any, paid scientific positions. Both were of independent means and came from established scientific families: Herschel had inherited money and telescopes; Darwin's father was a famous doctor and his grandfather, Josiah Wedgwood, was the chemist who founded the Wedgwood pottery works. Both Darwin and Herschel were well educated at home and at Cambridge, the incubator for so many English scientists, but their work always pursued independent paths, based on their personal interests, observations, and experiments. Neither worked systematically through one discipline; both drew heavily on a wide range of new scientific knowledge. The requirements of a paid academic post or the constraints of a professional position in the government or civil service might have limited their access to other fields – and would certainly have limited their quiet time for thinking, experimenting, and observing, which both men fought all their lives to protect. Financial anxieties in the 1850s led Herschel to take one disastrous appointment as Master of the Mint. It confirmed all his worst fears about professional posts.

Herschel's trip to the Cape was expensive, and several scientific patrons and societies offered to underwrite it. Herschel turned them down. He wanted the freedom to pursue his interests wherever he might, and he had already served on enough scientific committees to know how administrative duties could consume every working moment. He insisted on remaining an "amateur" scientist, despite his clearly "professional" record of achievements. In the nineteenth century the role of the amateur was prestigious due to its association with gentility. Like artists and authors, scientists had only recently become professionalized enough to have specialized societies and a range of paying work. Most scientific research throughout history was performed by amateurs, who were in many cases self-taught, like William Herschel.

In the 1830s the benefits of being an "amateur" were significant, if one could afford it. The independence and the freedom from the boundaries of academic specializations, which were newly emerging alongside professional societies, were crucial. And amateurs suffered no lack of prestige: with their extensive publications and extended networks of Cambridge contacts and family friends, Darwin and Herschel were well received everywhere they went. Science was a small world then: in the late 1830s nearly every scientist in England passed through Babbage's London salons, many of them amateurs mingling easily with the professionals and professors.[49] But by the 1860s, the professionalization of the arts and sciences had made it much more problematic for Julia Margaret Cameron to identify herself as an "amateur" photographer. The terms were in flux, and "amateur" was gradually becoming an inferior status, as salaries and professional degrees became more important than social status and pure talent. Being a woman, of course, complicated the picture. Being a "professional" woman meant playing a role in public, accepting money for labor, and competing with men in the marketplace – all things that were considered disreputable for middle-class Victorian women. Those gendered attitudes persist: Cameron is still considered an "amateur" photographer, though she sold and exhibited her work, and though Darwin and Herschel are never now called "amateur" scientists. All three of them described themselves as amateurs.

Like Darwin's and Herschel's work, photography itself grew out of an amateur tradition in the same decade. Its history was contested and complicated from the start: like Darwin's theory of natural selection the "invention" of photography arose out of the swirling currents of early-nineteenth-century culture. Curiously, photography came to light in France during the decades that Julia Margaret lived there. And, like Julia Margaret, it had a dual heritage from France and England. According to the standard history of photography, the first attempt to fix a camera image was by the chemist Humphrey Davy and Thomas Wedgwood, Darwin's relative, at the turn of the nineteenth century. They experimented with light-sensitive compounds on paper and leather, but they could never make the image permanent.[50]

A few decades later, Joseph Nicéphore Niépce, a French inventor, succeeded in using silver chloride, which is light-sensitive, to fix an image projected by an "artificial eye," or camera. Unfortunately, the background was black and the photographed images appeared white: Niépce had created a negative (though it would be years before that term was coined, by Herschel), and he could not figure out how to print a positive image from it. Niépce described this process in letters as early as 1816, and over the next decade he succeeded in fixing a hazy positive image on a metal plate. The exposure took eight hours and he called his invention the heliograph. The earliest surviving example dates from around 1827 and is now exhibited alongside Cameron's work in Helmut Gernsheim's photography collection at the University of Texas at Austin.

Niépce shared his invention with the theatrical set designer Louis Daguerre, who was interested in improving the effects of his illusions and in making money. The early decades of the nineteenth century saw an explosion of new optical devices, mostly for recreational purposes and mostly forgotten now except for photography.[51] On January 6, 1839 Daguerre announced his own invention: the daguerreotype, which fixed a photographic image onto a silver-coated copper plate. The image was not reproducible (it was not developed from a negative) but it was very clear – and permanent. Meanwhile, William Henry Talbot, another amateur English scientist, had simultaneously developed his own photographic process in England and was alarmed at the new competition from France. His "Talbotype" used light-sensitive paper to make a negative, which could then be contact-printed onto other pieces of treated paper to create multiple images. The images were initially very small and delicate, but they were distinct. Talbot practiced taking images of his home, Lacock Abbey, and when he first presented his work to the Royal Institution on January 29 he commented drily that "this I believe to be the first instance on record, of a house having painted its own portrait."[52]

Herschel, who was back in England by this time, heard of both Daguerre's and Talbot's processes in January and he instantly grasped how they could be improved. As early as 1819, Herschel had published a paper on the fact that sodium thio-sulphate (or hypo) dissolved silver salts. Since both Daguerre and Talbot used light-sensitive silver salts to make their images, they both faced the problem of how to fix the image permanently by stopping the silver salts from continuing to react to light. Herschel solved the problem within a week of hearing about it: indeed, if his friend Humphrey Davy had paid attention to Herschel's 1819 publication about "hypo" then photography might have been invented twenty years earlier.[53] Herschel immediately wrote to Talbot about his modification and Talbot visited Herschel on February 1 to view his experiments with hypo. Herschel gave the information to Talbot and Daguerre freely, but both men included it in the patents they filed to pro-tect their inventions. Daguerre had already given his process to the French nation in exchange for a lifetime annuity. When photography was publicly revealed in August, people swarmed to buy cameras and chemical kits to make their own first images of streets and buildings.

Herschel's important contributions to photography – discovering "hypo," coining the terms "negative" and "positive," and being among the first to use the term "photo-graphy" itself – have led some photographic historians to argue that he should be given as much credit as Daguerre, Talbot, and Niépce for the invention. It is certain that, as with Darwin's theory of evolution, there were many people conducting research along similar lines at the time. Photography was such an astonishing public marvel in the early years that others then came forward to announce their similar researches, all slightly different, but all trying to claim the important discovery as their own. Herschel himself continued to experiment with photography: he was perhaps the first to make a negative on a glass plate (in a variation of the process Cameron later used in the 1860s). Appropriately, it was a photograph of his father's mighty telescope. Perhaps Herschel's most invaluable contribution to photography, however, was simply his friendship with Cameron: the affectionate regard that developed in Cape Town led to decades of correspondence, in which Herschel relayed to Cameron the latest technological developments in the field. Later, when Cameron took up photography herself, Herschel was among her first advisers and supporters.

The earliest experimenters in photography – Wedgwood, Niépce, Daguerre, Talbot, and Herschel – were all first interested in its uses for artists. All were familiar with the camera obscura and camera lucida, devices employed by artists since the Renaissance. The camera lucida used a prism to "project" an image in great detail onto a traceable surface like drawing paper; Herschel made many drawings from the camera lucida that he carried on his travels. Niépce's experiments with light-sensitive chemicals were intended to make lithography easier to reproduce without the need for an engraver to trace each copy. Like the printing press centuries earlier, photo-mechanical reproduction allowed for virtually limitless copying of images and art. Throughout the nineteenth century, technical advances in photography and mechanical reproduction enabled the mass production of artwork and illustrations. Illustrated books were no longer collectors' items for the rich. These inventions did for the visual world what the printing press did for the literary and textual world: they created a consumer market in images that were cheap, plentiful, and, before long, omnipresent. Photographic historians have argued that the photograph quickly became a mass commodity of the new industrial age: available to all, it collapsed social distinctions and represented complex social relationships as abstractions.[54] This context would become important to Julia Margaret's career.

From its beginnings, photography had a divided heritage: was it English or French? Was it a science or an art? The confusion was intense and the picture only got murkier as the century progressed. By mid-century, people were not always sure what was being represented: was it fact or fiction? The invention of photography had exploded into the public arena in an unprecedented way: with the proliferation of magazines and newspapers and new masses of readers in the nineteenth century, technological inventions traveled faster than word of mouth and to a wider public than the clubby scientific circles that produced them. In March 1839, just after Daguerre announced his invention, Samuel Morse, the painter and recent inventor of the telegraph, compared notes with Daguerre and excitedly wrote home to his brother about the new process: "The exquisite minuteness of the delineation cannot be conceived. No painting or engraving ever approached it . . . . The effect of the lens upon the picture was in a great degree like that of the telescope in nature."[55] Morse's brother edited the *New York Observer* and he published Samuel's letter in an April issue. Even before the installation of telegraphs, news was travelling pretty quickly. Soon hoaxes like Locke's would be impossible to sustain for long.

In February 1838, while the Camerons were marrying in Calcutta, Herschel and his family were packing their bags. The trip to the Cape was finished and it was to provide the most important scientific work of his life. Herschel returned to England to write up his observations and make the calculations from his accumulated measurements. It was the close of one of the happiest periods in both Herschel's and Julia Margaret's life. Shortly afterward, Herschel and Cameron began what would become a long and affectionate correspondence. In one of the earliest extant letters Herschel wrote fondly

> I do assure you I feel very humbly the first kindness of your recollection of me and mine after so long and so distant a separation, a distance and length marked as much by events as by miles and months. The Cape has formed an influential point in both our histories and it is truly delightful to have such a point to look back on in which so much . . . real enjoyment has been mixed up with so little to regret.[56]

Their letters were filled with family news, comments on current events, and more surprisingly, scientific discoveries. They exchanged information and specimens as if the world-renowned scientist and the Calcutta matron were peers. Ten years into their correspondence Herschel was confident enough in Julia Margaret's knowledge and interests to write

> As I know you take an interest in scientific matters, I enclose two specimens of chemical novelties, lately sent me from Basle . . . – the one is <u>paper</u> rendered <u>transparent</u> and in an extraordinary degree electrical by a peculiar process which extends its application to any vegetable tissue. The other (which seems to be and in fact is a piece of cotton) has the explosive property of gunpowder and is even more powerful (weight for weight) with the additional peculiarity of not losing its power by immersion under water for any length of time. Neither of these processes are yet made public.[57]

Historians of photography have often taken cues from Cameron's photographic contemporaries and derided her technical knowledge of photochemistry, but her correspondence with Herschel demonstrates a broad fascination with science and implies knowledge that was unusual for a Victorian woman. Cameron herself paid tribute to Herschel's influence on her later work when she wrote: "For you were my first Teacher & to you I owe all the first experiences & insights which were given to me when you sent me in India a score of years ago . . . the first specimens of Talbotype, of photographs coloured by the juices of plants, &c, &c."[58]

Herschel and Cameron shared a deep fascination with harmonizing dualisms. When photography was invented, Herschel rejoiced (in a poem, suitably) that science and art had become one. Both believed that science and religion were fully compatible. They were optimists. They believed in science, art, and faith with equal devotion and so they could worship with the whole of their natures. They were lucky. Many Victorians were more like Charles Hay and Charles Darwin: caught between their training in rational skepticism and the pressures to conform to established religion. Others, like Carlyle or Eliot, diverted the force of their passionate faith from religion to secular beliefs. But for Victorians like Herschel and Cameron, there seems to have been little struggle in their spiritual life: their beliefs, their experiences, and their feelings ran together in one wide stream. They lacked the inner turmoil of many of their peers, torn between what they believed to be true and what they knew to be true. Their worship could take the form of counting stars or translating poetry, conversing with geniuses or kissing babies. When Cameron made a close-up photograph of two children's heads almost merging as one and called it "The Double Star," she was citing both Herschel's Cape Town observations and the biblical pairing of John the Baptist and Jesus. The science of stellar astronomy was like biblical exegesis was like childrearing was like making art, all springing from love and faith.[59] Both Herschel and Cameron used analogies between the natural and spiritual worlds in order to make religion and science consistent. It was a worldview based in Romanticism and traditional Bible scholarship, and it was already under attack. By mid-century, Herschel's harmonious world would be drawn despite itself into the raging debates over Darwinism; Cameron's ecstatic belief in the unity of art, religion, and science would take shape in photographs just as critics fought over photography's status. But in 1838 Cameron was in a state of grace, surrounded by family and new close friends and wading into the rich currents of Victorian intellectual life.

CHAPTER 3

Memsahib

W HEN JULIA MARGARET and Charles Hay Cameron stepped out of Calcutta
Cathedral as husband and wife on the evening of February 1, 1838, they
assumed a prominent place in Anglo-Indian society. Their marriage had overcome
religious differences and solidified a romantic attachment, but it also legally and economically united two prosperous and influential people in Calcutta society. In
drawing up their marriage contract, Charles and Julia Margaret each declared their
respective fortunes and named their prominent friends and relatives as trustees of a
new estate held in trust for a surviving partner or children. They appointed her father,
James Pattle, her brother-in-law Henry Thoby Prinsep, and their friend Sir Edward
Ryan to this important task of overseeing the financial stability of their family.

In 1838 their future must have looked very rosy. Julia Margaret contributed 85,400
rupees to their marriage settlement and Charles Hay contributed 50,000 rupees and
a bond for 50,000 more over the next three years. In 1841 the trustees duly noted that
the additional 50,000 rupees had been paid as promised and absolved Charles Hay
of the bond.[1] Julia Margaret's contribution seems to have come from a substantial
bequest made to her and her elder sisters by her late uncle, Thomas Pattle, a merchant in Canton.[2] It is difficult to assess the value, in 1838 or today, of Julia Margaret
and Charles Hay's fortunes, but they were clearly in the upper-middle-class bracket
economically. Though separated by two decades and a continent, a rough estimate
would equate their socioeconomic status with the Bingleys of Jane Austen's *Pride
and Prejudice*: not aristocratic but with excellent connections and substantial
incomes. Charles Hay also had a respectable salary from his position on the Law
Commission, and he had enough capital to buy several large estates in Ceylon over
the next decade.

The marriage settlement would generate investment interest for the couple while
one or both lived and the principal would be held in trust for their children after their
deaths. Julia Margaret's settlement contract specified that she would receive the

income from her own marriage portion herself and that her assets would not be liable for any debts that her husband might have at his death. This was an important protection when a married woman's legal status was defined by "coverture," the nineteenth-century notion that marriage subsumed a woman's legal identity into her husband's. Like other privileged women, Julia Margaret clearly had friends and advisors who made a careful, separate legal provision to give her some continuing control over the money she brought to the marriage. Without the marriage settlement, Julia Margaret would have been in the position of most Victorian women: without the right to her own income or inheritance and without the right to financial support from her husband. She could have found herself, for example, in Caroline Norton's unfortunate position.

Caroline Norton was born into a prosperous English family a few years before Julia Margaret's birth. Indeed, the two women may have met in England through their mutual friend Henry Taylor. Caroline was wealthy, beautiful, and talented: her poems were compared to Byron's. But she married a volatile and impoverished gentleman who denied her access to her money, sued for divorce by falsely accusing her of adultery, and took custody of their children. George Norton tried and failed to take her literary copyrights as well, but he succeeded in making his wife's life miserable and spurring her into activism for the reform of women's legal position. All through the 1830s and 1840s Caroline Norton campaigned in her novels, poems, and petitions to secure women's right to divorce, their right to their own earnings and property, and their rights as guardians of their own children. It was not until 1857, however, that the Divorce and Matrimonial Causes Act even established a civil divorce court outside of the Church or Parliament. Women's property rights weren't addressed until the 1870s and 1880s.

In the late 1830s money worries were far from the Camerons' minds. Julia Margaret and her well-married sisters were at the top of Calcutta society. Their father was a senior member of the Company's Board of Revenue; their husbands dominated the administrative councils of the Company and the British colonial government. British India at the time was still divided between Company rule and the growing influence of the royal government in London. The Governor-General of India was appointed by the Crown and Charles Hay too became a government appointee to the Council of India. James Pattle and Henry Thoby Prinsep, on the other hand, were high-ranking Company employees concerned with the administration of a trading empire.

Julia Margaret conceived almost immediately after her marriage: by July, she was writing a prayer for the child quickening within her and on December 5 that child, her only daughter, was born. In keeping with family tradition, she was named Julia after her mother. Like all her siblings, she would also bear the surname of Charles's aristocratic mother: Hay. In the prayer that Julia Margaret wrote in July she revealed her natural fear of dying in childbirth, alongside her anxiety about her husband's spiritual state. The four-page prayer concludes desperately:

> [S]hould I be spared to rise from my bed of sickness and know the fullness of a Mother's joy oh grant that I may live to praise and magnify Thy Holy name for all Thy mercies towards me. Grant me the assistance of Thy Spirit in enabling me to watch over the body & soul of my Infant & spare me to be a tender and loving wife to my husband . . .[3]

With the birth of that child it was as if Julia Margaret herself was born anew, in a swift, sudden change of identity that presaged her transformation into a photographer decades later. She was an intensely involved mother: devoted, anxious, vigilant. After a later birth in 1847, she wrote ecstatically to Sir John Herschel of her great domestic happiness:

> I have always since I have been a Mother felt, that it is worth living for, only to know what it is to be a Mother; it is worth going through all previous trials + sufferings of life to drink of that fount of pure joy which never flows so sweetly as when one's Infant is going to sleep upon one's bosom—[4]

Little Julia was followed closely by her brother Eugene in February 1840, but as the only daughter and namesake Julia Hay seems to have held first place in her mother's heart for a long time.

As she tended an ever-growing family, Cameron relied on the large household of servants that was one of the major perks of colonial life. A woman in Cameron's position could be expected to employ a head servant and several cooks, cook's assistants, waiters, grooms, gardeners, and ayahs (combination nursemaids and lady's maids). The rules regarding caste defined which tasks each Hindu servant could perform, so many jobs were very specific. Cameron would have had a sweeper, a water-carrier, messengers, a door-opener, watchmen, a washerman, and men to operate the cooling punkah fans in the extreme heat. Thomas Babington Macaulay reported that some colonial families kept their servants up all night pulling the punkah fans by a string from outside the master's bedroom.[5] The total number of servants in a middle-class household easily reached ten and sometimes exceeded a hundred. In 1850 Fanny Parks, a colonial writer who claimed to live a quiet life, recommended a minimum of fifty-seven servants, including three to wait at table, two to sew clothes, six to pull the punkah, eight to cut grass, and another eight to groom horses.[6] Labor was cheap and household work was difficult in the tropics, where water often had to be boiled before it could be consumed. Food supplies spoiled quickly and rooms were swept and inspected constantly for insects, snakes, and scorpions. Running a large and efficient household was a wife's main responsibility, and it may often have felt like a military campaign, especially for those who moved frequently.[7]

For British women who arrived in India to marry, setting up a home in a land where languages, religions, climate, and customs were so different was often overwhelming. Cameron and her sisters had the decided advantage of having known India from birth. Whereas memsahibs (the wives of the British masters, or sahibs) were well known for picking up just enough Hindi to command their servants, Cameron and her sisters could converse in Hindi and used it as a private language to communicate with each other after their return to England. Brought up on spicy curries and accustomed to life around elephants, tigers, and alligators, they were immune from many of the trivial fears and serious misconceptions of their compatriots. They were used to the daily routines necessary to avoid the midday heat; they took for granted the seasonal cycles of moving between the scorched city and the cooler hill stations of the Himalayas. If India had been what was called a settler colony, like Canada and Australia, the Pattle sisters would no longer have been "English" at all: generations of life in India meant that their English identity was maintained through sheer force of will in a close and mostly self-contained community. A marriage like the Camerons' made sense on many levels, not least of which was the fact that Julia Margaret brought to Charles an intimate knowledge of life and society in Calcutta, whereas Charles gave Julia Margaret closer ties to the mother country.

One thing that united all the British in India – both recent arrivals and old hands – was an obsession with health and disease. The assumption that India was unhealthy for Europeans was so widespread and unquestioned that it inspired strange fetishes. Many Britons insisted on wearing hard, protective "topi" hats for fear that the sun would fry their brains. Women were told to restrict all activity while they were menstruating. Some of these shibboleths used bad logic for reasonable ends: after all, it did make sense to wear hats and minimize activity in the heat. And there were real risks of disease in India that didn't exist at home in Great Britain, especially in the century before vaccines and antibiotics became available. Malaria was endemic in the tropics and left people shivering with sudden fevers. Everyone took preventive doses of quinine. Cholera was much more common in India than at home, where the Sanitary Acts of the 1830s were beginning to address the problem of contaminated water supplies. Typhoid, tuberculosis, and dysentery were always serious and often fatal. Deaths were frequent and, even more disturbingly, sudden. There were poisonous snakes and scorpions too; a British lady had to get used to shaking out her shoes before she put them on and carefully inspecting her bathroom before each bath.[8]

There were other dangers in India as well. In the late 1830s the British public was shocked and horrified by revelations about Thuggee, the worship of the violent goddess Kali (whose name contributed to the place name "Calcutta"). Thugs (the term was then appropriated into English) proved their devotion to Kali by strangling travellers at random. Although they often robbed their unwary victims, greed was not their main motive and so their behavior was hard to predict. Thugs operated as a small, secret society and it was only through long investigation that the British first discovered and then slowly rooted out the practice. In the meantime, it was sensational news: inspiring long exposés in British periodicals and a bestselling novel called *Confessions of a Thug* in 1839. Written by Philip Meadows Taylor, who superintended a police force at Hyderabad, it was based on Taylor's real encounters with crime and demonstrated the British obsession with imposing law and order on a society they viewed as essentially anarchic and unruly. The fictionalized narrator of the novel is a former Thug who confesses to a British policeman in exchange for a lenient sentence. The Thug displays little regret or unease about the violent history he recounts and the policeman rarely interrupts. The revelation of Thuggee in the late 1830s was convenient and timely for the British: a secret criminal underground helped justify continuing and extending British control over India. Also, in revealing this secret society to a British officer and, implicitly, to the British public, the novel allays anxieties about the mysterious "foreignness" of the new territory.[9] In the 1830s, especially, the British were consolidating their conquests and becoming alarmed by the increasing challenges of their new empire. India seemed to them to grow more and more complicated, and less and less familiar, as they explored and conquered it. Each new region brought new languages, religions, and traditions, all confusing and strange to them. In their eagerness to explain and erase India's difference, the colonial British applied all the familiar tools of the Western Enlightenment: they reasoned, they mapped, they counted and measured – and they made lots and lots of new laws.

It hadn't always been this way. When the British first arrived in India as Company traders, they settled in small seaside ports and negotiated with local rulers. They were outsiders, there on sufferance and without the numbers to form a society of their own. They were forced to fit in and the history of the early colonization is one of relatively easy and casual social relations between Indian and Briton. Many of the early colonists were adventurers and profiteers, but others were serious scholars who studied ancient Asian languages and established the Asiatic Society in Bengal. They admired Indian civilization for its long history and its achievements in arts and sciences.[10] True, they mostly believed that Indian religions were idolatrous, but they were still interested in them and eager to study anything new.

As Edward Said pointed out most memorably, Western ideas of the East always served the purpose of controlling and defining its threatening "otherness." The early Orientalists in India and the later utilitarian and evangelical administrators all shared the same goal of remaking India into a place that could be understood and governed only through Western interventions.[11] But despite this common purpose, the growth of the colonies and the arrival of missionaries did change British attitudes towards India. Ironically, the British became less tolerant and less interested in Indian culture the longer they stayed. They became convinced that their mission was to save India from itself and bring "civilization" and order to a chaotic land. The pantheism of the Hindus was no longer a matter of personal belief, provoking a shrug of the shoulders at the whims of foreigners; it was now a matter of duty to save as many immortal souls as possible. By the 1830s, the British in India had the numbers and the clout to create their own segregated societies and insist on their own customs. Isolated from the larger culture that might help them maintain their own traditions and feeling threatened by the profound differences all around them, the British in India held on all the more tightly to their Britishness. Sometimes their efforts seemed ridiculous, like when the women insisted on wearing crinolines, corsets, and petticoats in the Indian heat. Sometimes they simply seemed practical, if nostalgic, like when they formed "mutton clubs" to raise and butcher sheep in a land where beef and pork were mostly forbidden.[12] Cameron grew up during that change in the attitude of the British to the Indians. Her parents were shaped by the older, more tolerant culture, but she matured into the new, more repressive society.

This shifting political culture may help to explain one of the paradoxes of Cameron's experience in India. Although the colonial classes were often accused of being more rigid and intolerant than their compatriots at home, Cameron and her family were easily accepted, despite their eccentricities and their willful flaunting of expectations. One Company memoirist wrote that British colonial ladies were especially "high-spirited" and "quarrelsome" because they were in scarce supply and high demand.[13] Although Cameron tended to be bossy and insistent on her privileges, she was also more inclined to follow her own impulses and opinions than any social mandate. Living in the transition between the old freewheeling and entrepreneurial Company culture and the new governmental bureaucracy helped her to establish her independence from the colonial elite while staying within it.

Britain's newer attitude toward India was expressed in social behavior but also in concrete language and policy. In 1817 the utilitarian philosopher James Mill had written an influential history of British India, which explicitly argued that India represented a degraded and declining civilization and it was Britain's mission to civilize the country. The British East India Company was so pleased with Mill's work that it offered him a full-time job, providing him (and later his son John Stuart Mill) with a steady income to supplement their writings. For all their radicalism, the utilitarians, including John Stuart Mill later on, were remarkably unsympathetic to colonial cultures. When considering legislation, they could and did defend the rights of all people to the same, neutral laws. In matters of religion, they were often atheists or agnostics and tolerant of alternative faiths. But in questions of culture, they were as deeply committed to British superiority as their most conservative enemies.

The utilitarians were such an important influence on colonial India and on Cameron's life that it is worth a detour to consider the various people and ideas associated with the term in the 1830s and 1840s. As a movement, utilitarianism covered theories of economics, law, philosophy, politics, and education, often in contradictory ways. As a group, the utilitarians were close, even claustrophobic: James Mill rented lodgings from Jeremy Bentham and involved Bentham in the accelerated education of his gifted son. In general, all the utilitarians, or "philosophic radicals," agreed with Bentham's doctrine that actions be judged by their consequences: do they result in the greatest happiness of the greatest number of people? This philosophy suspended thorny discussions of "natural laws" or "God's will" and substituted a clear, human-centered, and rational calculation for the rightness or wrongness of every action. If it benefits the majority, then it is right. If it does not benefit the majority, then it is wrong. As simple as that.

Except, as John Stuart Mill was later to discover with great pain, this rational accounting of debits and credits gave scant weight to feelings or other unquantifiable pleasures like art or culture. John Stuart Mill's upbringing and education had been so relentlessly logical that that the prodigy suffered a mental breakdown when he was twenty years old. He recovered by immersing himself in Romantic poetry and afterward humbly declared that

> I never, indeed, wavered in the conviction that happiness is the test of all rules of conduct, and the end of life. But I now thought that this end was only to be attained by not making it the direct end . . . . Ask yourself whether you are happy, and you cease to be so.[14]

Utilitarianism also begged the question of who would be deciding about whose happiness. This question became especially important when the newest colonial administrators arrived in India steeped in utilitarian ideals. Suddenly they were part of a tiny European minority governing over millions of Indians in their own land. The utilitarian logic-by-numbers now became problematic and drew attention to conflicts between theory and practice. Lord William Bentinck, who was Governor-General in the early 1830s, was a strong advocate of James Mill's *History of British India* and declared that his goal was to base "British greatness on Indian happiness."[15] One of his first reforms was to abolish the Indian practice of *sati* (called suttee by the British at the time), whereby high-caste Hindu widows were burned alive on their husband's funeral pyres. By feminist and humanitarian standards, *sati* was clearly wrong. And yet its abolition was also a cultural imposition that ignored the religious and social traditions of a very different land.

The newly arrived British administrators like Bentinck were influenced by utilitarian theories, either through their education or through the animated public debates surrounding the Reform Act of 1833, which granted the vote to portions of the English middle classes. Naturally, the reformers drew on utilitarian logic to argue that increasing political participation benefited the majority of the population. Macaulay, who arrived in India in 1834 as the first legal member of the Council of India, was fresh from his triumphs as a parliamentary reformer. Although Macaulay had once publicly attacked the utilitarians' political ideas, he agreed with their laissez-faire economics and his legal and educational reforms in India would depend heavily on a close look at consequences. Macaulay was no radical – he did not approve of universal male suffrage because he felt the working classes were not sufficiently well educated to vote – but he believed that the landed aristocracy must share power with the new industrial middle classes or else England would face a revolution like the one in France.[16]

When Macaulay arrived in Calcutta, his reputation had preceded him and he was greeted with banquets and honors. By the time he left, four years later, he was perhaps the most hated man in the city. He had unfortunately landed in a hornet's nest of controversy and problems that predated him. At the time, the British Crown was pondering the future of India and realizing that it needed to make some claim over the possession and administration of the ever-growing colony. It was unseemly for a private trading company to govern it, but the solution was politically tricky. The British East India Company had lost its monopoly on trade with India in 1813, but it was still the de facto ruler of British India and powerful at home. In 1834, as part of a gradual movement toward assuming control of India, the English government ordered the British East India Company to cease its trading activities and divest itself of its commercial properties. The Company was allowed to continue governing India in exchange for taxes sent to London, but it was acknowledged that India needed a more structured administration. In the past, the court-appointed Governor-General had ruled the subcontinent by fiat. The Council of India was simply an advisory body and there was no legislature. Now, the English government added a legal member to the Council in order to begin to address the lack of lawmakers.[17] Macaulay was the first legal member, and Charles Hay Cameron succeeded him a few years later.

When Macaulay arrived, the Council and its committees were deciding how to spend 100,000 rupees designated by the British government for the education of natives in India. This small matter became enormously important for India's future as the newly arrived bureaucrats lined up against the older generation of scholars and

Company traders and made a decision that would determine language and education policies for the rest of the century. The so-called Orientalists, led by Cameron's future brother-in-law Thoby Prinsep, argued that the committee had always promoted the teaching and publication of works in India's literary languages: Sanskrit, Persian, and Arabic. India had a long and celebrated written tradition in these languages, the Orientalists insisted, and they should continue to be supported by the British. The more recent arrivals, led by the evangelical and utilitarian Charles Trevelyan, argued that it was only through familiarity with English traditions and the English language that the Indians could better themselves enough to earn their independence. The debates were fierce and often degenerated into name-calling and stone-throwing. Trevelyan accused the Orientalists of using British funds to publish Sanskrit "pornography."[18] Prinsep hotly denounced the naïve and ignorant newcomers. But the tide was turning against the older administration of Orientalists who wanted to study and observe India: the new administrators, partly influenced by James Mill's account of the British mission to civilize India and partly led by evangelical fervor to convert it, arrived in India intending to change it.

It was at this cultural turning point that Macaulay arrived, and Charles Hay Cameron soon after him. Macaulay was, in effect, to use his considerable rhetorical powers and prestige to cast the deciding vote. On February 2, 1835 he delivered his famous "Minute on Indian Education", a report to the Committee on Public Instruction of which he was a member. In deciding whether English or Sanskrit and Arabic should be encouraged with government funds, Macaulay muses, "Which language is the best worth knowing?" and proceeds to evaluate it by the numbers: how many students study each language and how much do they pay for it? What are the sales figures for books in each language? "The state of the market is the decisive test," he concludes in true utilitarian fashion. And yet the essay is also full of patently unprovable assertions, such as Macaulay's notorious comment that "a single shelf of a good European library was worth the whole native literature of India and Arabia."[19] Macaulay had come down firmly on the Anglicist side, in support of his new brother-in-law Charles Trevelyan. Governor-General Bentinck ratified the basic argument of Macaulay's speech in March. Macaulay and the Anglicists had won, and they are largely credited with the establishment of English as the lingua franca of India. They are also accused of the grossest cultural imperialism, though some argue that their open prejudices against Indian culture ironically helped set the stage for Indian nationalist movements.[20]

The controversy over English education was the biggest battle in a running war between Thoby Prinsep and Macaulay. As other scholars have noted, the two men did not differ so widely in their basic assumptions: for example, both men believed that England's role in India was to guide it toward self-government. But they argued fiercely over the means to that end. Prinsep, a lifelong conservative, resisted any sudden changes in policy and believed in following established precedents. Like the other Orientalists of the time, he felt that the path toward Indian self-government should come from within its own culture. Macaulay, on the other hand, believed with Bentham that precedent had no special authority in matters of right and wrong. India, the Anglicists argued, would benefit most by assimilating into a new, English way of life.[21] Their feud, fed by personal rivalries as well as philosophical differences, continued after Macaulay's triumph. Even in 1837, a later Governor-General, Lord Auckland, wearily wrote home that Prinsep and Macaulay "butted at each other like wild bulls, blind to everything but their own joust of brains and the contest was not advantageous to either."[22] His sister, Emily Eden, agreed that "the Prinsep" was "so contradictory that he will not let anybody agree or differ with him."[23] As a utilitarian and a Macaulay loyalist, Charles Hay Cameron's entry into the Pattle family must have fanned some flames, although there is no evidence of anything but harmony between Prinsep and Cameron later in life.

After his education policy success, Macaulay was put in charge of the Law Commission to reform the Indian penal code. It was a prodigious task for which he had little experience. Charles Hay's appointment to the Commission was crucial to its success: Cameron had experience of legal scholarship and some knowledge of South Asian law through his work in Ceylon. Moreover, he was another utilitarian who could be counted on to have legal views compatible with those of Macaulay.[24] Cameron arrived in Calcutta on August 12, 1835 bearing a letter for Macaulay from James Mill himself. Macaulay put the newcomer up in his own house while Cameron searched for lodgings. Macaulay wrote the senior Mill back with a good report of their mutual friend:

> All that I have seen of him satisfies me that the home authorities could not possibly have made a better choice. We agree perfectly as to all the general principles on which we ought to proceed, and differ less than I could have thought possible as to details.[25]

The two men started work immediately, and Macaulay optimistically, and quite wrongly, believed they would finish in a few months. Macaulay thought so well of Cameron that he also recommended his junior colleague for a vacant seat on the Committee for Public Instruction, where, like Macaulay, he sided firmly with the Anglicists against his soon-to-be brother-in-law Thoby Prinsep.

It was partly Cameron's ill health, which led him to the Cape of Good Hope and to marry Julia Margaret, that delayed the completion of the penal code, which Macaulay finally delivered to the government in May 1837. As Macaulay complained in many letters home, he finished the code almost single-handedly as illness decimated his

Commission. The new penal code drew on the same Anglocentric, utilitarian, and rational assumptions as the debate over Indian education. In place of the heterogeneous and flexible Indian laws, based often on Islamic law and conducted in local languages, it established a single, unified legal system conducted in English. Characteristically, Macaulay had insisted on creating a new penal code from scratch, without building upon any existing laws but based instead on philosophical principles.[26]

In devising the ambitious new Indian penal code, Macaulay and Cameron must have drawn heavily on Cameron's recent work in Ceylon. In 1829–30 the British government had appointed Cameron and William Colebrooke as commissioners to inquire into the state of colonial administration in Ceylon. Their recommendations for legal reform, submitted in 1832, were largely carried out in 1833 and resulted in the replacement of local, sometimes conflicting, legal traditions with one standard, English-based legal system that uniformly applied to every race, religion, and class. Cameron and Colebrooke were radical in insisting that no legal distinctions be made between the British and the native populations. While the goal of equality before the law was admirable, in practice the imposition of the English language and bureaucracy made the courts difficult for local people to navigate.[27]

As in India later on, the reformed, anglicized legal system was intended to be unified, rational, and fair, but it hoped that people would change to suit the laws instead of creating laws to suit the people. In their campaigns against the privileges of birth (either class or caste) and the abuses sanctified as tradition, the utilitarians sincerely tried to remake the world into a more democratic and more reasonable place. But if something was sacrificed – comfort, differences, alternatives – they didn't always notice. It would all be for the best in the long run, they argued, as they compelled others to match their own commitments to education, industry, political participation, and self-improvement. Their logic was at once humanitarian and imperialist. As Charles Hay wrote in 1832,

> I can conceive no tie which will bind the lower people so strongly to their government, as a judicial establishment so contrived as that the very same attention and discrimination should be employed upon their causes as upon those of their affluent neighbors.[28]

Cameron favored the education of natives and their admission to the civil service (at lesser salaries, though) for similar reasons: it was right, it would bind the colonized to their colonizers, and it would help prepare them, slowly and gradually, for eventual self-government. It was a paternalistic attitude, but its intentions were benevolent within the conventions of the time.

Macaulay was an acerbic observer of Calcutta society and it is no wonder that with his unconventional views and intellectual pretensions he made few friends there. He was clearly fond of Charles Hay and also befriended Edward Ryan, then Chief Justice of the Supreme Court in Bengal and Charles Hay's childhood friend from Eton. The three men were all avid classicists and Macaulay couldn't resist poking fun at the ill-educated ignorance of the company clerks in their classical examinations. He lived and socialized with his beloved sister and her husband, Charles Trevelyan, and went out as rarely as possible, complaining,

> the public diversions are of a miserable sort, –vile acting, –viler opera-singing, –and things which they call reunions, – a sort of subscription balls. These and great dinners of between thirty and forty people constitute the dissipation of Calcutta. I avoid all these amusements, – if they deserve the name, – the dinners excepted. I am forced now and then to be a guest, and now and then to be a host. Last week we had a party of thirty six, and next month we must have another. Nothing can be duller. Nobody speaks except to the person next him. The conversation is the most deplorable twaddle that can be conceived; and as I always sit next to the lady of highest rank – or in other words next to the oldest, ugliest, proudest, and dullest woman in the company – I am worse off than my neighbors.[29]

Macaulay's open impatience with colonial society made him unpopular, and his success inspired envy as well.[30] It was well known that Macaulay had been tempted into this job with the exorbitant salary of 10,000 pounds per annum and during his four years in India he managed to live well and still save enough money to return to England a rich and independent man. This had been his personal motive for taking the job and his letters home are filled with running accounts of his savings and expenses. As he himself pointed out, he was lucky to have come to Calcutta after the bank failures early in the decade. Calcutta society was noticeably quieter and Macaulay was much more careful than his peers about living within his means and avoiding debts.

Julia Margaret's position at the pinnacle of Calcutta society and government necessarily involved her in political events. With Charles Hay holding an influential position in the government and with members of their extended family occupying high offices within the East India Company, Julia Margaret and her sisters appear to have taken a natural and enthusiastic interest in current events. This is best demonstrated by surviving letters between the family and Captain (later Major) George Broadfoot, a good friend of theirs and a hero of the First Afghan War.

The early 1840s saw the opening moves of what became known as the "Great Game" between Britain and Russia for influence over Central Asia. After the Napoleonic Wars, it became clear that Russia was Britain's only imperial rival in Asia, and as the colonies became more and more important to Britain the British became more and more uneasy about Russia's influence, especially in the unstable lands to the northwest of India. England had made a precarious alliance with Ranjit Singh, the powerful leader of the Sikhs in the Punjab region (now divided between India and Pakistan and still under dispute). But beyond the Punjab lay Afghanistan, where competing tribal leaders were fighting for control. With rumors of Russian influence in Kabul swirling around, the British decided pre-emptively to create an Army of the Indus and forcibly return the exiled and enfeebled Shah Shuja to the Afghan throne. With the British and East India Company army, some 9,500 men strong, went Julia Margaret's brother-in-law Major Colin Mackenzie and their friend Captain George Broadfoot.

The invasion of Afghanistan in 1839 seemed surprisingly easy and the British promptly restored Shah Shuja to his throne and left Sir William Macnaghten and Sir Alexander Burnes, respectively British Envoy and Resident, in charge behind the scenes. They left a small force on the plains outside Kabul, and the rest of the army retreated to India. Mackenzie was left in charge of a fort near Kabul and Broadfoot ended up at the fort in Jalalabad, which guarded the Khyber Pass and the border of India (now Pakistan). There were some who thought the whole invasion reckless. Little was known of Afghanistan in the West except for the fact that it was in a state of almost constant unrest and it did not easily suffer foreign occupations. Colin Mackenzie was apparently uneasy with the tense quiet of 1840; he wrote: "Our gallant fellows in Afghanistan must be reinforced or *they will all perish*."[31]

He was right. The Afghans rose up against the British in Kabul in November 1841, killing the British Resident and his assistant, George Broadfoot's brother. The fort outside Kabul was besieged. The indecisive British commanders finally decided to open negotiations with the Afghan leader: Macnaghten promised to remove the British army from Afghanistan if the Afghans provided them safe conduct to the border. Mackenzie accompanied Macnaghten to the parlaying point, but the Afghans had heard that Macnaghten was still scheming to avoid the humiliating treaty and they turned on him. Macnaghten was killed and Mackenzie and another officer were taken hostage. The British army in desperation began the retreat from Kabul to Jalalabad on January 6: a sick and hungry party of some 16,000 British and Indian soldiers, their families, and camp followers began a 150-mile march through snowy mountain passes. Frost and hostile Afghan horsemen decimated their numbers. On January 13 the one and only survivor stumbled into Jalalabad with the terrible news. For the British, it was one of the worst military disasters of the nineteenth century.

George Broadfoot had been assigned to secure the failing defenses of the old fort at Jalalabad, and he now advised holding out against the surrounding Afghans until reinforcements could be sent from India. He and others like him prevailed with their anxious commanders and together they managed to defend the fort and send the

Afghan army back to Kabul. In April British reinforcements arrived, and by September they had recaptured Kabul. During this tense and frightening time, Broadfoot wrote continually to Julia Margaret and her sisters as well as to Charles Hay Cameron and Thoby Prinsep, exchanging news of Colin Mackenzie for news from Calcutta. The family was clearly worried about Colin, who was eventually ransomed when the British returned to Kabul. While being held hostage by the Afghans, he had been made an emissary for negotiations and his courage in keeping his word to return to captivity when the negotiations ended made him a hero. "Anxious about him we cannot but be," Broadfoot wrote to Julia Margaret's sister Louisa Bayley in May 1842,

> yet I know the [Afghan] men with him are desirous to protect him, and I believe them able to do so, for they are relations of the principal chief, near relations, and the esteem they perceive Colin enjoys here has confirmed their opinion, already very high, of his value as a hostage in their hands.[32]

Louisa's husband, Henry Vincent Bayley, was another scion of a prominent colonial family – he eventually became a justice on the Supreme Court of India – so his influence would have been useful to Broadfoot as well.

Broadfoot was much concerned that Colin's heroism be acknowledged with some honor, in spite of the general disaster.[33] The letters, though addressed to Julia Margaret and her sister Louisa Bayley, include asides intended for Charles Hay or Thoby Prinsep and reveal how influential the Pattles were in Calcutta. The sisters report on Broadfoot's reputation in Calcutta by carefully watching the new Governor-General, Lord Ellenborough, for signs of favor. In return, Broadfoot sends the Pattle clan inside information on the state of affairs on the front line. When the reinforcing army arrives in Afghanistan ill equipped, Broadfoot makes sure that his influential friends in Calcutta hear about it. He was candid in blaming the previous Governor-General, Lord Auckland, for the disaster at Kabul and frank about British "ignorance of the institutions and manners of the country."[34]

In 1843 Charles Hay became the legal member of the Council of India – Macaulay's old post. As such, he was responsible for the legal interpretation of treaties and colonial policies, so he was often consulted in territorial matters. He investigated the Kabul disaster and wrote up a Minute (or report to the Council) on it. He was well positioned to evaluate the successive Governor-Generals in character and ability and he didn't hesitate to judge them. Of Ellenborough he wrote in 1843 to Broadfoot:

> The Governor-General is civil to me, and continues to show those good qualities which we both agreed in thinking he possesses; nevertheless, I wish he may not remain here, for he is not steady enough for enterprises which take a long while in the concoction and in the execution.[35]

Julia Margaret agreed in even stronger terms in another letter to Broadfoot a few days later:

> Lord Ellenborough, if it be not treason to say so, is flighty and unmanageable in all matters of business; shrewd enough, but wholly without ballast; violently enthusiastic on all military subjects, and they alone seem to occupy his interests or his attention.[36]

Later in the same letter, Julia Margaret expressed anxiety about Broadfoot's health and urged him not to sacrifice himself to his duties. "For I (although a woman) am a lover of public good," she wrote, and in the long term the public good would not be served if good men wore themselves out and suffered "early decay."[37] Cameron had an ulterior motive in these warnings: even as early as 1843, five years into marriage, she was worried about Charles Hay's health and the strain of his responsibilities in Calcutta. In addition to his Council work, he was the President of the Council for Education in Bengal. His friends, she confided to Broadfoot, wished him to stay in Calcutta for as long as it took to finish his legal reforms, but Julia Margaret protested that Charles Hay was too often unsupported in the Council and that he was sacrificing himself in "this vile climate" for nothing. She swore to Broadfoot that

> I have never sought to persuade or bias my loved Charles either in favor of going home or remaining here. With so little ambition as he has with so much taste for literary leisure & retired life I think he would be far happier at home but he might think he was wasting abilities that he ought to have devoted to public life & to public good and therefore I think that on this subject he alone can decide & that a Wife incurs too great a responsibility when she lets the devotedness of her love urge her Husband to do that about which he has a shadow of a doubt as regards the conscientiousness of the step.[38]

Cameron may have been protesting too much: it is hard to believe, regardless of her best intentions, that she didn't make her preference for a life in England well known to her husband. She continues her letter by stating, rather melodramatically, that she merely hopes her own health will allow her to continue living in Calcutta with Charles Hay.

But Cameron did have real cause to campaign for a return to England, besides Charles Hay's health. Her three-year-old son, Eugene, had just been sent to live in England and her beloved daughter Julia would join him the following year. Cameron dreaded these separations with an agony that she could barely contain. The voluble and candid letters to Broadfoot in September included a long sigh of relief that little Eugene, who had been ill when he was put on board ship, was now recovered and thriving on the long passage. Even the usually acerbic Emily Eden had to admit that "the real calamity of the life [in India] is the separation from home and friends. It feels like death, and all the poor mothers here who have to part from their children from five years old to seventeen are more to be pitied than it is possible to say."[39]

Relocations and separations were a constant feature of family life. Sara and Thoby Prinsep had recently moved back to England and Julia Margaret watched their adjustment with great interest. In the same letter to Broadfoot in September 1843, she complains that her outgoing younger sister was too taken with fashionable society in London and she hopes that she would soon settle down into better company. "Her heart," she wrote, "so warm as it is meets with constant disappointment from the worldliness, the pride, & the arrogance of those in whose circle she moves & yet she has not the courage to renounce at once all these vanities."[40] Her own life in Calcutta, she wrote, was more sociable than she wished and she often went out alone to spare her husband the exhaustion of stifling ballrooms. Whether her complaints were completely sincere or not, it appears that Julia Margaret was not as wholly enamored of her role in Calcutta society as some accounts suggest. Also, the distinctions she makes between fashionable society and smaller, select gatherings of special friends will later be borne out in her preference for her own close and eccentric circles at Little Holland House and Freshwater over the salons of the London elite.

It is often observed that Julia Margaret enthusiastically arranged picnics and boating parties, entertained visiting dignitaries, and generally organized Calcutta society until her departure in 1848. If there were awkward introductions to make, Julia Margaret could make them. If there were strangers in need of anything, Julia Margaret would care for them. It was a social pattern established early in her life and driven by a personality at once loving, generous, and eager for attention, but her letters to Broadfoot show her social life in a different light. Socializing was clearly an important duty for the wife of a colonial administrator and Julia Margaret tried to balance this responsibility with her own social nature and her love for her family. She also recognized her need for activity when she was feeling depressed and anxious.

It may have been the emotional demands of motherhood alongside the absorbing political events of the time that made Julia Margaret impatient with social claims. Letters exchanged with the Herschels reveal domestic tidbits about little Julia, called Juley, and Eugene. Another son, Ewen Wrottesley Hay, was born in December 1843. It so happens that several letters between the Camerons and George Broadfoot survive from December 1844 and early 1845 and these reveal how intensely the parents dreaded the looming separation from six-year-old Juley. In the surviving letters they never mention Eugene, which seems to imply that Juley's departure felt like a new and particularly heart-wrenching experience. Perhaps because Juley was their first child and only daughter, this separation felt different than the rite of passage that uniquely and distinctively marked the life of every colonial Briton. On December 5 Charles Hay wrote: "Today is little Julia's birthday & my retreat is invaded by many fair enemies [–] fair in aspect I mean[,] not in the mode of their hostility. Do not therefore expect much Law or Reason from me–."[41] Julia Margaret added a postscript lamenting that this was her daughter's last birthday in India: "what that thought brings to my heart you who <u>know</u> my heart can know & tell."[42]

The countdown had begun and Charles Hay's letters of December 12 and 26 each conclude with Julia Margaret too depressed and preoccupied to write to Broadfoot herself. His letter of February 9 begins with the bald fact that little Juley sailed in January. They had seen her to the sandbanks and said goodbye and Julia Margaret had promptly fallen ill, which Charles Hay attributed to grief. There is no evidence that they saw Juley again until their return to England in 1848, three years later. Eugene would not see his parents for more than four years. Julia Margaret's long postscript reveals her struggles to make sense of this

> very great loss–the loss of my first born & best beloved Child the darling of my soul . . . . [N]o tears but those of joy did I ever shed over my Julia till the hour of parting approached and came–of the anguish of that hour I will not trust myself to speak here . . . –for how few who part in India meet again!!
>
> But this is not the view I allow my mind habitually to take. And even under this view a strong sense of duty of having in plain words, done what was right to be done, still consoles me. I have told my husband that of all my life of devotedness to my Child [no] act has so strongly marked my love for her as this parting with her–[43]

She believed that sending Juley away was best for her, and she comforted the crying child with accounts of the healthful and energizing air of Europe. But her pain was not much relieved by the fact that every expatriate mother went through this same parting. Does every mother devote herself to her child as she had done, preferring the nursery to the throngs of dancing, singing, smiling revelers at the illuminated balls in Government House? she asked rhetorically. Julia Margaret's grief was natural and understandable, but when she describes how she will keep a daily journal so that Juley will later appreciate her mother's devotion, how they never spent one hour apart, and how she lived for and in her daughter, it begins to sound like an excessive reaction. She had other children who seem to have received less than their share of her love and attention. Indeed, she mentions at the end of the letter that little Ewen is well and dear

> but I dare not now trust myself to give him all my love. One fears to love after a great trial, and one thinks by raising a sort of bulwark round one's heart that one cannot suffer so much under another separation or trial, but yet I do not feel sure that there is wisdom in this . . .[44]

There was only one love that trumped her love for Juley and that was her love for Charles Hay: she wrote Broadfoot that her husband wanted her to accompany Juley to England but she couldn't bear to leave him.

Eugene and Juley were sent to Margaret Hay Cameron, Charles Hay's unmarried sister, who lived by the sea in the south of England near their widowed sisters Isabella Darling and Mary Wodehouse. Julia Margaret's concern to shelter her children from worldliness as well as dangers must have been assuaged by the quiet, devout life that they led with their protective aunt. Margaret kept a journal to chronicle the daily chatter and play among the two Cameron children and their Wodehouse cousins, presumably for Julia Margaret's benefit. They had visits from their Calcutta aunts and uncles, and Eugene, at least, was photographed by daguerreotype in 1846, perhaps at his mother's request.[45] The children also had their portraits painted regularly. One visitor from Calcutta reported back to Julia Margaret in December 1846 that Juley was

> a sweet looking pretty little girl rather French looking and strikingly like her Aunt Virginia. Eugene is a very fine boy with such remarkably good manners that he quite delighted me, and he is moreover the living image of yourself.[46]

In that letter it was clear that the Camerons were already making plans to return to England.

Julia Margaret kept up a constant flow of letters and trinkets to the two children. In one letter that survives from April 1845 she lists the enclosures: a figure of the Infant Samuel, a fan depicting babies and their mothers (to remind Juley of her fond Mama), and a box painted with a visual trick and containing imitation almonds.[47] In another packet she sent an ornament symbolizing faith, hope, and charity; a doll's necklace with a turquoise cross; a tiny purse; a silver whistle; a book called *The Story Without an End*, about divine love and providence; and an illuminated Sermon on the Mount. The letters betray a deep anxiety about illness and accidents. In the April missive six-year-old Juley is reminded not to run, not to put any berries in her mouth without permission, not to fall off the donkey, and not to eat any of the imitation almonds that her mother had sent in case she chokes on them. Julia Margaret cannot seem to keep from her small child how grief-stricken she is at their parting: she pleads for letters, even misspelled, and she brags about how many pages she has filled in the daily journal she has kept since Juley's departure. She tracks the separation day by day into weeks and months and she candidly tells the child that she has made a shrine of her little bed. All of this is loving and attentive, and typical of Julia Margaret's ardent nature, but it casts a long shadow: Julia Margaret continued to send long, affectionate, and rather querulous letters to her daughter long after the girl had grown and the intimacy between them seems to have been both close and claustrophobic. Even as a young woman, Julia Hay Cameron was being warned to take care on the beach lest she sit on something wet.

But for all her passion, Julia Margaret was practical too, and she needed to turn her energy to good use. The effusive letter to Broadfoot ends with Julia Margaret forcibly turning her attention from Juley's many graces and determinedly reporting on the latest gossip at Government House. As in the rest of her life, she needed a new and absorbing project in which to immerse herself for the next few years. She found two such that drew upon her social and artistic talents as well as her generosity and her desire for attention. The most pressing was the growing awareness in the British world of the miserable plight of the Irish in the mid-1840s. Several years of potato crops had failed, and by 1845 the situation was desperate: in a country already poverty-stricken and dependent on agriculture famine was everywhere. Utilitarian theory favored the laissez-faire economics of David Ricardo. Governments must not interfere with imports and exports, he argued, and the inevitable economic cycles should be left alone to correct themselves naturally. With this in mind, and facing its own disgruntled population of poor and newly unemployed during the "Hungry Forties," the British government ignored the crisis in Ireland for years: dairy products continued to be shipped out of Ireland and starving peasants were told that imports would start when they bought goods and created demand. Alms would be left to private benevolence.

Which is exactly where Julia Margaret stepped in. It would have been impossible to be ignorant of the Irish famine in Calcutta, where the Irish dominated the rank and file of the British and East India Company armies. The officers' ranks and the civil service were also filled with Anglo-Irish and Scots (like Charles Hay). So Julia Margaret had a ready pool of sympathizers when she set up a relief fund for Ireland during the year 1845–46. It may have been the first such fund;[48] it was certainly among the most successful. Julia Margaret raised around 14,000 pounds to send to Ireland. This extraordinary sum earned her much praise. When her son traveled to Ceylon for the first time in 1860, the people on board remembered his mother for this feat from fifteen years before.[49] Back in England, Lord Hardinge wrote to Julia Margaret to thank her for a prayer she sent him and mentions that he had just finished collecting 1,600 pounds for an Orphan's List: "nothing like your Calcutta sweep, but we were well pleased."[50]

Henry Hardinge, later Viscount Hardinge, had arrived as Governor-General to replace Lord Ellenborough in 1844. He was a military man with little interest in social pretensions, and the Camerons got along well with him. They thought highly enough of him to name their fourth child Hardinge Hay Cameron. This son arrived in August 1846 and the Governor-General was his godfather. Lord Hardinge and Charles Hay seem to have agreed on many important matters, including the reform of Indian laws to apply to British, Hindu, Muslim, and other residents uniformly. Hardinge was in charge during the next imperial war in India: this time with the Sikhs over the Punjab. George Broadfoot had recently been appointed to the prestigious and now sensitive post of political agent to the northwest frontier, and he was among the first killed when the war broke out. The wars in the Punjab and Sind were aggressive imperial conquests; by their conclusion, Britain had added most of what is now Pakistan to its empire.

Meanwhile, Cameron was absorbed in study, working on music and German, and continuing her correspondence with Herschel on developments in photography. Herschel wrote to Julia Margaret that the monuments of India would be perfect photographic subjects, and since Hardinge encouraged the photographing of some Indian antiquities in the mid-1840s, perhaps she passed along the idea.[51] In June 1841 Herschel's wife and daughter had written to Cameron mentioning their sun-prints of leaves (now called photograms) and referring to Talbot's new "Calotypes." Herschel himself enclosed some examples of these early photographs and assumed she was already familiar with daguerreotypes.[52] In 1842 he sent her two dozen calotypes. Herschel's samples are believed to be the first photographs Cameron ever saw.[53] They were certainly among the first photographs to arrive in India. Although Talbotypes (or calotypes) and daguerreotypes trickled into India soon after the announcement of their invention in 1839, historians of photography guess that the first daguerreotype portraitist opened for business in Calcutta in 1844 and the first calotype photographer in 1848.[54] Interestingly, one source identifies the first photographs taken in India as the work of another amateur English lady living in Uttar Pradesh in 1843.[55] So Cameron's access to photographs in India in 1841 placed her in the scientific and artistic vanguard.

Julia Margaret's next major project, in 1847, was her first known creative endeavor: a translation from German into English of Gottfried Bürger's popular Romantic poem *Leonora*.[56] Written in 1773, the poem had already been translated many times, most recently by William Taylor (whose version greatly influenced Samuel Taylor Coleridge and William Wordsworth) and by Sir Walter Scott. In her preface to her translation Julia Margaret takes care to differentiate her work from both of these rivals, with surprising modesty: "These distinguished men have infused their own genius into their translations; and Bürger is forgotten, whilst Scott and Taylor arrest the attention . . . . In this instance the case will be found to be far different. Bürger must here be felt throughout."[57] Interestingly, this rhetoric mirrors Charles Hay Cameron's argument in his *Essay On the Sublime and the Beautiful* that true artistic genius always effaces itself.[58] This may be an oblique explanation as to why Cameron never made a self-portrait as a photographer.

Cameron's self-effacement was tactical, however: it inferred that she was the better translator for being the more transparent and "true" to the original, while also avoiding any unseemly direct competition with men. The ambition and confidence that it must have taken for an unpublished colonial society matron to compete with Sir Walter Scott in the literary marketplace was managed through canny rhetoric of submission and deference. She opens her preface with the first shot: "The following translation of Bürger's Leonora was made before the Author had seen any other version of this justly celebrated ballad. As she does not profess to have added any thing to the original, the sole merit of her version (if it have any) must consist in accurately and vividly representing the German poem . . . ."[59] In the very first sentence she identifies herself as an "Author," while simultaneously defending herself against arrogance or rivalry with other versions. In the second sentence she again makes modest claims that in fact infer her superiority and skillfulness.

As Cameron biographer Amanda Hopkinson has aptly noted, the translator's role that Julia Margaret claimed in 1847 anticipated the photographer's role that she adopted seventeen years later. When Julia Margaret writes in the preface that "the present Translator, not aspiring to create, has studied only to catch the likeness of a beautiful picture, and to copy faithfully each feature and expression of the original,"[60] she uses almost the same phrases that she will use in her 1874 autobiographical fragment to describe her goals as a portrait photographer. By insisting on the mere "copying" functions of translations and photography, she deflects any possible criticism of being too ambitious and competing on men's terms with (male) geniuses. These were not just the usual self-deprecations of a novice; they were part of a strategic plan to make Julia Margaret's grand ambitions palatable to the public, and perhaps to herself. There is nothing in her letters or in the early accounts of her life to indicate that Julia Margaret was driven by a strong creative impulse or by a desire for fame, but her forays into art, while slow to start, were always ambitious.

The translation of *Leonora* does indeed read well. While the Romantic poets admired the ballad for its antiquated language and gothic elements, Julia Margaret's translation uses plainer vocabulary and syntax and claims to follow Bürger in focusing on the "broken-heartedness of the afflicted maiden."[61] The plot follows Leonora, whose lover, William, has gone off to war. When the war is over and he fails to reappear, she descends into hysterical grief, despite her mother's efforts to persuade her to trust in God's will. When William returns in the middle of night to take Leonora off to be married, she complies eagerly, although the portents are ominous. The snorting, pawing steed, the whistling wind, the long cold ride through the night, the two planks he promises her as a bridal bed – all these signs forebode ill to the reader accustomed to gothic tropes and themes. Indeed, she arrives to find that she will be wed at her graveside to her fallen fiancé as ghosts scold her for bemoaning her fate. The last stanza of Taylor's translation ends with

> "Be patient; tho' thyne herte should breke,
> Arrayne not Heven's decree;
> Thou nowe art of the bodie refte
> Thie soule forgiven bee!"

Over forty years later, Julia Margaret's translation is simpler and clearer:

> "Endure! Endure! Though break the heart,
> Yet judge not God's decree.
> Thy body from thy soul doth part,
> Oh! May God pardon thee!"[62]

In the *Biographia Literaria*, written in the year Cameron was born, Coleridge famously distinguished between the primary imagination, the secondary imagination, and the fancy in what became a highly influential Romantic theory of aesthetics. The primary imagination he described as "the living power and prime agent of all human perception."[63] That is, when our minds encounter and make sense of reality, we use our primary imagination, and we reflect, on a human scale, the divine creation of the world. The secondary imagination is the creativity of the poet or artist, which "dissolves, diffuses, dissipates, in order to recreate . . . . It struggles to idealize and unify." It is an echo of the primary imagination, which was itself an echo of God's supreme creativity. Both kinds of imagination can create something new and alive, even if they work with "fixed and dead" realities.

Fancy, on the other hand, lies at the bottom of the hierarchy: lacking any inventive power, it simply rearranges existing facts and objects. It produces inferior work and its authors have no claim to the exalted, semi-divine status of poets and artists. "The fancy," Coleridge sneers, "is indeed no other than a mode of memory emancipated from the order of time and space." Yet this definition could also describe the as-yet-uninvented photograph. It is easy to see how this aesthetic inheritance could cause conflicts for Cameron later, in her pursuit of an artistic career and identity. With her deep faith in photography as an art and even a form of worship, she spent her life resisting its description as mere verisimilitude. Coleridge's Romantic aesthetic helps to define the attitudes she grew up with and also explains the conflict that ensued. The Romantic poets provided the philosophic underpinnings for the newly exalted status of artists and poets: the development of consumer markets liberated artists from patrons, but Romantic aesthetics also contributed to the cult of creative genius, which gave artists and poets enormous prestige in the nineteenth century. Cameron wanted to share in that prestige, as her translation of *Leonora* demonstrates. But when she took up photography to establish herself as an artist, she also enlisted in a battle that raged on long after her death – the battle of photography's relationship to art. Romanticism taught Cameron that creativity was divine, but it also insisted that mere copying was never creative.

Julia Margaret was proud of her translation: she sent it to Herschel, who was bi-lingual in German, with the more genuinely modest wish that she was as good a German scholar as his two daughters.[64] The translation was favorably reviewed by at least one London journal[65] and sumptuously produced in a large-format book with engravings after illustrations by the well-known painter and illustrator Daniel Maclise. Maclise designed several different leafy borders to frame each page of text and added beautifully drawn illustrations of the major scenes. A member of the Royal Academy, Maclise was already very successful and well connected. He was a friend and portraitist of Charles Dickens and later an illustrator for an 1857 edition of Tennyson's poems. Cameron and Maclise may have become acquainted through their mutual friend Thackeray, but the genesis of the whole project is unclear. Cameron implies in her preface that she had translated the poem as a hobby and later decided to publish it, but she gives no further details. Nor does she seem to have had any contact with Maclise after moving to England, although she too would famously attempt to illustrate Tennyson's poems. Indeed, one of her photographs for the *Idylls of the King* closely resembles one of Maclise's illustrations of the same scene.[66] Much of Tennyson's work also drew on old ballads like *Leonora*, and Julia Margaret was always drawn to the more romantic and supernatural of his poems. In illustrating Tennyson's poems, she was also always envious and resentful of the greater profits that illustrators like Maclise and Gustave Doré earned for their contributions. Her photographs, and probably her earlier translation, never earned much money.

Like Tennyson's similar ballad "The May Queen," *Leonora* is largely composed of a dialogue between a mother and a daughter. In both poems, the mothers counsel the daughters against despair and abandonment to love. In both, the mothers fail to save the daughters. Julia Margaret seems to have been drawn to this poetic subject, for she also made many photographic illustrations later on of "The May Queen." The timing of her translation of *Leonora* may have been significant: as she came to terms with her daughter's departure, she turned toward a poem about a mother who also loses a daughter, through no fault of her own. Julia Margaret had sent her daughter away, but she remained a hovering, counseling presence in the letters to Juley, just as Leonora's mother is a righteous, admonishing presence in the poem. The girls complain and protest, but in the end mother is proven right. That could well have been a very useful message for Julia Margaret at that moment and one that would remain powerful for her even after her daughter was grown.

Maclise's illustrations include a double portrait of Leonora and her mother at the height of Leonora's grief [see figure]. The two women are positioned in a pietà pose, with the seated mother bending over the younger woman, who collapses against her mother's lap and turns her face toward the heavens. The illustration looks self-consciously artistic: the pietà allusion feels baroque; the rich background of intertwining, overgrown foliage lends a gothic touch; and the pillars and arches behind the pair evoke classical art. The calm and austere mother is covered by a cowl and raises an admonishing finger at the stricken girl. Curiously, the only known photograph of Julia Margaret and her daughter [see figure] bears a striking similarity of pose and composition to this earlier illustration by Maclise. While Julia Margaret was unlikely to have composed either image, she may have influenced the presentation of one or the other, or simply kept this photograph instead of another one because of its haunting evocation of connection and separation between mother and daughter.

Like Maclise's figures, Julia Margaret and Juley appear before a dense frame of leaves. The photograph is an odd one to have survived for over a century because it shows Juley in a rather unflattering pose: mouth slightly open and eyes definitely closed, apparently asleep against her mother's seated, reading figure, probably in the garden of Sara and Thoby Prinsep's home at Little Holland House in London. A few other portraits of Julia Margaret exist from the same sitting: she wears the same trimmed dress, with her hair parted in the center and pulled down and back over her ears *à la* Emily Dickinson. Each includes a book as a prop, perhaps in reference to Julia Margaret's own literary and creative interests or perhaps as a generic emblem of portraiture. The photographer for these portraits is still unknown: one possibility is Cameron's brother-in-law Lord Somers, an amateur photographer and member of the Photographic Society. They were taken some time in the late 1850s, well before Cameron took up photography herself, and the double portrait perhaps marks Cameron's ambivalence about the loss of her daughter to marriage in 1859. Indeed, Julia Margaret revisited that past grief a few months after Juley's wedding to Charles Norman in a letter of consolation to a bereaved father: "Ah me! If when I parted with my little Juley on a sea voyage her empty garments were more than I could bear to see, can I not understand what is and will be for ever your aching memory –."[67]

It is arguable that Julia Margaret's intense investment in her only daughter and namesake gave the first emotional impetus to her later photographic work: by her own admission, it was Julia and Charles Norman who gave her a camera. It was the agony of separation that framed her career, bringing her to England and then sending her to Ceylon, and it was an obsessive, repetitive compulsion to photograph women and children that fuelled most of her work. Photography is an art to conjure up the absent and to preserve the present. Her decade of married life in India was one of almost continual losses: her grandfather died in 1840; three of her sisters and Eugene left for England in 1843; Juley left early in 1845; Broadfoot was killed in the Sikh wars later that year; and then her parents both died that autumn. She may have felt unable to face new and prolonged separations from the children and feared the ultimate separation from her husband if he continued to exert himself in that climate. She may have given up her ideal of disinterestedness and begun to use her considerable influence and powers of persuasion to convince Charles Hay to retire early and relocate to England. In 1848 at least one letter of business from the Ceylon plantations spoke of a promising and profitable crop of coffee.[68] The Camerons must have felt sufficiently financially secure to make the expensive move.

When Macaulay, rich and unpopular, left Calcutta for England in January 1838, just before the Camerons' wedding, he sent his letter of resignation from the Council of India to his old nemesis Thoby Prinsep and wrote privately to a friend about the difficulties of his post. The fourth member of the Council, expected to cover legal affairs, was the only appointee of the Crown. The other members were drawn from the East India Company and the East Indian army. He was an outsider where they were insiders. His areas of expertise were different from theirs, and his ignorance of Indian affairs could seem contemptible to his colleagues. Macaulay concluded by noting that under the circumstances he felt that he had been well treated and his appointment successful.[69] But it was a fair warning for Charles Hay, who would soon succeed Macaulay in this delicate and difficult position.

Macaulay and Cameron were relatively unusual in their eagerness to leave India. Macaulay called his stay in India a "banishment," "an exile," and compared himself to Ulysses. He was exceptional in his homesickness. He observed, with bemusement, that the typical British civil servant comes out to Calcutta at seventeen or eighteen and experiences independence for the first time. He suddenly has money to spend and no family around to supervise him. He can live like a lord, with fine horses, twenty servants, and a mistress. He can quickly become a Man of Consequence. This expansive, yet provincial, life renders him unfit for England, Macaulay argued.

> In Europe he knows that he will be considered as an old, yellow-faced, bore, fit for nothing but to drink Cheltenham water and to ballot at the India House. He has acquired, it may be, a great deal of valuable information on Indian affairs,– is an excellent Oriental Scholar,–knows intimately all the interests of the native Courts,–is as well acquainted with the revenue-system of Bengal as Huskisson was with the revenue-system of England,–is as deeply read in Hindoo and Mahometan jurisprudence as Sugden in the law of England. He knows that these acquirements which make him an object of admiration in Calcutta will procure for him no applause–nay not the smallest notice–in London.[70]

No wonder, Macaulay said, that so few company employees took their home leaves.

This was the transition that the Camerons faced in 1848. They followed Sara and Thoby Prinsep home, so they had a community in England already, but they were giving up a great deal: ten years of family life in India; a generous income; a privileged position in a tight-knit society. In addition to Julia Margaret's anxieties about health and separations, there are hints in the letters that it may have been Julia Margaret's social and creative ambitions that drove them to the move. Charles was always happy in the East, though his ill health may have necessitated an early retirement. Certainly he had worked very hard to defend Macaulay's penal code: after its publication in 1837, Charles Hay was put in charge of collating and responding to all the commentary it received. In addition to his regular Council work, he submitted lengthy reports, endorsing the original code, in 1846 and 1847 and drafted a new code of criminal procedure for India before he left in 1848. The zeal for reform had died down with Macaulay's departure, though, and the work must have been slow and frustrating at times. Charles Hay never did see the original code enacted in India. It remained mired in committees and partisan politics until 1859.

When Macaulay left India, Calcutta society breathed a sigh of relief. Two months before his departure, five hundred residents of Calcutta gathered in a public meeting to protest his most recent regulation and generally malign him. Dwarkanath Tagore, a wealthy and influential Hindu merchant who had supported the British in some of their reforms, called Macaulay a *sub janta*, or know-it-all, and scorned him as an interloper.[71] But when Charles Hay left in 1848, a group of Indians commissioned his portrait to commemorate his work as President of the Council of Education to improve native education.[72] Nonetheless, Cameron's education policies were based on the same utilitarian, rational assumptions as Macaulay's and James Mill's. He believed that the introduction of Western thought in India would gradually make the Indians first conscious of the superiority of British civilization, then eager to obey their colonizers, and eventually fit for self-government. As Cameron argued a few years later in a letter recommending that the East India Company appoint the first native to the Indian Medical Service,

> We do not doubt that a time is fast approaching when, by the general diffusion of that liberal education which you are giving to the people of India, the advantages of your government over any that could be expected from the sway of any Asiatic prince will be so fully appreciated by the Indian nations, that it will be perfectly safe and very beneficial to place your native troops under the command of native officers.[73]

At that time, Cameron, like the other utilitarian administrators brought to India, sincerely and completely believed that British rule in India produced the greatest happiness for the greatest number, and he seems to have left in 1848 with complete confidence in British policies and his own beliefs. It was just as well that he left when he did, because in 1857 the Indian Mutiny, or First War of Independence, would change everything.

CHAPTER 4

Lion-Hunting in London

T HE YEAR 1848, when the Camerons left India for England, began with a bang. Responding to the rapid changes of industrialization and colonialism, populations all across Europe were soaring and shifting. People were migrating from old countries to new, from farms to cities. Living in crowded conditions, some starved, some sickened, and many agitated for new political rights. Both the working and middle classes were newly aware of themselves as "masses" – as workers, as readers, as consumers, and in some cases as voters. In February Karl Marx and Friedrich Engels anonymously published *The Communist Manifesto* in London. That month, as Charles Hay was receiving tributes from the Indians of Calcutta for his work on their behalf, the people of Paris rose up against the Bourbon monarchy and established a republic. Revolutions followed in Austria, Italy, and the German states. In London Chartists rallied to present their petition for six radical reforms: universal male suffrage, the secret ballot, equal electoral districts, abolition of the property qualification for Members of Parliament, salaries for Members of Parliaments, and annual elections. Although the Reform Act of 1832 had extended some rights to the middle classes, political life in England was still largely dominated by landowners. The growing middle classes and the struggling working classes both demanded increased participation in public life.

The Chartists were set to present their massive petition, with an expected five million signatures, to Parliament on April 10 – around the time the Camerons would have arrived back in England. Londoners, expecting riots and looting, deserted the streets that day and police constables lined the route from the rally on Kennington Common to the Houses of Parliament. But for whatever reasons – British reformism, government restraint, rainy weather – fewer than 20,000 people showed up and the proceedings remained orderly. Parliament rejected the petition, and Chartism as an organized alliance of the working classes was over.

On their way home from India, the Camerons had stopped in Ceylon. Charles Hay, still devoted to the island after his sojourn there in 1830, had bought several

Ceylonese estates, probably between 1844 and 1848. The Colebrooke–Cameron legal reforms were implemented in stages, and by the mid-1840s restrictions on foreign ownership of land in Ceylon had been loosened.[1] It seems that Charles Hay took advantage of these legal reforms, which he had recommended years before, to become a major landowner. One transaction in 1841 entailed the purchase of over 1,000 acres near the hill station of Nuwara Eliya for an average price of 5 shillings an acre.[2] His intention was to turn the estates into coffee plantations, but first he needed to clear the hilly and heavily forested land and build access paths, housing for the native workers, sheds for the bullocks, and a bungalow for the manager. He seems to have had hopes from the start that his family might relocate there to the Edenic paradise in central Ceylon. In 1846, when he commissioned a bungalow on the Rathoongodde plantation, his estate manager in Ceylon warned him about the remoteness of the location and added tactfully that "a jungle life may not prove equal to your expectations."[3]

When the Camerons moved back to England, they had four children: Julia, Eugene, Ewen, and Hardinge Hay. Two more sons would be born in England. There were many mouths to feed, and coffee, Charles Hay hoped, would feed them all. He certainly believed that this investment in land was to provide his sons' patrimony. In this he reflected the assumption of his generation that political and economic power was based on ownership of land, but perhaps he also wanted to reverse his family's slow decline from aristocratic landlords to salaried civil servants. Indeed, he later wrote: "I feel no doubt that the boys will one day be very thankful to me for providing them with this resource against dependence and place-hunting."[4] He would have preferred a simpler and more economical rural life in Ceylon, but he confided candidly in the same letter, Julia Margaret preferred literary society; if she could not bear an extended stay in Ceylon and trips back and forth were too expensive, then how would they manage? Clearly, Julia Margaret and England won out in 1848, but the matter was far from settled, as their futures would demonstrate.

The pull of England was strong: Sara and Thoby Prinsep had established themselves on Chesterfield Street in London, and Maria Jackson had first sent home her eldest daughters and then, in 1848, she too returned to England with her youngest, Julia Prinsep Jackson, while her husband stayed in Calcutta and worked his way up through the Indian Medical Service. The youngest Pattle sisters, Sophia and Virginia, had been living with the Prinseps, but Sophia had recently married another prominent Anglo-Indian civil servant, John Warrender Dalrymple, in June 1847 and the new couple had returned to Calcutta late in the year. Julia Margaret's translation of *Leonora* had perhaps made her eager to capitalize on her literary connections too. Besides, there was always Charles Hay's health to consider. The attack that had sent him to Cape Town and kept him from working on Macaulay's penal code had permanently weakened his kidneys and his health was rarely good for long.

The Camerons returned some time in early spring: by June, Julia Margaret was writing letters from a visit to the country home of Charles Hay's old friend George Warde Norman in Kent. They settled first at 10 Chesham Place, in affluent Belgravia in London. But their life in England would prove to be nomadic: they moved five times over the next twelve years and they shuttled constantly between extended stays with friends and relations. The move to England put them back in the midst of some of Charles Hay's oldest friends, who may not even have met Julia Margaret before this move. Neither Charles Hay nor Julia Margaret seems to have visited England in the ten years since their marriage. Charles Hay eagerly sought out Norman, an old friend from his childhood in Bromley, Kent, and now a director of the Bank of England, and Samuel Jones Loyd, later Lord Overstone; the three men had all attended Eton and they had become firm friends. His extended family in England included his three unmarried or widowed sisters and his cousin the Earl of Erroll, though Charles Hay was not close to that side of his family. His parents had died decades earlier and he had inherited only debts, which he had since cleared. Lord Hardinge, Sir Edward Ryan, and Sir John Herschel were all back in England as well and the Camerons renewed their acquaintances. Charles Hay rejoined the Political Economy Club, which put him back in touch with the philosophic radicals of Bentham's school and also probably gave him news of his first son. Charles Henry Cameron had been raised in London by Charles Hay's friend John Cowell and was just embarking on his own career in the Indian civil service. In fact, he left for India just as the Camerons arrived back in London.[5]

Julia Margaret had connections of her own: her aunt Julie Impey had settled in Bath after the death of her husband, and Thackeray was rattling about London, Paris, and Brighton with his two daughters in tow. He had married Isabella Shawe, from another colonial family, in 1836 and settled within an expatriate community in Paris for the sake of economy.[6] By 1840, they had two children, but Isabella was already descending into the mental illness that would confine her to institutions for the rest of her life. By the end of the decade, Thackeray had reclaimed the girls from his mother in France and set up house in London. In 1847 the completion of *Vanity Fair* had turned the Pattles' old friend into a literary lion. Soon after the Camerons' arrival, the author brought his daughters to meet his old friend Julia Margaret. Annie Thackeray reminisced much later about this first encounter:

> I remember a strange apparition in a flowing red velvet dress, although it was summer time, cordially welcoming us to a fine house and some belated meal, when the attendant butler was addressed by her as 'man', and was ordered to do many things for our benefit; to bring back the luncheon dishes and curries

for which Mrs. Cameron and her family had a speciality. When we left she came with us bareheaded, with trailing draperies, part of the way to the station as her kind habit was. A friend of mine told me how on one occasion she accompanied her in the same way, carrying a cup of tea which she stirred as she walked along. My father, who had known her first as a girl in Paris, laughed and said: 'She is quite unchanged,' and unchanged she remained to the end of her days; generous, unconventional, loyal and unexpected.[7]

Julia Margaret was disappointed not to see more of Sir John Herschel, whose work and ill health kept him close to his estate in Kent. But the arrival of another son, Charles Hay junior, in February 1849 kept her busy, and indeed her domestic life seems to have become a great deal more complicated in England. Her letters from Calcutta, once full of concerns for Charles Hay's health, the agony of separation from children, and political or literary events, suddenly revolve around the receiving and paying of visits. The next decade was full of domestic logistics: sick children were isolated from the family and sent to recover with friends at the seaside; well children were sent away to country estates while Julia Margaret nursed the sick one; children needed to be escorted back and forth between these lengthy stays away from home and between home and boarding schools; friends and relatives from out of town were put up and given dinner parties. It was a full life of a different sort: with little time for reflection or repose and involving many urgent demands. Throughout it all, the Pattle sisters crisscrossed to and from each others' homes. And, increasingly, Julia Margaret worried about money, borrowed from her sisters, and despaired of finding train fares. Her itinerant life was heavily dependent on the growing network of railways.

Julia Margaret was eager and impulsive in making new friends and this was nowhere more in evidence than in her own account of her first encounter with Henry Taylor, the poet who became her lifelong friend. According to letters written later on, they met on July 30, 1849, a date whose anniversary they both marked for at least the next six years,[8] while the Camerons were visiting Tunbridge Wells, near the Taylors' summer home. Julia Margaret went walking and saw a tall man with long white hair and beard in a flowing cape and a "wide-awake" hat and, she wrote later, she felt as if a dagger had struck her heart. Her deep and devoted friendship with Taylor, who like Cameron was already married, had romantic overtones without any actual impropriety taking place. In fact, Taylor seems to have been at first a common bond with Charles Hay – Julia Margaret wrote that it was Charles Hay who first introduced her to his literary work. The fact that both Camerons were fans of Taylor's work before they met him makes the "accidental" meeting seem improbable, but it was the only account Julia Margaret ever gave.[9]

Annie

Julia Margaret Cameron, *Annie, My First Success*, January 1864.

In her autobiography Cameron identified this photograph
as the first she completed entirely by herself.

Julia Margaret Cameron, *Charles Hay Cameron*, 1864.

_____

This early portrait of Cameron's husband was included in the album
given to his friend Lord Overstone.

Henry Herschel Hay Cameron took two photographs of his mother at
the same sitting in 1874. One is used on the jacket of this book.
This is the other.

Fresh Water   *April 1864*

The Double Star

Julia Margaret Cameron, *The Double Star*, April 1864.

————

This striking early portrait refers to the infant Jesus and John the Baptist
but also to Sir John Herschel's catalogue of double stars,
which he was working on when he and Cameron met at Cape Town.

Julia Margaret Cameron, *Paul and Virginia*, 1864.

———

An illustration of a French novel popular when Cameron was a girl,
this photograph was an early example of Cameron's interest in portraits of
children and literary subjects.

This photograph from the late 1850s of Julia Margaret Cameron with her two youngest sons, Charlie and Henry Herschel Hay, has been attributed to Charles Dodgson (Lewis Carroll) and to Cameron's brother-in-law Lord Somers, but the evidence is inconclusive.

This double portrait of Julia Margaret and her daughter was probably taken in the garden of Little Holland House around the time of Juley's engagement and marriage in 1858–59.

Watts painted this portrait of Cameron in 1852, during the heyday of her sister's salon at Little Holland House. Henry Herschel Hay took this photograph of it many years later.

1.

The mother to her comfort flies:
"Oh! why this grief so wild?"
She clasps her daughter in her arms,
And cries "God calm my child!"

Cameron's 1847 translation of Bürger's romantic poem *Leonora* was her first creative project. The illustrations were drawn by Daniel Maclise.

Julia Margaret Cameron, *The Whisper of the Muse/Portrait of G. F. Watts*, April 1865.

For this famous portrait Cameron transformed her painter friend
Watts into a musician.

Throughout most of his friendship with the Camerons, Taylor was a high-ranking clerk in the Colonial Office, but his fame rested on his poetry and plays from the 1830s. The best known, *Philip Van Artevelde,* was a tragic drama set in the Renaissance era and it was so full of "poetic beauty, moral vigour, soundness + elevation of feeling" that it was "second to none but Shakespeare," according to the Camerons.[10] Julia Margaret took up Taylor with all the enthusiasm and ardor of her nature. She lavished presents on him and his wife, Alice: "India shawls, turquoise bracelets, inlaid portfolios, ivory elephants, &c," Taylor wrote to his father less than two months after meeting her.[11] The Taylors were at first baffled, and then charmed by this onslaught. Cameron praised Henry to the skies, promoted him shamelessly to her friends, and entered into feuds with anyone who disparaged him. She so closely associated Taylor with the hero of his best-known work that she usually called him "Philip." Though Taylor's work is not much read or admired today, Julia Margaret held it in higher esteem than Thackeray's or Tennyson's and his friendship was more important to her than theirs too, as occasional disputes made clear. The depth of this passion was often aggravating to her literary friends, but it had an earnest and innocent sincerity that rescued it from the ridiculous.

By November, Cameron was writing to Sir John Herschel begging him to read and recommend a German translation of the first part of *Philip Van Artevelde* so that the translator could drum up enthusiasm for a second volume. She admitted she was a "hardened beggar" and suggested that Taylor would appreciate some kind words from the renowned Herschel – could he include an autographed copy of one of his works? And could he address the signed book to Taylor without letting him know she asked for the gift? In reply, Herschel judiciously praised the German translation and acknowledged Taylor's gifts but ignored the request for the autographed book. The exchange was typical of Cameron: she was really quite shameless in her avid promotion of her friends and her interests and she was always intent on getting her celebrity friends together for mutual exchange. Often the exchanges she had in mind were real intellectual debates; at other times, the exchanges seemed to be of flatteries designed to appease insecure egos or of trinkets intended as relics in a growing cult of celebrity. All her life Cameron yearned for mementos of genius: her treasures included original letters, signed portraits, books inscribed to her by Tennyson and other authors, gifts from her family. She believed in the aura of genius as an almost tangible force that could distinguish these mass-produced commodities, especially for those "in the know." The value of her collection of celebrity mementos was incalculably increased by personal knowledge and the blending of public accomplishment with private affections.

Cameron, of course, shared Herschel's praise for Taylor with her husband and with Taylor himself, and Taylor's reply, again through Cameron, reads as a calculated counter-move in a complicated game. He acknowledges that Herschel's praise is well worth having but then rather undermines his own counter-flattery by claiming that a poet is less able to evaluate a scientist's work than vice versa. He despairs that he found Herschel's work "impenetrable" when he tried to read it. Julia Margaret exulted over this mutual admiration without seeming to notice the subtlety of Taylor's distancing maneuver. Taylor may have been embarrassed, especially so early in their relationship, at Julia Margaret's trumpeting of his talents; certainly his ambivalence shone through the civilities. Julia Margaret, interestingly, announced that she too was writing poetry at the time, though none from that period has survived. She particularly admired Taylor's efforts to "soothe and cleanse" English poetry after the maddening and polluting effects of the Romantic poets (presumably this refers to Byron).[12] Taylor had argued in his 1835 preface to *Philip Van Artevelde* that "no man can be a very great poet who is not also a philosopher" and he had criticized Byron for favoring emotions over ideas.[13] Wordsworth, the only canonical Romantic poet still alive at the time, was a personal friend of Taylor's. Cameron was supposed to have corresponded with Wordsworth herself, but if this is so, no letters have survived.[14]

It would have been characteristic for Cameron to have pursued Wordsworth, however, especially as she and her sister Sara Prinsep began their "lion-hunting," or pursuit of celebrities. As Julia Margaret had noted in 1843, soon after her sister's relocation, Sara was an energetic, social, and generous woman who liked being surrounded by people. One of her granddaughters later wrote that "she was the kind of woman who would have turned a convent into a scene of tumult. There was no such thing as quiet where she was."[15] She had opened her home to her youngest sisters, several of her husband's nieces, and several of her late sister Adeline's children at times too. Some time in 1848, a momentous meeting gave her the entrée she wanted into artistic and literary circles. The painter George Frederic Watts had begun his career as a protégé of Lord and Lady Holland at their residence in Florence. After several years of commissions and hospitality from them, he appears to have worn out his welcome and he returned to London in 1847, taking a studio on Charles Street. According to much-repeated legend, one day Watts saw an especially lovely and graceful young woman walking in his neighborhood and he recalled having declined a friend's offer to introduce him to a local beauty. On a hunch, Watts rearranged the meeting and made the acquaintance of his mystery woman, Virginia Pattle, by repute the most beautiful of the beautiful Pattle sisters and now living with her sister Sara on Chesterfield Street.

Watts was both a gifted artist and a delicate, sickly man in need of mothering; the combination suited Sara perfectly. Soon "Signor," as he was always called, was a regular at Chesterfield Street, and in 1850, when the Prinseps needed to find larger accommodations, it was Watts who suggested they consider Little Holland House, a farmhouse on the grounds of the Holland family's estate in Kensington. Thoby and Sara drove out to see the house in what was then rural farmland. The roads were unpaved and heavily rutted from coaches; cows grazed in open fields; and the house itself was like something out of a nursery rhyme, with low ceilings, uneven floors, and a thatched-roof porch. Several buildings had been merged into one, making a higgledy-piggledy assortment of rooms and corridors. It was not elegant, but it was spacious and eccentric and it clearly appealed to the bohemian Prinseps. They fell in love with it and took a twenty-one-year lease. They made it into a destination.

Little Holland House was not the only London salon of the 1850s. Women, in particular, often aspired to lead literary and artistic salons, in the Parisian tradition of Madame de Recamier and Madame de Staël. It was an established route into power and public life for women: wives of ambitious politicians cultivated allies and hostesses connected artists to patrons and sitters. Until recently, writers had needed patrons too, for most literature was published by subscription before the development of a reading public in the early nineteenth century. Then, of course, people with intellectual and cultural interests liked to share their ideas and projects with like-minded colleagues, both amateur and professional. While Sara Prinsep was building a coterie around Watts, Jane Carlyle was hosting "at homes" around her husband. The two women also had competition from cultured aristocrats, like the Countess of Airlie, and wealthy merchants like Arthur Lewis, both of whom hosted cultural salons near Kensingon. By the 1860s, the area was becoming both convenient and fashionable after the extension of the subway line and the design of new red-brick houses, commissioned by artists like Val Prinsep and Frederic Leighton. Lewis, who married the actress Kate Terry, entertained musicians, artists, and actors with singing and oysters. The Countess of Airlie went after the same literary lions as Sara and Julia Margaret: Thackeray, Tennyson, and Carlyle.[16] Later, Marian Evans and George Henry Lewes would create a salon around "George Eliot" in the 1870s.

Watts's relationship with the Prinseps benefited both parties: Sara got a resident artist as a star attraction for her salon and a genius to fuss over; Watts got a home and a studio that came fully furnished with carefully prepared meals for his queasy stomach, nursing on demand, and inexhaustible adoration. Even better, he had a ready supply of beautiful models to sketch and paint. He began painting Virginia Pattle as soon as he met her, and rumor has it that it was his portrait of her, displayed at the Royal Academy exhibit of 1849, that caused Charles Somers Cocks, Lord Somers, to fall in love with her. Rumor also claimed that Watts was in love with her himself, but couldn't compete with her titled admirers.[17] Throughout the 1850s Watts painted all of the Pattle sisters, including Julia Margaret, and over time he added the second generation of Prinseps and Jacksons to his stable of models. He was unusual in calling upon women friends as models instead of the professional working-class models favored by most artists.[18] It was part of his eccentricity and provided some of the thrill of unconventionality in the society at Little Holland House.

Watts believed in the importance of idealized art about historical and allegorical subjects. His reputation has risen and fallen in step with the interest in epic art, but as William Rothenstein, an artist who knew him, wrote after Watts's death, the epic spirit came naturally to him

> and the mention of his name evokes a luminous world of his own creation. This in itself is proof of his genius. Carlyle said, of great talkers, that they may talk more nonsense than other men, but they may also talk more sense. So Watts may have painted more tedious pictures than men less copiously endowed, but he painted more splendid ones.[19]

Watts was always in demand as a portrait painter, and he was a very fine one, as a trip to the National Portrait Gallery in London will confirm. But he only accepted portrait commissions when he needed money; the rest of his time he devoted to allegorical frescoes for private homes and government buildings, as well as canvases for the annual Royal Academy exhibition. He was adept at cultivating influential and moneyed clients and he entertained them through long sittings with conversations about Truth, Beauty, and Art, which charmed and stimulated socialites used to the extremely limited boundaries of acceptable discourse. He could assume different roles: as a protégé of aristocrats like the Hollands he acted the dandy, but at Little Holland House with the Prinseps he donned monkish robes and was photographed barefoot.[20] This was a lesson that Julia Margaret must have consciously or unconsciously absorbed: an artist who cultivates eccentricity and good conversation can enthrall patrons and sitters alike.

Watts was a model and mentor for Julia Margaret in many ways. When she took up photography, he was one of the first people she turned to for help in composing and framing the images. Their scant surviving correspondence is filled with terse suggestions from Watts, jotted down between portrait sittings. Both Watts and Cameron are often accused today of sentimental and overly didactic work. Both were definitely saturated with their culture's belief in the importance of art as a civilizing and improving force in an industrial society, but both spent most of their careers cloaking their lessons in allegory and symbolism. One of the younger generation around the Little Holland House and Freshwater circles asked Watts late in his life about his artistic goals and he answered that he tried "not to teach a moral lesson, but to suggest some emotion or thought by his pictures, as is done by music."[21] Both Cameron and Watts loved music, and perhaps used it as their ideal form of non-verbal communication. Cameron's most famous portrait of Watts, called *The Whisper of the Muse* [see figure], is then particularly appropriate: the artist becomes a musician flanked by two blurry children as he awaits inspiration from his child-muse. The visual interest in the photograph comes from the interlocking set of gazes. Watts and the child over his shoulder look down to our left; the child on his knee looks directly at us. It is a tri-angular composition squeezed tight to fit into the frame and overflowing at the edges with foliage, tumbling hair, and folds of clothing. There is a variant of this image, but the basic composition remains the same, with Cameron exploring different ways to balance and condense the three figures with the violin.[22]

Watts designed and painted the dining room at Little Holland House, which was a marvel remarked upon by everyone who saw it. A small, low-ceilinged room, it was filled by Watts with large figurative frescoes of the history of civilization. Dressed in long, flowing robes, perhaps inspired by the Elgin Marbles, Virginia Pattle posed for Mother Earth (or Chaos), Maria for Assyria, and Julia Margaret for Hindustan. Sophia modeled for Art, while the adolescent Adeline Jackson posed as Truth.[23] The ceiling was painted dark blue with twinkling stars. Other rooms had walls painted in clear, bold colors like green and purple. It was as far as imaginable from the typical Victorian décor of patterned wallpaper, carpets, and knick-knacks. As a popular author on interior decoration lamented a decade later, the prevailing style usually consisted of fussy ornamentation, "gaudy chintz," and walls covered with "silly representations of vegetable life."[24] It is hard to know now who was responsible for Little Holland House's unique style, but, like the salon itself, it was probably a creative collaboration between Sara's Eastern-trained eye and Watts's predilection for the tones and themes of Venetian painting. A gift for interior design was shared by several of the sisters: Julia Margaret was an early fan of William Morris's wallpaper, which she used in her home on the Isle of Wight, and she extensively remodeled her house after her own designs.[25]

During the peak of Sara's salon, the house was open to friends and artistic acquaintances every Sunday afternoon. Many commented on the literal breath of fresh air that a visit to Little Holland House offered: for Victorians expected to observe the Sabbath with greater or lesser severity, it was a relief to have entertainment that was at once innocent and stimulating. The gardens were beautiful and allowed to run a little wild and overgrown, with shade-giving elms and brightly colored flowers. In the afternoons Sara had the servants carry the sofas out onto the grass and people wandered about at will, played croquet on the rolled lawns, or shared a *tête-à-tête* with Thoby on his special sofa in a dark, quiet corner. Sara would approach a select few with a whispered invitation to dinner, and as most of the guests departed, those favored would quietly stay on as the furniture was brought back into the house and the entertainment shifted to the long, informal tables under the sky-painted ceiling, with music after dinner by famous instrumentalists like Hallé and Joseph Joachim on piano and violin. Adelaide Kemble Sartoris, a family friend and once a professional singer, shared her voice on occasion too.

The salon soon became a meeting place for up-and-coming painters, as well as taste-makers like the editors and illustrators of *Punch*. The English art scene was dominated by the Royal Academy and was, by definition, rather conformist and cautious because of its close ties to that institution. Huge history paintings and sentimental domestic scenes replete with dogs and horses were exhibited regularly every year at the Academy's annual exhibition in May. The English public had limited access to art: mass reproduction of engravings created a market in cheap prints, but there were few public art collections early in the century. But times were changing: puritan and evangelical suspicions about art's idolatry and sensuality were lessening. Newly wealthy industrialists were creating formidable art collections out of the wreckage of the Napoleonic Wars in Europe, as old-world art changed hands or came to light amid the turbulence of war and revolutions across the Continent. Cameron's old friend Lord Overstone was an assiduous collector and an early sponsor of important art exhibitions like the Manchester Art Treasures Exhibition of 1857.[26] In this climate, John Ruskin's passionate and erudite defense of J. M. W. Turner's impressionistic paintings was a revelation: here was an art critic who defended the distinctive and eccentric vision of a bona fide English genius.

In mid-century London, Turner was an aging champion and Ruskin was a rising critic, but in general artistic taste remained conservative. Thus the sudden appearance of a rebel group of young artists who professed themselves opposed to all the conventional, dull art of the day struck like a bolt of lightning. In 1848 four very young artists (three more joined later) wrote up a very brief manifesto and called themselves the Pre-Raphaelite Brotherhood (or PRB, as they signed their early paintings). Ambitious, audacious, and extremely talented, Dante Gabriel Rossetti, William Holman Hunt, John Everett Millais, and Thomas Woolner were students at the Royal Academy at the time. Determined to view art and nature afresh, without merely copying established conventions as to how art should look, they shocked critics and public alike with their highly colored, painstakingly detailed representations of biblical and literary subjects. Before Raphael, they argued, painters had drawn carefully from nature, and recorded exactly what they saw, whether "realistic" or not.[27] They determined to do likewise. In the 1850 and 1851 exhibitions of the Royal Academy their art was vilified as ugly, unnatural, and vulgar. Although they claimed to have had little knowledge of Ruskin before starting the PRB, their works had much in common with Ruskin's adherence to truth as the first concern of all art.

As Ruskin explained in the four volumes of *Modern Painters*, if artists looked carefully and represented what they saw faithfully, beauty would necessarily follow. It was the pursuit of beauty as an end in itself that revolted the puritanical and earnest Ruskin.

Needless to say, the pursuit of beauty did not offend the Pre-Raphaelites, but they did agree that truth came first. The problem, of course, was what truth? Artists like Watts and, later, Cameron also believed in representing truth, but they felt that truth was an inner quality not necessarily reflected in outer forms. Watts's idealized paintings of nymphs and knights were also based on a "truth" according to Watts, though they had little in common with the *plein air* studies of light, shadow, and foliage that Ruskin and some of the Pre-Raphaelites advocated (though none of the PRB devoted much attention to landscape, to Ruskin's dismay). Watts and Ruskin were friends, and Ruskin admired his work sincerely enough to commission Watts to paint a portrait of his wife, Euphemia Gray Ruskin, early in their short marriage. But their notions of truth diverged, as Watts admitted when he wrote to Ruskin: "I am inclined to give truth a wider range, and I cannot help fearing you may become farsighted."[28]

Similarly, the Pre-Raphaelites did not always cleave to Ruskin's rigid standard of visual truthfulness either. Rossetti was always more interested in fanciful subjects and the truth of his inner vision. His work was highly saturated with bold colors and evocative of sensual delights. Edward Burne-Jones, who became the most famous follower of Rossetti, was likewise interested almost exclusively in medieval and mythological subjects treated in a light and ethereal manner. It was Millais and Holman Hunt who bore the torch for naturalism for as long as they could. In 1850 Millais shocked Christian England by exhibiting a painting entitled *Christ in the House of his Parents* which represented Jesus as a regular boy in a carpenter's shop. Dickens was so incensed even years later that he complained that the Mary of the painting was so

> horrible in her ugliness that (supposing it were possible for any human creature to exist for a moment with that dislocated throat) she would stand out from the rest of the company as a monster in the vilest cabaret in France or the lowest gin-shop in England.[29]

When *The Times* attacked the PRB again for their contributions to the Royal Academy exhibit in the spring of 1851, Ruskin officially entered the fray with a letter to the editor defending the group. He argued that their noble intentions and conscientious fidelity of painting should earn them at least the respect of the press; he also acerbically pointed out that the technical faults they were accused of were much more prevalent among established Academy painters.[30]

Soon, the Pre-Raphaelite artists and Ruskin were frequent guests at the Little Holland House salons, drawn by the conversations about art and the easy hospitality. Edward Burne-Jones later wrote of his first visit there with Rossetti:

> One day Gabriel took me out in a cab – it was a day he was rich and so we went in a hansom, and we drove and drove until I thought we should arrive at the setting sun – and he said, 'You must know these people, Ned; they are remarkable people: you will see a painter there, he paints a queer sort of pictures about God and Creation.' So it was he took me to Little Holland House.[31]

In a society bound by strict rules of etiquette, the Pattle sisters were relatively casual. One American guest was so overcome by the kindness and informality of Sara and her sisters that she burst into tears: "nobody since I left home has treated me as these people did, so lovingly, so frankly – neither looking at me formally, because I was a stranger, nor curiously, because I was an American . . . ."[32] It is perhaps hard to imagine how stifling respectable English society could be: the presentation of visiting cards at the appropriate hours and intervals; the parade of paired-off guests into dinner, ranked carefully by status. Virtually all the middle and upper classes of society dressed for dinner, even at home, but at Little Holland House you might stay on and dine in your afternoon clothes, though Thackeray was known always to keep a formal suit at hand in a suitcase for such occasions. The hospitality was open and sincere: once, when the absent-minded Tennyson accidentally invited the art critic William Michael Rossetti to stay on for dinner when only his brother Dante Gabriel was expected, Julia Margaret quietly gave up her seat at the table for the extra guest and roamed around the gardens until the table was cleared. William Michael realized the faux pas after the fact and was both embarrassed and touched by her tact and kindness.[33]

In addition to their social graces, all of the sisters had formidable visual talents: they were particularly known for their fashion sense. Although some London socialites snickered, many of their peers admired the Pattle sisters for their unconventional refusal to wear crinolines and corsets or bother with formal gowns. They made striking figures on a Victorian street in loose bright robes, tied with gold cord at the waist and covered with Indian shawls. They wore batches of gold and silver bracelets that jangled as they talked with animated gestures. They all had dark hair, skin, and eyes – Sophia was said to have more auburn coloring and she and Virginia were tall and slender as well – and they emphasized their Anglo-Indian heritage by adopting Eastern fashions. One contemporary described their habit when together of sitting up late into the night gossiping in Hindi and cutting and re-sewing their own clothes.[34] This departure from the prevailing standards of English beauty did bring down upon them some racist slurs: at least one contemporary called Virginia's looks "nigger."[35]

The open-minded, bohemian spirit of Little Holland House served the Pattle sisters well with artistic and literary society. But it may have hurt them in the more conservative realms of politics, religion, or the military. Throughout the 1850s, Henry Thoby Prinsep repeatedly tried to win a seat in Parliament, as his father before him had done. In 1851 he tried for a seat in Harwich, Essex and failed. It was a difficult time to be a Tory, as liberal coalitions dominated the government.[36] His efforts are believed to have eventually cost him and Sara their fortune, as parliamentary elections were extremely expensive for unknown candidates. It is interesting to imagine how generous, impulsive, and unpredictable Sara Prinsep might have fared as the wife of an MP. Despite excellent connections, almost no one in their circle ended up as an elected official, although the most famous English politicians of the century – William Ewart Gladstone and Benjamin Disraeli – were habitués of the Little Holland House salon.

There were certainly scandalous whispers about Little Holland House.[37] The American guest who had been so charmed by Sara's sweetness was later appalled at her laxness when a mutual friend behaved badly in a love affair.[38] In the spring of 1858 Julia Margaret and Sara were involved in the dissolution of an engagement between Miss Georgina Treherne and Merthyr Guest, son of their friend Lady Charlotte Schreiber. Miss Treherne was found to be spending time alone at Little Holland House with the widowed Lord Ward and the engagement was broken. Lady Charlotte made sure that her own unmarried daughters were always chaperoned on their visits there.[39] Other guests hesitated before bringing their wives and sisters there at all: after George Du Maurier, then a rising young illustrator, first visited Little Holland House in 1862, he wrote to his mother wondering "*if they are all right*–for there seems an atmosphere of looseness about this aristocratic lot–people say that Mrs. Dalrymple and Lady Somers are all sorts of things."[40] When Sara and Thoby's only daughter, the beautiful Alice Prinsep, married young in 1861, she took up with the Prince of Wales's fashionable and racy "Marlborough House set," which made her seem questionable company for respectable ladies.[41] The power and influence of the Pattle sisters over their husbands and Watts also gave rise to snickers and sneers: people laughed at Sara's sway over her "dog Toby" and questioned the masculinity of Watts and the Pre-Raphaelite artists who surrounded them.[42]

Despite the rumors and innuendoes, the Pattles did, however, succeed in marrying back into the aristocracy that they had left two generations ago in France. Virginia Pattle was the toast of the London elite: stories tell that when she and Sophia attended a London costume ball as "Night" and "Dawn" respectively, Virginia received sixteen proposals of marriage the next day.[43] She was a celebrity as a beauty: people jostled on the sidewalks to get a glimpse of her and waited to see her leave parties and shops.[44] Her beauty was said by many to be matched by her goodness and sweetness of temper. Thackeray, who had been in love with her (among others), was one of the few ever to comment on her personality. In April 1849 he wrote to his close friend Jane Brookfield: "I saw my lovely VIRGINIA to day – she looked rather yellow though, but was as kind & merry as ever." Mrs. Brookfield wrote back that she had heard gossip that Virginia had eclipsed another woman in the "Duke of D–'s admiration."[45]

In June of 1850 Thackeray published a satiric poem in *Punch* called "On a Good-Looking Lady." The poem suggested that an elder poet was infatuated with his muse "Erminia," who was endowed with

> a charming face, a perfect form, a pure heart, a fine perception and wit, a pretty sense of humour, a laugh and a voice that are as sweet as music to hear, for innocence and tenderness ring in every accent, and a grace of movement which is a curiosity to watch, for in every attitude of motion or repose her form moves or settles into beauty.[46]

The poet wrote a paean to her beauty that caused Erminia to burst into tears and exclaim "nobody cares for anything but that." Everyone saw through the veiled references to Henry Taylor and Virginia Pattle, and the Pattle sisters were not amused. Much to Thackeray's annoyance, Julia Margaret was so indignant that she exercised that most Victorian gesture of disapproval: she cut Thackeray when she ran into him. Perhaps it was even because of some spreading gossip about Virginia and her admirers that Virginia soon afterwards accepted the proposal of Charles Somers Cocks, Lord Somers, an aristocrat with artistic ambitions and a close friendship with Ruskin. Thackeray, still in the family's bad graces, was "ordered" by Sara to attend the wedding on October 2, where he ran into the Taylors and expected to see them again at the country house of a mutual friend. Mrs. Brookfield took Thackeray aside and told the oblivious author frankly that he couldn't go to the country house without creating an awkward scene and that he had better apologize at once for the article. Thackeray delayed his trip and wrote an apology to Henry Taylor the following day:

> I have long been aware, by the reports of some friends, the estrangement of others, and the demeanour of some acquaintances, that a certain article of my writing had given great offence; but as I meant it in the most good-humoured spirit, and was actually proud of the absurd composition, I would not acknowledge that anybody had a right to be offended, and was quite indignant and angry that any one else should be so . . . . But just before I came to the railroad I was referred to the unlucky paper in question by a friend of mine who is not likely to be a very willing judge against me, and then, and not till then, I saw that I had been wrong . . . and I ask your forgiveness . . .

He went on to the country house as planned, but Jane Carlyle, who was there as well, reported to her husband that the Taylors were exceedingly uncomfortable and that Henry "sulked." The authors made up, but the Taylors left early and Thackeray may never have been fully forgiven by Julia Margaret for his insult to her idol.[47]

Nonetheless, over the next decade Thackeray was an occasional guest at Little Holland House, which he described once as a "Fairy Palace,"[48] and Julia Margaret became increasingly close to his eldest daughter Annie. During the 1850s, Thackeray turned his attention to the British community in India that he knew well and wrote and published *The Newcomes*, a serial novel about an Anglo-Indian colonel's return to English society. Colonel Newcome is an upright, naïve, and old-fashioned gentleman who runs foul of the pretensions and petty hypocrisies of his English relations. He is accepted as an eccentric curiosity while he has money, but when he is ruined in a bank failure only his son stands by him. The novel develops that most Victorian of preoccupations: what is the relationship between inner natures and outer appearances? What is real gentility in an age of shifting class boundaries? These are questions that Cameron too would explore visually. George Du Maurier believed that Colonel Newcome was modeled on Thoby Prinsep,[49] but most scholars today think that Thackeray's stepfather, Major Carmichael-Smyth, was a more likely source.[50]

Soon after Virginia's wedding, Julia Margaret was introduced to Alfred Tennyson for the first time, at Henry Taylor's house. The newly married Emily Tennyson wrote in her diary of that first meeting on October 14 that Julia Margaret "was a delightful picture in her dark green silk with wide open sleeves, the dress fastened by a silk cord round the waist and having the courtly charm of manner . . . which became her well."[51] Three weeks later, Tennyson was offered the poet laureateship, vacant since Wordsworth's death earlier in the year. It was a turning point for him: in 1850 the laureateship and the emotional authority of his new elegiac poem, *In Memoriam*, suddenly made Tennyson the voice of Victorian England, for both critics and public. At Little Holland House in the 1850s, he would read aloud *Maud* and early versions of the *Idylls of the King*, reciting the verses in his deep, Lincolnshire accent with customary solemnity. Like many of Julia Margaret's friends, he was known for his lack of social graces, and his curt simplicity often seemed rude, but he was basically shy, gentle, and melancholy in character. Julia Margaret became a close friend of the whole family, but especially Emily. It was to Julia Margaret and to Alice Taylor, his neighbors near Richmond Park, that Alfred turned when Emily went into labor unexpectedly on August 11, 1852. The Tennysons' first child had been stillborn the year before and the laureate was frantic. Julia Margaret went herself into the city to fetch the doctor and was present later at the child Hallam's christening. Alfred responded, "I shall never till the hour of my death forget your great kindness in rushing off to Town as you did in the hour of my trouble. God bless you ever."[52]

Some time in October, perhaps before the meeting with the Tennysons, Charles Hay left on the first of his extended trips back to Ceylon to oversee the coffee plantations. By November 3, he was writing to Julia Margaret from Alexandria. These trips were the bane of Julia Margaret's life and perhaps the only serious drawback to her life in England. She coaxed and cajoled and argued, but there were times when, despite ill health and familial devotion, her husband had to inspect the estates himself. Charles Hay's letters from that trip to his wife, addressed to "Juley love," survive and they are long, fond epistles filled with the details of his daily life. They imply a tender and close bond between the two. Charles Hay teases her about economizing and reassures her about his health and comforts. After landing in Alexandria, he took a boat up the Nile to Cairo and then crossed the desert by camel or coach to board another steamer in Suez. The journey was long, hot, and crowded, but he would have been happy if only Julia Margaret and the children were with him. He slept wrapped in a plaid that Julia Margaret gave him and read *In Memoriam* on board, commenting on "the immense crowd of deep reflections and practical images which T.[sic] has made to spring out of the sentiment of sorrow."[53] On this trip, perhaps their first long separation, Charles Hay carried with him a daguerreotype of his wife.

Charles Hay was worried about his investment. His estate manager at Rathoongodde and his distributor in Colombo were squabbling over the quality of the coffee crop, with each blaming the other for dry, discolored, and shrunken beans. There was no coffee cultivation in Ceylon until the 1830s and 1840s, when speculation in coffee began as the world's agricultural markets responded to the abolition of slavery in the British Empire and the growing popularity of coffee drinking. Free-trade utilitarians had abolished many import duties and coffee was cheaper than ever, at the same time that Caribbean plantations could not supply the demand. The land grab in Ceylon, which has been compared to the California gold rush, reached a peak in 1840–41 and resulted in the sale of nearly 300,000 acres of Crown lands.[54] But coffee cultivation in Ceylon meant clearing forests, growing plants in new conditions, managing a rainfall that alternated between drought and monsoon, and training a new local workforce. The trees had to be harvested of their cherry-like fruit and the beans removed, dried, and peeled before shipment to Europe. In 1845 import duties were reinforced and freight charges soared. Many speculators went bankrupt in the late 1840s, forced out by the usual vagaries of agricultural commodities: blight, wildly fluctuating prices, and unpredictable conditions. Cameron's estates ate up as much profit as they produced, and Charles Hay became alarmed. Already the Camerons were running up debts and the letters to Julia Margaret cite the importance of economizing in order to pay back the Normans and other friends. For Charles Hay, who had diligently paid off all his father's debts after his death, the looming shadow of insolvency must have been very stressful.[55]

Charles Hay loved Ceylon – its cool, lush forests, sparkling streams, and dramatic waterfalls and vistas – but this was a business trip; he inspected the apparatuses for peeling and drying the coffee and met with his various agents. The trip from Kandy, the nearest town to his estate, to Rathoongodde took nearly eight hours by cart and pony over narrow dirt roads. When he arrived, he was astonished and delighted by the progress of the estate and its beauty. On December 16 he rhapsodized to Julia Margaret, "O Juley! Juley! How I wish you could see all that I have been seeing for the last five days–I must try to describe this place to you." He drew her a picture of the setting of the bungalow, "like a Swiss Cottage," described the layout of all the rooms, and led her visually around the landscape:

> If you follow the path which winds round the grassy hill on the right you come in about 200 yards to a deep ravine down which flows a lovely mountain stream which I have christened the Julia oga . . . . When it crosses the path it forms a beautiful cascade falling in two white and foaming sheets of water, over the smooth face of a huge and solid mass of granite rock. At the bottom of the cascade it forms a pool about five feet deep, always cool and clear as crystal. This I have selected for my bath and Macleod is now putting up a little thatched room for me to dress in with wooden steps descending into the pool . . . . You see nothing on either side but the steep and wooded banks of the ravine with ferns and wild flowers in profusion . . . . The side of the valley so rising in front of you, is covered, for about two thirds of its height, with fine coffee, then comes a belt of forest, above that is a grassy ridge seen over the tops of the forest trees and above that the bright blue sky or the floating clouds. You may ride for some miles, by steep and winding paths, through my woods which the sun never penetrates[,] through my coffee fields and over my grassy fields, the sweet murmur of falling waters for ever in your ears, and from the coffee fields or the grassy hills or from occasional openings in the forest boundless and glorious prospects of mountains and valleys lie before you. It would be nothing less than an eternal shame to you to be the owner of such a place and not to come and see it . . .[56]

To prevent that shame, Charles Hay suggested that they economize by moving the family (except Eugene, who was at school) to Ceylon for a year and a half. He calculated the cost of food (from eggs at a halfpenny each to fowls for sixpence) and argued that even with expensive passages they would still come out ahead. The climate (or the contentment) seemed to be good for his health, for he boasted to Julia Margaret of his freedom from digestive problems. Indeed, his good spirits practically overflow from the pages of his letters: he writes to his daughter Julia often too, correcting her Greek exercises and gaily promising to make her queen of a rocky island in his stream, "crowned with a beautiful chaplet of wildflowers."[57] He was setting his heart on a return to Ceylon and he admonished his wife in another letter in January:

> I hope, Juley, it will never be said that I have a Swiss Cottage built by my own architect and carpenter and laborers, with my own wood, my own bricks, my own thatch, my own varnish, but which my own wife will not inhabit. If you really and sincerely desire to revert to our Garden Reach life [in Calcutta] this is the place to do so. For here I shall never be absent from you a day.[58]

He seemed confident that he could persuade her to the compromise of a temporary stay in Ceylon and he hinted mysteriously at "two bribes" that he held in reserve for her. Now fifty-six years old, he wanted to seize his remaining years of vitality. He was always under consideration for another colonial appointment, but he commented ruefully in a letter to Julia Margaret that since the East India Company thought the government should give him one, and the government thought the East India Company should give him one, he had resigned himself to not getting one.

Despite the steady stream of correspondence, Julia Margaret was disconsolate in his absence. She turned again to her oldest friends and wrote Herschel a melancholy letter, reminiscing about the sorrow that his friendship had alleviated in Cape Town and hoping for another favor of a visit during this lonely time. Herschel had just been appointed Master of the Mint, a civil service position that he perhaps solicited out of anxiety about providing for his large family. He had turned to Cameron and the Prinseps for help in placing his eldest son advantageously in the British East India Company and they were only too happy to oblige.[59] In April, Julia Margaret hastened to France to meet Charles Hay on his way home. Their reunion was happy and complete: Julia Margaret was delivered of her sixth and last child, Henry Herschel Hay (her Benjamin, as she often called him), barely nine months later.

In early May Julia Margaret and Charles Hay Cameron returned to London from their reunion in Paris to find the art world full of interesting developments. As John Ruskin wrote his letter to the editor defending the Pre-Raphaelite Brotherhood, the English public were turning toward art with new enthusiasm. The Great Exhibition of the Works of all Nations, already known as the Crystal Palace, had just been opened by the Queen in Hyde Park. It displayed the arts and crafts of over 13,000 exhibitors in a monumental cathedral of glass and steel. It was an engineering marvel and it drew over six million visitors. Ruskin and Burne-Jones hated it, but they were a decided minority.[60] At least one art historian has argued that the real reason for the existence and popularity of the PRB was the Great Exhibition with its "paraded ugliness and vulgarity of every single object."[61] The Great Exhibition was the nation's candid assessment of the state of its art, and it had mixed results. The popularity of the exhibit was considered a credit to the English people and their interest in culture and self-improvement. In particular, the enthusiasm and good conduct of working-class visitors helped to fuel arguments for public libraries and museums. But despite the high quality of many British contributions, the exhibit as a whole seemed to mark a low point in British taste and sensibility to art. *The Art-Journal*'s catalogue to the exhibition included a prize-winning essay called "The Exhibition as a Lesson in Taste," which railed against the "prevailing gorgeous taste of the present day, which gives the eye no resting place, and presents no idea to the mind, from the want of individuality in its gorged designs."[62] The author then proceeded frankly to assess the merits and demerits of British design in every category displayed. This national anxiety helped contribute to the growth of national design schools.

Ruskin's defense of the Pre-Raphaelites led him and his wife Effie into a friendship with them, especially Millais, who shared Ruskin's passion for landscapes painted with a close, accurate observation of details. Millais asked Effie to pose for him for a painting entitled *The Order of Release*, exhibited at the Royal Academy in 1853 to great acclaim. But Effie's posing, while commonplace to members of the Little Holland House set, was unseemly to old-fashioned bourgeois families like the Ruskins, and Effie was criticized by her in-laws for provoking gossip.[63] Ruskin himself seemed immune to the talk and set off on a long summer's vacation to Scotland with his wife, Millais, and Millais's brother, during which Millais struggled with a portrait of Ruskin standing astride a painstakingly painted waterfall. It was during this trip that Millais fell in love with Effie Ruskin, eventually marrying her after the annulment of her marriage to Ruskin in 1854.

Early in the 1850s, around the same time that Watts painted Effie Ruskin's portrait, Watts also painted Julia Margaret's portrait; it is now owned by the National Portrait Gallery [see figure]. Cameron is shown in much the same pose and expression as in the few surviving photographic portraits of her from the 1850s and 1860s, looking surprisingly meek and morose. The photographs were necessarily limited by the long exposure times and thus all Victorian portraits are characterized by steady, solemn expressions. But for Watts to paint Julia Margaret with such pathos is surprising: the woman everyone described as willful, imperious, lively, and bursting with energy is represented as a wan, drooping Romantic heroine. In the painting she looks very young, though at the time she was in her late thirties and had just delivered her sixth child. Compared to the photographs of her that have survived, Watts has made her nose smaller, her coloring fairer, and removed the small mole near her nose. Perhaps Watts thought he was doing his friend a favor by idealizing her face and expression to fit the standards of the day. If so, he did her an injustice; the portrait has none of the power of the two taken in 1874 by her son Henry Herschel Hay. It may have been Watts's portrait that inspired Sara to tell Julia Margaret one day that she was looking sick, but much more like her picture than ever before.[64]

If Julia Margaret was depressed in the middle of the decade, it was over the family's continuing financial problems. The letters of the 1850s are filled with anxiety about expenses, notes of borrowing money from her sisters and brothers-in-law, and trouble on the Ceylon estates. This constant strain was made worse by the ordinary hazards of Victorian life: disease was everywhere and daily life could be life-threatening. The Camerons' house twice caught fire during the 1850s: once from a candle held carelessly by Charles Hay and once by sparks from the chimney that caught fire inside the walls of the house and filled the rooms with smoke. No one was hurt, but the fire engines were called and the house evacuated each time. Vigilance – against disease, against fire, against penury – was a way of life.

Julia Margaret herself suffered intensely from something she called "*tic douleureux*," manifested in headaches and dizziness. She took quinine treatments and convalesced with the Normans, with Maria, and with Virginia at Brighton. At other times she had relapses of her bronchial ailments and once she was diagnosed with a lack of blood in the brain, caused by heavy menstrual periods and resulting in fatigue and memory loss.[65] All of her ailments worsened under stress and some of them may have been related to menopause. Watts fell ill and sought out the famed water cure at Malvern. Charles Hay was chronically ill with diarrhea and rheumatism. Julia Margaret nursed him devotedly and ministered the Jeremie's opiate drops that lessened his pain but increased his dependence on laudanum. Charles Hay was a difficult and obstinate patient. It took all of Julia Margaret's ingenuity and perseverance to tend him to her own satisfaction. He distrusted doctors and surviving letters chronicle a running feud between husband and wife about when and whether to send for Dr. Headland, Julia Margaret's favored physician. Julia Margaret believed that everyone should consult Headland about everything, and urged him on all her friends whenever she heard of any trouble. She also took it upon herself to nurse chronic invalids as a charitable cause.

Early in 1854 anxieties worsened as Britain entered the Crimean War to support Turkey against Russia. It was another sortie in the ongoing power struggle between Russia and Britain over influence in Asia, with Britain propping up the fading Ottoman Empire in order to defend its Mediterranean shipping routes and trade with the Middle East. Although Britain eventually "won" the war in 1856, the English military suffered several embarrassing losses like the one immortalized by Tennyson in "The Charge of the Light Brigade." Over the long, cold winter of 1854–55, British soldiers in Turkey were left with insufficient food, clothing, and ammunition as the central administration in London struggled to solve supply problems. This war was well publicized by the first war correspondents on the front lines and by Roger Fenton's photographs. The British public, which had at first clamored to enter the war, now turned on the government and denounced these indignities: the only light in the disaster was the pioneering work of Florence Nightingale and her well-trained nurses.

It was during these years that photography began to become established as a discipline. In 1853 Fenton and Sir Charles Eastlake were among the founders of the Photographic Society, later the Royal Photographic Society. Eastlake was appointed its first President after Talbot declined the honor. Fenton became the resident photographer for the British Museum and encouraged Queen Victoria's and Prince Albert's interest in the field. His portraits of the royal children in that decade were bestsellers, perhaps in part because of their surprisingly natural and informal presentation. Charles Somers Cocks, married to Julia Margaret's sister Virginia, was another early enthusiast for photography and also joined the new society. He too was a friend of Ruskin's, and seems to have remained loyal to him after the scandal of Ruskin's annulment divided the art world.

Somers Cocks managed to bridge artistic and aristocratic society. He was a member of the Photographic Society and Lord-in-Waiting to the Queen. He was the Member of Parliament for Reigate and a close friend of Henry Layard, the archaeologist of Nineveh, whose excavations he visited avidly. It has been claimed that he wanted to be an artist himself but his family wouldn't countenance it.[66] He and Virginia seem to have had a satisfactory marriage, although contemporaries commented that, having won her hand over many rivals, he didn't seem all that interested in her.[67] It was also said that she ruled the marriage.[68] Together they commissioned Watts to paint frescoes for the dining room of their London home on Carlton Terrace. Watts based his design on Greek mythology and called it *The Elements*. It was considered some of his best work and it gave an added attraction to their dinner parties.

The easy and eccentric informality of social life at Little Holland House may be compared to the rigid requirements of aristocratic society that Virginia Pattle entered upon. Although Lord and Lady Somers enjoyed the company of artists and writers, the couple's social life was made up of the obligatory events of high society: formal balls in stifling rooms; dinner tables flanked by political friends and potential allies; stiff afternoon visits with their respectable wives. Virginia, who had been carefully educated to play the lady in cultivated drawing rooms, fitted in surprisingly well, despite her unorthodox background. Madame de l'Etang had educated the girls with a sense of noblesse oblige: they believed kindness and charity were as much a part of being a lady as fashion, sketching, and a good singing voice.[69] Sara Pattle reportedly regretted that she had "no education,"[70] but Virginia apparently had learned all that she needed to for her future life, and she worked hard to pass those skills and priorities along to her own daughters.

George Du Maurier was good friends with Val Prinsep and attended both Sara and Virginia's dinners in the early 1860s. At Little Holland House one undressed for dinner, he joked, about Watts's appearance in a velvet jacket and slippers, and at parting Sara "almost embraced me." Lord and Lady Somers, on the other hand, served dinner for twelve *à la russe*, which was the fashion. It was, he wrote, the

> greatest state of sweldom these rustic eyes ever had the pleasure of beholding with mild surprise & of inwardly laughing at. Milor is a jolly sort of a little fellow with a squeaky voice. Miladi very handsome woman; but she & all the women were decolletées in a beastly fashion – damn the aristocratic standard of fashion; nothing will ever make me think it right or decent that I should see a lady's armpit flesh folds when I am speaking to her . . . . It would be something too absurd for me to be patronised by people whose dinner conversation was such as I heard last night.[71]

Du Maurier was a keen-eyed satirist, as demonstrated by his popular novel *Trilby*, which drew on these acerbic observations of cosmopolitan culture. He doubted the sincerity of the Pattle sisters but Sara grew on him as he got to know her better and he enjoyed his visits to Little Holland House. Virginia he candidly determined to use in whatever way would prove advantageous to his career.[72]

Although the sisters remained very close, Virginia's marriage into the aristocracy divided the family, especially in the next generations. The cousins were often close too, but their lives were very different. To begin with, only Julia Margaret's two youngest sons and Virginia's daughters, born in the early 1850s, had no experience of India. The eldest of the second generation were all born in India and were adolescents by the time the Little Holland House salon was holding sway. They had already seen a good deal of the world. Maria and Julia Margaret's eldest daughters, Adeline Jackson and Julia Hay Cameron, were almost the same age and very good friends. Adeline and her sisters Mary and Julia all modeled for Watts, Holman Hunt, and other artists in the circle. So did their Prinsep cousins. They enjoyed surprising freedoms for Victorian children and spent a lot of time with adults. Bourgeois Victorian children were usually kept separate from their parents' society in a world of their own. Virginia's daughters, Isabel and Adeline, had a standard, sheltered aristocratic upbringing. They spent all their time with a series of nurses, maids, and governesses (Isabel had had seven by the time she was five years old).[73] When their parents vacationed in Europe or toured the Mediterranean on a yacht, the girls were left at home. Their infrequent visits to their great-grandmother Madame de l'Etang in Versailles were the only times when the reins loosened a bit.[74] Whereas Julia Margaret's Juley was tutored in Greek by her father, Isabel and Adeline learned only the sorts of things that would be useful later in a drawing room: music, poetry, and a little German.[75] When Isabel eventually inherited Eastnor Castle, she had no training in estate management or book-keeping and was, unsurprisingly, considered a bad businesswoman.[76]

Adeline and Isabel Somers were of an age with Cameron's youngest children, Charlie and Henry Herschel Hay, born in January 1852. The similarities and differences in their upbringings are remarkable. Like all the Pattles, Julia Margaret and Virginia were obsessed with the health of their children and Julia Margaret's letters from the 1850s are sprinkled with descriptions of rashes that might be small-pox, admonitions about not drinking too much cold water, and accounts of the endless shuffling of households as sick people rotated in and out of her care. Virginia too was vigilant, but from a distance: one cannot imagine her putting the sick child in bed with her for easier night-time nursing, as Julia Margaret was wont to do whenever Charles Hay allowed it. Virginia lost her four-year-old youngest daughter, also named Virginia, to diptheria in 1858; in her grief she became compulsive and terrified about the well-being of the surviving Adeline and Isabel. The girls were sent to the seaside with a carriage full of servants whenever they showed any slight sign of illness. Their mother wrote doting letters filled with staccato commands:

> *Come well wrapped up* you must on no account allow any window to be open in the railway – put on your worsted veil – have yr large shawl round your knees – yr sealskin and grey cloak over it, you need not keep your veil down in the train.[77]

And always the girls were admonished to try harder, harder, harder to please and obey their mother because she loved them so much.

Julia Margaret wrote similar letters to Juley throughout the 1850s – demanding, gushing, and pleading. As Juley migrated from one extended visit to another in the usual custom of bourgeois young women, her mother wrote her letters daily – sometimes a few lines just to say that she loved and missed her and sometimes twenty pages of directions and news. Towards the end of the decade, the letters seem to shift, naturally, onto discussion of the futures of the eldest children. Eugene began studying for the entrance exam for the Royal Artillery, where he eventually made a career. The Crimean War was over in 1856: young officers returned from abroad, and society turned again to matchmaking. Juley turned eighteen that year and began attending balls, though it is unlikely that she had an official debut. Her cousins Isabel and Adeline Somers, on the other hand, were given weeks of lessons in curtseying in order to be presented to the Queen upon their coming out. The Prince of Wales attended their debut balls.[78] Still, Juley also needed guidance in the ways of high society, and Julia Margaret's letters begin to include reminders to write to so-and-so promptly, suggestions for tipping the maids in the homes she visits, and enigmatic commands like: "Don't be imprudent about the Duchess in any way to night."[79] As impecunious relations in a close-knit family, socializing

could be difficult. Julia Margaret often reminded Juley to economize and sometimes had to deliver disappointing news:

> Don't be eager to go to the Woolwich Ball. First remember what fatigue and
> expense these expeditions occasion for whoever takes you – next reflect how
> much Scarlet fever there is at Woolwich – + 3rd if Signor has been so ill however
> much Sara may be disposed to indulge you she cannot be attuned to going her-
> self . . . . I am sure you will be a considerate child + remember the object for
> which you remained at home + not be out all day long.[80]

The letters reveal a close and loving relationship, but inevitably mother and daughter fought too. Julia Margaret's intense and passionate nature demanded similar
returns from her daughter, and Juley's nature seems to have been calmer and more
temperate. Such serenity often seemed to her mother to indicate an absence of emotion, and then she lashed out in pain. One such contretemps that survived in letters
may have been typical. Julia Margaret and Juley were staying with the Normans at
Bromley in December 1856. When it was time to leave, Juley asked permission to
extend her stay, which Julia Margaret granted reluctantly, believing that the Normans'
home was "improving" to Juley and knowing how much she enjoyed it there. Julia
Margaret kept to her plans to leave and once home she sent her daughter a stinging
and bitter letter rebuking her for her behavior at parting. These separations are always
painful, she wrote, but this one especially: did she not realize what a sacrifice it was
to her mother to return home alone? Could she not thank her mother for the sacrifice? Was it too much to look for some concern and inquiries about her mother's
departure, even if she has given up expecting any help? Wouldn't a dutiful and loving
daughter have spent their last moments together? "All absences," she wrote,

> even those of 24 hours have some touch of seriousness to loving + anxious
> hearts – I was to be absent from you a week as you knew – but it gave you no
> sort of emotion + hence the conduct which seems to you only to have been
> carelessness + forgetfulness but don't deceive yourself. The root lies deeper
> dearest Child + if you had one spark of the love for your Mother that burns ever
> in her heart for you such conduct wd have been purely <u>impossible</u> to you –
> Therefore my tears flowed and flow– not from anger – nor need you ask my for-
> giveness – you have it most entirely – but seek to give us more love or there will
> be more + more of that sorrow you have more than once caused me – Nothing
> makes up for the <u>absence</u> of love – and where it is not absent mistakes can't
> arise –[81]

Juley's reply has not survived, but three days later her mother's next letter is reassured
and trying to understand her daughter's more restrained personality:

Outward + visible signs do cheer us in our somewhat dreary life even as we are cheered by beholding the glory + feeling the warmth of the Sun – but when obscured the Sun is still there and your Light + warmth of Love will I am sure as you say shine out to bless when most needed.[82]

It was around the same time that the family tearfully said goodbye to Sara and Thoby's son Arthur, who followed his elder brother Henry into the East India Company army. Arthur had been the golden-haired lad whom Watts bribed and cajoled into growing his hair into long curls so that he could paint him as the young Sir Galahad.[83] Watts remained very fond of the young man, and took the unruly teenager on a trip to Europe with him in 1855–56, effectively disciplining him by stating: "If you do that I shall have a headache."[84] In early 1857, as news of the Indian Mutiny started trickling back into England, the Prinseps spent the better part of the year worrying about Henry and Arthur's safety. Both sons survived; Arthur was wounded but remained in the Bengal Cavalry.

The Indian Mutiny, or First War of Independence as it is called in India, was probably the inevitable result of thousands of British attempting to rule over millions of Indians in their own land. British domination had always depended essentially on Indian co-operation and collaboration: in 1857 the East Indian army consisted of 34,000 European soldiers and 257,000 Indian sepoys.[85] The trend toward anglicizing India had only continued after the Camerons' departure and the subcontinent was becoming a pressure cooker. When rumors circulated that the newly issued rifles used cartridges greased with pig and cow fats, which observant Hindus and Muslims would have to tear open with their teeth, those sepoys began a chain reaction of mutinies that spread down the Grand Trunk Road from Delhi toward Calcutta. It started with a massacre of the European residents in Meerut in May, and the looting, killing, and vandalism soon brought the northcentral regions of India into chaos. At Cawnpore (now Kanpur), a thousand European residents took refuge in two barracks buildings and were besieged by mutinying soldiers for three weeks of broiling heat and desperate hunger. A parley between the forces agreed on an evacuation plan, but on June 27 the surviving men, women, and children were attacked by their escorts as they boarded boats to row downstream to safety. Four men survived to tell the tale. The fort at Lucknow, filled with the entire European population of that city and hundreds of loyal Indians, was besieged for months over the summer before finally being relieved and evacuated in November.

In the meantime, sensational news of butchered women and children, gallant officers, and maddened sepoys was igniting the public at home. The British just didn't seem able to take it in: their rule, so civilized and sensible as it seemed to them, overtaken by violence, anarchy, and evil. It seemed to confirm all their most racist anxieties about the East and their colonial subjects. They had believed and trusted in the bonds of loyalty that existed between officer and sepoy, between master and servant, and it had never occurred to them to think about the price that such a divided loyalty might cost their native "friends." Pursuing their own self-interests, they were shocked and dismayed to see Indians rise up to defend their own interests and identities.

The Pattle clan took the news hard. Julia Margaret was depressed and literally fell ill as the terrible news spread over all England. Besides worrying about Arthur Prinsep, in July they heard that Sophia's husband John Dalrymple was among those being recalled from their home leaves in England to return to India during the crisis. The family was heartbroken and worried and rested its hopes on the expectation that the mutiny would be quelled before he finished the long sea journey there. In July and August Julia Margaret went with first Eugene and then the Dalrymples to the Photographic Institution on New Bond Street to take commemorative photographs of everyone before John sailed. Eugene too would be called up for his commission in the Royal Artillery soon, though he was not expected to serve in India. She wanted him photographed before he "loses the look of peace! . . . . Badinage apart as we never know when he may be ordered off – + where – it is a gain + comfort to get a good Photograph whilst we can."[86] All her life Julia Margaret used photographs to mediate absence and separations.

Although Cameron's own account in her unfinished autobiography implies that she instantly fell in love with photography early in 1864 and worked steadily and rapidly over "many and many a week" at her craft until her "first success" in January, new evidence suggests that she took up photography much more erratically or slowly over the course of several years.[87] Cameron did not mention any teachers in her autobiographical fragment; yet she is known to have met or consulted with the photographers Reginald Southey, David Wilkie Wynfield, and Oscar Rejlander prior to beginning her own career, in addition to whatever she might have learned from Herschel and her brother-in-law Lord Somers. Clearly Julia Margaret was intent on representing her career and her talent as entirely her own. She implied that photography struck her like a thunderbolt and her transformation was sudden and complete. In reality, it seems to have been a more gradual and collaborative process, although it is still remarkable how comparatively little evidence survives of her interest in photography before 1864.

The evidence that does exist consists of references in her letters to taking or commissioning photographs in the late 1850s and the early photographic albums that she gave to friends. Beginning in 1857, around the time of her first recorded visit to a photography studio in July, Cameron gave albums partly filled with photographs to her closest friends and relatives. These albums, which art historian Joanne Lukitsh has studied in detail, include studio portraits of those friends and family as well as more artistic portraits and reproductions of artworks by favorite artists like Watts. Cameron's first known gift album may be one given to Watts, now called the Signor 1857 Album. It has no inscriptions by Cameron but it includes a portrait of her two youngest sons taken by photographer Reginald Southey during an April 1857 visit to the Isle of Wight. The Camerons were probably visiting the Tennysons at Farringford; Southey photographed them while also taking portraits of the poet's sons. Southey was a nephew of a former poet laureate, Robert Southey, who had been good friends with Henry Taylor and who made Taylor his literary executor. It is unclear whether Southey's visit to the Isle of Wight was at Cameron's or Tennyson's invitation.

Southey was also friends with Charles Dodgson at Oxford, where they had both recently taken up photography. Dodgson, still a decade away from writing *Alice's Adventures in Wonderland* as Lewis Carroll, had to work hard and steadily to master the complicated manipulations of light and chemicals necessary to produce a recognizable image. To produce a successful composition was that much harder, as Cameron would also come to understand. Later that summer, Dodgson met and photographed Tennyson's niece Agnes Weld. This gave him an entrée to introduce himself to the Tennysons in September while they were on a visit to the Lake District. He too took portraits of Hallam and Lionel, as well as a group portrait of the Tennysons with their hosts, the Marshalls.[88] Southey and Dodgson's photographs were unlike either the studio portraits of the time or Cameron's later work. They were informal and at ease, revealing people in ordinary dress in their own homes. Except for their extreme stillness and their conscious manipulation of light and shadow, they looked like snapshots. Dodgson also took a solo portrait of Tennyson in which the laureate looked rather small and tense. Emily Tennyson wrote the photographer a few months later to ask him to destroy all but his own copies.[89]

The Signor 1857 Album contains other photographs of the Cameron boys dressed as the Tennysons often were, in lace collars and velvet tunics. Another well-known portrait of Cameron and her two youngest sons [see figure] comes from this period and used to be attributed to Charles Dodgson. No definite evidence has turned up to confirm that attribution, but the boys wear lace-collared outfits similar to the ones worn in the Signor 1857 portraits and the portrait shares the informal style of Southey's and Dodgson's work. Despite these similarities, no one is sure who took or presented the photographs in the Signor 1857 Album. Tantalizingly, however, some betray themes that Cameron would explore later in her own work, like portraits of half-clad children or adults in fancy dress.[90]

Another early gift album was probably given in 1859 to Sibella Norman, wife of Charles Hay's old friend George Warde Norman. It was filled with over three hundred portraits of the royal family, mutual friends, and family members, but only a few are inscribed by Cameron.[91] Charles Hay had a long history with George Warde Norman, from the stretch of Cameron's childhood when he lived in Kent, from their schooldays at Eton, and from their shared interest in radical philosophy at the Political Economy Club. Along with George Grote, later an eminent historian of ancient Greece, the friends pursued an earnest and erudite companionship, staying up late to read and discuss Kant and Bentham. When Norman had a mental breakdown in 1822 Cameron was there to support him. Norman had originally gone into his father's timber business, but in 1821 he joined the Bank of England, where he eventually spent fifty years as a director. His estate at Bromley, filled with a large and happy family after his marriage, was a frequent retreat for the Camerons when ill health or fatigue wore them down. Norman was a loyal friend to the family for his whole life, and he acknowledged Charles Hay's considerable gifts, but he also speculated about his friend's worldly failures. Despite his intellect and achievements, Cameron was never as successful professionally as his old friends Norman, Grote, or Samuel Loyd, Lord Overstone. In his autobiography, Norman speculated that "he has not the art of making his way with official men, so as to obtain and to keep his place and salary."[92]

By the fall of 1857, Julia Hay Cameron's extended stays at the Normans' home in Bromley had taken a new turn, perhaps an intended one. She formed a deep attachment to their eldest son Charles, who had probably been named after her father. According to Julia Margaret's letters to Juley, it seems that her mother knew of Juley's feelings for Charles Norman and she warned her daughter frankly that Charlie seemed to have a prior attachment. She spent September at Bromley for her health, temporarily escaping the horrors of news from India while Juley and the rest of the family stayed in London. She watched Charlie carefully and conferred with his mother, concluding that he was in love with a Catholic Miss Ellis who would never marry a Protestant. She wrote sympathetically to Juley, "He is very sad – very sweet in his nature + I am very sorry for him but young men are smitten with a thousand cross-bows before the one that is to fix happiness lodges its safe point into their hearts . . . ."[93] Presumably she was proven right, because Charlie Norman proposed to Juley a year later; they were married in January 1859, to the great joy of their families. Julia Margaret wrote an ecstatic letter to Herschel detailing the perfect union of the two families and inviting him to the wedding. Her gift of a photographic album to Sibella Norman some time that year was perhaps intended to unite the two families into one commemorative album and cement the ties between the two mothers.

Julia Margaret wrote another, serious letter to Juley herself on the occasion of her twentieth birthday on December 5, 1858. Juley had decided to take her first communion and her fiancé was going to accompany her. Julia Margaret stayed up late into the night reminiscing about Juley's birth at 4 in the morning twenty years before and about her own first communion at age seventeen. Engagement and communion were important rites of passage and Julia Margaret showered sixteen pages of advice and blessings upon her. She was proud and happy for her daughter, and surely relieved that Juley was so well settled in life when the family finances were so precarious. Her advice on marriage was sensible and romantic at once, belying her reputation for hyperbole and drama:

> You will have a good and a darling Husband, and I hope and believe it will be an easy duty to you to 'love – to cherish – and to obey him, till death you do part' but you are too well <u>taught</u> in life's experiences to suppose that uninterrupted happiness <u>can</u> fall or <u>should</u> fall to any lot in life even the brightest . . . . [M]arried life whilst it doubles our blessings and enriches, and exalts <u>all</u> of good or of ill that happens to us, <u>does not halve</u> our sorrows – It is a delusion to suppose that it does –

She continues to emphasize the doubleness of marriage: the tending of body and soul, the preparing of two souls for heaven, the inextricable connection between joy and pain. You must be vigilant, she told her daughter, in rooting out evils, but also quick to confess and forgive weaknesses. "Take this cup of joy," she concluded, "as you will take the Sacramental Cup today with a <u>careful</u> hand not to waste or spill sacred good."[94]

Henry Taylor, who knew Juley well, singled her out in his autobiography for particular, and insightful, praise. After commenting on the charms of originality, simplicity, honesty, understanding, clearness of purpose, and liveliness, he adds that

> in Julia Cameron they did not appear in any likeness that was to be met with elsewhere. And when I try to make out what it was that distinguished her from other natural and original persons, I can think of nothing capable of being written down except this, – that having been born of parents who were no more ordinary in their ways than in their gifts and faculties and powers, there occurred in the case of the daughter that sort of resilience which is so often observed that it may almost be regarded as a provision of Nature, and her originality took, along with other forms, the form of a determination to be commonplace. Commonplace otherwise than externally she never could be, let her determination be what it might; but I think the intention to be like other people in all things possible gave a peculiar colour and distinctness to the inborn individuality which no outward conformity could conceal.[95]

One can well imagine a child in Juley's circumstances developing inner reserves of calm and strength. Her mother was fond and attentive, but needy and histrionic; her father was warm and amiable, but ailing and depressed. The family moved often and, due to continuing financial problems, was falling out of the socioeconomic class into which it had been born. It was a slow and agonizing process and Juley acquitted herself well through it, ultimately finding a happy and secure home of her own within their extended circle.

Meanwhile, as Juley got settled, Julia Margaret worried more about the boys. By the end of the decade, Eugene had been posted to Haiti and while his sister was on her honeymoon in Paris he was defending against a revolution there. Hardinge and Henry Herschel Hay both squinted and Julia Margaret devoted much energy to diagnosing and attempting to cure their eye troubles, with intermittent success. But the worst came when six-year-old Henry was discovered to be blind in one eye. Julia Margaret was frantic. The doctors wanted to operate and warned her that the good eye might fail too. She insisted on more opinions, consulted everyone she could, and took the boy to see Professor Richard Owen, the prominent anatomist. The letters contain no resolution but Julia Margaret's restraint in vetoing surgery may have been proven right, because Henry Herschel Hay retained sufficiently good vision to become a photographer like his mother.

Cameron's days at Little Holland House, and the friendships she made there, immersed her in the major currents of the Victorian art scene. Her association with the Pre-Raphaelites stood her in good stead a few years later when they were among her first models and earliest advocates. Although they are better known for painting beautiful women than for encouraging their art, the "second-wave" of Pre-Raphaelites did include many significant female artists too, like Rebecca Solomon and Evelyn DeMorgan. Some art historians have included Cameron among their number, though she worked with light instead of paint. They note that her work observed the same interest in literary subjects and in balancing romance and realism.[96] Cameron did sometimes acknowledge the influence of the Pre-Raphaelites on her work, as in an 1864–65 image of women and flowers entitled *Decidedly Pre-Raphaellete* [sic].[97] Besides a fondness for women and flowers, Cameron shared with the Pre-Raphaelites certain langorous poses of women draped or drooping over furniture.[98]

The Pre-Raphaelites were also perhaps the first major art movement in England to arise after the invention of photography, so their work was among the earliest to show its influence. As art historian Lindsay Smith has noted, the early Pre-Raphaelites demonstrated an extreme literalism about representation that resulted in curious paintings. In *The Scapegoat* and *The Light of the World*, for example, William Holman Hunt made religious metaphors into a literal goat and a lantern, earning him critical jeers.[99] Cameron's work would later explore the same questions from the photography side, as when she used light as a physical, tangible presence in her compositions.

Cameron's work, however, always insisted on photography's moral purpose. For artists like Cameron and Watts, art could not be stripped of its idealizing, moralizing function without it ceasing to be art at all. Cameron, Watts, and the Pre-Raphaelites may have started out in a similar place, in Little Holland House, but they pursued different paths afterwards as the PRB turned more toward the aestheticism that would inspire other critics and artists to insist on "art for art's sake."

In the long view, what makes Little Holland House stand out from the crowd of London salons was its paradoxical sense of excludedness. Little Holland House seems to have been a place where outsiders were made to feel comfortable and included, even powerful and influential. Led by colonial families like the Pattles and Prinseps, who wore their privilege easily but never quite fitted into English society, Little Holland House attracted people like Watts, the son of a piano maker, and Tennyson, the son of a vicar with a family history of "black blood." Like the Pre-Raphaelites, the artists and writers of Little Holland House all stood a little outside the circle of respectability and conformity. Despite their gifts and successes, none of them felt fully accepted by their social class. And at Little Holland House the relationships and exchanges were more mutual and balanced. There wasn't one patroness exchanging her social standing for a patina of art; the Pattle sisters were as ambiguous in their status as their so-called "followers," and vice versa. But as the various artists and authors became more successful – as the radical Pre-Raphaelites earned a following and joined the Royal Academy, as they married, built houses in developing Kensington, and "settled down" – they needed Little Holland House less and less. Sara's salon declined through the 1860s and ceased operating altogether in the early 1870s.

CHAPTER 5

Idylls of Freshwater

I N OCTOBER 1859 Charles Hay received alarming news about his coffee estates in Ceylon. They were slowly failing and bringing down the family finances with them, as well as jeopardizing the Cameron sons' futures. It may have been the first sign of the blight that would decimate the coffee crops of Ceylon and turn the island toward the cultivation of tea.[1] Though he would soon be sixty-five years old, Charles Hay resolved to go back out to Ceylon himself to see to the problems, taking his two eldest boys with him to introduce them to estate management. Eugene was committed to the Royal Artillery, but he managed to obtain six months' leave to accompany his father. But first Charles Hay had to get past Julia Margaret's resistance to the idea. Needless to say, she was not pleased. She hated his absences, when she worried ceaselessly about his health and suffered from loneliness even in the midst of her tight-knit clan. When Charles Hay suggested this plan, she begged and pleaded with him to consider his health, to consider her happiness, to consider the dangers of climate and rough living. He replied that he would be spared an English winter. Over the years, she had developed an antagonism to Ceylon: it was her nemesis and arch rival and she even described it in one letter as a seductress who enchanted her husband and lured him away from her. Bluntly she wrote to Sir John Herschel that "his reigning passion for his Ceylon properties . . . has held him in sway + weakened his love for England for the last 20 years!"[2] Charles Hay did love the island and couldn't fathom why Julia Margaret refused to acknowledge its charms. Whereas Charles Hay believed the tropical climate was always healthful and beneficial to him, Julia Margaret believed obstinately that it was only the sea voyage that did him good: the rough food, heat and damp, and laborious life, she insisted, were treacherous.

Julia Margaret tried everything to convince him not to go. She asked the boys to plead with him, she asked Dr. Headland to give his medical opinion against it, she wrote to old friends like Lord Overstone and begged them to use their influence. She enlisted Charles and Julia Norman to reason with him. Juley was pregnant with her first child and Charles Hay would miss the birth of this grandchild while in Ceylon. It was all to no avail. As Julia Margaret caustically remarked, "Charles speaks to me of the flower of the coffee plant. I tell him that the eyes of the first grandchild should be more beautiful than any flower."[3] Charles Hay could be stubborn, especially when reason could be set against irrational feelings. He loved the island, but the real purpose of the visit was practical: owning estates was a responsibility that included occasional visits. He became quite sick with his old kidney complaint before the voyage and Julia Margaret hoped that it would be put off, but Charles Hay insisted that he would be well enough to travel. Julia Margaret nursed him with beef tea, poached eggs, port wine, and mulligatawny soup, alongside doses of creosote zinc, gum arabic, and quinine.[4] As Julia Margaret eyed the trunks standing ready in the hall, the dreaded day grew nearer.

The trips to Ceylon, though infrequent, were clearly a continuing source of tension for the Camerons, but they seem to have reflected a deeper conflict about responsibility. Julia Margaret wrote to Overstone that fall that Charles Hay was insistent on developing the Ceylon estates for his five boys and he felt it was his duty to provide for them generously. Surprisingly, she thought that ridiculous: "I think it his chief duty," she wrote Overstone, "to consult their higher interests in preserving his life for them to the longest term of life he can – by care – and all those means which regular life at home & only regular life at home supply . . . ."[5] She added that Charles Hay himself had inherited no fortune and that no able-bodied young man needed one to get along well in the world:

> I only urge upon Charles one thing, which is to take care of his health, to educate his Sons, + to leave the rest without an anxiety giving them what we have to give, which is more than he ever himself started with.[6]

Julia Margaret wrote proudly of her sons, but she clearly placed her husband's well-being above their worldly success. What Overstone made of this rather unmaternal argument is not known, though it is doubtful that he intervened on her behalf with Charles Hay. The logic is indeed puzzling: after all, the Ceylon estates were crucial not only to the boys' future inheritance but also to the family's current subsistence and, indeed, the cost of schools. What exactly did Julia Margaret think they would live on if the estates failed? They still earned interest from the funds in their marriage settlement, but not enough to support the family. Clearly the issue was more emotional than rational, which is why Charles Hay persisted stubbornly in overruling her anxieties. Julia Margaret simply wanted his presence: she wanted it now, she wanted the boys to have it as they grew up, and she wanted it for as long as possible. Absence and illness put that emotional need at great risk.

The obvious solution would be for Julia Margaret to accompany him. She claimed she could not because her nerves were already shattered from her ten years' residence in Calcutta.[7] Her own health, she admitted readily to Overstone, was not up to the voyage and the climate; why could Charles Hay not admit the same? Ultimately, the conflict boiled down to a power struggle in which they both lost sight of reality. Julia Margaret was certainly well enough to travel if Charles Hay was, but she did not want to co-operate with any plan involving those troublesome estates. Charles Hay really was, perhaps, too old and sick for such a trip, but he absolutely refused to give up on the Ceylon property as a refuge for himself and an investment for his sons.

Before he left, Charles Hay was forced to borrow another 2,000 pounds from Lord Overstone, probably to finance the expensive passages by steamer. It was not easy, but he justified his request by assuring his friend that his 5,000 acres in Ceylon had been yielding £1,200 on average each year and that they were worth far more than that. Besides, his marriage settlement would provide for his sons and wife after his death: he implied but did not quite state that the estates needed only to yield an annual income to live on.[8] This, however, was not easily managed (especially as debts accrued), and it was clear from Cameron's letters to Overstone that he was also actively seeking another colonial appointment. Before sailing, he again forwarded testimonials about his qualifications to the Colonial Secretary, the Duke of Newcastle, to put himself forward for a governorship of Ceylon or Malta and the Ionian Islands in the Mediterranean. He had been on a shortlist of candidates for the past six years but never appointed. In writing to Overstone again in 1859 on the subject he clearly wanted his friend to understand that he was doing all he could to augment his income. He probably also hoped that Overstone would recommend him to his friend the duke. Overstone would have been only too happy to do Charles Hay another favor, as his continuing loans confirm, but the major obstacle was Cameron's health. He did in fact speak to the duke on the subject later in the year; he remained staunchly loyal and generous to Charles Hay out of his deep respect and affection for him: the letter that accompanied the loan made Charles Hay burst into tears and cover his face with his hands, as Julia Margaret later reported to Overstone.[9]

Charles Hay left his credentials and his hopes in Overstone's and Newcastle's care and sailed for Ceylon with Eugene and Ewen on November 20. Tennyson kindly accompanied Julia Margaret and the three youngest boys to Southampton for the wrenching goodbyes, and afterward swept them off to his home on the Isle of Wight. She gave her Putney Heath house to an agent to sublet and spent several lonely months with Tennyson and visiting Juley and Charlie and friends. Meanwhile, England receded into the distance for Charles Hay, Eugene, and Ewen: on November 28 they were in the Mediterranean; on December 27 they were in Colombo; in January they arrived at Rathoongodde. There they received the belated but very welcome news that Juley was safely delivered of a healthy baby, Charlotte. Charles Hay promptly named the waterfall on his property after her.

Julia Margaret continued to watch vigilantly over Charles Hay's health, and she must have charged Eugene and Ewen with monitoring their father's condition and relaying details to her at home. The young men would turn twenty and sixteen, respectively, while on the voyage, and they struggled to please both parents during the long and anxious absence. When Eugene wrote his sister to congratulate her on Charlotte's birth, Julia Margaret rebuked him for not using the occasion to report on his father's health. When Charles Hay did become seriously ill, first in February and then in June, the young men were left to decide when to send for the doctor by cart and pony from Kandy and how much to tell their mother. Almost alone on their estate in the forests of Ceylon, with only an ailing father, a local steward, and a cousin at hand to guide them, they must have felt the great pressure of each decision.

It began with a short attack of fever in Colombo. But by February, Charles Hay was complaining of fever, ague, and chronic diarrhea that kept him up at night. He resorted to the strong medicine (perhaps the "green draught in the wooden bottle") that Dr. Headland had prescribed in case of dire need, as well as fifteen drops of the laudanum that Julia Margaret disapproved of so heartily.[10] The news trickled back to the family by the end of the month, and Julia Margaret panicked. Her reports came from Charles Hay himself, and the accounts that she quotes to Juley are surprisingly candid about his weakness and pain, considering how upset he knew she would become. She considered rushing out to Ceylon herself but knew that she would be at least two months behind the latest developments. She wished that he would head home right away, but she knew that he would not. She scolded everyone, especially Charlie and Juley, for not helping her prevail against Charles Hay's ill-considered plan. She blamed the inevitable disaster on their refusal to listen to her good sense and prescient concern. Before the departure, she had tried to be careful not to use arguments that would be painful to remember later if she was proven right in forecasting danger; now, she forgot her scruples and let fly with recriminations and lamentations. The three youngest boys tried to comfort her by reminding her that the danger may have passed by the time she received the letter, but she resisted:

> In Children such springing hope is natural – but those who have seen the shadow of the valley don't think only of stationary sunshine + steady prosperity of which I for one never knew much – when I was a Child I feared + now I am a Grand Mother I fear. Yet hitherto death has not seized very many of my most beloved ones at least not that I yet know but it seems to hold my heart in its bondage today –[11]

By March, Julia Margaret's letters had turned to new topics; the danger appeared to have passed, as her family and friends had reassured her. She was still staying at Freshwater Bay on the Isle of Wight, near the Tennysons, and she was growing attached to the island, with its milder winter climate and sea air. It seemed healthful and quiet to her, two benefits that she prized highly. She wrote Juley ruefully that she was surprised to learn she had only 15 pounds in the bank, and she was forced to borrow another 100 pounds from the Normans. She hoped that the future rent of the Putney Heath home would enable her to repay the loan, but her agent hadn't yet found a tenant for the house. She visited Juley and the Normans at Bromley toward the end of the month and delighted in her new grandchild. Nonetheless, she wrote that she cherished Charlotte but she was building "bulwarks round my heart to prevent myself from getting too fond of her . . . ."[12] As with Ewen's birth many years before, enduring separations made her loath to commit to new attachments. She missed Charles Hay so much that she couldn't bear to read his letters aloud, and tried to assume her usual good spirits and energy to distract herself from her loneliness and anxieties.[13]

Julia Margaret spent April back at Freshwater Bay with her sister Louisa Bayley, the least social of the six sisters. The two women nursed their children through sore throats and tensions began to run high as everyone was stuck indoors in separate quarantines. For relief, Julia Margaret went up to Little Holland House at the end of the month and saw Sara and Juley in London. Eugene returned home from Ceylon in May, having exhausted his six months' leave from the Royal Artillery. Julia Margaret found him rather low and rather disappointed in her island home, perhaps in comparison to the one he had just left. As usual, she urged him to be grateful for the blessing of a safe return, but he pined for a permanent home in England, to which his mother replied curtly that in that case he "should have married the Black Princess with the $40,000 who the Major says was desperately enamoured of him –."[14]

In May Julia Margaret also wrote to Charles Hay of the welcome news that the Governor-General of Ceylon, Sir Henry Ward, was retiring and that Charles Hay was under consideration as his replacement. She urged her husband not to count on the appointment and reminded him of the importance of peace and quiet to his health. "I know how near it lies to yr heart," she wrote, "but I think nevertheless that official life would be a burden to you now and that you are more sure of inward peace <u>out</u> of public excitement + official responsibility than <u>in</u> it." Again, she made no mention of financial considerations in her letter, but she closed it very fondly:

> Life is not so very full of years to any of us – and long absences dwindle away what is already in the course of nature dwindled to a short span–So come home
>   —your affectionate Wife, Julia Margaret Cameron[15]

In June Overstone wrote to their mutual friend George Norman that "I have brought all the circumstances of Cameron's case fully under the notice of the Duke – but I do not profess to be sanguine as to the result."[16] That summer, another candidate was named

Julia Margaret Cameron, *Angel of the Nativity*, 1872.

One of Cameron's great-nieces, either Rachel or Laura Gurney,
modeled for this portrait of angelic childhood.

This portrait of the Pattle family was painted in France by J. F. Garneray when Julia Margaret was about three years old.

Cameron bought two adjacent houses in Freshwater and joined them with a tower of her own invention. She called the combined home Dimbola Lodge, after one of the family's coffee estates.

This photograph is one of a series of possible collaborations between Cameron and the photographer Oscar Rejlander at Cameron's home in the spring of 1863, though Cameron didn't officially take up photography until early 1864.
Mary Ryan is on the right in a white apron; Cameron is to the left in a dark dress.

Julia Margaret Cameron, *Hardinge Hay Cameron*, May 1864.

This early portrait of Hardinge resembles David Wilkie Wynfield's Renaissance-style portraits of artists.

Julia Margaret Cameron, *Pray God Bring Father Safely Home*, 1872/1910.

This photograph is an example of Cameron's narrative photographs, which echo
Oscar Rejlander's interest in dialogue and everyday scenes.

Julia Margaret Cameron, *Alfred Tennyson*, May 1865.

Tennyson called this portrait of himself "The Dirty Monk".

Julia Margaret Cameron, *Sir Henry Taylor (A Rembrandt)*, 1866.

Cameron consciously experimented with modeling her photographs
after Old Masters paintings.

Julia Margaret Cameron, *Grace Thro' Love*, 1865.

Cameron's maid, Mary Hillier, modeled for this and many other
Madonna portraits.

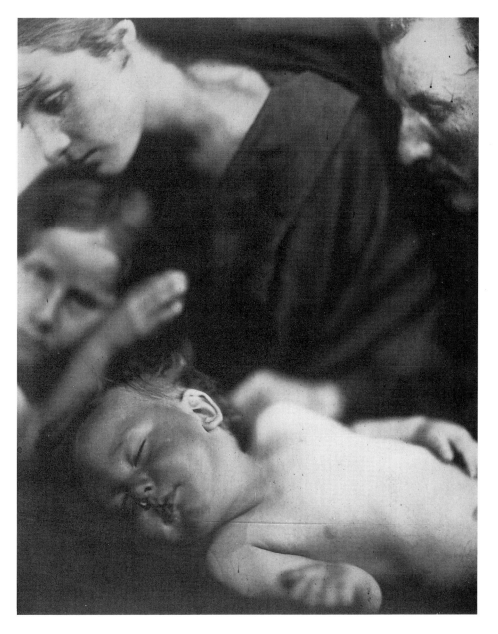

Julia Margaret Cameron, *Prayer and Praise*, 1865.

With its radical cropping and intense, hazy close-up, this photograph is an example of
the unconventional techniques that earned Cameron the disapproval
of photography critics.

Julia Margaret Cameron, *The Shunamite Woman and her dead Son*, 1865.

Mary Ryan was again the model in this photograph
of a biblical scene.

to the position. A year later, Henry Taylor wrote a testimonial for Cameron when the governorship of the Cape colony fell open, but again he had to be frank about Charles Hay's health.[17] In 1864, when the governorship of Ceylon again fell open, Charles Hay once more put himself forward fruitlessly. Overstone sighed, "He will not, I fear, settle down in tranquil contentment until the question has been finally and absolutely disposed of."[18] Charles Hay never did obtain another colonial appointment.

As Julia Margaret wrote that letter, and Overstone and the Duke of Newcastle conferred about him, Charles Hay was beginning to relapse into another unfortunately timed illness. Ewen kept a journal of his Ceylon trip from May to August 1860, with a few entries from later in the autumn, and notes of his father's ill health begin to appear in mid-May. He seems to have had no supervised instruction in estate management: he simply conversed with the manager and took long walks through the forests to visit other plantations or observe the Ceylonese workers. He often accused himself of idleness, but by this he seems to have meant he did little reading. He didn't do much writing either, for his daily entries range from a few sentences to a paragraph, but he did produce regular letters home to his extended family. On May 24 Ewen was sufficiently worried about his father's condition to remonstrate with him that they ought to head home. Charles Hay demurred, and Ewen was left in an awkward position, torn between obedience to his father's expressed wishes and duty to his mother's implied directions. At the time his cousin Willie Wodehouse and the estate manager Mr. Rose were out visiting another plantation and Ewen was alone with his father and their servants. The area was experiencing a drought that was damaging the coffee crops; Ewen waited for rain while he watched his father, hoped for his cousin's return, and tried to avoid being trampled by elephants on his walks.[19]

Despite doses of laudanum, Jeremie's drops, and many bottles of claret, Charles Hay continued to weaken, with only occasional good days. When Willie Wodehouse returned, he too urged his uncle to leave but Charles Hay was adamant. They did succeed in getting him to "half consent" to a doctor, so they promptly sent for one from Kandy. The doctor arrived the next day, examined the patient, and warned Willie privately that they must telegraph Charlie Norman of his father-in-law's life-threatening condition. Ewen sent Willie off in secret to Kandy on June 4, but when his father told him to write home and proclaim his health pretty good, Ewen repented of the anxiety a telegram would cause and sent a "coolie," as they called their local servants, in the hopes of catching and forestalling Willie's errand. The young man anxiously watched his father for any sign of worsening or improvement, but the signs must have been difficult indeed to read, and the consequences of a wrong decision disastrous. It turned out that Willie did not telegraph, but he did write to Charlie Norman from Kandy, and Ewen agonized over the family's reaction to the bad news.

He was right to be worried. By July 17, Julia Margaret was writing frantic letters to Charlie and Juley from Freshwater, asking them to book her a berth for Ceylon on the steamer leaving on the twentieth. She had already been to Southampton to reserve a room but had failed to find one and was relying on Charlie and Juley to pay her fare and secure her passage. She resolved to go alone, leaving the three younger boys with her sister Maria and trusting only to God to support her in her trial. Charlie and Juley must have been in a quandary about what to do, for they sent no response and they prevaricated about forwarding news to her. Julia Margaret wrote again to them the next day from the docks, opening her letter bluntly: "It overwhelms me with distress not to have any answer yet to my Letters."[20] Brief, urgent, and full of underlined sections and dropped words, the letters from this terrified week speak of Julia Margaret's panic at being so powerless in the face of disaster. She always sought refuge in action, and here – over 5,000 miles from her dying husband – there was nothing to be done but race across the oceans to him, even though she acknowledged to Juley that she might cross him in transit. The trip was somehow forestalled; they must have received word, perhaps by telegram, that Charles Hay and Ewen had started for England on July 5.

Charles Hay was still ailing but well enough to be carried by palanquin for the first leg of the journey from Rathoongodde, then by carriage as they neared the small city of Kandy. They hired another coach to get to Colombo and then Galle at the southern tip of Ceylon, where they departed by steamer on July 16. Ewen was terribly seasick, and the ship had to veer south over the equator to avoid summer storms, but the trip was otherwise uneventful. Charles Hay rarely left his cabin and often stayed in bed all day, but he was comfortable except for the extreme heat of the Red Sea in July. At Aden steamers always refueled and all the windows were closed to keep out the coal dust, making the rooms intolerable. They disembarked at Suez and traveled overland to Cairo, then by barge down the Nile to Alexandria, where they boarded the SS *Ceylon* for the final leg home. Charles Hay often needed laudanum to sleep and could barely swallow the food.

The travelers landed in Southampton on August 17, at which point all letters and diary entries cease. Ewen later commented that his mother was "dreadfully shocked" at her husband's appearance. In fact, Charles Hay was still very ill and required constant attendance from Julia Margaret and Dr. Headland for his first three weeks in England. He was given laudanum twice a day and made a slow recovery. Julia Margaret also suffered fainting spells and dizziness that were attributed to overexertion and anxiety. Throughout the fall, Charlie and Juley nursed Charles Hay at Putney Heath, while Julia Margaret moved to Little Holland House under the care of Sara and her daughter Alice.[21] In November Charles Hay was still writing letters addressed from "Bed–Ashburton Cottage,"[22] but he was clearly out of danger by

December. Ewen went for an extended stay at the Norman home in Bromley until his parents were well enough to make plans for his interrupted education. He did some desultory work with a local tutor and played a lot of billiards.

That fateful trip to Ceylon had important consequences. First, it almost certainly precluded any later trips, though some scholars have speculated that Charles Hay was absent in Ceylon when Julia Margaret took up photography in 1863–64. Given the disastrous results of this trip, it seems unlikely that Charles Hay would have made another one, or that there wouldn't be references to it in surviving letters. The next time the Camerons went to Ceylon they went together. The second important result of the Ceylon trip was Julia Margaret's increasing intimacy with the Tennysons and her extended stay on the Isle of Wight. The Tennysons had moved to Freshwater in 1853 when, in their frequent house-hunting, they came across a gabled Queen Anne house called Farringford with a glorious view of the sea. Freshwater was relatively remote then: it has been said that at the passenger ferry to Lymington porters used to call out, "This way to England!"[23] Emily Tennyson was often immobilized by a spinal complaint and she never liked travelling, so she settled there while Alfred roamed among friends and literary salons, with frequent returns to Farringford for work and solace. It was there in March 1854 that their second and last child, Lionel, was born. Over the course of the decade, the Tennysons and the Camerons had grown close. They visited at Freshwater and met often at Little Holland House, where Tennyson would recite *Maud* (which he considered underappreciated) or some of his works in progress. Tennyson always liked to compose his poetry while walking and speaking the lines out loud, so over the years Julia Margaret probably had first-hand knowledge of his writing process. Only later would he commit the verses to paper, and then his revisions often continued after publication. His memory was prodigious: he knew all of his own work by heart, ready to recite at a moment's notice, and he loved to quote other poets' verses as well. His work was always meant to be heard as well as read: it was renowned for its musicality (though Tennyson himself wasn't as interested in music as Julia Margaret and Emily were) and it still wins over its audience first by its sonorous and melodic qualities before its story or argument.

In the late 1850s Julia Margaret and her sisters were privileged to hear Tennyson declaim drafts of "Guinevere" and "Merlin and Vivien," two books of the first installment of the *Idylls of the King*. On one occasion Virginia Somers made the faux pas of keeping and copying one of the manuscripts that Tennyson had passed around. The poet was predictably annoyed: both he and Emily were very careful about the business side of his career. He wrote playfully but no less seriously to Sara Prinsep, calling her Principessa (his and Emily's nickname for her) and urging her to "hint to the Goddess of Eastnor Castle and Little Holland House that she must really burn or hermetically seal up that copy of Guinevere taken surreptitiously under cloud of night."[24] The poems were published in June 1859, and by July, he was comfortable enough to give a copy of the manuscript of "Guinevere" to Julia Margaret with the words "she shall have it if anyone has it."[25]

During Charles Hay's absence, Julia Margaret and the younger boys stayed with the Tennysons at Farringford for part of the time and probably rented a cottage nearby for the rest of the winter and spring. It must have been fairly close by, because one day Emily Tennyson noted in her diary

> I hear a tramping on the drive while I am resting and think it is Americans coming as seven did the other day to ask for admittance but find that it is Mrs Cameron's Grand piano which she has most kindly sent for Mr. Lear. It is pleasant to see the surprise of each one coming in and seeing it.[26]

As with the Taylors, Julia Margaret showered the Tennysons with gifts, sometimes of questionable relevance. During the early years of their friendship, she gave Emily Tennyson a bound copy of Taylor's poems. She gave Hallam a bound copy of his father's poems, though it turned out to be Lionel's birthday. She gave the family blue wallpaper trimmed with a border depicting the Elgin Marbles. Once she arrived at their house with two legs of Welsh mutton from Eastnor Castle.[27] And of course, she gave them photographs, in ever increasing quantities as she began making them herself.

It was during this stay that Julia Margaret fell in love with the Isle of Wight, and probably began scouting for houses there for herself. In May she eagerly described its spring beauties to her husband in Ceylon, quoting a line from Tennyson's "Guinevere":

> This Island might equal your Island now for richness of effects. The downs are covered with golden gorse + beneath them the blue hyacinth is so thickly spread that the valleys look as if 'the sky were upbreaking thro' the Earth' – the sea on one side is cool and tranquil like a child asleep that may awake to cry but sleeps that <u>all over</u> sleep which is granted only to the Child . . .[28]

Her rhapsodies echo those of her contemporaries. When Annie Thackeray tried to describe her magical introduction to the island, she too turned to a sort of poetry in prose:

> Farringford I first knew in autumn, but perhaps it is most beautiful in the spring when the woods are full of anemones and primroses; narcissus grows wild in the lower fields; a lovely creamy stream of flowers flows along the lanes; and then, with a later burst of glory, comes the gorse, lighting up the country round

about, and blazing round the Beacon Hill. From High Down . . . you come at last to the Needles, and may look down upon the ridge of rocks that rise crisp, sharp, shining, out of the blue wash of fierce, delicious waters.[29]

Tennyson shared Cameron's love of the island's natural beauties; the two would often stand on the beach together watching the sea in silence. Tennyson's land was partly wooded and Cameron treated the estate as her own until the poet tetchily told her not to pick his wild hyacinths. Emily apologetically sent some over to her the next day. Nothing daunted, Julia Margaret recognized Alfred's sensitive and irritable temper as a part of his character that had nothing to do with his affections. She marveled that he could carefully observe the riot of color across his lawn and yet grumble incessantly about workmen and tourists. The most popular and arguably the most acclaimed poet in England, he had a litany of complaints: tradesmen cheated him; strangers took souvenirs from his grounds; fashionable ladies sought autographs. Julia Margaret was bemused and sympathetic, but she refused to indulge his distemper. She briskly ignored or overruled his complaints and held her place in his heart through sheer perseverance and loyalty. She mused, "If he would only live in his own <u>divine</u> powers and not suffer the merest terrestrial trifles to magnify themselves into misfortunes heaped on him."[30]

She saw Alfred's generosity beneath the scowling façade: she reported to Charles Hay that Alfred had volunteered to tutor Hardinge in Greek. Much of her letter chronicles the poet's near-comic sensitivity to other people: he could never forgive her for introducing him to the local officer to whom he had lent a horse. He was very near-sighted and often took fright at the approach of people he could barely see.[31] He would beg Julia Margaret to see him to his gate because someone was coming. "Alfred, it is only a poor old woman," she would reply, and he would relax again. Interestingly, Julia Margaret early on noted that

> the <u>looking</u> at him would be the most capital offense of all if he were Ruler of the Universe and yet he is so worth looking at – so grand in form + character + even in his shrinking there is a sad + serious helplessness – + <u>no offensiveness</u> – None is meant.[32]

Yet Tennyson was one of the most painted and photographed celebrities of Victorian England, and he sat frequently for Julia Margaret in later years, though reluctantly. It was perhaps his relative comfort with her looking at him that made the photographs successful.

Tennyson's fame since being made poet laureate in 1850 had only grown: *Maud* sold well enough to enable him to purchase Farringford in 1856 and by the end of the decade the first four books of the *Idylls of the King* were generating large royalties.

Critical opinion was mixed – Elizabeth Barrett Browning, for example, felt that with the Italian risorgimento happening all around her in Florence, these archaic tales of King Arthur's England seemed pale and lifeless.[33] But the public loved them and eagerly awaited the next installments, though the last of the twelve books was not published until 1885. Tennyson had become a bona fide Victorian celebrity and he was constantly sought for sittings by people eager to commemorate his genius, or trade on his popularity. Watts painted his "moonlight" portrait of Tennyson in 1859 in a pose and style much like Cameron's later work: he depicted the poet's head and shoulders at a three-quarter angle, with eyes downcast. The effect, as in Cameron's portraits, is slightly softened by blurring the edges of his body, omitting any props, and making the background severely blank. Thomas Woolner sculpted a medallion of Tennyson's profile in 1856 that made him into a fierce Roman patrician, with relatively short and combed curls. He was sketched by everyone: from friends like Edward FitzGerald and James Spedding to professionals like Richard Doyle (of *Punch*) and D. G. Rossetti. Many photographers associated with Cameron photographed Tennyson before she did, including Lewis Carroll (in 1857) and Oscar Rejlander (in 1863). The most famous portrait of the poet in his lifetime was probably J. E. Mayall's 1867 image, about which Tennyson once infuriated Cameron by claiming to prefer it over her own. "The comparison," she wrote in her autobiographical fragment years later, "seems too comical. It is rather like comparing one of Madame Tussaud's waxwork heads to one of Woolner's ideal heroic busts."[34] Nonetheless, in 1855 she had liked one of Mayall's portraits enough to frame it and give it to Tennyson.[35]

As early as October 1859, Julia Margaret had written to the American publisher James T. Fields to send him photographs that she had "had taken" of Tennyson. Fields and his wife Annie had visited the Tennysons at Farringford and had been to Little Holland House, but Julia Margaret had not yet met them when she sent off the photographs. It seems, then, that the idea to commission and forward the images was her own and she took some explicit credit for them in her letter, referring to "my photographer" and praising his abilities and his discretion in not profiting off copies of the laureate's portrait. She was aware of the commercial potential of the work, for she also insisted that Fields not allow the images to be reproduced.[36] One imagines that Tennyson would not have been pleased by the circulation of his portrait in the United States, since he always felt plagued by American fans. By inference, Julia Margaret was sophisticated enough in her knowledge of photography to know that even without owning the negative a person could rephotograph an existing image and make copies that way.

Besides commissioning photographs of Tennyson, Julia Margaret had something of a history of mediating in portraits of and by others. Late in 1858, when he was painting Tennyson, Watts wrote Emily Tennyson a letter apologizing for Julia Margaret's interference in the work in process. Apparently, Emily had somehow criticized the painting and Julia Margaret had rushed to its defense, leaving Watts helplessly to distance himself from her overeager efforts: "Pray do not in any degree identify me with it . . . I hope neither of you have [sic] been seriously vexed by your joust with Mrs. Cameron. You know how she delights in a passage of arms!"[37] A month after Cameron sent the Tennyson portraits to Fields, William Holman Hunt wrote to tell her he had found the photograph she wanted and was going to forward it to her. Perhaps it was a portrait of himself that she asked him for; his wording is ambiguous:

> I believe it will be found to be tolerably successful altho as one always wishes to look honester than one is it would not get the premium were such offered for the first photograph that turned out in all respects satisfactory to the sitter. In truth however it is very flattering as to the appearance of the outer man and very possibly to the inner man too.[38]

The fragmentary evidence from the years 1857 to 1863 points to Cameron's gradual interest in collecting photographs of loved ones and famous friends and her increasing involvement in their production. Since it is also known that she assembled and gave photographic albums as gifts during this period, it seems likely that her interest in photography grew first out of her desire to circulate mementos of shared affections and interests with those in her circle. These albums, like the ones she gave later on that included examples of her own work, were probably intended to cement existing ties and foster the exchange of favors. The albums probably given to Watts in 1857 and Sibella Norman in 1859 consolidated long-lasting friendships and family unions. The album she gave to Lord Lansdowne on February 9, 1859 probably signaled an exchange of some kind: Lansdowne had given Juley and Charles Norman a wedding present the month before and Charles Hay was in the midst of his efforts to gain a colonial appointment, for which Lansdowne would be an important personal reference. In the Lansdowne Album Cameron captions the portraits of Hardinge Cameron "your protégé," which might perhaps imply that Lansdowne paid the boy's tuition at Charterhouse, where he had just enrolled that month.[39] In December 1862 Cameron gave her daughter her own photo album; like the one given to Sibella Norman, it was filled with portraits of the united Cameron and Norman families, though no one is sure who chose the photographs or when they were added.[40]

Cameron's close ties with Tennyson also made her an influential contact for people trying to get access to him, especially artists. The painter Samuel Lawrence wrote to Cameron in 1863 to report on a favor she asked of him and to ask for one for himself, in a move that was typical in the correspondence of Cameron's circle. The personal and the professional were entirely mixed up and even the supposedly separate spheres of male work and female domesticity were more often than not intermingled. Lawrence hoped that Cameron would ask Emily Tennyson to loan him back his own painting of Alfred so that he could "make one from it." It is not clear what he wants to make, but likely another painting. Lawrence has asked Alfred to sit again but he has refused. In desperation, he hopes that Cameron will intercede for him. He continues:

> The photographs of him that I have seen are not so good as to provoke me to buy one, and with all the great merit of that port't by Watts there is not his color or the robustness of his brains. It has delicacy of sentiment but delicacy and strength unite in Tennyson more than any man I know of and it is to be seen in his look as much as his works . . .[41]

People who met Tennyson often commented on his character as a union of opposites: strength and sensitivity; courage and cowardice; complexity and simplicity. Inevitably, this perception of duality led them to make gendered comparisons, and Tennyson's personality was often considered a particularly androgynous mix of masculine and feminine traits, according to the assumptions of the time. It is worth remembering that such comments were considered high praise by the Victorians, because there was a profound, prevailing assumption in Christian England that Jesus Christ himself was a perfect union of male and female natures, and he was the archetype for all humankind. Tennyson himself believed that men should be more like women and vice versa; both should be more like the "double-natured Poet." Like many of his peers, Tennyson believed that poets needed to be especially empathic and sensitive to all human feelings. Henry Taylor also wrote of Tennyson that "there is much of a woman's nature in him, as there ought to be in a poet: who should represent humankind rather than mankind."[42] Their contemporary Algernon Swinburne referred to Tennyson when he wrote approvingly that "great poets are bisexual."[43]

Cameron's contribution to the representation of Tennyson's "double" nature is best seen perhaps in her well-known portrait of him [see figure], which he called the "Dirty Monk." She took it in May 1865 as one of a set of new photographs of Alfred and in the same month as another of her best-known works, *The Whisper of the Muse*. Cameron used it later on as the frontispiece for her volumes of photographs illustrating Tennyson's *Idylls of the King* in 1874–75. It is famous in part, no doubt, because of Tennyson's sardonic description of himself as the "Dirty Monk." Everyone who knew Tennyson commented on his sloppiness: his clothes were soiled; his hair was long and uncombed; his fingernails dirty. His grooming improved after Emily took over his laundry and household, but he was both vain about his great height and strong frame and oblivious to the details of his appearance. Cameron's photograph and Tennyson's caption make the most of his paradoxical combination of high and low: the grandeur of the poet-genius worshiped by readers and the physical presence of an unkempt body. Though he called it the "Dirty Monk," she allegedly captioned one print "a column of immortal grandeur – done by my will against his will."[44] It is quite a claim for a budding photographer to make about the poet laureate of England. Her eagerness to identify with Tennyson is reinforced by its now iconic title: Cameron too had a reputation, both personal and photographic, for messiness.[45]

This example of Cameron's work is well focused and it reveals the coarse cloth of his monk-like cowl, the straggling hair, the pouches of skin around eye and cheek, the thick fingers. The pose is styled after Renaissance portraiture of great men: like Hans Holbein's *Sir Thomas More*, it shows the upper body at a three-quarter angle, though the face is more in profile. The poet's hand aptly holds a book, a prop denoting his identity and status like those used by Renaissance portraitists. Other contemporary photographers, like David Wilkie Wynfield, were experimenting with this format of heroic portraiture too. Later on, Cameron would turn towards a radically blurred and impressionistic style of portraiture for her images of great men, but she seemed pleased with this more sedate and respectful view of the laureate. Aware of its commercial potential, she had Tennyson autograph copies by the score. It was a measure of his great affection for her and, again, her force of will that he grumbled but usually complied.

Cameron liked to compare her two favorite poets – and friends – Taylor and Tennyson by calling the former the "practical poet" and the latter the "contemplative poet."[46] By practical, she meant that Taylor had a life in the world, with an office job and daily responsibilities. She loved them both but she preferred Taylor, perhaps because his character, like her own, was more sanguine and social. Perhaps she also liked to root for the underdog, for she was fond of promoting Taylor whenever she could, whereas Tennyson needed no assistance from her in that respect. She took many photographs of Tennyson but she took far more of Taylor [see figure], and Taylor sat both as himself and as characters from literature and the Bible, whereas Tennyson only ever posed as the laureate. In his autobiography, Taylor writes of his stays at Freshwater in the 1860s that he believes he was photographed almost every day.[47] In December 1860 Cameron wrote to Watts begging him to paint Taylor's portrait as part of his gallery of famous men. Watts wrote back in January to suggest some times for Taylor to sit for him that winter and, interestingly, asked whether Cameron could persuade Professors Owen and Faraday to sit for him too.[48] Clearly, acquaintances and connections were exchanged within the circle of artists, and Cameron was not the only one to mix business and pleasure with her friends. More surprising is Cameron's comment in her letter that "there is small use in my struggling and striving with pen and hand which <u>can't</u> do it to shew you how you might paint Henry Taylor as great + grand as Alfred Tennyson aye grander + greater too . . . ."[49] Cameron may have been referring to her abilities to convince Watts by her eloquence in the letter, but it is also possible that her interest in photography liberated her creative impulses from a lack of skill or training in drawing.

Taylor and Tennyson were bound to compete with one another, especially as one reputation waned and the other waxed, but Julia Margaret may have consciously or unconsciously enjoyed fomenting the rivalry. Some time around 1861 she wrote Taylor candidly from Freshwater that

> Alfred has grown, he says, much fonder of you since your last two visits here. He says he feels now he is beginning to know you and not to feel afraid of you, and that he is beginning to get over your extreme insolence to him when he was young and you were in your meridian splendour and glory. So one reads your simplicity.[50]

Nonetheless, the two poets enjoyed sparring and they could spout quotations from verses by the hour. After one dinner party Cameron wrote of their conversation: "they were like two brilliant fencers crossing their rapiers or flashing their foils, both giving and evading clean thrusts."[51]

By the fall of 1860, she and Charles Hay were almost fully recovered from their illnesses relating to his Ceylon trip. By October 3, Julia Margaret had somehow scraped together the money to buy the lease for two adjacent houses at Freshwater from Jacob Long, a local fisherman.[52] They called the home Dimbola Lodge, after one of their Ceylon estates, and eventually built a tower to link the two buildings [see figure]. It shared a private path and gate to Tennyson's grounds nearby. It had large bay windows facing the main road down to the beach and was covered with climbing ivy and roses. The house still exists and is being restored and opened to the public. The town was filled with stone cottages and farmhouses; local trades included blacksmiths, wheelwrights, and soldiers and gunners from a nearby fort. There were two local churches: one, with a thatched roof, was established in the seventeenth century and the other, dating from the eleventh century, has a stained-glass window designed by Watts. The beaches below the high downs roared with the sounds of crashing waves on the rocks. Shipwrecks along the coast were common.[53] It was a place well suited to the contemplation of natural beauty and to examinations of natural life: among Tennyson's and Cameron's friends were professors of astronomy and amateur fossil hunters who came to Freshwater for their summer vacations.

The move to Freshwater may have been Julia Margaret's doing, but Charles Hay came around quickly this time. A few months after their arrival, Julia Margaret wrote to Juley that her father was feeling ill but

> I think he likes the place very much. He won't say how much but he has observed that it is curious how many points of resemblance there are between this house + the one at Rathoongodde which is much like a Bridegroom saying his Bride is like the loveliest of Raphael Madonnas–[54]

Charles Hay liked to walk along the terrace path, or pace through the garden, reciting Greek poetry to himself. When he once complained that there wasn't enough lawn for his walk, Julia Margaret impulsively pulled up the kitchen garden one night and had new green turf rolled out by morning to surprise him when he woke up.[55] When it rained, he paced indoors, while his son Charlie watched and advised him to hold up an umbrella to improve the illusion.[56]

Both Camerons benefited from the constant stream of visitors to the island, some attracted by Tennyson and others seeking country retreats from the polluted air of industrial England. There were plenty of cottages in Freshwater that could be rented for short periods of time and the Camerons seem to have had arrangements to keep some of these on reserve for their company. They also continued to rent out their London home in Putney Heath and sometimes rented Dimbola and moved into cheaper lodgings when it paid to do so. It was a chaotic way to live, and Julia Margaret bemoaned the trouble and work that fell to her.

There is evidence that at various points in her life Cameron tried her own hand at creative writing, especially poetry. One such occasion arose when she rented one of the neighboring cottages to the poet Arthur Hugh Clough and his wife Blanche in March 1861. "The Porch," named after Socrates' gathering place, was regularly rented to Benjamin Jowett, Master of Balliol College at Oxford, who was translating Plato. All three were very interested in the problems of translating Greek and Latin verse into English, since classical verse was dominated by a six-footed line (hexameter), counted in syllables, whereas English verse mostly used a four- or five-footed line, counted by stresses. Clough tried to write and translate into English hexameter, with some success. Amateur classicists (and this included a wide swath of English gentlemen) like Sir John Herschel translated Homer in their spare time. Charles Hay would have taken a keen interest in these conversations too.

Apart from their shared interest in prosody, Clough and Tennyson had little in common poetically. Clough was good friends with Matthew Arnold, whom Tennyson considered a prig,[57] and both Clough and Arnold's poems were much more earnest and argumentative than Tennyson's. Swinburne, who was even less earnest and even more of an aesthete than the laureate, had little patience for Clough and skewered him with the limerick: "There was a bad poet named Clough, whom his friends found it useless to puff: for the public, if dull, has not such a skull as belongs to believers in Clough."[58] Clough was ill during his visit to Freshwater and he died that fall in Florence, where he had repaired for his health. Julia Margaret was fond of both Cloughs and kept up with the widow after her husband's death. The following July, the Camerons had an exchange of letters with Blanche Clough in which she sent them her husband's posthumously published work; Charles Hay responded with appreciation and Julia Margaret, surprisingly, responded with a poem of her own.

Entitled "On Receiving a Copy of Arthur Clough's Poems at Fresh Water Bay," it is a competent and generous poem that depicts Clough as a man of learning and domestic devotion. Its most memorable part is when Julia Margaret compares the poet's wife, who collected his thoughts and works into a posthumous volume, to a bird who roams the skies collecting treasures to line her nest. The metaphor awkwardly compares the flying bird to the seated wife, and then strains toward a resolution when the readers are given the "nest" as a memorial. It concludes more conventionally with the poet's soul itself winging toward "Home and Heaven."[59] Stylistically, it reads much like Julia Margaret's letters – with run-on sentences and no punctuation except dashes – and it contains much of her warm-hearted love of nature and people. It is one of four poems written by her that have survived, not counting her translation of Bürger's *Leonora*, and it was a kind and thoughtful response to the widow. It was not ambitious as a poem, perhaps, but it was ambitious as a thank-you note for a gift received.

Cameron refers to writing poems elsewhere in her letters and it is unsurprising that she should take up poetry when everyone around her seemed to be immersed in it. During the early years at Freshwater, Tennyson was also helping his friend Francis Turner Palgrave assemble poems for *The Golden Treasury*, published in May 1861 and destined to be perhaps the most popular anthology of English poetry ever produced. The volume was intended to be perused for both pleasure (by those already familiar with English poetry) and instruction (by those presumed to know little about the English canon, like the working classes). Palgrave, who was a poet and a professor of poetry himself, was not particularly systematic in his editing: he wrote a preface in which he rather threw up his hands about how to define lyrical poetry and why he excluded dramatic, humorous, and religious verse.[60] Like Matthew Arnold in "The Function of Criticism at the Present Time," he relied on a stable and widely understood notion of the "best" work to give unity to his selections. The "best" work seemed to be self-evident. Indeed, the anthology was tremendously popular because its taste (formed in great part by the ever-popular Tennyson) was able to both reflect and shape the taste of the Victorian public. It included no work by living poets, so Tennyson and Palgrave were under no obligation to choose among their own and their friends' work, and it had an avowedly national aim of celebrating the English-language tradition.

Julia Margaret must have known Palgrave well, for he was one of Tennyson's most loyal friends and followers, but she seems never to have photographed him.[61] She surely would have made her opinions known, however, in any discussion of the poems and poets to be included in the volume. When the Irish poet William Allingham, another friend of Tennyson's, edited a volume of poetry in 1859, Julia Margaret complained to Woolner about the absence of Taylor's work. Woolner promised to pass on her opinion to Allingham and urged her to send along any other suggestions she had.[62] In 1866 Henry Taylor reported that Julia Margaret was among four of his women friends who had started writing novels. No other evidence of this project survives, but it is intriguing to speculate about it. Taylor felt that Julia Margaret's effusive and impulsive creativity was not suited to literary craft: "Her genius (of which she has a great deal) is too profuse and redundant, not distinguishing between felicitous and infelicitous."[63] But perhaps her fertile imagination would have reveled in a picaresque novel of adventure or a fantastic children's tale like Lewis Carroll's *Alice's Adventures in Wonderland* or Charles Kingsley's *The Water Babies*. Though of different generations, Julia Margaret developed a close friendship with Annie Thackeray (later Ritchie), who became a novelist like her father. Annie later reported that Julia Margaret once offered to be William's scribe: "Nobody writes as well as I do," she told him, "let me come and write for you."[64]

In 1861 Tennyson was also looking for a subject to write about. Unlike Julia Margaret, he found it hard to find subjects but easy to execute them. After their marriage, Emily Tennyson often resorted to soliciting their friends for suitable topics for Alfred, and it was Woolner who nagged him to write the story of a fisherman that he had heard while on board a ship to Australia.[65] The poem was published as "Enoch Arden" in 1862 and was another commercial success. The English public's appetite for poetry, especially Tennyson's, seemed insatiable. People were profoundly moved by his work, especially when it dealt with sentimental and pathetic themes like this one of a sailor who returned home after being presumed lost at sea. The effect can be judged by Tennyson's reading of the poem at Freshwater on June 14, 1862, when Maria Jackson "went into hysterics" as the poem neared its conclusion.[66] The reaction was noted by Emily Tennyson in her diary that night too, where she added presciently about Maria's daughters, Mary and Julia: "Her two dream girls haunt one. They seem to come out of some Niebelungenlied."[67]

Julia Margaret had spent the year involved in a marriage even closer to home. Her son Eugene had become engaged to Caroline Browne. Like Charles Norman, Caroline was the child of old family friends of Charles Hay's in Kent. Throughout the summer of 1861, there are occasional references to the problem of chaperoning the

125

couple adequately alongside continuing problems with money as the Camerons waited for the quarterly interest income from their marriage settlement. How, for example, could the couple travel to London from Freshwater at the smallest expense of train fare without sacrificing the propriety of an escort? To send a maid in the second-class carriage would defeat the purpose. To send anyone in first class was a great expense.[68] This dilemma was solved in a typical fashion: by Julia Norman's enclosure of 5 pounds in her answering letter. Eugene had applied for a colonial appointment and throughout the fall the family waited to hear the outcome, which would determine the couple's wedding plans. He had served four years in the Royal Artillery but his army salary could not support a wife, and he and Carry depended on this appointment. Eugene did obtain the appointment, as a private secretary to Governor Walker in the West Indies, but the salary was still small and his parents counseled him to go out alone, save money, and then send for Caroline when his finances improved.

But the engaged couple saw no reason for delay and Julia Margaret had some "very hard words" with her soon-to-be daughter-in-law. The Camerons settled 3,000 pounds from their marriage settlement on Eugene, but he wouldn't receive it until after their deaths. They made it clear, however, that they could do nothing further to help the couple. Eugene reconciled himself to his parents' financial difficulties and offered to give up the £52 that they gave him as an annual allowance so that they could apply it toward Ewen's education instead. However, he insisted on marrying Caroline before he left for the Caribbean. Julia Margaret feared his getting into debt and hoped that assiduous labor in Walker's service would make his colonial career. She was greatly suffering from her recurring attacks of giddiness and felt forlorn and angry over Eugene and Carry's opposition.[69] In December came the news of Prince Albert's sudden death and the whole nation seemed sunk in gloom. After her bereavement, the Queen retreated more and more to Osborne House on the other side of the Isle of Wight, which contributed to the development of the island through the 1860s.

The question of Eugene's future was complicated by everyone having a conflicting opinion. Julia Margaret wanted Eugene to rise in colonial administration, perhaps eventually becoming a governor-general, which by custom entailed knighthood. Charles Hay continued to wish for his sons to settle in Ceylon and take over the coffee estates that he had purchased with such high hopes decades before and had held on to so precariously. He persisted in thinking that "a good crop or two" would set him and his sons up, even as the coffee plants succumbed to the blight that finally killed off the whole industry.[70] What Eugene wanted is unclear, but what he would do seemed certain: he had overcome parental opposition years before to enter the Royal Artillery and he would soon overcome parental opposition again in marrying Caroline before he had secured a stable income. One of Julia Margaret's complaints during this family struggle was that Eugene had not originally taken her advice to join the Royal Engineers, where promotion and salaries were better able to support early marriages.[71] There is some evidence that the family's friends were getting impatient with their continued financial problems. Around this time Lord Overstone wrote George Norman commending him for his good advice to Charles Hay and adding sharply, "I trust he will properly appreciate his present position, and make the little effort which is requisite for the discharge of the duty as regards his monetary position, from which he cannot shirk without discredit. You cannot be too explicit with him on this matter."[72] It is unclear what effort the two bankers specifically recommended, but they continued to lend the family money for more than a decade.

The Camerons counted on Caroline's parents to support them in delaying the marriage, so they were annoyed and disappointed when Eugene and his Aunt Margaret appeared on New Year's Day in 1862 bearing a letter from Mr. Browne stating that he had decided the couple had better marry immediately. He believed delay would literally kill his daughter and his medical advisor agreed. Charles Hay was very unhappy and Julia Margaret was indignant: "What answer to <u>such</u> views thus expressed can be given by rational Parents on the other side–" she asked rhetorically.[73] Mr. Browne would also settle 3,000 pounds on his daughter (for her support if Eugene predeceased her) and Eugene announced he was ready to marry with or without their consent. As Eugene paced up and down the room outlining his plans to marry immediately and sail with his new wife to take up his appointment with Walker on February 3, his parents struggled to absorb this turn of events. They refused their consent to the marriage but they agreed to attend the wedding. Julia Margaret, at least, blamed Caroline and her family for the conflict. Eugene and Caroline's absence from England over the next few years proved significant: when Julia Margaret took up photography, they were not around to sit for her, though Julia Margaret did take photographs of their son Archibald in 1865 and she took one known portrait of Eugene [see figure]. Of Caroline, nothing: no letter, no portrait, hardly even a reference to her. Eugene and Caroline, more than any of Julia Margaret's children, strayed furthest from her intimate circle and from her control.

By 1862 the charmed circle at Freshwater was complete. It revolved around Tennyson as its sun, and it included many lesser luminaries: the poets Aubrey DeVere, William Allingham, and Edward Lear; scholars like Benjamin Jowett and James Spedding; and churchmen like Arthur Stanley, the Dean of Westminster, and William G. Ward. Artists such as Holman Hunt and Woolner continued to visit, but the center of interest had shifted from Little Holland House's pursuit of artists, with Watts on the pedestal, to

Freshwater's worship of poetry. Sara Prinsep continued to reign in her London salon, but it was no longer the center of Julia Margaret's cultural and social life. She had found her own lodestars in her twinned poets, Tennyson and Taylor. The shift, for Cameron, may have signaled her eagerness to follow popular taste. Artists were finding audiences but, especially after Dickens's death in 1870, no one could compete with the laureate's popularity. In taking up photography she was also following what had become a fashionable trend.

It would be hard to overestimate Tennyson's importance at Freshwater. For a time, he was the Prospero of an enchanted isle, though it was Taylor whom Cameron later photographed in that role. Another contemporary spoke of Tennyson as "the well-head of an enchanting river of song; the charm of his personality and the beauty of his surroundings at Farringford came in addition to make a precious setting for the jewel of his genius."[74] At first the remoteness of the location and the select company made the community seem like a shared secret, a communal devotion to the grand and the good. But as time went on, crowds came to gawk at Tennyson and some indignant onlookers made fun of the whole circus. Wilfred Ward, the son of Tennyson's good friend, grew up in Freshwater and later wrote:

> Outsiders with little appreciation of literary greatness – who merely lionized Tennyson as a famous man – were sometimes irritated at the quality of our enthusiasm, and almost incredulous of its sincerity. They could not enter into the feelings of those who felt genius to be a far greater thing than wealth or position . . . . They took stock of all they could see – namely, the external signs – and traced them to the only source their categories supplied, describing them as 'adulation' of the poet. The distinction between lionizing and hero worship was unintelligible to them.[75]

Lionizing idolizes the man, whereas hero worship honors the genius itself, Ward seems to argue – but wasn't Tennyson the man hounded and praised as often as his work? Was it always possible to distinguish between the dancer and the dance? It is certainly the nature of a celebrity culture to confuse the two, and the mid-nineteenth century saw the birth of celebrity culture. It was a fact that Julia Margaret took advantage of in becoming a portrait photographer and it was a fact that shaped Tennyson's life and work. Tennyson's intense ambivalence about his astounding fame appears in an anecdote told by Henry Taylor, who must have himself felt some envy or chagrin at Alfred's complaints:

> He said he believed every crime and every vice in the world were connected with the passion for autographs and anecdotes and records, –that the desiring anecdotes and acquaintance with the lives of great men was treating them like

pigs to be ripped open for the public; that he knew he himself should be ripped open like a pig; that he thanked God Almighty with his whole heart and soul that he knew nothing, and that the world knew nothing, of Shakespeare but his writings; and that he thanked God Almighty that he knew nothing of Jane Austen, and that there were no letters preserved either of Shakespeare's or Jane Austen's, that they had not been ripped open like pigs. Then he said that the post for two days had brought *him* no letters, and that he thought there was a sort of syncope in the world as to him and to his fame . . .[76]

Taylor must have been aware of the irony of Tennyson's complaints: Taylor himself had recently given up poetry altogether and had never achieved even a fraction of Tennyson's financial success; Tennyson himself counted desperately on the fans he despised. And surely Taylor exacted his revenge by publishing exactly the sort of "anecdote" that Tennyson dreaded in an autobiography that dissected his friend's greatness. Ironically, Tennyson has bequeathed us one of the best-documented lives ever to fall to an author: in addition to his poetry and plays, he is survived by letters, diaries, memoirs, reminiscences, photographs, paintings, sketches, and even early audio recordings. Julia Margaret was perfectly placed to take advantage of Tennyson's fame and of his good nature. Soon she would follow Watts's example of building a portfolio of England's great men and Tennyson would be the cornerstone. Her photography in turn would transform her into a celebrity, and before long she would herself become one of the luminaries of Freshwater.

PART TWO

Priestess of the Sun

CHAPTER 6

Domestic Arts

O N JANUARY 29, 1864 Julia Margaret Cameron produced her first known photograph: a portrait of Annie Philpot that she called "my first success" [see figure]. The story of that photograph, and Julia Margaret's transformation into a photographer, is told in the autobiographical fragment she wrote in 1874. Julia Margaret implies that she took to the camera instantly and eagerly:

> my first [camera and] lens was given to me by my cherished departed daughter and her husband, with the words, 'It may amuse you, Mother, to try to photograph during your solitude at Freshwater.'
>
> The gift from those I loved so tenderly added more and more impulse to my deeply seated love of the beautiful, and from the first moment I handled my lens with a tender ardour, and it has become to be as a living thing, with voice and memory and creative vigour. Many and many a week in the year '64 I worked fruitlessly, but not hopelessly . . .
>
> I began with no knowledge of the art. I did not know where to place my dark box, how to focus my sitter, and my first picture I effaced to my consternation by rubbing my hand over the filmy side of the glass. It was a portrait of a farmer of Freshwater, who, to my fancy, resembled Bollingbroke [sic] . . .[1]

Significantly, her account of the origins of her work emphasizes the issues that will matter most to her later oeuvre: her signature focus, her technical abilities, her penchant for cross-class role-playing and costume dramas, and most importantly, her insistence on photography as an "art" from the beginning. The autobiography also emphasizes the family origins of her career in the gift of the camera from Juley and Charles Norman and the assistance of her sons Hardinge and Henry Herschel Hay in her early apprenticeship. The picture that emerges is of a determined and gifted Artist overtaken by a Muse and instantly transformed, as in a Greek myth. This has been the standard account of Cameron's career for over a hundred years, but more and more evidence points to it being a carefully constructed legend that served Cameron's own aims. Nonetheless, the autobiography probably reflects an emotional truth: the acquisition of the camera and the resulting photographs marked a shift in identity as well as a more serious immersion in the field. Even ten years after the fact, Cameron's elation at the onset of her artistic career shines through her writing.

Recent scholarship has turned up two surprising new contexts for Cameron's early work. First, she had much more contact with professional photographers before 1864 than she admitted or than has been previously known. Second, it now seems that she had much more experience with photography herself prior to taking her own images. As discussed in the previous chapters, she collected photographs that she assembled into her own albums and presented as gifts perhaps as early as 1857. These albums included family portraits, reproductions of artworks by Watts and others, and formal portraits of celebrity friends like Tennyson and Taylor. In the past Cameron scholars were stymied by the scarcity of direct evidence of her early career in letters from the early 1860s: there are few references to the gift albums, to the first camera, or to any training or lessons in photography from her correspondence of 1862–64. It now looks as though the gift of the camera, almost certainly at Christmas in 1863, was a natural return gift for the photographic album Cameron had given her daughter for her birthday the year before.[2] It reflected the interest Cameron already had in the field: her interest gradually evolved over many years toward greater and greater participation until she finally produced her first independent image in January 1864. When she called *Annie* her "first success," she probably meant that it was the first image for which she had prepared the glass plate, positioned the camera, posed the sitter, focused the lens, opened the aperture, soaked and rinsed the negative, toned the paper, and printed and dried the photograph all by herself to produce a result that pleased her. It now seems likely that she had practiced many of these steps before she owned a camera or completed a single photograph.

Oddly enough, while the gift of the camera and whatever early lessons Cameron took are all mired in mystery, that first photograph itself is carefully documented. Cameron was never meticulous about her work but she was very emotional about important personal events. She always kept certain anniversaries and she seems to have been fully aware that *Annie* was a breakthrough and the beginning of something important. In the 1970s Cameron scholar Colin Ford found Annie Philpot's descendants and discovered an original print of the portrait in their family album, alongside other Cameron works given later. The back of their print bears an inscription from Cameron that reads: "given to her father by me. My first perfect success in the complete Photograph owing greatly to the docility & sweetness of my best & fairest little sitter. This Photograph was taken by me at 1 PM Friday January 29th

Printed – toned – fixed and framed all by me & given as it is now by 8 PM this same day."[3] Cameron did not stumble into photography: her interest in it may have evolved over time, but the speed and eagerness with which she took it up, added to her single-minded insistence on mastering the techniques, bespeak a clear intention to make it her own from the start.

Personally, Cameron's new obsession with photography probably arose out of the changes occurring in her domestic life: first, the Camerons were increasingly desperate for money and it now seems certain that Julia Margaret took up photography at least in part in the hopes of making money from it.[4] It is unlikely that she ever made a profit, for various reasons that will become clear, but it is no longer possible to imagine romantically that she was solely driven by beauty and art. Her own offhand comments, often in ingratiating letters to well-placed friends, candidly present herself as a woman with "sons to educate."[5] Her familiarity with the world of art and literature, through Watts and Tennyson especially, was intimate enough for her to know precisely the monetary value of every creative endeavor. She understood from the heyday of Little Holland House that art was inextricably bound up with commerce, with finding sitters, with cultivating patrons and public, with negotiating prices, and with creating an "artist's" persona. By the early 1860s, it was clear that Charles Hay was never going to obtain another colonial appointment and Julia Margaret must have wanted desperately to save the family finances, and perhaps forestall a move to Ceylon. Through sheer determination she probably did succeed in delaying the move for ten years.

The other important emotional motive for Cameron's career was probably her growing freedom from childrearing duties. By 1863, Juley and Eugene were both married and even Cameron's "Benjamin," Henry Herschel Hay, was eleven years old. Boys could be tutored at home until they were about twelve, as were Hallam and Lionel Tennyson. Soon, Henry and Charlie Hay would follow their older brother to Charterhouse, the elite boarding school that Hardinge was attending, and Ewen would leave for Ceylon to manage Rathoongodde. By the beginning of 1866, Julia Margaret was complaining of an empty nest.[6] The heavy expenses incurred in the education of upper-middle-class adolescent boys and her sons' absence from home may have combined to motivate Julia Margaret to turn her interest into a professional passion. Perhaps the gift of the camera, famously destined to relieve Julia Margaret's "solitude," was intended to replace growing children, not a travelling husband. Between the separations that Cameron always found difficult to bear and the finances that required urgent attention, some sort of energetic action was inevitable in those years. Her subsequent obsession with representing women and children, as family portraits or as allegorical or religious subjects, becomes an almost overdetermined necessity.

As a "late-bloomer," Cameron was typical of many women photographers: her contemporary Lady Clementina Hawarden took up photography in her late thirties, as did Cameron's best-known stylistic successor, Gertrude Käsebier, in the 1890s. They too had children to raise before they took up creative careers toward their middle age; they too made their names as photographers of children and family and their professional identities remained consistent with their domestic lives. In the mid-1850s, when many of her photographic contemporaries – like Charles Dodgson, David Wilkie Wynfield, and Oscar Rejlander – took up the new wet collodion technique, Julia Margaret still had a house full of children, which delayed her serious pursuit of the art.

Frederick Scott Archer had invented the wet collodion process in 1851 and gave it freely to the public, though at first it was embroiled in legal disputes with William Henry Talbot's calotype process, still under patent in England. While Talbot's technique used a paper negative to produce a soft and finely grained image, Archer's wet collodion process refined the technique to use a glass negative treated with collodion (or diluted gun cotton) to make it light-sensitive. The glass negative produced a sharper image that was especially appealing to portraitists trying to compete with the small, shiny metal surfaces of daguerreotypes. Glass plates produced prints that were larger, sharper, and easily reproduced so the wet collodion process grew popular, especially after the materials became cheaper late in the decade. The new process enabled the production of small, cheap, and precise *cartes de visite* – photographic visiting cards that could be collected and displayed like today's baseball cards. J. E. Mayall set the trend when his *Royal Album* of *cartes* of the royal family sold 60,000 copies in 1860. From 1860 to 1867 an estimated 300–400 million *cartes* were sold in England each year.[7] This proof that photographs and photographers could make money led many new entrepreneurs into the field and the professionals gradually began to dominate the emerging discipline instead of the older generation of gentleman amateurs.[8]

Charles Dodgson, just beginning his academic career at Oxford, was one of those drawn into the field by the new advances in ease, precision, and lower costs. He and his friend Reginald Southey had taken photographs of the Cameron and Tennyson boys in the late 1850s. In April 1862 Dodgson visited the Isle of Wight and took more photographs of the Camerons. In September he traveled to East Sheen to photograph Henry Taylor's family; while there, he also took Ewen Cameron's portrait and copied two photographs of Julia Jackson that Watts had hand-colored.[9] Dodgson makes an interesting point of comparison for Cameron's career, especially in terms of style and temperament. Like Cameron, he aimed to make artistic photographs and he concentrated on children. Like her, he often posed them in costumes or narratives. But unlike Cameron, his style was so much more sharply focused and "objective" that the works tend to direct the viewer emphatically toward the "real" child and

Dodgson's relationship with him or her. These children, often named by Dodgson on the print, sitting in the middle ground of the composition, at ease on Victorian furniture in recognizable rooms, were undeniably *there* before his camera. Their "thereness" makes them available for all sorts of projections by viewers: they are victims or aggressors, innocent or seductive, before we know anything about them. Cameron's children, on the other hand, are often unrecognizable and indefinite in the haze of light, shadow, and emulsion that obscure and reveal them. Without the markers of their everyday life, they temporarily lose themselves. Cameron gloats in the changeability of children, whereas Dodgson tries to stop the clock. Moreover, Dodgson was a prickly, cautious, methodical man, whereas Cameron was impulsive, ebullient, and emotional. While it is unlikely that Dodgson encouraged Cameron to pursue photography (their styles and personalities were incompatible), it is possible that his example helped her to conceptualize a career as an artistic portraitist who avoided commissioned sittings.

The Swedish photographer Oscar Gustave Rejlander was an even better role model in that regard. He had been a painter who first took up photography to make studies for other artists. He believed that photography could help artists improve their draftsmanship and knowledge of anatomy.[10] In 1853 he took a one-day lesson in photography at a studio, bought a camera, and took it home to set up shop as a photographer. To his chagrin, it took him a while longer to learn the craft, but he persevered and by the mid-1850s his contributions to photographic exhibits were earning praise as artworks. He came to the Isle of Wight to photograph in the spring of 1863, and this visit has often been described as Cameron's first significant encounter with photography, although we know now that she met other photographers and made albums earlier. Rejlander's influence on Cameron's early work, though, is clearer than Dodgson's or Southey's. He too favored narrative photographs: with titles like *I Pays!* or *Don't Cry, Mama*, his sitters often appeared as characters delivering a line. He also made studies of children, but his interest in Old Masters paintings led him toward images like Cameron's: children posed "after Raphael's Sistine Madonna," for example.[11] Rejlander also experimented with extreme lighting, sometimes limiting the light for an image from one corner, although he never ventured as far as Cameron would into the shadows. He had little background in science and probably less of an understanding of the photochemical principles than Julia Margaret. Like her, he was also known for his technical carelessness and was (like her) often praised for his artistry while scorned for his sloppy prints.[12]

Rejlander took many photographs during his stay with the Tennysons and Camerons that spring. The best-known is an image of the Tennyson family walking in their woods, backlit by sunlight and holding hands. But he also took many genre photographs in the manner of the French and Dutch naturalists: maids at a well;

servants hanging laundry; the arrival of the postman [see figure]. These images often ended up in Julia Margaret's albums, indicating an approval that she withheld from Dodgson's work.[13] The photographs appear staged: members of the household are posed in static scenes, with each person playing a role marked by costume and posture as clearly as if he or she were facing an audience. In one, entitled *At the Well*, Hardinge leans negligently against a ladder, the very picture of the young man of the house, while two winsome maids draw water from a well. In another, Julia Margaret appears at her front door, conventionally attired for a change, and accepts her letters from a jovial, bearded postman, perhaps Rejlander himself. Several smiling maids surround her, making this daily event into a special occasion.

As other scholars have noted, the presence of Rejlander in some of the images presents the tantalizing possibility that in at least some cases Julia Margaret may have been the one behind the camera.[14] The production of this series of photographs at her home in the same year that she took up photography herself certainly suggests that there was some sort of collaboration or apprenticeship between the two photographers. The titles of several photographs refer to Julia Margaret in the third person, but one, a portrait of her four youngest sons entitled *My Cameron Clan* in Julia Margaret's characteristic possessive voice, implies that she could be the photographer, just as later images will be entitled *My Grand-child* or *My Ewen's Bride*. Several Cameron scholars have identified stylistic evidence to support the possibility of collaboration between the two photographers.[15] In fact, some of these photographs used to be attributed to Cameron, then were reassigned to Rejlander and are now inching back towards Cameron.[16]

This emerging evidence of Cameron's involvement with photography before she obtained a camera in 1864 may bear out a statement that has long been ignored or discredited by Cameron scholars. In 1890 the prominent landscape photographer P. H. Emerson brought out an early posthumous selection of Cameron's photographs in a series called *Sun Artists*. This volume includes an interview with her son Henry Herschel Hay, then running a portrait studio himself, about his mother's work. Henry Herschel Hay told Emerson that before taking up photography his mother had spent "hundreds of pounds" paying commercial photographers to take portraits of her friends, "often under her immediate supervision. The best of this vicarious photography was Rejlander's portrait of Tennyson, taken at Freshwater."[17] This extraordinary comment, which provides more evidence for arguments about collaborations between Rejlander and Cameron early in the 1860s, was dismissed by Helmut Gernsheim in his first biography but now seems more and more credible. The most astonishing part now seems to be the possibility that Cameron had actually hired Rejlander for those images. On the other hand, Rejlander was a professional photographer, so it is not so far-fetched to assume that he was paid for that work.

Certainly the extravagant expenditures and the tendency to "stage-manage" productions as if they were amateur theatricals are in keeping with Cameron's later practices.

The photograph from the series produced that spring which appears the most likely to have been collaborative from its style is a small, indoor image now known as *Irish & Isle of Wight peasants*. This image, now named after an inscription believed to be in Cameron's own hand, was published in the Mia Album as *The Three Graces*. In this composition three of her favorite maid-models hold hands in a circle and look off in different directions.[18] It has classical references that both Cameron and Rejlander would enjoy, but it is only half-heartedly symbolic. The women wear their everyday print dresses and stand in an ordinary room. On the whole, the 1863 photographs do not presage Cameron's work in style: they are smaller than her photographs and taken outdoors with a crisp, almost documentary focus. They are well-composed group shots, whereas her group compositions often suffered from an awkward massing of too-close bodies. They look professional and somewhat conventional: Rejlander's family portrait of the Tennysons is more radical – with its sun-limned bodies and expressive faces – than these generic tableaux. The figures do not slide off the frame, nor do the faces loom out of the dark.

Generally, Cameron's aesthetic was more impressionistic and subjective than Rejlander's, but she would later make a few images that bear the mark of his style and subject matter. In a work like *Pray God Bring Father Safely Home* [see figure], Cameron uses a spoken title, as Rejlander often did, and depicts a generic working-class scene of a fisherman's family. Even here, however, Cameron overstuffs her frame. Unlike Rejlander's more spare and empty outdoor scenes, Cameron's fisherman's cottage is chockfull of four family members, utensils, and a cascading net. The people cling to the edges of the picture, while the lowly teapot, iron, and jug upstage them in perfect focus at the center of the image. It is an odd choice that could almost serve as a perfect illustration for art historian Lindsay Smith's well-known analysis of "focus" as a gendered term that derives from the Latin word for "hearth."[19] Here it seems to work in part because of Cameron's typically dramatic lighting. The photograph is boldly divided in half on a vertical axis drawn straight through the kettle on the hob: the seated woman and girl are lit as if from within by bright light, absorbed in each other, while the older man and boy huddle together and confront the viewer from the darker corner. Although the father is absent (perhaps inspiring the hole in the middle of the composition, which forces the other figures to the margins), the photograph is a gendered image of Victorian domesticity that succeeds on formal terms, instead of sentimental ones.

On July 7 Julia Margaret assembled an album of photographs and gave it to her sister Maria with the inscription: "For my best beloved Sister Mia from Julia Margaret Cameron. With a blessing on the New Years and the old."[20] It was Maria's forty-fifth birthday and birthdays were important to the extended family. Whether together or apart, the Cameron clan made a point of drinking each other's health on their birthdays and sending letters of congratulations. When Juley and Eugene were sent away from India to England, they honored their parents' birthdays by treating the servants to cakes and fruit wines.[21] The choice of Maria as Julia Margaret's favorite sister is surprising. By all accounts, Julia Margaret was temperamentally more like Sara: vivacious and social. Maria was usually in ill health and struck her grandchildren as querulous and cranky. A doctor's wife, she was interested in diseases and cures and offered her opinion freely (like Julia Margaret). She passed along this interest in nursing and caretaking to her youngest daughter, Julia.[22]

In 1863 Maria, like Julia Margaret, was making the transition from mother to grandmother: her eldest two daughters, Adeline and Mary, had both left home. Adeline had married Henry Halford Vaughan, an Oxford historian, and had already borne and lost children. Her marriage was rumored to be unhappy: her future brother-in law Leslie Stephen believed that Adeline, like the fictional Dorothea Brooke, had chosen Vaughan to devote herself to his genius and found herself saddled with a cold Casaubon.[23] Mary had recently married Herbert William Fisher, tutor and private secretary to the Prince of Wales. The birth of their first son, Herbert Albert Laurens Fisher, would be commemorated in the Mia Album in 1865. H. A. L. Fisher, later an eminent educator, described his mother as "a saint," and indeed his cousin Virginia Woolf reluctantly agreed, adding dryly that "the Fishers would have made Eden uninhabitable."[24] The remark was emblematic of the differences among the family's next generation. In 1863 seventeen-year-old Julia Jackson was still living at home, declining proposals from William Holman Hunt and Thomas Woolner.[25]

The Jackson family was if anything even more closely knit than the Camerons. Maria and her three daughters had spent a great deal of time alone together, while John Jackson finished his medical career in Calcutta. It wasn't until 1855, only a few years before Adeline's marriage, that the doctor retired to England and rejoined his family. "Somehow," Leslie Stephen mused, "he did not seem to count as fathers generally count in their families."[26] H. A. L. Fisher added that his grandfather had been in India so long that he found he had been totally forgotten when he came home.[27] Thus the four women were used to being on their own and they shared interests in art and culture as well as their famed beauty. Their lives were shaped by the habitués of Little Holland House: Maria became good friends with the poet Coventry Patmore and she let the nine-year-old Julia model for Edward Burne-Jones's *Annunciation* and a sculpture by Baron Marochetti. All of this background was reflected in the Mia Album, which contained portraits of the growing extended family, portraits of artists like William Holman Hunt and G. F. Watts, and photographic reproductions of paintings. Julia Margaret probably gave the album to her sister half-filled and she seems to have dictated its arrangement. The book is intended to be viewed in two relatively distinct sections: first one opens the cover and sees Cameron's photographs on the right-hand side, then at the end one flips the book over and reads it again with other photographers' images on the right-hand page. Over the years, as Cameron added her own work to the album, she included specific instructions to her sister as to where to place the new images.

The album was then, necessarily, an evolving project that Julia Margaret and Maria could collaborate on during many exchanged visits and letters. The version that survives today, now disassembled, opens with one of Cameron's photographs of Maria's daughter Julia – sixteen of the approximately 120 images in the album today are of Julia Jackson – and charts familiar terrain through Cameron's portraits of Mary Jackson Fisher, Thoby Prinsep, Charles Hay Cameron, John Jackson, Alfred Tennyson, Aubrey DeVere, Henry Taylor, William Michael Rossetti, William Holman Hunt, Robert Browning, and neighboring children on the Isle of Wight. The celebrities of Little Holland House are well represented, but the bulk of the portraits are of family, with several allegorical and narrative "high art" photographs by Cameron as well. The second section features photographic reproductions of Watts's portraits of Julia Margaret and Virginia, portraits of their sisters Louisa's and Virginia's children by Rejlander, and Rejlander's genre photographs taken outside Cameron's home in Freshwater, perhaps in collaboration with Cameron.

As other scholars have noted, the Mia Album seems designed to construct and celebrate a specific notion of bourgeois femininity.[28] It shows the Pattle women and their daughters as conventionally successful: as honored mothers and dutiful daughters, as beloved sisters, as beauties, and as cultivated women in a circle of eminent men. It documents the success of their husbands – in pictures like a group portrait of the High Court of Calcutta that includes Louisa's husband, Henry Vincent Bayley, or a photograph of Herbert Fisher with the Prince of Wales – and commemorates marriage and childrearing in portraits of Ewen's future bride Annie Chinery and Mary Fisher with her newborn son. Surprisingly, it includes no portraits of Maria herself, Cameron's other sisters Sara and Sophia, Maria's daughter Adeline Vaughan, nor Virginia's husband Lord Somers. Adeline's family is represented only by one portrait of her husband Henry Halford Vaughan; it is possible, though speculative, that the Vaughans were left out because their marriage was not considered successful.[29] Sophia Dalrymple is represented only by a portrait of her daughter by Rejlander. The Norman family is included in a joint portrait of Julia and Charles Norman by an unknown photographer and by Rejlander's portraits of their daughter Charlotte.

In August 1863, soon after Cameron presented the Mia Album, the painter Samuel Lawrence wrote to her confirming that he had obtained a photograph she requested but that he was sending a daguerreotype and not the "negative" that she desired.[30]

The fact that Julia Margaret was now requesting negatives may be significant: Cameron scholar Joanne Lukitsh has recently argued that Cameron may have begun her experimentation with photography in the darkroom before attempting to take any images herself. Lukitsh examined the pre-1864 albums and found evidence of Cameron's manipulation of photographs by rephotographing and reprinting them, presumably to conform more closely to her taste and vision. Cameron may have requested a negative from Lawrence so that she could better shape the final image by printing it herself. If so, then it was perhaps only when her creative ambitions outran her ability to manipulate already-photographed images that she decided to take her own photographs with her own camera. As Lukitsh points out, in mid-century a camera was an expensive investment usually associated with commercial studios, and therefore it is not so surprising that Cameron entered the field through printing.[31]

The Mia Album marks the first major project of Cameron's photographic career. Even if it was incomplete and filled with others' work when she gave it to her sister, it was the germ of the notion of herself as a photographic artist. From the summer of 1863 the album was there, waiting to be filled, full of potential. After this collection Julia Margaret began producing albums more frequently. On October 5 she presented her niece Adeline MacTier, Louisa Bayley's daughter, with an album filled with Rejlander photographs (or possibly collaborations) like Maria's. The album included the genre photographs from Cameron's home and one image of Julia Jackson standing under a tree, tantalizingly captioned: "from Life year 60 printed by me J.M.C."[32] It provides further evidence that Julia Margaret began her career by printing works before she graduated to making and developing her own negatives.

Cameron followed the MacTier Album with another album, given to her sister Virginia for Christmas that year and only discovered in the 1990s. The so-called Somers-Cocks Album probably contained only about twenty photographs when Cameron gave it to her sister and there are many duplications with the Mia Album. Cameron inscribed the album: "For my beloved sister Virginia (Photographs of my own printing) with every fond Xmas wish from Julia Margaret Cameron Xmas Eve 1863."[33] The Somers-Cocks Album is an important piece of evidence in the chain of Cameron's gradual immersion in photography because, as Lukitsh has discovered, at least one image seems to have been reprinted by Cameron from a Rejlander photograph. Between July and December, Cameron rephotographed and reprinted Rejlander's portrait of Henry Taylor to make it larger and heighten the contrast: in other words, to make it conform more closely to the style she would later adopt when she took up her work.[34] For some unknown reason, Virginia never added any of Julia Margaret's own images to her album and for over a hundred years it remained in close to its original state, filled with family portraits taken mostly by Rejlander and perhaps printed by Cameron. Eight images in the Somers-Cocks Album are identical to photographs in the Mia Album, prompting Lukitsh to argue that the albums were designed to transcend the distances between the sisters by enabling them to peruse their family portraits simultaneously even when they were not together.[35]

Generally, the family albums were given to women, while the later professional albums were given to men as a return for favors and friendship.[36] Men like Overstone, Herschel, Watts, and Taylor were close family friends who were also able to further Cameron's career artistically or financially. The exceptions to this general rule were Lord Lansdowne, whose favors benefited the whole family, and Annie Thackeray, a close friend and also a well-connected author and critic, who received an album from Cameron around 1865. The albums served a dual and often divided function: they promoted her professional career and cemented her personal ties. In some cases those aims aligned in the recipient and the oeuvre; sometimes different recipients would receive albums customized to suit their interests. Herschel and Overstone's albums, for example, included photographs of their daughters that were absent from other albums. As another scholar has noted, their albums were indexed and the photographs in them were signed with Cameron's trademark flourish, whereas the "family" albums came with less commentary.[37] Cameron gave Sir Coutts Lindsay, a family friend and later founder of the Grosvenor Gallery, an album with a large percentage of literary and allegorical images.[38]

The albums must have been significant to Cameron. Before 1864 she seems to have given albums to Lord Lansdowne, Julia Norman, Adeline MacTier, Virginia Somers-Cocks, and at least one to Watts (inscribed "JMC to GFW"). The Signor 1857 Album may or may not have been given by Cameron and did not contain her work. The Mia Album of 1863 was given by Cameron and eventually contained some of her work. In the eleven years of her photographic career in England (1864–75) she made at least ten albums of her full-size photographs (for Watts, Herschel, Overstone, Lindsay, Annie Thackeray, the Tennysons, the Normans, and two for the Taylor family). In the 1870s she also compiled and bound books filled with small-scale copies of her work for friends and relatives. The albums were usually bound in leather and personalized with embossed names or titles. They entailed enormous amounts of work in developing, printing, and then mounting and inscribing hundreds of images in each book. Cameron scholar Julian Cox argues that the sheer effort Cameron put into this work implies that the albums were at least as important to her as producing individual prints for exhibit and sale.[39] If this was so, she was not alone. Charles Dodgson also compiled his work into albums, which he gave to prospective sitters and friends but also kept scrupulously as a record of his achievements. At his death his estate included thirty-four albums, though only about a third of these seem to have survived. Like Dodgson, Cameron would have carefully assembled the albums to display the range and quality of her work, while customizing each one to suit the interests and purposes of its viewers. Like her, he often composed his albums leaving blank spaces to fill in with later photographs.[40] The two photographers had typically diverging priorities: Dodgson was methodical about recording and cataloguing his output but delegated the printing of his negatives to a London company; Cameron always claimed to print photographs herself but was careless about record-keeping.

On Christmas Eve, 1863, as Julia Margaret was inscribing and presenting an album to her sister Virginia, their friend Thackeray died suddenly in his London home at the age of fifty-two. The literary world paused in shock and he was mourned as much as a man as a writer. His two daughters, Annie and Harriet (known as Minnie), were devastated. His widowed mother, who had been staying in the room above his, collapsed.[41] He had been sick, and he was exhausting himself in the editorship of *The Cornhill Magazine* and the writing of *Denis Duval*, but he had always been resilient. The accident of fate that meant Cameron was never able to photograph her old friend has often been remarked upon, but the timing may not have been coincidental. If Cameron was gradually immersing herself more and more in photography, moving from collecting photographs to printing her own, from occasional albums to three gift albums in 1863, what was the turning point that led her to take up the camera with sudden zeal and identify herself as a photographer? The gift of the camera, possibly on Christmas Day when she heard the news of Thackeray's death, could well have sparked a chain of familiar feelings and associations: love and flesh cannot withstand time; only art and the soul are immortal. It seems quite possible that the sudden death of her old friend would have struck at the emotional roots of her passion for photography: to preserve the presence of loved ones and to stave off the specter of the final separation. Whatever the cause, it was as if a switch was thrown in her life. With the new year, 1864, she would be reborn as a photographer.

The Camerons and Tennysons were at Freshwater when they heard the news. Emily recorded her shock in her journal and she and Alfred raced into town to see if he could be of service to the women. Annie and Minnie were besieged with well-wishers and struggling to deal with the emotions and logistics of their loss. There was the simple funeral to manage, then the unfinished manuscripts, the magazine, the magnificent new house on Palace Green, now empty, and their finances. Raised without a mother, the girls had always been extremely close to their father, who was in turn devoted to them. Annie had been his amanuensis and had recently begun publishing her own work. Cameron offered them an empty cottage in Freshwater, and after the funeral Tennyson whisked them away for a grim New Year.

Cameron turned her affections and benevolence on Annie and Minnie, whom she hosted at Freshwater regularly over the next year. She also lent them the home she still kept in Putney Heath when they needed it. They were temporarily homeless as they waited for their father's affairs to be settled. That first month of grief was a dull blank. "We arrived late in the afternoon," Annie wrote later,

> It was bitter weather, the snow lying upon the ground. Mrs. Cameron had lent us a cottage and the fires were already burning, and as we rested aimlessly in the twilight, we seemed aware of a tall figure standing in the window wrapped in a heavy cloak with a broad rimmed hat. This was Tennyson, who had walked down to see us in silent sympathy.[42]

They stayed a month, as Cameron must have been experimenting with her camera next door on her maids and farmers, her angels and Bolingbrokes. Hardinge Cameron [see figure] was home from Charterhouse (not Oxford, as Cameron would write later in her autobiography) and tried to distract and entertain the young women.[43] They left on January 28 and on January 29 Julia Margaret produced her own now-famous *Annie*, the portrait of a daughter of the Reverend William Philpot who frequented the island for vacations with his sister's family, the Bradleys.

Cameron continued to work steadily and intensely at photography throughout that winter and on February 26 she wrote to her old friend Sir John Herschel to announce her new work. In the letter she reminisces about first learning of photography through his letters to Calcutta and also states decisively that

> at the beginning of this year I first took up Photography ie. my kind and loving son Charlie Norman gave me a camera + I set to work alone + unassisted to see what I could do all thro' the severe month of January I felt my way literally in the dark thro' endless failures, at last came endless successes![44]

This account of the origins of her work already sows the seeds for the account she will publish in the *Annals*: she worked alone and her interest in photography was new and sudden and the result of the gift of the camera. Cameron sent Herschel a book containing specimens of her early work, along with a letter of praise from Watts, and then makes a confession that does not appear anywhere in the *Annals* or in other letters: "I have had one lesson from the great amateur Photographer Mr. Wynfield + I consult him in correspondence whenever I am in a difficulty but he has not yet seen my successes."[45]

David Wilkie Wynfield was an artist who had recently turned to large-scale photographic portraits of celebrities. In fact, that winter he exhibited a series of photographs, called *The Studio*, consisting of portraits of prominent artists like John Everett Millais and even Watts himself. The portraits clearly influenced Cameron, for they are much like the work she soon pursued: soft-focus, close-up heads of celebrities in fancy dress, modeled on Renaissance portraiture. Cameron and Wynfield seem to have had little contact later in her career and she must have been sensitive about his help and influence because she never acknowledged it publicly. In another private letter, this one to the art critic William Michael Rossetti in January 1866, she complains that Wynfield had not attended one of her exhibits yet praises his work and credits it for her success.[46]

Like Cameron, Wynfield was admired for his elevation of portrait photography into art, as opposed to the cheap *cartes de visite* that were sold on every street corner by this time. Joanne Lukitsh notes that the reception of their work had class implications: critics argued that it was because Cameron and Wynfield were in fact upper-class that their portraits seemed so artistic and so sensitive to the essential class distinctions that most *cartes de visite* elided.[47] Interestingly, in her letter to Herschel Cameron calls Wynfield an "amateur," further associating him with a gentlemanly tradition even though he was a professional artist and a founding member of the St. John's Wood clique.[48] Wynfield's series *The Studio* represented rising young English artists as a brotherhood, as the Pre-Raphaelites had done fifteen years before. Juliet Hacking, an art historian who has written virtually the only book on the long-neglected Wynfield, notes that the recent admission of women to the Royal Academy art schools may have also motivated this sudden interest in reaffirming the exclusive and masculine realm of a bohemian art world.[49] Perhaps the new possibility of women enrolling in establishment art schools encouraged Cameron's career too. Annie Thackeray and Julia Norman had set up a fundraising booth on behalf of the Female School of Art at the South Kensington Museum in 1861, so Cameron definitely knew about opportunities for women artists.[50]

Cameron turned her coalhouse into a darkroom and a glass-covered chicken shed into her studio, which drew from her a characteristic burst of good humor and bravura:

> The hens were liberated, I hope and believe not eaten. The profit of my boys upon new laid eggs was stopped, and all hands and hearts sympathized in my new labour, since the society of hens and chickens was soon changed for that of poets, prophets, painters and lovely maidens, who all in turn have immortalized the humble little farm erection.[51]

It was clearly important for Cameron to emphasize her family's support for her endeavor: she mentions each member's praise or assistance in the autobiography. This may, paradoxically, provide additional evidence for Cameron's financial motivation from the start: it was the fact that she wanted to photograph professionally and earn money from her work that would have made it potentially suspect to her peers. Between the lines she seems to be defensively saying: yes, we lose the income from the eggs, but we will all gain from my art and my family encourages me to do this! In her career she had to walk a fine line between two poles: self-effacement would satisfy her public persona of self-sacrifice and devotion to her family but deny her ambition and personal talent; self-promotion would serve her art and career but potentially threaten her identity within her family and community. Professional work was certainly not impossible for Victorian women, especially in the cultural fields, but it was difficult and strewn with obstacles. For a bourgeois woman suddenly to take up a paying job might imply that her husband could not support her, that the family was in dire straits, that the wife was insubordinate . . . Cameron's autobiography, many of her letters, and her portraits of Charles Hay and her children function rather like a signed permission slip that Cameron could present upon demand.

Beginning a photographic career entailed a sizeable investment of time, energy, and money. Cameron had been given a large wooden box camera intended to take 11 by 9 inch glass plates. It probably came with a rudimentary darkroom kit but every photographer needed a great many other supplies: pre-cut glass plates, pre-coated albumen paper to print on, and chemicals like pre-mixed iodized collodion, silver nitrate, a developing solution of acids, sodium thiosulphate (or "hypo"), gold chloride for toning, potassium cyanide, and varnish. The darkroom needed access to water (from a well in Cameron's case) for the frequent washing of prints as well as a fireplace to heat the varnish on the glass plate into a hard protective coating. There was little standardization, so different suppliers could produce different effects on the final image, and photographers usually experimented until they found a few manufacturers that pleased them. Helmut Gernsheim, the first major collector and scholar of Cameron's work, recounted that her first camera and lens were examined in 1890 (they were still owned and maybe even used by her son Henry Herschel Hay in his photographic studio). A well-known English lens-maker concluded that her early lens had aberrations that made it impossible for Cameron to achieve a perfectly focused image.[52] Gernsheim studied the evidence and agreed: the prints from 1864 to 1866, when she changed cameras, vary dramatically in definition because the large plate size, built-in fixed stop, and faulty lens limited her control over the image.

In her autobiography Cameron herself stated that she believed

> what my youngest boy, Henry Herschel, who is now himself a very remarkable photographer, told me is quite true – that my first successes in my out-of-focus pictures were a fluke. That is to say, that when focussing and coming to something which, to my eye, was very beautiful, I stopped there instead of screwing on the lens to the more definite focus which all other photographers insist upon.[53]

Gernsheim interpreted this passage to mean that Cameron was unaware of the faulty lens and "blamed herself" for her inability to focus. But far from expressing self-doubt, Cameron's words seem instead to take a gloating pleasure in her difference from (perhaps superiority over) other photographers. From the start she emphasizes her eye, her vision, her artistic control, though Gernsheim was right to point out her technical constraints. Other scholars have suggested that her radically out-of-focus photographs were the result of vision problems that ran in her family.[54] In the generations of heated discussions over Cameron's focus, one can lose sight of the obvious: whatever Cameron's original intentions were, she clearly loved and approved of the results. She praised, exhibited, and sold "out-of-focus" photographs and defended them vigorously from the disapproval of photography critics. She staked her reputation on them and that soft, blurred, impressionistic portrait became her trademark. As Cameron began her career, Wynfield was earning praise from artists for his "out-of-focus" photographs and his work set the terms for the critical debates that would soon follow hers.[55]

At first, however, her signature focus may have been the combined result of her lens, her artistic vision, and her eagerness to differentiate herself from other photographers. This is not inconsistent with her son Henry Herschel Hay's perceptive comments on the subject, made decades after his mother's death:

> It is a mistake to suppose that my mother deliberately aimed at producing work slightly out of focus. What was looked for by her was to produce an artistic result, no matter by what means. She always acted according to her instinct; if the image of her sitter looked stronger and more characteristic out of focus, she so reproduced it; but if she found that perfect clearness was desirable, she equally attained it.[56]

This statement, given to a journalist in 1897, loyally defends his mother and bolsters her (and his) artistic credentials, but it also correlates to the evidence in her body of work. Cameron's work does in fact cover a wide range of definition, as Gernsheim acknowledged too: some photographs are very soft, some are very crisp, and some have a differential focus where one feature is clear and the rest of the composition is hazy. In 1866 Cameron bought a new camera for taking 15 by 12 inch plates with a Rapid Rectilinear portrait lens, which corrected for aberrations. With this camera Cameron was now able to adjust the aperture opening, although working with large plates required as much light as possible – otherwise the exposure time would be unendurable for sitters. She was largely indifferent to cracks on her negatives and marks on her prints, but she also made fewer mistakes as she gained practice. The technical problems that persisted later in her career were often the result of damaged negatives that she refused to discard. She did consider some photographs failures, as evinced throughout her letters, but her criteria were her own. Nonetheless, her work after 1866 still exhibits the same range of focus – from the blurred, moving Thomas Carlyle to the pristinely clear Annie Thackeray [see figures], which leaves us back where we started: Cameron could make perfectly focused images but she did not always want to.

At the end of March Herschel answered Cameron's letter, commented on her photographs, and requested some prints. That letter has not survived but Cameron's response is effusive. She barrages him with technical questions, complaining, "I get into difficulties + I cannot see my way out of them from ignorance of the scientific causes of those failures miscalled 'accidents.'"[57] Her list is a testament to the extreme difficulties of Victorian photography: white lines appear on the print; the film peels off the glass plate; the plate seems scratched as she takes it out of the bath; some prints turn green; and the silver nitrates turn red on the albumen paper. Worst of all, she worried about her health and the potential effects of contact with so many toxic chemicals. "When my hands are as black as an Ethiopian Queen's can I find no other means of recovering + restoring them but this dangerous Cyanide of Potassium[?]" she asked Herschel.[58] She wasn't feeling well, but hoped it was the result of her fatigue and hard work and not the chemicals she worked with every day. Herschel's reply is missing, but he is known to have sent her articles about alternatives to the potassium cyanide and he warned her often to be extremely careful with her chemicals.

Despite the dangers and difficulties, Cameron pursued photography as if suddenly driven by furies. She gave the first album of her own photographic work to Watts on February 22, less than one month after producing her first "success." The photograph of Annie was prominently displayed in two prints facing each other on the first page.[59] The thirty-nine photographs in this album included both Cameron's family (especially the Normans) and her Isle of Wight neighbors. Many of the photographs look homely and familiar, the prints cut with a shaky hand into curved arches or circles. Some are cropped or even retouched.[60] All of Cameron's later subjects – portraits, allegorical and religious images, literary illustrations – were present in her work from the first month and are included in this album alongside some of Watts's own drawings and sketches. Cameron acknowledged the value of Watts's influence and support with her inscription: "To The Signor to whose generosity I owe the choicest fruits of his Immortal genius. I offer these my first successes in my mortal but yet <u>divine!</u> art of photography–Julia Margaret Cameron."[61] Her early awareness of photography's "double" nature – as science and art, as evanescent and permanent, as physical and spiritual – is also there from the start. In describing her work as "mortal but yet divine!," she refers not only to debates about photography's status but also her own emotional need to use photographs to avoid loss and bereavement. Photographs provided her subjects with an afterlife as surely as her faith did.

The album celebrated Cameron's new achievements and honored one of her earliest supporters and advisers. It was a birthday present – Watts was turning forty-seven – but it was probably also timed as a wedding gift. On February 20 Watts had married Ellen Terry, a week before her seventeenth birthday. The story of their incongruous marriage has been well told, and more will be related in the next chapter, but

---

it is worth a short digression. Terry was the second daughter of the illustrious acting family. Her elder sister Kate had just made the transition from child actress to leading lady; in a few years she would retire from the stage to marry the wealthy merchant and art patron Arthur Lewis. Ellen had grown up on stage, playing Puck, Cupid, and little boys until adolescence. It was Tom Taylor, editor of *Punch* and friend of both the Terrys and the Little Holland House set, who brought Kate and Ellen Terry to Watts for a sitting as *The Sisters* in 1862.[62] It was not so surprising that the sensitive, melancholy Watts took to Ellen's ebullient charm, but it is surprising that the confirmed bachelor decided on marriage to a woman thirty years younger and already quite independent. It is not at all clear what motivated Watts. He wrote pompously to his friend Lady Constance Leslie that he had

> determined to remove the youngest [Miss Terry] from the temptation and abominations of the stage, give her an education and if she continues to have the affection she now feels for me, marry her . . . . To make the poor child what I wish her to be will take a long time and most likely cost a great deal of trouble, and I shall want the sympathy of all my friends.[63]

This Pygmalion impulse could easily have been disingenuous, the defensive reaction of a middle-aged man afraid of making a spectacle of himself in front of his friends. But if even partly true, it presages the failure of the marriage from the start, for Ellen was already quite happy the way she was. On another occasion Watts was reported to have had a similar exchange:

> *Watts*: I am thinking of adopting Ellen Terry; what do you think of this?
> *Friend*: I think she is too old.
> *Watts, later*: I have thought over your advice and I am thinking of marrying Ellen Terry – what do you say?
> *Friend*: I think she is too young.[64]

Clearly, Watts was having trouble sorting out his own motives.

Terry, however, was optimistic and enthusiastic, at least at first. She took to Little Holland House at once, perhaps because of its similarity to the fantasies she played out on stage and the contrast with the precarious, itinerant life she led with her family. "It seemed to me a paradise," she recalled, "where only beautiful things were allowed to come. All the women were graceful, and all the men were gifted." She accepted Watts's proposal eagerly and later wrote:

> The day of my wedding it was very cold. Like most women I always remember what I was wearing on the important occasions of my life. On that day I wore a brown silk gown which had been designed by Holman Hunt, and a quilted

white bonnet with a sprig of orange-blossom, and I was wrapped in a beautiful Indian shawl. I 'went away' in a sealskin jacket with coral buttons, and a little sealskin cap. I cried a good deal, and Mr. Watts said, 'Don't cry. It makes your nose swell.'[65]

Terry's most recent biographer, Nina Auerbach, rightly sees a Pre-Raphaelite somberness to this account in the emphasis on beauty over happiness, on static models over feeling people. "Theirs was no ordinary wedding," she concludes, "it was a ceremonial dedication to beauty."[66]

The newlyweds honeymooned at Freshwater, where they were quickly absorbed into the daily rounds of visits, walks on the downs, and now sitting for photographs. Despite her own formidable talents and her eagerness to fit in, it is hard to overestimate how oddly out of place Terry was within that group. "At Freshwater," she wrote later,

> I was still so young that I preferred playing Indians and Knights of the Round Table with Tennyson's sons, Hallam and Lionel, and the young Camerons, to sitting indoors noticing what the poet did or said . . . . He and the others seemed to me very old. There were my young knights waiting for me; and jumping gates, climbing trees, and running paper chases are pleasant when one is young.[67]

If there is some lingering spite in this passage, who can blame her? She had always been a tomboy and these active games must have been a necessary relief after the hours of immobile posing that were also expected of her in her new role as artist's wife. With the boys she could play at different roles, exercise her limbs, and stick out her tongue at the grown-ups. She was in a strange position betwixt and between: she was an actress in a circle that loved play-acting and make-believe, she was gifted in a circle that worshiped talent, but she never understood what was expected of her. Perhaps she was too much of a professional actress to believe wholeheartedly in the charades that Cameron, especially, promoted.

There were plenty of children for Terry to consort with at Freshwater. In addition to the Tennyson and Cameron boys there were the Bradleys, children of the master of Marlborough College (which Hallam later attended), and their cousins the Philpots; the children of the officers at the local fort; and the children of the local fishermen and tradesmen. Cameron drew on the whole range of them when selecting her sitters and she was known to lurk near her door ready to waylay a passing child (or even an attractive tourist) for hours of posing in her studio. Edith Bradley Ellison recalled that "the children loved but fled from her;" they would call out, "She's coming! She'll catch one of us!" when they saw her. She often did catch them, and they were bribed with sweets to pose.[68] The children who left memoirs later on pretty much all agreed that it was an ordeal. Her great-nephew H. A. L. Fisher complained of it.[69] Her great-niece Laura Gurney Troubridge remembered sitting along with her sister for hours with swan's wings attached to their shoulders [see figure]. Julia Margaret tousled their hair with an "ungentle hand" and brooked no denials. "No wonder," Troubridge continued,

> those old photographs of us, leaning over imaginary ramparts of heaven, look anxious and wistful. This is how we felt, for we never knew what Aunt Julia was going to do next, nor did any one else for the matter of that. All we were conscious of was that once in her clutches, we were perfectly helpless. 'Stand there,' she shouted. And we stood for hours, if necessary, gazing at the model of the Heavenly babe (in reality a sleeping child deposited in a property manger). The parents, anxious and uneasy, were outside, no more able to rescue their infant until Aunt Julia had finished with it, than we should have been.[70]

To Troubridge Aunt Julia was

> a terrifying elderly woman, short and squat, with none of the Pattle grace and beauty about her, though more than her share of their passionate energy and willfulness. Dressed in dark clothes, stained with chemicals from her photography (and smelling of them, too), with a plump, eager face and piercing eyes and a voice husky, and a little harsh, yet in some way compelling, and even charming . . .[71]

Cameron's combination of eagerness and carelessness explains the often-told story of her meeting with the Italian patriot Giuseppe Garibaldi. Garibaldi had gone to the Isle of Wight in the spring of 1864 to meet Tennyson, and while there the two men had talked and smoked and (rather pretentiously) planted a Wellingtonia tree to commemorate their meeting. The meeting made the cover of the *Illustrated London News* and the tree was later shorn of many of its branches by tourists seeking souvenirs. As the statesman left, he was accosted by a disheveled woman who fell to her knees in supplication. It was Julia Margaret hoping for a portrait sitting. But Garibaldi dismissed her as a beggar, as Julia Margaret looked down at her blackened hands and (in some versions) cried after him, "This is not dirt but art!"[72]

She lost Garibaldi, but by the spring Julia Margaret had worked steadily and doggedly to produce a serious body of work. On May 30 she took ten successful photographs up to London and registered them for copyright. They included portraits of Holman Hunt, Taylor, Tennyson, and Tennyson's friend James Spedding, as well as four studies of Madonnas and children.[73] This was probably in preparation for her participation in the annual exhibit of the Photographic Society of London, where she displayed five photographs that month. It was a considerable achievement for some-one who had taken her first photograph less than four months before. The five she chose (or the Society chose – it is unclear whether she submitted other work) were portraits of G. F. Watts, William Holman Hunt, and Henry Taylor, and two unidentified photographs entitled *Study from Life* and *Portrait*.[74] Appropriately enough, the exhibit was held at the former rooms of the Society of Female Artists on Pall Mall and was on display from May to June. Lady Clementina Hawarden's photographic studies of her daughters were also in the show and received excellent reviews, though she (like many a woman artist) must have grown very tired of hearing the word "charming." Cameron's photographs were immediately compared to Wynfield's signature soft-focus, close-up celebrity portraits.[75] Wynfield himself, always diffident about promoting his work, did not exhibit anything.

Cameron's work received mixed reviews. The Society's own *Photographic Journal* encouraged her in following Wynfield but withheld judgment; the *Athenaeum* praised her superior artistry in contrast to most photographers; the *British Journal of Photography* urged her to overcome her technical flaws.[76] The *Illustrated London News* advocated the artistic use of "soft-focus" as long as the most important part of a picture stayed in clear focus. For this reason the critic condemned Cameron's por-traits as bad examples, because no part was in focus.[77] Some critics didn't seem to know what to make of her work. The *Photographic News* commented on her "rather extraordinary specimens of portraiture, very daring in style," but wasn't sure whether they succeeded or not.[78] A later review in that journal again cites her "bold" work, filled with "force" and "power," but without true excellence.[79] Part of the problem seemed to be that although women had exhibited with the Society from its inception, Cameron's work did not appear to fit easily into the gendered assumptions of what a "lady's" work should look like. Whereas Hawarden's work was praised with words like "tenderness," "delicacy," and "taste," Cameron's was described uneasily in much stronger terms.

Following so closely upon Wynfield's pioneering series of portraits, Cameron's work set off a controversy about focus. As early as 1853, Sir William Newton had advo-cated photographing out-of-focus to achieve a painterly effect.[80] Until the 1860s, however, the evolving field of photography was dominated by gentlemen and ama-teur scientists who valued precision and whose experiments were aimed at improving verisimilitude, or commercial photographers who needed to earn a profit on each image. When Wynfield exhibited his soft-focus portraits of artists, art critics naturally rejoiced and praised them as superior to the banal recordings of features that passed for portraiture in the commercial studios. Just as naturally, other photo-graphers resented this criticism and defended themselves by insisting on what they felt was most essential and unique to photography: the sharp focus that enabled its "objective" realism. When the *Reader* complained that most photographers could not represent fine distinctions such as those between a lady and a maid, the *Photographic News* retorted that the fault lay in "nature's" deceptive appearances. When the art establishment praised Wynfield's allusions to Old Masters paintings, photography critics denied that "the only mode in which a recognized 'artist' can confer dignity even upon men of mark in the world, in the nineteenth century, is by ransacking the chests of the costumier for the moth-eaten drapery of a bygone, but more picturesque age."[81] As Joanne Lukitsh has rightly pointed out, these arguments surfaced at this time because portraiture was in flux: inexpensive *cartes de visite* made portraits available to everyone and suddenly it became important to draw distinctions between "vulgar" portraits and "artistic" ones.[82] The focus point for this struggle over the definition of photographic portraiture was focus itself.

In this context the *Athenaeum*'s praise for Cameron's first exhibited works in the spring of 1864 was incendiary.[83] The more the art and literary establishment commended her artistic "out-of-focus" work, the more the photographic establishment balked at her faulty technique. The *British Journal of Photography* was typical of the latter response, commenting patronizingly that "this exhibitor being one of the very few ladies whose works adorn the walls of the room, it would be ungallant to say more in this strain . . . ."[84] The criticism was not "sexist" per se (Clementina Hawarden was always well reviewed, Wynfield too was panned by the photographic press, and Cameron received good reviews from art critics) but it was certainly gendered: Cameron did not produce work that conformed to the institution's prevailing expectations and so it was convenient to patronize her and accuse her of incompetence.[85]

Not that it discouraged Cameron one whit. On June 7 she joined the Photographic Society and the following year she was elected to the Photographic Society of Scotland. The bad reviews stuck with her enough for her to mention them in her autobiography with a sniff:

> The Photographic Society of London in their *Journal* would have dispirited me very much had I not valued that criticism at its worth. It was unsparing and too manifestly unjust for me to attend to it. The more lenient and discerning judges gave me large space upon their walls which seemed to invite the irony and spleen of the printed notice.[86]

She copyrighted over thirty more photographs at the end of June and she continued to turn out new work at a prodigious pace. By the end of that first year, she had copyrighted more than a hundred photographs and was a member of the most prestigious photographic societies in the country, if not Europe.[87] The art establishment remained her most consistent allies throughout her career – even after many photographers had been won over. Perhaps it was inevitable that Cameron's background at Little

---

Holland House and her "artistic" aims for photography would align her with artists and not photographers, but this occurred quickly and enduringly. The association of "art" photography with softer focus and "documentary" photography with sharper focus has also proven to be an enduring legacy of these Victorian debates.[88]

As for the ongoing debates about focus that divided the periodical press in the early 1860s, Cameron dismissed them with a wave of the hand in a letter to Herschel on the last day of that pivotal year: "What is focus and who has the right to say what focus is the legitimate focus –." It is a bravura statement for a year-old photographer and a woman. It is a remarkably post-modern statement in its acceptance of alternative, subjective truths (Cameron would rarely make such admissions about anything else: her personality, her culture, and her faith leaned toward absolutism). In context, it comes after a blunt plea for his help

> [to] induce an ignorant public to believe in other than mere conventional topographic Photography–map making–& skeleton rendering of feature & form without that roundness & fullness of form and feature that modeling of flesh & limb which the focus I use only can give tho' called & condemned as "out of focus".[89]

It is not, technically, her focus (or lack thereof) that provides the lifelike flesh and round modeling that she desires: it is her virtuoso use of light and shadow that creates the illusion of three-dimensionality. But the limited light, the technical specifications of her camera, her preference for close-ups, and the large-format plates did affect the consistency of her definition, and clearly she liked the results. The faint fuzziness also implied motion (sometimes the sitters did move), which further improved the illusion of lifelikeness in an art always associated with death, an art Cameron wanted desperately to associate with immortality. Motion was a constant problem during the long exposures of Victorian photography, but Cameron refused to use the headrests and braces that could have minimized it.

Focus was a divisive issue between Cameron and Dodgson too. Once Cameron had taken up photography, her relationship to Dodgson inevitably changed. In June Dodgson viewed Cameron's photographs at the Photographic Society exhibit and "did *not* admire them." Like most photographers, he preferred Hawarden's work.[90] In July he wrote to Cameron requesting an introduction to Watts and she ignored him. Perhaps she was anxious not to share her sources now that she too was pursuing celebrity portraits. Dodgson asked the sculptor Alexander Munro, who asked Val Prinsep, who finally offered the coveted letter of introduction. Dodgson visited Signor in his studio at Little Holland House, where Watts showed him a photograph that Cameron had made of a painting by Watts of Ellen Terry. Watts hinted at coming to sit for Dodgson but never did. Later that summer, Dodgson took a vacation to the Isle of

Wight and he and Cameron exchanged their portfolios. Dodgson admired some but concluded that they

> were all taken purposely out of focus–some are very picturesque–some merely hideous–however, she talks of them as if they were triumphs in art. *She* wished she could have had some of *my* subjects to do *out* of focus–and *I* expressed an analogous wish with regard to some of *her* subjects.[91]

For her part, Cameron wrote to Taylor that she had heard Dodgson's portrait of him described as looking like "a sea monster fed upon milk" and that the Tennysons hated it. She blamed poor printing, and actually had some praise for the negative, but refused to order a print.[92] Whether through the smallness of the tight circles they both moved in, or through rivalry, the two photographers did photograph some of the same sitters, including the Tennysons, Ellen Terry, and more importantly, Alice Liddell, the inspiration for Dodgson's *Alice's Adventures in Wonderland*.[93] Dodgson had not yet become "Lewis Carroll," but he had already told the story to the Liddell sisters during a boat trip in Oxford in 1862 and he was conferring with his publisher on the title. Cameron, who also knew the Liddells from their summers on the Isle of Wight, did not photograph Alice until she was grown; her fierce, direct gaze in *Pomona* suggests a very different character than the whimsical child of the story.

Dodgson's visit to Cameron also sheds light on their different approaches toward the same material: portraits of children. He was clearly the "amateur" in the old-fashioned sense of a gentleman pursuing a hobby out of love (the Latin root for amateur). He did not exhibit his work in shows or join the Photographic Society, though he did sell it occasionally. He had a consuming, full-time career that took up most of his time, in addition to his literary work, which would compete with photography after the *Alice* books were published. It is perhaps for these reasons that he unexpectedly stopped taking photographs altogether in 1880. Dodgson was also shy and diffident. When he was at Freshwater with Cameron, he noticed an attractive "gypsy" of a girl whom he wanted to photograph but he didn't know who she was. Cameron briskly advised him to ask the girl her name, but Dodgson was too shy and he asked the landlady of his hotel for help instead.[94] His indirection, driven perhaps by fear of his attention to girls being misconstrued as well as his own timidity, was at odds with Cameron's assertive candor. Dodgson had every reason to be confident in approaching sitters: he was a gentleman, a successful academic, an expert photographer. Cameron had every reason to be insecure: she was a "lady amateur" to most of the field and still a novice photographer. And yet temperamentally she was the brash and extroverted promoter of herself and her work. She may not have been popular with children, as Dodgson was, but she was not self-conscious with them. As other scholars have noted, the two photographers have been constantly compared to each other and put into opposite camps on every subject as if they were rival siblings, but their differences say more about the complexities of the Victorian photographic world and its legacy than about their works, which share some marked similarities.[95]

Cameron's eager adoption of her new career and her new identity as an artist led her back to her old friendship with Herschel. Herschel was in ill health and she rarely saw him despite the short distance from his home in Kent. When she took up photography, she naturally turned to him for advice and criticism, sending him portfolios of her work for comment and printing copies for him of the images he admired. She followed up that autumn by presenting him with a major album of her new work, now at the National Museum of Photography, Film, and Television in Bradford, England. On November 26 she inscribed the gift "with a grateful memory of 27 years of friendship" and on September 8, 1867 she added photographs and reinscribed it in "renewed devotedness of grateful friendship."[96] The insistence on her gratitude is important: Cameron was grateful in 1836 when Herschel and his wife took her up in Cape Town and cheered her in her distress there, but now she must have been doubly grateful for his support and encouragement in her growing career. The gift of an album must have been motivated by that deep well of feeling for him but also by some hope of gain: Herschel's goodwill, like Watts's, would be very convenient to her as she began to photograph. In 1864, when she was embroiled in controversy with the photographic establishment about her use of focus, she needed an ally from the scientific side of the field as well as the artistic side.

The Herschel Album, now disassembled, contained ninety-four photographs: half from 1864 and half from 1865–67. Cameron indexed the album and emphasized that the photographs were taken from life, with no retouching or enlarging, by her own hand at Freshwater, with a few exceptions. She was conscious of their commercial value, even in sending them to Herschel, and noted in a letter that they were all copyrighted and not to be copied.[97] The portraits from 1864 include Watts, Taylor, Aubrey DeVere, James Spedding, and one of Holman Hunt in Eastern dress. The album includes many of her best-known works: Madonnas and children, illustrations from Tennyson's "The May Queen," *Paul and Virginia*. Cameron was always careful about the placement of her photographs and would probably have opened the album with her best work, just as the Watts Album opened with two facing prints of Annie Philpot. The 1864 album probably opened with the works that she had recently displayed at the Photographic Society: portraits of Taylor, Watts, Holman Hunt and James Spedding are near the front after some inserted work from 1867. The first image in the revised album of 1867 is naturally Herschel himself, the photograph informally known as "Paterfamilias": she finally took Herschel's portrait in April 1867 and that would have been a key reason for updating his album.

Cameron carefully customized her albums for their recipients and the Herschel Album is no exception. The Mia Album is filled with family portraits; the Lindsay Album is filled with Christian allegories; the Overstone Album includes portraits of Overstone's own family that aren't found elsewhere; and, likewise, the Herschel Album includes a photograph of Herschel's eldest daughter made during the same trip to Herschel's home in April that yielded the portraits of her father. Though a scientist, Herschel had an interest in all of the subjects that Cameron favored: he was devoutly religious, interested in classical and literary topics, and familiar with many of the celebrities she knew and photographed. He had also met most of her family over the years, which explains why Cameron's own extended family (as usual) comprises a significant portion of the album. He was a godparent to Henry Herschel Hay, as Julia Margaret was to his daughter Julia, and he took his responsibilities seriously.

It is clear that the gift of this album was at least partly tactical, because all that autumn Cameron wrote Herschel insistently asking for comments, favors, and, boldly, publicity for her work. She asked him to write out some verses of his translation of Homer in his own hand so that she could photograph them. Perplexed, he sent her some in a letter. Then, in December, she sent him some more new work (probably the *Fruits of the Spirit* series that she would soon donate to the British Museum) and wrote the defense of her use of soft-focus that has already been quoted. In that letter she refers to Sir David Brewster's speech on photography and frankly urges Herschel to write something of the sort that would praise and defend her work.[98] Brewster had made great claims for photography's moral and social value: it could carry one "magically" to the far parts of the globe, cheaply decorate one's home, document scientific work, describe different races, preserve artifacts and manuscripts, catalogue anatomy, and solve crimes.[99] Although she claimed in her autobiography that she was unconcerned by the photographic establishment's contempt for her style and technique, clearly she was looking for reinforcements in the battle with them. Who better than Sir John, revered by the public and honored by photographers as a pioneer in their field? Herschel's reply has not survived; however, on other occasions he told her gently that if he could find an appropriate opening he would be only too happy to compliment her work in public, but he hesitated to do so out of the blue.[100] Cameron must have ground her teeth in frustration, but she persevered in her requests.

The history of photography, like the history of art with which it is now identified, is usually thought to be a procession of gifted innovators who tried to express themselves visually and earn a living at the same time. The fact that the materials of a medium – in this case, camera, negatives, photochemicals, paper, albums, even light itself – define one's options is usually considered secondary to the human drama of an artist wrestling with a subject or an audience. The camera is a crucial part of that narrative for photographers and historians of photography: it is generally thought to be the essential tool that produces the photographs. In Cameron's case, the question of when she first received her camera and when she began using it has been absolutely central to the story of her career. That seems natural until one considers recent discoveries: it now looks as though Cameron's photographic career did not begin behind the camera. Nor, for that matter, was it the invention of the camera that inaugurated the field of photography – it was the discovery of photochemicals that could fix the image. Likewise, it was not necessarily the gift of the camera that marks the official beginning of Cameron's career as much as her experiments in printing and album-making.

To privilege the camera is convenient for the field of photography because it emphasizes the moment of interaction between artist and subject in which the spiritual and magical side of the art must somehow take place. It seems to be the moment when the photographer has the most choices: where to place the camera, how to focus and frame the image, who and what to photograph. But in fact the developing and printing are at least as important to the final image as the opening of the aperture. For the sitter or the consumer, those parts of the process occur in private, some of it in the dark; they are at least as magical in their transformation of light into emulsion, but they are little understood and unwatched by others. Other photographers have had whole careers without using a camera: the most important in Cameron's case was Anna Atkins, the nineteenth-century British botanical photographer who worked almost exclusively in photograms, or images printed directly onto light-sensitive paper when placed in the sun. Around 1862 Cameron made a photogram that she entitled *My printing of ferns*. In a second photogram she experimented further by adding a border of silhouetted leaves to a Rejlander photograph of a girl in profile. The girl was photographed in front of foliage and the added frame adds texture to the portrait.[101]

Increasingly it seems that what was radical about Cameron's photographic work was not simply that it was produced by a Victorian woman. There were other Victorian women photographers, including owners of commercial portrait studios, though there weren't many.[102] But Cameron's work now seems especially interesting for its perhaps unconscious disregard for our preconceived notions: that photography begins with a camera; that photographs should be "in focus;" that artists have a vision and then produce it. Even the possibility that Cameron began her career by collaborating with other photographers undermines our assumptions about the independent, solitary artist, though the latter is known to be a creation of Romantic ideologies. Cameron herself worked hard to fit herself into that Romantic notion of art and the artist. With photography's status always in doubt, she couldn't afford to question the very definitions of art itself without risking her newborn identity and work. She insisted that she worked alone, although there are repeated accounts by others of her maids and sons assisting her, as well as the possibility of collaborations.

Perhaps, as Joanne Lukitsh also suggests, Cameron's "career" really began some time between July and December 1863, when she rephotographed and reprinted other people's work.[103] In that moment she became a photographer: in 1863, that meant a person able to represent the world in black, white, and gray, using only light and chemicals. Her work changed remarkably little in subject, style, or format over the fifteen-odd years of her career. From the start she seemed to crave intimacy, bringing her camera up next to the faces of her sitters as if to embrace them. It is tempting to understand Cameron's work in terms of a proto-Freudian assertion of personality as the key to identity, instead of the traditional markers of class, gender, religion, or trade. In Cameron's decontextualized heads, the subjects are left with nothing but their features to show for themselves: they are all eyes and the impression of interiority behind them. Given the length of Victorian exposures, their expressions are enigmatic at best. The palette of emotion is extremely limited: despair, sorrow, melancholy, contentment, calm, thoughtfulness are possible; anger, joy, scorn, hatred are not. One can see the bourgeois liberalism of her age in Cameron's belief in the individual, her attention to its interior life over its exterior life. And why not? In this she echoed the realist novel too as it turned toward the representation of thoughts and feelings over events. In Cameron's work one sees the same tug of war that was occurring in the novel between character and plot. Character would win the battle on both fronts, but the real winners in the high-stakes war for high art would soon be the media themselves: the rich, evocative language loved for its rippling sounds and the rectangles of color, light, shadow, and shape admired for their sheer beauty. One can see the change coming already in Tennyson's and Cameron's works.

Julia Margaret Cameron, *Ellen Terry at Age Sixteen*, 1864/1875.

This portrait of Ellen Terry was taken during her
short-lived marriage to Watts.

Julia Margaret Cameron, *Thomas Carlyle*, 1867.

———

Carlyle wrote that sitting for this portrait was an "inferno", but Cameron recognized the
audacious portrait as one of her best works in her autobiography and it is still
among her most celebrated photographs.

L. F. W. Herschel

Julia Margaret Cameron, *J. F. W. Herschel*, April 1867.

It was several years before Cameron found an opportunity to photograph her old friend Herschel.
She brought all her equipment to his home and insisted on washing and
fluffing up his white hair.

Julia Margaret Cameron, *Romeo and Juliet*, 1867.

Cameron used her maid Mary Ryan and Ryan's fiancé, Henry Cotton,
as models for this romantic pair.

Julia Margaret Cameron, *The Bride (Annie Chinery)*, November 1869.

Cameron eagerly welcomed this new daughter-in-law into her family and photographed her
several times around the time of her wedding to Ewen.

Julia Margaret Cameron, *Anne Isabella Thackeray (Lady Ritchie)*, c.1867.

———

Cameron was good friends with William Makepeace Thackeray and after his death
became increasingly close to his daughter Annie, also a writer.
This portrait is typical of Cameron's more formal or studio-like photographs.

Julia Margaret Cameron, *Ewen Wrottesley Hay Cameron*, 1865.

———

Ewen Cameron managed and then owned Rathoongodde, Charles Hay's beloved estate in Ceylon.

Julia Margaret Cameron, *Henry Herschel Hay Cameron*, 1870.

———

Henry Herschel Hay tried to establish himself as a coffee planter with his brothers in Ceylon. He eventually became a photographer like his mother.

Julia Margaret Cameron, *My Son Eugene of the R.A.*, 1867.

———

Cameron's eldest son, Eugene, made a career in the Royal Artillery.

Julia Margaret Cameron, *Charlie Hay Cameron*, October 28, 1867.

———

Cameron took this portrait as her son Charlie Hay left home for the first time.

Julia Margaret Cameron, *Mrs. Herbert Duckworth*, April 1867.

———

Cameron took a series of photographs of her niece Julia Jackson
just before her first marriage.

CHAPTER 7

Muses, Models, and Mothers

W HEN PHOTOGRAPHY emerged from the amateur tradition in the 1840s and
1850s, becoming commercial and popular in the 1860s, it was inevitably compared to painting, but it was just as insistently compared to the theater. In an age
when the theater included a broad range of professional and amateur occasions and
covered forms from Shakespeare's newly canonical high art to travelling vaudeville
companies, circus performers, freak shows, and acrobats, the theater touched many
more Victorian lives than painting or sculpture. From the start, critics compared
photographs to contemporaneous *poses plastiques* (or living sculpture) and *tableaux
vivants* (or living pictures) and photographers struggled to define their practice
within a very wide range of possibilities across the arts and sciences.[1] For Cameron
and her friends, the theater meant attending plays and meeting actors as well as a
heightened form of self-expression that pervaded both public and private life.

Theatricality entailed self-consciously playing roles of all kinds, including femininity, maternity, class affiliations, and "character" parts like those of artist and
eccentric. In a society where public roles were relatively fixed and inflexible, the
world of theater and fantasy allowed room to explore other selves and identities.
Playing roles helped make the relatively rigid boundaries of Victorian identities more
bearable. Though Victorians may come across as serious and intolerant today, they
were more playful and experimental than we generally assume, and the theater was
a place where they could mock their most serious selves and try out dangerous roles
safely. In Charlotte Brontë's *Jane Eyre* Mr. Rochester and his gentry friends play a version of charades while the governess Jane watches from the sidelines. There, the
amateur theatricals served a matchmaking purpose: playing a role helped courting
couples to express feelings that were officially unspeakable while preserving the
appearance of propriety.

Cameron and her circle, like most Victorians, entertained themselves at home in the
days before television and radio with frequent performances of plays, pantomimes,

charades, and other parlor games. Like music, Bible reading, and family prayers, amateur theatricals were a regular part of a middle-class family's evenings at home. They were perfectly suited to large families and even larger house parties. The more the merrier, the more melodramatic the better. In a letter from the early 1860s Hardinge Hay Cameron describes a visit to the theater with his sister and brother-in-law that conveys the anarchic, surreal quality of popular theater at the time. They attended a burlesque of the Greek myth of Hercules and Omphale in which

> one sees the terrible tyrant Eurystheus appear like a buffoon in [a] fairy tale, whilst the brazen gates of the palace are shattered by an india rubber club wielded by a woman dressed in a lionskin of Hercules who afterwards plays the bones whilst Philocletes dances the cure and Mercury plays the caduceus as if it were a banjo . . .[2]

The description goes on in that vein for another two paragraphs, including an account of a Houdini-esque escape trick and other clever "artifices." Thackeray's family performed a version of William Makepeace's own play *Lovel the Widower* in the winter of 1862, with gentle Minnie Thackeray playing Lovel's mother-in-law and dramatically revealing that her daughter had once – gasp! – trodden the boards.[3] Minnie was also a star of the private performance the Thackerays put on that year of another version of the play, called *The Wolves and the Lamb*.[4]

So Cameron photographed people who were accustomed to posing and performing for each other. They loved reciting lines and donning costumes. In her first year behind the camera Cameron made studies of Holman Hunt in Eastern dress, Henry Taylor as Friar Lawrence, and female friends as sibyls. She photographed Bernardin de St. Pierre's *Paul and Virginia,* and Charles Kingsley's *Water Babies*. She draped her models in cloaks and posed them with bows and arrows. She seems to have self-consciously repeated some of the genre tableaux taken by or with Oscar Rejlander at her home in 1863: she photographed several versions of women drawing water from a well, culminating in an image of Rachel from the Old Testament. Even the artists themselves enjoyed dressing up: in the 1860s some London artists, including members of Cameron's circle, formed a volunteer rifle group as reservists and spent their weekends designing their uniforms and marching around in costume.[5]

The faintly scandalous nature of the theater – which grew more and more respectable as the century progressed – was part of its appeal. Acting permitted flirtations, rebellions, and all sorts of exceptional behavior under cover of a costume. Even Julia Margaret, permitted many eccentricities in her everyday life, enjoyed the liberties of a few more. One of her child sitters chronicled Julia Margaret's love of theater and how she built a studio near her house to stage plays, often for charitable causes. In January 1867 Emily Tennyson records the Camerons and the Tennyson boys producing a melodrama called *Ici On Parle Français*.[6] Thoby Prinsep's niece Louisa was another proficient amateur actress and she starred in a private theatrical three days before her wedding at Freshwater.[7] It was intended to be her farewell performance (much like Kate Terry's before her marriage to Arthur Lewis) before she entered the confines of respectable domesticity, but it may not have been. One summer the Freshwater crew put on a romance called *Our Wife* and Julia Margaret was so displeased with her son Henry's love scene that she leaped to the stage and enacted the passionate scene herself. "'There!' she exclaimed, rising out of breath and triumphant. '*That's* the way to do it!' 'All right, mother!' replied her son, a comical gleam in his eye. 'All in good time!'"[8]

Henry Herschel Hay was supposed to have been a remarkable amateur actor, who attempted a professional career. Cameron was proud of him and praised his abilities in letters, including one to Mrs. Bateman, whose daughter Isabel was an actress whom Cameron had photographed. Cameron notes that Isabel was admirably simple and anti-theatrical in her acting and compares her to the famous opera-singer Madame Malibrau of her youth in Paris. "I very much appreciate this reserve of power in everything– in painting – in poetry – in acting," she wrote.[9] However, acting was not a respectable career for a young man related to earls and countesses; the conflict over Henry's career would cause much strife in the next decade.

Surprisingly, the only professional actress to join the Freshwater circle was exiled soon afterwards. By the beginning of 1865, the marriage of Ellen Terry and G. F. Watts was over. It had lasted under a year and the Pattle sisters, often blamed for instigating it, have been blamed for its failure as well. In the swirling legends that arose about Terry after she had become a star of the Victorian stage, it was said that Sara Prinsep and her sisters had decided that the melancholic and lonely Watts needed a wife, and set out to find a biddable girl for him. It was Kate Terry, they said, who was primed for the role, but Ellen upstaged her elder sister and won the part. As both Terry's and Watts's biographers point out, the Pattle sisters were high-handed and marriage-minded, but they must share some of the responsibility with Tom Taylor, the drama critic who introduced the Terry sisters to Little Holland House and enjoyed escorting them around society.[10] Nor was Watts, who seems to have exerted his will enough to choose the younger sister over the elder, as passive as legend suggests. Besides, when writing of the "disaster" it is worth remembering Terry's own comments in her autobiography: "'The marriage was not a happy one,' they will probably say after my death, and I forestall them by saying that it in many ways was very happy indeed."[11]

From the start, Watts seems to have had no intention of setting up his own household with Terry, and instead simply incorporated her into his routine at Little Holland House. They honeymooned at Freshwater within the same extended circle of artists, writers, and their acolytes. She modeled for his celebrated painting *Choosing* and he painted her in armor for *Watchman, What of the Night*, during which she famously fainted during the long sitting. She never had domestic responsibilities and seems to have left all household management to Sara Prinsep. Yet, according to everything she wrote then and afterwards, she was happy. Nina Auerbach, Terry's biographer, argues that both Watts and Terry believed that they could make a marriage out of a mutual devotion to art and beauty.[12] Terry reveled in her new womanhood and Watts wanted a muse of his own. Their relationship may or may not have been sexual – stories later circulated that the marriage was unconsummated, that Watts was impotent, that Terry was found crying outside her bedroom door on their wedding night – but it was filled with the very real pleasures of looking, posing, and creating. Unconsciously, they abjured the usual bourgeois function of marriage to establish a home, produce children, and control sexual relationships in favor of a partnership that enabled them both to play roles and create illusions. In fact, they tried to live out the ideals of art and beauty that were also expressed in Cameron's art: they made their little world into their stage.

Predictably, perhaps, their efforts were not well received in what passed for "real life" at Little Holland House and Freshwater. Terry's power in the relationship clearly came from her role as muse and model, not as wife, so she disdained to act the lady and continued to play the tomboy. As Auerbach put it, "out of the studio, not knowing who to be, she fell back on the stage child who had won so much applause."[13] At dinner parties she allegedly shocked the Pattle sisters by appearing in costume as Cupid. At an afternoon visit to Watts's friend, the artist Roddam Spencer-Stanhope, she was left with the women in the drawing room while Watts and Spencer-Stanhope discussed art in the garden.

> With an air of supreme boredom, [Terry] leant back over the arm of the chair in which she was seated, and, shaking her head to and fro, loosened the pins from her hair which tumbled about her shoulders like a cloak of shining gold . . . . Mrs. Prinsep was horrified. 'Ellen! Ellen!' she cried, 'Put up your hair instantly!' And Ellen, flashing a wrathful glance at her tormentor, grasped the waving mass of gold, coiled it carelessly upon her head, and, stabbing it with pins, sat there looking lovelier than ever, a petulant, scolded child.[14]

Terry had not signed up for a supporting role.

Soon, however, she found herself ignominiously sent back to her parents: "I wondered at my new life, and worshiped it because of its beauty. When it suddenly came to an end I was thunderstruck; and refused at first to consent to the separation, which was arranged for me in much the same way as my marriage had been," she wrote later.[15] Spencer-Stanhope frankly blamed Sara Prinsep for the failure of the marriage, and she must surely have had a hand in the decision to send Terry away. By

Christmas 1864, Terry was gone, and by January Watts had drawn up a legal separation agreement in which he agreed to provide her with 300 pounds per year for as
long as she remained "chaste," or 200 pounds per year if she returned to the stage.[16]
She did, of course, return to the stage, but she forfeited her financial support when
she ran off with the architect Edward Godwin in 1868 and bore him two illegitimate
children. She lost contact with Watts and his set for decades, but she always wrote
kindly of her ex-husband and even swallowed whatever animus she may have had for
the Prinseps and the Camerons, graciously supplying them with boxes at her shows
when they asked.

Terry's story illustrates the ambivalent role that the theater played in Victorian society, especially in Cameron's elite circle. Auerbach argues that Sara and Julia Margaret
thought that an actress wasn't good enough for their Signor and that the theater was
excluded from the arts they cultivated.[17] But while class distinctions at Little Holland
House were certainly as fine as she suggests, the circle's attitudes toward the theater
were contradictory. They were avidly interested in stage people and would surely have
countenanced Terry if she had been willing and able to add bourgeois wife and hostess to her many roles (as her sister Kate did when she married the industrialist Arthur
Lewis). Julia Margaret and Sara seemed unable to understand that there was little to
recommend the role when they had stripped it of its privileges and powers. Terry's
story, filled with sexual innuendoes, had an all-too-"Victorian" denouement with her
"fall" into adultery and illegitimacy, but she defied expectations, and the melodrama's
typical plot, by refusing to disappear. In 1875, after seven years of exile from society
with Godwin and their children, she made another triumphant return to the stage,
where she specialized in the tragic heroines that she never played in real life.

According to copyright registrations, Cameron took about seven photographs of
Terry during the short spring of her marriage to Watts. Only four are known to have
survived.[18] In one, she poses as the Southwest Wind and she seems childlike and
ethereal. In the other often-reproduced image, sometimes called *Sadness* [see
figure], she is all too real: more than most of Cameron's portraits, this one represents
a living, feeling person in a realistic setting (supposedly the bathroom at Farringford).
Terry clings to the wall, averts her face from the viewer, and covers her body with her
arms. She is dressed in a shift, and seems posed for display, but the tension in her posture makes viewing uncomfortable. As Auerbach has written, it is an emblematic
portrait of a young girl's coming of age into a femininity defined by constraints and
self-consciousness.[19] But Terry was an actress and a photograph is not simply a reflection of reality; the image does not necessarily represent Terry's emotional state,
though it is tempting to read it as a morning-after portrait. Victorian marriages of a
young girl to an older man were both popular (older men were revered as heroes)
and practical (older men could afford wives and children), but they were also slightly

titillating. Terry and Watts's marriage would have come under extra scrutiny even if it had lasted. Such marriages, like Julia Margaret's and Sara's too, were often ideal for ambitious women: they grew into their powers as their husbands let go of theirs. But, unfortunately for Terry, Watts already had a powerful partner in Sara Prinsep.

In 1877 Ellen Terry and G. F. Watts were officially divorced, ending a separation of over ten years. Terry wanted to return yet again to the stage and was considering marrying a man who could give her illegitimate children a legal name besides Craig, which she had picked for them. Watts testified in the divorce proceedings that his "restless and impetuous" wife had been spoilt by the "exaggerated romance of sensational plays," making it impossible to have a quiet life with her. Her "insane excitability" kept him from his work, he claimed, and so the separation ensued. The nature of this evidence meant it would necessarily be painful and perhaps unjust, but Watts's belated demonization of Terry as a madwoman was undoubtedly related to her career, which had once seemed attractive and compatible to his.[20] The same high spirits and strong wills that kept both Terry and Cameron persevering in creative professions always threatened to damn them as lunatics in Victorian England. Theatricality was both enabling and dangerous for them.

Terry returned to the stage in 1878, joining Henry Irving's rising Lyceum Theatre and playing Ophelia to his Hamlet. It was a long-lasting partnership and a role that would make her famous. Again, this boisterous tomboy was adept at playing tragic heroines, and this one in particular fascinated Victorians. Watts painted a series of Ophelias around the same time, based on old sketches of Terry. Millais's *Ophelia* two decades before had started the cult of Pre-Raphaelite women by merging Elizabeth Siddall's beauty, victimization, and tragic ending into one exquisite canvas. Ophelia was, of course, an archetype of the creative woman: fallen (as Mike Weaver suggests) through no fault of her own. She was the Lady of Shalott, Elaine, and all the women who have loved not wisely but too well. Her creativity was expressed in her own body: she made herself into an artwork to be admired and sighed over. One can see the physical and dramatic possibilities for Terry, whose body was the tool of her trade, but it was just a role, a convenient role that opportunistically merged her onstage and offstage legends.

Back in 1868, when she ran off with Godwin, Terry had disappeared so completely that she wrote rather gleefully in her autobiography

> a dreadful thing happened. A body was found in the river,–the dead body of a young woman very fair and slight and tall. Every one thought that it was my body.
>
> I had gone away without a word. No one knew where I was. My own father identified the corpse . . .[21]

Her sisters went into mourning before her mother re-examined the body and realized the mistake. Terry came rushing back from her rural hideaway to prove she was still alive, but she seems to have enjoyed the melodrama. Ophelia was her twin, but she was ever escaping the fallen woman's fate, which Watts had painted decades before in a work called *Found Drowned*. As Auerbach points out, the irrepressible Terry just laughed in the face of disaster, returning insouciantly to her "life of sin" in Hertfordshire.[22]

Unfortunately for Cameron, photography was often associated less with high arts, or even with professional theater, than with popular melodramas and amateur theatricals, such as those that Cameron and her circle themselves produced. It is a natural connection to make: in the mid-nineteenth century both photography and amateur theatricals were very popular with middle-class families. The association of photography, especially narrative compositions, with the theater also stemmed from the popularity of *tableaux vivants*, which shared characteristics of both arts. Like the theater, these performances displayed real people who were present in person. Like photography, the actors held fixed poses and the action was frozen in time.

Victorian "artistic" photographers, like Cameron, may have composed these narrative tableaux to strengthen their claims for photography's status as an art. By drawing on literary and historical subjects, and the artistic conventions of European painting, they aimed to prove that photography could transcend mere mechanical reproduction and aspire to high art. But, as historians of photography have pointed out, the result was sometimes paradoxically ridiculous.[23] Instead of ennobling photography by relating it to the high arts of literature and painting, they unintentionally seemed to create parodies of those arts. In short, the photographs seemed theatrical, like representations of representations of high art, rather than the thing itself. This was especially true of Cameron's narrative tableaux, which were often criticized by Victorian and contemporary critics for their lack of realism, though of course the models were just as present and "real" in these photographs as in the portraits.

By the 1850s, *tableaux vivants* were starting to seem vulgar.[24] Rejlander had pro-voked a flood of criticism in 1857 for a large work entitled *The Two Ways of Life* that appeared to be a photograph of a *tableau vivant*. In fact, the photograph, which showed a large group of people acting out lives of virtue or vice, was a collage of sep-arate negatives printed together into one photograph. Nonetheless, Victorian viewers were shocked by this representation of what appeared to have been an orgy-like scene, with clothed and unclothed bodies juxtaposed indiscriminately. Still, the moral lesson of the image was so appealing that even Queen Victoria bought a copy.

A photograph like Rejlander's *Two Ways of Life* raised difficult interpretative prob-lems for the Victorians. Not only were most viewers unfamiliar with photographic techniques like combination printing, but the novelty of the medium made it hard for them to read the image. Photographs insist on their subjects: those models were really there in some fashion, but how? And who were they? The women especially were provoking. Typically, middle- and upper-class women who modeled for paintings were named in the title of the work. They were posing as themselves for portraits. Artists needing other female figures used working-class or professional models, who were unnamed and posed as a character or a type. Photographers tended to follow this convention: Cameron never made a photograph entitled *Mary Hillier* but she made several named after her niece Julia Jackson. Female models were like actresses: they shared an ambiguous class status that was intricately bound together with their role-playing. If models and actresses were always changing identities, how could they be trusted? If they were paid for their work, how could they be respectable? Being paid, playing roles in public – this excluded models and actresses from the Victorian ideal of middle-class femininity. In fact, it made them uncomfortably like . . . prostitutes.

After all, how could one tell the difference between a lady and a maid, or between a virgin and a prostitute? This was a matter of great urgency for mid-century Victorians, when class boundaries were threatened by a Reform Act that extended the vote to parts of the working classes and when industrialization was wreaking havoc with gender roles. There were conventions for visually differentiating virtuous women from their fallen sisters: loose, unbound hair, an uncovered head, showy dress, direct eye contact – all these signaled depravity to respectable Victorians; but these clues became less reliable in mid-century. Victorians liked to think that the boundary between vice and virtue was absolute and visible, but historian Judith Walkowitz has shown that in fact most Victorian prostitutes fell in and out of respectability rather than turning to "vice" once and for all. In other words, prostitution too was a role that could be played rather than an identity to be assumed forever. Most prostitutes had been and would again be maidservants.[25] And middle-class Victorians couldn't always tell the difference.

The question of how to read an image of a working-class woman has particular significance for Cameron's work because her most frequently used models were her own housemaids, especially Mary Hillier, often known as "Madonna Mary" after her best-known role. Two photographs she described on the copyright registration forms in May 1864 as "Mary Hillier as Madonna" were among the first ten photographs that Cameron ever registered and they figure in the Watts album of her earliest work as well. Hillier was a Freshwater native whose sister and brother worked for Tennyson at Farringford. In 1861, at age fourteen, she started in service for Cameron.[26] Cameron was generous about sharing credit with her, and paid tribute to her beauty of mind and face in *Annals of My Glass House*: "The very unusual attributes of her character and complexion of mind, if I may so call it, deserve mention in due time, and are the wonder of those whose life is blended with ours as intimate friends of the house."[27]

Cameron was unusual in considering the personality of a model as well as his or her appearance, but it was consistent for an artist who was trying to represent inner as well as outer truths. Furthermore, her relationship with Hillier, founded on over ten years of modeling and shaped by the daily interactions within a household, was necessarily intimate. She clearly liked to believe that Hillier was an honored and eager participant in the role-playing and art-making, but an interview with Hillier in the 1920s made it clear that she considered the sittings just one more duty imposed by a rather eccentric employer.[28] Indeed, Hillier and Cameron's other maid-models seem to have spent little time doing housework; guests at Dimbola often complained about the untidiness and the disarray. Annie Thackeray visited over Easter in 1865 and wrote to a friend that "we have shocking bad dinners, and are obliged to have eggs and bacon to make up for almost every meal." Cameron was in a full flurry of work at that time, and Thackeray, herself a haphazard homemaker when she was busy with a novel, described it indulgently: Julia Margaret up every night until two in the morning soaking her photographs in cold water; the procession of young men with candles and maids carrying photographs across the lawn one evening; and the community of students, poets, painters, and old-fashioned eccentrics (like Thoby Prinsep in a cone-shaped hat, veil, and many coats).[29] No wonder meals were a low priority.

Choosing Hillier to play the Virgin Mary was not as radical as it may seem. Artist's models often came from the working classes, and Victorians were especially interested in the holy family's humble origins. Cameron would have been well aware of the controversies over Millais's carpenter's son in *Christ in the House of his Parents* and George Eliot's translation of *The Life of Jesus*, a German account that portrayed him as a historical everyman rather than a divine hero. In the Gospel of Luke, when an angel appears to Mary with the news of her destiny, she says: "*Ecce ancilla Dei,*" or, "Behold the handmaid of the Lord." This naming as a maid marks Mary's perfect submission[30] and it was the phrase that Dante Gabriel Rossetti used to title his famous painting of the Annunciation, for which he used his sister, the poet Christina, as a model. Cameron also relished the punning of names: in a photograph called *The Three Marys*, who in one version of the Gospels witness Jesus's resurrection, she uses three maids named Mary for the models.[31] For Cameron, casting Hillier as a Madonna would have strengthened her religious faith in miracles and transformations: the metamorphosis of Mary into Madonna at the Annunciation could be reaffirmed in her own transformation of another Mary into another Madonna. Just as she enjoyed the literal duplication of the name, Cameron relished the symbolic reference to the miracle of divine intervention, to the low becoming high and the mortal becoming immortal. And, of course, such transformations supported her sense of her own divine calling and her own creative powers. As a photographer, she could change natures and reveal the heroine lurking inside the peasant. Indeed, as at least one critic has noted, it may have been easier to imagine "universalizing" a working-class woman who would seem (to Cameron) to have less of a name and a history of her own.[32]

Hillier had a perfect face for a Madonna: it was round and symmetrical, with even features and full cheeks that suggest a postpartum body. If Julia Jackson seemed to reflect the classic beauty of ovals and lines, Hillier was all fleshly curves, and the children and babies she holds melt right into her voluminous drapery. She looks rather childish herself, with a curious blankness of expression that inspires calm. In images of Madonnas and children, Cameron's attention is equally interested in the child and the woman. She seems, as other scholars have noted, to bring a mother's eye and hand to those images in which the soft-focus lingers on the plump arms and tousled heads of sleepy children. Art historian Carol Mavor emphasizes the representation of touch in Cameron's work: the women and children always in contact, and the poignant evidence of Cameron's own handiwork in the scratches that have transferred from negative to print.[33] The touch is homoerotic and polymorphous, expressing a pleasure in flesh against flesh that is neither conventionally romantic nor sexual but located somewhere on the same continuum. Mavor rightly points out that Cameron's work is just as obviously erotic as Charles Dodgson/Lewis Carroll's, but Cameron has remained safe from accusations of pornography and the exploitation of children because of her position as a heterosexual bourgeois mother.[34]

There is no point in arguing whether Cameron intended her photographs to be erotic or not. Our post-Freudian, self-conscious definitions of intention and sexuality are inevitably different to hers. It is clear that Cameron's critics did not read her images as overtly sexual – they did sometimes express indignation at artworks that crossed some undefined line into "indecency" and they never levelled this accusation at her work. Nonetheless, the "beauty" that she sought so eagerly and that she was praised for so insistently is so closely entangled with sexual desire that there is no way of stating definitively that she or her sitters or her viewers kept the two things in distinct categories of their minds, hearts, and bodies. Beauty itself is erotic. Bodies are sexual. The draped women and half-clad children, the unbound hair and close-up faces easily suggest sexuality, even if they stay within the realm of allusion. The stillness and smallness of photographs (even Cameron's large ones) make them ideal for fetishization, and Cameron's repetitive representations of women and children lend themselves even more to voyeurism of all kinds.

Then there are the erotics of power, rarely discussed in relation to Cameron's work: Cameron almost always took photographs of people who were not her social equals, so her sittings were also performances of domination and submission in that rigidly hierarchical society. In posing and "taking" maids, children, and younger relatives, Cameron played the "mistress" of the house, whereas with older and more famous men she could play more ambiguously at being both "master" and "servant" to their geniuses. Her language often reflected those ambiguities, as when she itched to try her "master hand" on the now eighteen-year-old Annie Philpot, or when she decides she is finally worthy of photographing "my great Master," Sir John Herschel.[35] There are erotic pleasures in posing too, as Ellen Terry knew: Julia Jackson was always said to have been perfectly unconscious of her great beauty, but one imagines that she must have got something out of the long and uncomfortable sittings that she agreed to endure so often.[36]

Recent feminist scholarship on Cameron's work has emphasized her "maternal" vision, perhaps in part to deflect the problem of the erotic in her work. The obsessive representations of young women, the many variations on the Madonna, the profusion of heroines all seem intended to create a matriarchal lineage for photography that echoed the powerful matriarchy of Pattle sisters. Where once art critics saw Cameron as a puzzling anomaly in the history of photography's forefathers, now art historians look back to Cameron as "the Mother of all art photography," in a parade that ends with Sally Mann.[37] Some argue that by becoming a photographer Cameron took on a male role and a male position as viewer, which automatically makes her work radical and subversive of patriarchy.[38] Others argue that the photographs of women create a "composite portrait" of Victorian womanhood.[39] Mavor makes an interesting argument that Cameron is radical in the very breadth of her vision of the maternal: she can let mothers into the picture as active players and she can also let them out (in cropped photographs that push the mother to the edge of the frame).[40] This range of roles is in sharp contrast to the Victorian bourgeois ideal of a mother who is passive and yet ubiquitous – a matrix, so to speak, but not a player. It was a role that Emily Tennyson, for example, was often praised for, despite her efficiency in managing her husband's life and career.

What seems clear, at least, in these muddied waters is that to be a Victorian woman photographing Victorian women upset stereotypes. Instead of the classic cultural narrative of a young male artist producing art to re-create an idealized mother, Cameron presents us with an older female artist creating art to recover idealized children. By replicating her daughter figures and clinging like Mary to the sons she will lose, she wrote her own story into the history of art.[41] In this sense, the Madonna and child images dramatize the essence of Cameron's photographic project: to track the process of loss. Her letters full of longing for her children and her photographs full of close-up faces illustrate an urgent desire for presence. When it was time for Charlie Hay to leave home, she wrote Lord Overstone a long mournful letter complaining that soon all she would have left of him was his photograph [see figure].[42] These photographs imply an umbilical cord stretched to snapping point, as mothers gaze on children they know will eventually leave them.[43] Every

Madonna and child implies a pietà, especially for Victorians who faced high infant mortalities.

The power dynamics are important, though, in part because lurking behind the long-suffering mother (an expression Cameron actually used as the title for one of her Madonna portraits), waiting for the inevitable pain of loss and death, is the figure of another mother: Cameron herself, who as a photographer is powerful and authoritative. As Jeannene Przyblyski argues in a critique of recent scholarship on Cameron's "maternality," mothers are controlling as well as tender. They might be outside the law of the Father but they too could rule, as any Victorian knew well.[44] Cameron and her work lend themselves especially to this vision of the imperious Mother: she assertively sought out subjects and actively managed her sittings. Her well-known "bossiness" and the ensuing anecdotes combined her roles of eccentric artist and managing mom.

"Mother," then, could be a role like any other, and Cameron and Hillier both played it. The role bridged the gap between Cameron's secular work – her literary illustrations and portraits – and her religious allegories. Performances of religious allegories and biblical narratives were not a routine part of Victorian amateur theatricals; they trace their lineage to older, traditional folk cultures of pantomime, Christmas pageants, and passion plays. The Victorians were eccentric and theatrical, but they did not ordinarily dress up as Jesus or Mary unless they were posing for high art. Nonetheless, the rediscovery in England of Old Masters paintings from the Continent sparked enthusiasm for Catholic art and its iconography. Lord Lindsay, a member of Cameron's extended circle through his cousin Sir Coutts Lindsay, wrote a book on the symbolism of Christian art that included a table of visual references to spiritual things. Heaven, for example, was represented in art by the color blue.[45] The prominent art critic Anna Jameson also wrote many books on religious art, including *The Poetry of Sacred and Legendary Art* and *Legends of the Madonna*.

Cameron scholar Mike Weaver was the first to look closely at the role of Christian iconography in Cameron's work. He concluded that she was a "typologist," or one who "is endlessly preoccupied with the possibilities of relating persons and events from different times and places in history for moral and religious purposes."[46] Typology was originally a Protestant method of Bible scholarship that emphasized the ways in which the Old Testament foretold the New Testament. That is, Old Testament heroes like Noah were seen as "types" of Jesus Christ. It was exegesis by analogy – this character is like that character – and it organized the sprawling and diffuse Scriptures into a pattern of recognizable figures, particularly Jesus, the Virgin Mary, and Mary Magdalene. Not coincidentally, these figures are often found in Cameron's work, although she emphasized the women and she found their "types" everywhere: in Tennyson's poetry, in Shakespeare's plays, and in the people around her. Noah is a type of Christ but so are her friend Colonel Loyd-Lindsay, King Arthur, and Tennyson himself.[47]

Yet Cameron made some interesting revisions to accepted interpretations of the Bible. For example, she played with androgynous representations of Jesus, John the Baptist, and angels, often using female models to portray them. Cameron's great-niece Florence Fisher posed as the child John the Baptist and Mary Hillier modeled several times as *The Angel at the Tomb*, who was male in the Bible.[48] Weaver sees this as evidence of a "typological feminism."[49] Mavor too suggests that Cameron's blurred focus and her blurring of boundaries were also subversive of her orthodox subjects.[50] But it is possible that these practices seemed less radical at the time, when actresses like Ellen Terry routinely played boys' parts until their bodies developed.[51] Emily Tennyson's biographer, Ann Thwaite, discovered an account of a young visitor at Freshwater who reported that Tennyson took a fancy to dress up one of Cameron's nieces as a man: he lent her his coat and drew a charcoal moustache on her face with great delight.[52] Also, typology encouraged a sort of universalist view of humanity in which "details" like time, place, class, and perhaps even gender were less important than the essential natures of individuals. This will be discussed in more detail in the next chapter. If one's "real" nature was internal then one's external self could wear any sort of costume without necessarily being transgressive.

In December of 1864 Cameron turned her attention from personifications of female saints, Madonnas, and children toward her first series of allegorical representations of religious virtues. Again using Mary Hillier as model, she copyrighted images entitled *Grace Thro' Love*, *Meekness*, *Faith*, and *Joy*, and called the series *Fruits of the Spirit* [see figure] after a biblical text from the Epistle to the Galatians. In January she gave the nine photographs to the British Museum, her first entry into an institutional collection. Another pair of photographs from the same time, the *Five Foolish Virgins* and the *Five Wise Virgins*, have been much maligned as examples of her inferior compositional skills and her vague storytelling, but they are ambitious attempts to group several figures into a crowded frame. Cameron favored female subjects for these allegorical portraits but sometimes pursued men too. Emily Tennyson tells a story in a letter that winter of Cameron interrupting a conversation with a friend to rush out into the road shouting

> 'Stop him! Stop him! There he is, Time.' An old man was brought in with white hair . . . he was undressed, had no shirt on. Wanted scrubbing very much. Mrs. Cameron wraps him up in best shawls, puts an egg cup in his hand, turns him into 'Time,' but talks to him so much about his beautiful face that he is supposed to have grown very conceited at last . . .[53]

Interestingly, this anecdote suggests that Cameron did not always have her image in mind and then seek models for it, but rather found models and then developed roles for them to play. She also seemed to be always working, and Emily Tennyson marveled too at the "endless" stream of Madonnas and queens and virgins who poured forth from her fertile camera.

These allegorical works owe much to Watts's work, and it is clear that Watts was an early and influential advisor. It was Watts who supported himself with his Hall of Fame portraits while painting idealized visions of *Time and Oblivion*, *Hope*, and *Love and Death*. Cameron first of all owed that division in her own oeuvre to him, although her portraits were not as profitable. Watts felt ambivalent about the term "allegory" and preferred to think of his paintings as expressing abstract universal truths, not "mere pictorial forms, combined as in a kind of cryptogram," in the later words of G. K. Chesterton.[54] Cameron's best allegorical work also avoids the trap of looking like a rebus: in most of them one or two figures pose together with only the vaguest of narratives to give flesh to their grand titles. This abstraction, however, was essential to her mission of elevating photography into an art form. By the aesthetic criteria of the day, photography could only be considered an art if it could represent abstractions and ideals as well as physical reality.

Watts and Cameron shared a common devotion to idealism that grafted Protestant ethics onto Platonic aesthetics: in his preface to *Sketches of the History of Christian Art* Lord Lindsay wrote earnestly of the ideal as a striving toward perfection that balanced the beauty and strength of the body, the reason and the imagination, and the submission of passion in the spirit. Through intuition, the individual could progress from the bodily senses through the enlightened intellect to reach spiritual truth. This progressive, normative worldview was applied to individual lives and also whole civilizations.[55] For Watts, this philosophy was represented by his motto "The utmost for the highest," a phrase he invented for his bookplates and which Virginia Woolf mocked mercilessly in her play *Freshwater*.

In their surviving correspondence, now mostly held at the National Portrait Gallery in London, Cameron sends Watts her work and he scrawls back a critique dashed off between sittings. Watts hated writing, but it is his replies, not her effusive missives, that survive. His comments were encouraging but curt and candid: "I have received with your letter two beautiful photos more like old pictures than ever. I don't know that they are your very best but they are certainly amongst the most artistic," he wrote, characteristically, in June 1865.[56] Most of his notes are undated and some are filled with very specific advice about how to pose sitters (with sketches) and what effects to seek and avoid. In one letter he recommended dressing her grandchild in a yellowish shirt because his white shirt spoiled the picture. In several he complained about her technique and urged her to practice copying Wynfield's and others' work until she could effortlessly produce images free from scratches, spots, and smears. He was motivated by a striving after perfection but also by the art market, which, he reminded her, would not care for imperfections or too much repetition. He urged

Julia Margaret to vary her subjects more, to focus on the most important part of the face, and to experiment with studies of draped figures (she may have been following his advice in her later series of photographs after the Elgin Marbles). Ever practical, he admonished her not to waste her best, mounted prints on his critiques but to send him defective prints which he could judge just as easily. Always, he urged her on to better and better things: after a letter of high praise, he concludes, "you must not be satisfied there is more to be done & whilst that is the case we must never think anything done, I know your difficulties but the greatest things have been done under difficulties. Yours most sincerely GFW Signor."[57] Watts often painted from photographs and it is likely that Cameron's work influenced him as much as his did hers, though he was much further along in his career. They shared the same models on occasion and sometimes similar compositions in their portraits. Both loved and referred to the same Old Masters: Titian, Raphael, Perugino, Rembrandt, Michelangelo, Leonardo, Reni, and Giotto.[58] It was to these artists that Cameron and her reviewers always compared her work.

In the winter of 1865 Cameron sent another batch of photographs, including a "Raphaelesque Madonna" and a portrait of Henry Taylor, to the Photographic Society of Scotland. Her works did not win any prizes, and Cameron reacted with typical bravado:

> The picture that did receive the prize, called 'Brenda,' clearly proved to me that detail of table-cover, chair and crinoline skirt were essential to the judges of the art, which was then in its infancy. Since that miserable specimen, the author of 'Brenda' has so greatly improved that I am content to compete with him and content that those who value fidelity and manipulation should find me still behind him. Artists, however, immediately crowned me with laurels . . .[59]

The "author" in question was the photographer Henry Peach Robinson, who later wrote influential books on photography as well. Ironically, he shared her messianic zeal for photography as an art form, but he was on the other side of the battle line about focus. Even writing much later on, in 1874, Cameron was still clearly indignant about the slights she received from photographers about her use of soft-focus and she defended herself vigorously.

She was right to feel somewhat persecuted. Though the photographic establishment continued to accept and display her work, they invariably belittled it in reviews. One year into her career, the criticism of Cameron was so severe that the *British Journal of Photography* hoped in print that she had the hide of a rhinoceros – "for never has any photographer been subject to greater criticism than this lady." His or her sympathy ended there, however, for the critic considered her work unpresentable.[60] In February the *Photographic Journal* mourned: "we must give this

175

lady credit for daring originality, but at the expense of all other photographic qualities . . . . We are sorry to have to speak thus severely on the works of a lady, but we feel
compelled to do so in the interest of the art."[61] With this review the Photographic
Society tried to take back the ground of high art that Cameron seemed decisively to
have won. In April it awarded her an honorable mention in portraiture after Robinson's
prizewinner, but in May they were back on the attack:

> Admiring the enthusiasm of Mrs. Cameron, the committee much regret that
> they cannot concur in the lavish praise which has been bestowed on her pro-
> ductions by the non-photographic press, feeling convinced that she will herself
> adopt an entirely different mode of representing her poetic ideas when she has
> made herself acquainted with the capabilities of the art.[62]

The non-photographic praise that drew this response was almost surely a glowing
review of Cameron's work in the *Reader* in March. That art critic had compared
her work to Raphael and Leonardo and distinguished it from vulgar, professional
photography.[63]

In June, when Cameron's photographs again appeared in the annual exhibit of the
Photographic Society in London, the *Photographic News* weighed in with another
patronizing assessment of Cameron's ignorance,[64] and in July, when her work was on
display at Colnaghi's printsellers, the *Illustrated London News* retorted with more fulsome comparisons to a long list of Old Master painters, concluding that in her union
of science and art her images "afford a pleasure differing not only in degree, but
wholly in kind, from that to be derived from ordinary photographs. Many of them
startle the artistic spectator with a thrill of strange delight as at an unsuspected
discovery in nature."[65] As the struggle between art and photography critics continued
over the summer, it is hard not to conclude that Cameron was simply caught in the
middle. Being a woman clearly intensified the hostility she aroused. This clash of
values was bound to happen and Cameron and her work were just the flashpoint. If
so, she was not necessarily unlucky: the controversy provided a great deal of publicity
for a still inexperienced artist and encouraged a lot of her friends and fans to gather
forces around her. While mentioning her debt to Wynfield, the *Illustrated London
News* presented her as a solitary, self-taught pioneer fighting a hostile establishment.
For all its difficulties, that role was one that Cameron adopted eagerly.

Cameron pursued international notice in 1865 too, submitting her work to a
photographic society in Berlin (where she earned a bronze medal) and exhibiting her
work in a photographic exhibition in Dublin, which earned her more head-shaking
from the *Photographic Journal* in August. Clementina Hawarden, who had died suddenly early in the year, was posthumously praised, but the reviewer admitted to
having "very little hope" for Mrs. Cameron. Some photographs, he or she complained,

were so dark as to be illegible; Tennyson's features were indistinct; the Wise and Foolish Virgins looked "equally foolish."[66] Reviewers of both the Dublin and Berlin exhibits struggled to balance their perception of her artistic intentions and effects with their irritation at her "faulty" technique.[67]

Throughout the year Cameron had been assiduously pursuing publicity and sales using all of her connections: in May she took a series of portraits at Little Holland House of several influential friends in the art world, including William Michael Rossetti, Henry Cole, and probably Sir Coutts Lindsay. Cole was the founder of the South Kensington Museum (now the Victoria and Albert) and a friend and neighbor of the Thackerays (it was to Cole that Annie and Minnie first sent for help when they found their father dead in his room). He had also worked with Watts and Val Prinsep on murals for the new museum.[68] Cameron temporarily set up her studio at her sister's home and photographed many London celebrities there, including Robert Browning and her friends Lord and Lady Elcho. She worked doggedly, writing to Cole that one day she took twelve portraits and printed six dozen through the night. She seems to have hoped from the start that Cole would include her work in the new museum: she gave him a complete portfolio of her work from Colnaghi's and urged him to accept it for the museum. Her efforts succeeded and on August 10 the museum paid her £22 4s. 4d. for eighty prints. It was her first major sale, and, typically, Cameron forwarded another batch of thirty-four prints in September, gratis.[69]

Under Cole, the South Kensington Museum was one of the first museums to embrace photography. It undertook an ambitious campaign to photograph artworks and then hung these reproductions next to original paintings, sculptures, and objects. Cole was one of the original commissioners of the Great Exhibition of 1851, and he had a lifelong commitment to improving British design. When the Great Exhibition surprisingly yielded a large profit, he and Prince Albert advocated using the funds to support a new cultural center south of Hyde Park, which eventually became the complex in South Kensington. At the South Kensington Museum he created a Circulation Department which lent out parts of the museum's permanent collection (including Cameron's work) to regional museums across the country. He kept photographers on staff to document the collection; the photographs were then sold to the public or lent to other collections. Mark Haworth-Booth, curator of photography at the Victoria and Albert Museum, speculates that Cole may have acquired Cameron's work as inspiration for the designers who were then ornamenting the museum with decorative figures in terracotta.[70] The association with Cole and the museum was certainly advantageous to Cameron: her work was widely displayed and circulated, and in the next few years Cole even lent her two rooms in the museums as a studio. Though she was never employed by the museum, she seemed to be temporarily under its wing, and Cole may even have recruited sitters for her.[71]

Cole and Cameron were fashioned from the same pattern: he was indefatigable and had a finger in every pie. As "Felix Summerly" he wrote popular children's books, catalogued art collections, and designed bestselling tea sets. As Henry Cole he organized the Great Exhibition, reorganized the national schools of design, founded the South Kensington Museum, built the Royal Albert Hall, and established the Royal College of Music. In his spare time he wrote pamphlets, chaired committees, and raised eight children with his wife. He was a born reformer, criticized by people like Dickens for promoting culture through rules and committees but effective nonetheless in his practical goals. Among his causes he also encouraged the broadening of middle-class occupations for women by using them as engravers and working to get them admitted to the national schools of design.[72] As in Cameron's case, the result of all this prolific energy was a remarkable legacy of accomplishments but very little money. Despite his successes and his knighthood for public service, Cole left his widow and children in precarious financial straits.

While she was cultivating Cole and the South Kensington Museum, Cameron was simultaneously pursuing reviewers. In April Annie Thackeray published an anonymous piece on Cameron's work in the *Pall Mall Gazette*. Thackeray was just beginning her writing career, but she had excellent connections with journalists and publishers. In her short article she emphasized what can only be described as the "aura" of a photograph, despite Walter Benjamin's well-known claim that mechanical reproduction destroyed the aura of originality that clung to older art forms. Thackeray mused suggestively on the "interest and sentiment," so hard to describe in words but so distinct in one's apprehension, that characterize great art, though she goes out of her way to avoid critical judgment. Cameron's latest work, she noted, has the "indescribable presence of this natural feeling and real sentiment" that transcends the "mere inanimate copy." Thackeray's argument is consistent with other praise for Cameron in the art and general press, but is formulated in a very different style: it is glancing and seemingly effortless. When she describes a typical portrait sitting in a commercial studio, she makes it clear, by contrast, that Cameron is "*not* a popular artist," but she is not issuing the call to arms that characterizes Cameron's other reviews.[73]

It was around this time that Cameron gave an important, undated album of early work to Thackeray, inscribed: "Fatal to Photographs are Cups of tea and Coffee, Candles & Lamps, & Children's fingers!"[74] Joanne Lukitsh, who has worked extensively on this album, notes that unlike Cameron's reverent inscriptions to Watts or Herschel, this inscription places Thackeray's album in a domestic context. It is a gift between women and clearly to be viewed and shared in a family home. Since the Thackeray Album contains only one of the new portraits taken at Little Holland House in May 1865, Cameron probably gave Thackeray her album late in 1864 or early the next year.

The Thackeray Album does include a few portraits of mutual friends like Watts, Taylor, and Tennyson, but it emphasizes portraits or studies of women and children.[75]

With Cole and Annie Thackeray already secured as friends and professional allies through gifts of albums or sales of prints, Cameron continued to work systematically through her connections in the art world. Some time that year she gave a large undated album of 142 photographs to Sir Coutts Lindsay, friend and later founder of the Grosvenor Art Gallery.[76] As the South Kensington Museum made their major purchase of her work in August, she was busy assembling another significant album: this one to be given to her husband's old friend and the family's most loyal backer: Samuel Loyd, Lord Overstone. Overstone had made and inherited his large fortune from banking, but he spent it collecting art and keeping impecunious friends and relatives afloat. He was an earnest and scrupulous man. In February 1875 he summarized his wealth and examined his conscience carefully:

> Upon making up my Accounts for the year 1874, I am arrested by the magnitude of the Fortune which I appear to have accumulated. My first feeling is a moral fear that I have permitted myself to be overcome by a mean and unworthy love of mere wealth, valuing it not for its proper use, but solely for the sordid pleasure of contemplating its constant increase.
>
> I trust this has not been the case–And indeed upon a careful, and I hope candid, judgment of the circumstances, I do not think myself justly open to this censure.

His fortune was indeed staggering – the *Dictionary of National Biography* estimated that he died one of the richest men in England, with an estate of over two million pounds.[77] In the 1870s his annual income reached 100,000 pounds, of which he spent less than half and gave away some 21,000 pounds to his extended family and 15,000 pounds to churches and schools in 1874 alone. Over the years the Camerons received over 6,000 pounds thanks to his generosity.[78]

In May Overstone had quietly given the Camerons another thousand pounds to pay off debts[79] and the album – 111 photographs mounted with a carved wooden binding presented on August 5 – must have been a personal undertaking designed both to thank him and to interest him in her work. Her work, after all, was expensive, and it seems clear that Cameron was often pressured to cease or limit this unprofitable career. Though a collector and connoisseur, Overstone does not seem to have been impressed by her accomplishments. For the rest of the year he corresponded with their mutual friend George Norman about Charles Hay's health and Julia Norman's latest pregnancy, but he never mentioned the album that has come to be known with his name. "Every photograph taken from the Life & printed as well as taken by Julia Margaret Cameron," Cameron assured Overstone in the inscription. She provided a table of contents as well, which grouped the images into the now-familiar categories of her work: portraits, Madonna groups, and "fancy subjects for pictorial effect" (meaning illustrations from the imagination, or the fancy).[80] It included portraits of Overstone's extended family – his daughter and son-in-law and Sir Coutts Lindsay – but the portrait of Overstone himself had to wait until 1870. It included portraits of Cameron's family as well: Overstone's dear friend Charles Hay, but also Hardinge and Ewen, though the other Cameron children were surprisingly absent. There were also new portraits from that productive spring: Robert Browning, William Michael Rossetti, Lord and Lady Elcho, Charles Norman, Lady Adelaide Talbot, Minnie Thackeray, and Tennyson as the "Dirty Monk." These portraits had the effect of confirming the many connections within a privileged circle of class and culture. "We share the same world," Cameron was implying on the one hand.

On the other hand, she was fiercely defending her professional credentials: the album included portraits of the artists who praised and supported her work, like Holman Hunt and Watts. The art critic William Michael Rossetti was a potential reviewer of her work as well as a link in a chain to his famous brother and sister. In May, around the time she took his portrait, she wrote him urgent letters pressing him to review her work at the annual Photographic Society exhibit. He admired it, but wrote to his friend and colleague Frederic George Stephens delegating the request to him and urging him to see the show, collect the prints Cameron had left at Colnaghi's, and write up something. Stephens obliged with a short complimentary piece in the "Fine Art Gossip" column in the *Athenaeum*.[81] Cameron attempted to photograph all three of the Rossettis, whom she knew socially through Little Holland House, but succeeded only with William Michael. In 1867 Dante Gabriel growled a refusal through their mutual friend William Allingham.[82] Cameron gave him some of her photographs anyway and he wrote her an appreciative thank-you note.[83] Christina is known to have sat for Cameron but, tantalizingly, no print has survived.

Browning was a coup: Tennyson brought him to Little Holland House for a sitting, and legend has it that Cameron told him to stay still, left to look for something, and forgot all about him until she returned much later to find the poet still frozen in place.[84] Swathed in a cape, Browning was surprisingly resistant to idealization: the dapper, worldly man didn't seem to adapt readily to gloom and shadows and the proportions of the photograph somehow make him look smaller than life. Perhaps, under the circumstances, it was impossible, even for Cameron, to ask for another sitting. She did, however, photograph scenes from his poem "Sordello" the following year.

The album also included some two dozen images of Mary Hillier in Madonna and child poses, each variant with a slightly different name to evoke the noble qualities of the suffering, tender, expectant, loving, peaceful, patient, watchful, good woman. Alongside the cherubic children, they are a canny sample of her work to give to a renowned collector of Old Masters paintings. It is clear that Cameron felt the need to defend her expensive "hobby" to her family's creditor; the album was, among other things, an important piece of propaganda in that campaign. In June she had written candidly to her friend Jeanie Senior that their finances were so dire that their life in England was at risk: Australia and Bombay had been considered but dismissed, and they were once more considering a retreat to Ceylon to save money: "What will come to pass I know no more than those unborn creatures of the year 2000 who perhaps are already surveying with pity the world as it is now . . . ."[85] She worried about her sons' futures and complained that her expenses for photography were double her income from it, despite her hard work.

That summer Cameron seems to have been fighting desperately to preserve her professional life, which she must have pursued as least in part in the hope that it might help support the family. Or so she told herself and others, as she worked like a dynamo and ignored her balance sheets. Overstone's loans made their life in England possible but they were also a constant danger for Cameron, who must have known that Overstone was not one of her greatest fans. If he had decided to make her abandonment of photography a condition for one of his loans, her career would have been over. Hence the importance of the well-chosen gift that August. Perhaps it worked: Cameron did buy herself ten more years in England and the only condition Overstone and the Normans ever seem to have imposed on the Camerons in exchange for their loans was that Charles Hay consent to sell his beloved Rathoongodde. Like Julia Margaret's photography, the estate had been running up debts; the managing agents charged more to run it than the coffee crops brought in. Yet Charles Hay had vetoed every offer for the land until the fall of 1866, when Charles Norman described his father-in-law as "utterly penniless" and insisted that the sale be written into the agreement for the loan of another 1,500 pounds. The Camerons somehow avoided the inevitable in this as in other crises, and Rathoongodde was not sold. Norman also made it clear to his mother-in-law that this was positively the last time their friends would pay their debts and loan them money. Luckily, the 1865–66 coffee crop had been a good one, and the Bank of Bengal had just paid a higher-than-usual dividend on the invested money of the Camerons' marriage settlement.[86]

This was the context for Cameron's complete immersion in her work in 1865. She copyrighted ninety-one photographs,[87] pursued critics, and gave away promotional albums. She entered contests and exhibited everywhere she could. The photographs she sold to the South Kensington Museum were shown there that fall. Cameron was feeling low: money troubles were aggravated by anxiety about Julia Norman, who was sick from another difficult pregnancy. Her friend Kate Perry wrote to a mutual friend in November that

> Mrs. Cameron looked wretchedly aged, and quite broken down were it not for Annie Thackeray getting Mr. Cole to put her photographs into the K[ensington] Museum, where she took me to see them. They are very beautiful, and as usual she treats the many-headed monster, the public, as her dear familiar and gossip, writing in large hand on these photographs MY GRANDCHILD, JULIA MARGARET NORMAN, aged 6, with her nurse and so on . . .[88]

Around this time, Cameron began using Colnaghi's as her London agent for sales. Although all the records of this business relationship were destroyed during the Second World War, scholars speculate that she could have deposited negatives with Colnaghi's and had them make reprints to order, or she could have also deposited her own prints for them to sell for her, which she did late in 1865.[89] They could mount them and she could then sign or inscribe them, or have them autographed by the sitter. Although she always professed to do all her own printing, there is evidence that she sometimes had assistants and she did use the services of Colnaghi's throughout her career.[90] Later on she also entered into an arrangement with the Autotype Company, which made and sold long-lasting carbon prints from her negatives.

In November she put on her first one-woman show, renting a room from Colnaghi's on Pall Mall at her own cost, but it is unlikely to have been a financial success. She staffed it with one of her maids as a gallery assistant, printed up a flyer to serve as a catalogue, and offered artists half-price on any photographs they bought.[91] The *Illustrated London News* seems to have been the only journal that reviewed the show, strongly recommending it in two short pieces in successive issues. The critic praised the artistry, as usual, and then went on to praise the models, especially "the young ladies of various types of rare and refined female loveliness, or, at all events, possessed of a charm of expression which we suspect ordinary male photographers would fail to educe." One woman, he or she felt, was photographed rather too often, but the *Prospero and Miranda* she exhibited earned the highest praise.[92]

The best and most important of her reviews came out, unfortunately, just as the exhibit was closing. In January another of Cameron's literary friends took the trouble to praise her to the public in an unsigned notice. The poet Coventry Patmore was friends with Tennyson and with Cameron's sister Maria Jackson. Patmore was best known as the popular author of the poem cycle *The Angel in the House*, which gave rise to a name for the stereotype of Victorian femininity. A few years before, however, his beloved wife (upon whom the fictional Honoria was modeled) died, leaving Coventry with six small children. The Freshwater circle sprang into motion to help the family through their bereavement, as they would do for the Thackeray girls and many others: Maria Jackson temporarily took in the children and Emily Tennyson petitioned the Royal Literary Fund for a grant for Patmore. But this time the plan backfired. Patmore proudly rejected any financial assistance and in the crisscrossing of letters a serious estrangement grew between him and the Tennysons. They were never reconciled, although the split does not seem to have hindered his goodwill toward Cameron.[93]

In his review, Patmore is the first to accept that Cameron's work is art and to apply the terms of art criticism to it, instead of struggling with photography's status in general. He argues that her photographs – hovering between realism and idealism – radically challenge the assumption that idealism is the essential quality of art. He must have been familiar with Cameron's rhetoric about her work, because in his first sentence about it he seems to be echoing her later claims in her autobiography: "An amateur photographer, Mrs. Cameron, was the first person who had the wit to see that her mistakes were her successes, and henceforward to make her portraits systematically out of focus."[94] His critique of her work, instead of repeating the tug of war occurring between art and photography critics, anticipates the reception of Cameron's work in the early twentieth century: the group compositions and *tableaux vivants*, he claimed, were "grotesque," but the heads in the "grand style" were fine. He concludes rather anticlimactically by suggesting that Cameron's works would be excellent aids for artists and primly comments that they have been appreciated only in proportion to the artistic cultivation of the viewer.

Cameron was naturally pleased with this review and used it in her next offensive that month against two more potential supporters. She wrote William Michael Rossetti again on the twenty-third, scolding him for never commenting on her portrait of him, hinting that he should intervene to obtain some praise for her work from his brother, and asking outright if he couldn't find "any paper of <u>good</u> circulation" in which to publicize her exhibit. She added desperately that

> I am under a promise to stop Photography till I have recovered my outlay that is to say to take no <u>new</u> pictures + content myself to printing from the old + depend upon their sale–but this is duty–+ my delight therefore can only be in the past till a lucrative present gets me afloat again.[95]

Clearly, she had not escaped the financial crisis unscathed, and, just as clearly, her natural optimism resurfaced. She responded with an all-out campaign to maximize her sales and reputation.

A few days later she wrote Sir John Herschel a twenty-page letter, enclosing Patmore's review. Again, she dutifully referred to her gratitude to him for all his attentions and tried to explain her career in terms he would approve of:

I have now taken up Photography as something more serious than amusement. When I started Photography I hoped it might help me in the education of one of my Boys. I soon found that its outlay doubled its returns so that it became [a] matter of duty to me first to recover my Expenditure –and latterly my success in this hope is marvelous. Since I have acquired reputation if not fame in the Photographic world I sell as fast as I can print . . .[96]

This account of her motives was probably disingenuous; she was trying hard to impress Herschel and, perhaps, counter the boldness of the favor she was about to ask of him. In short, she again begs him at length for some "observations" about her work that she can use to promote sales. She assures him that her husband approves of her career and pre-empts Herschel's objections by suggesting that his daughter could take down his dictation at little trouble to him. She cites Patmore and Rossetti, and other artists' praise; she mentions medals from Germany; but, she pleads, "hitherto I have had no scientific notice." Her desperation is painful to read as she offers him any of her more than four hundred negatives from which to choose prints for himself and pretends that she has had no notice from him yet because she has been too diffident to ask. The pleas of the year before must have lain between them awkwardly.

In fact, Herschel was not unsympathetic, but whether from natural reserve or from a disapproval of her frank self-assertion he again denied her the favor. He wrote back without preamble on February 5: "My dear Mrs. Cameron, I really wish I saw any way in which I could quietly and without as it were stepping forth apropos to nothing at all express my opinion of the really great merit of your photographs."[97] He claimed ignorance of the language of art criticism – although of course it was precisely because he was not an artist that his opinion was so desirable to her. He insisted that his contributions to photochemistry were few now, without seeming to understand that his name alone would be valuable. He concluded, oddly, by suggesting that she do a group study in whiteface, with the models' hair, hands, and faces powdered to look like sculpture.[98] Perhaps Herschel was unable or unwilling to read between Cameron's lines and acknowledge her financial difficulties and her professional milieu. As a representative of an eroding amateur tradition in science, he may have been unable to see Cameron's photographs for what they were: products in the marketplace as well as studies in Truth and Beauty. Cameron's ambivalence in this regard may not have helped: she wanted it both ways – commercial and critical success – and her letter to Herschel may have lost some impact through this division of her energies.

Cameron wrote back immediately to thank him for his encouraging comments on her work and to boast anew about her latest efforts: "a series of Life-sized head [sic]–They are not only from the Life but to the Life and startle the Eye with wonder

& delight."[99] She dropped the question of his public comments again, and changed the subject to something safer: health problems – hers, his, Henry Taylor's, and now her friend Philip Worsley's. Worsley was a poet and translator who had suffered ill health for the past ten years. He had come to Freshwater for the sea air and during that winter and spring Cameron and his sisters nursed him through the last stages of tuberculosis. In her letters Cameron also commented that she was without children in the house for the first time in twenty-six years. Henry Herschel Hay and Charles Hay junior were at Charterhouse. Hardinge had started at Oxford and Ewen had left for Ceylon to manage Rathoongodde. Perhaps because she suddenly had no one to "do" for, as she complained in a letter, she devoted herself to Worsley. Though she doesn't mention it, that January Cameron's grandmother Madame de l'Etang finally passed away peacefully at Versailles. She had lived to meet her great-great-grandchildren.

The new "life-sized" heads were taken up at Watts's urging and they absorbed her attention that winter alongside Philip Worsley. They were made possible by Cameron's shift to a new lens and plate size around this time. The old camera used 11 by 9 inch glass negatives; her new camera took 15 by 12 inch plates. The new Dallmeyer Rapid Rectilinear lens had a longer focal length, enabling her to fill much more of the large plate with her image. Her exposures may have been longer, but the greater control over the focus and the impressive size of the print were worth it. On February 20 she copyrighted several photographs of children's heads that she described as "life size." The next day she crowed to Henry Cole that he must find her an occasion to present the twelve prints in the new series all at once to "electrify you with delight & startle the world. I hope it is no vain imagination of mine to say that the like have never been produced & never can be surpassed! I am waxing mad in my own conceit you will say–."[100] Her letter again shifts abruptly to a discussion of Worsley's slow decline:

> These great successes have come like meteors out of anxious troubled times–! I have been for 8 weeks nursing Philip Worsley on his dying bed– + I have been with him a great part of every day + also a great part of the night. The heart of man cannot conceive a sight more pitiful than the outward evidence of the breaking up of his whole being . . .[101]

It is hard to imagine that the abrupt daily contrast between life and death was not significant for her. As she attended Worsley, her new work strove after greater and greater lifelikeness, especially in rounded form and intimate close-up. She exclaimed to Cole: "Talk of roundness I have it in perfect perfection!"[102] From the beginning her work defied what she considered the "skeletal" outlines of sharp-focus photographs in favor of the round modeling of flesh out of light, shadow, and soft-focus. Critics too contrasted her work with the "death-like 'sharpness'" of other photographs.[103] Her words in describing Worsley's failing body are very similar to the vocabulary of outer form and inner nature that she used in describing her own portraits. One imagines she watched Worsley's disintegration carefully, already planning a portrait . . . Indeed, she would photograph him shortly before his death in May.[104] The portrait is much like one of her new life-sized heads: Worsley leans into the camera from what appear to be bedlinens with a grimly set mouth and staring eyes. He gazes upward at the viewer and the photographer, but his expression implies a fierce resistance to death and submission.[105]

Cameron was very proud of the new "life-sized heads" and liked to exhibit and sell them as a series of twelve close-up heads of children, named *Freddy, Alice, Katie, Beatrice,* and *Lizzie,* after their models.[106] She collected and bound them into a special two-volume set called *Photographs from the Life* that she gave to the Tennysons.[107] Containing forty-seven prints but few inscriptions by Cameron herself, these volumes occupy a middle ground between the earlier presentation albums and the later published photographs of the *Idylls of the King.* Cameron was not alone in being struck by the lifelikeness of these works: when she sent Herschel a copy of the intense close-up head called *The Mountain Nymph Sweet Liberty,* he responded that it was "a most astonishing piece of high relief–She is absolutely alive and thrusting out her head from the paper into the air."[108] This was exactly the effect Cameron wanted to achieve.

The association of photography and death was more than a cliché for the Victorians; it was an important part of the experience of a photograph. Though theorists like Roland Barthes have lately traced the metaphorical connections between the frozen image and the passing of time, in the nineteenth century photographs also literally recorded the dead in mourning portraits and albums. People collected photographs of memorials, and even of death announcements themselves. Of course the most frequent subjects were children, who left the fewest physical traces and often the deepest wounds in those who loved them. They were photographed as if they were sleeping, often tucked into their own beds.[109] For grieving parents, a photograph of the dead child could become a fetish, as when a man in New York wrote desperately to the *Photographic Journal* in London to ask how to improve the quality of the only photograph he owned of his only child whom he had lost.[110]

Cameron made several portraits in the summer of 1865 that bear an uncanny resemblance to the genre of postmortem photography. Most of them share the same composition of a young woman leaning over a prone, sleeping child so that the two bodies form rectangular and horizontal lines across the frame. In several, variously titled but usually modeled by Mary Hillier and Cameron's two-year-old grandson Archie, she has actually combined the woman and the child from two different negatives to experiment with a combination print (a technique her colleague Rejlander was well known for). In others, like *Prayer and Praise* [see figure], an extreme close-up of a family is organized around a prone child in the foreground, while the faces and bodies of the sibling, mother, and father bleed off the frame. It is a radical experiment with a fragmented, cropped image that anticipates Degas' paintings and photographs. Most obviously, she photographed one of her maids hovering over a still child and titled it *The Shunamite Woman and Her dead Son* [see figure]. In this photograph too the child's head is partly cropped off the frame. As Carol Mavor notes, these images play with deep-seated taboos, especially the pleasure of looking at death.[111] Although the dead child is posed for viewing, the mother does not herself look at him. These images unsettle our confidence in boundaries, especially those between life and death, reality and theater. We know the "sleeping" child in the post-mortem photographs is dead, but we still wonder if it could be asleep; we know the "dead" child in Cameron's portrait of the Shunamite Woman is asleep, but we still wonder if it could be dead. The paradox is reminiscent of the famous biblical passage that Cameron and her sisters inscribed on their father's memorial at St. John's Church in Calcutta: "And all wept and bewailed her, but Jesus said Weep not she is not dead, but sleepeth. (Luke VIII, 52)."[112]

Most theorists of photography's relationship to death have looked at the two as similar experiences: Christian Metz, for example, notes that photography marks the passage of time, thus documenting the very process of our dying, bit by bit.[113] For Roland Barthes, however, it is not process that links photography and death but their presentation – at heart, they are both theatrical: "photography is a primitive kind of theater, a kind of *Tableau Vivant*, a figuration of the motionless and made-up face beneath which we see the dead."[114] Nina Auerbach provocatively cites a line from Tennyson's *In Memoriam* ("men may rise on stepping-stones/of their dead selves to higher things") to argue that for the Victorians, death was the culmination of a life of fluctuating selves and thus eagerly sought and fetishized as much as feared. Victorians were anxiously aware of the fluidity of roles and identities: they expressed their anxiety in a fascination with theater and they believed that death would free them to become their essential selves, fixed for all time.[115] Arguably, it was these fluid, mobile, ever-dying selves that Cameron created and documented in the course of her career.

The height of theatricality was therefore the death of a child, who Auerbach suggests embodied the changing, mobile self more effectively than adults. The theater's endless transformations had to be visible to audiences, so the emphasis was placed on deathbed "conversion" scenes in more senses than one: these climaxes presented the spectacle of the changeable child becoming a fixed and stable icon, usually a visible illustration of a moral lesson.[116] In 1872 it was the death of a child, her great-niece Adeline Clogstoun, who inspired Cameron's only known postmortem portraits.

Adeline and her sisters Blanche and Mary were the granddaughters of Cameron's eldest sister Adeline Mackenzie. They were orphaned around 1870 and the girls were distributed around the extended family: Blanche became the adopted daughter of Watts and lived in the Prinsep household, and Mary and Adeline seem to have spent time with various families, including Cameron's.

In June 1872 Cameron recounted to Annie Thackeray the bizarre accident of Adeline's death: when their governess was sick, two of the sisters and a cousin were left unsupervised and in climbing and jumping on each other Adeline so injured her back that she died a few days afterwards. In the letter Cameron wrung her hands over her warnings to them and decided against an autopsy to determine the cause of death, out of pity for the feelings of the other girls. But her "reading" of the tragedy was entirely religious: it proved, she wrote, that Adeline had only been lent to her as a "bright example of her angel-like patience and endearing love."[117] She stressed the beauty of the dying girl and took four images of her after her death. She inscribed them: "From death." As Julian Cox has noted, in representing death as both beautiful and sentimental the photographs bear a striking resemblance to the most famous deathbed scene in Victorian literature: the death of Little Nell in Dickens' *The Old Curiosity Shop*.[118]

In an anecdote that may or may not be about Adeline's death, the American essayist Thomas Wentworth Higginson described observing a deathbed scene on a visit to Cameron and Tennyson at Freshwater. He recounted the usual eccentricities – Charles Hay "picturesque" in a blue dressing gown "with black velvet buttons and a heavy gold chain" – and then noted that the housemaids were all upstairs attending at a sick bed. Higginson

> was ushered into the chamber, where a beautiful child lay unconscious upon the bed, with weeping girls all around; and I shall never forget the scene when Tennyson bent over the pillow, with his sombre Italian look, and laid his hand on the unconscious forehead; it was like a picture by Ribera or Zamacois. The child, as I afterwards heard, never recovered consciousness, and died within a few days.[119]

The verbal description is startling in its dependence on the visual and theatrical. Clearly, dying had to be visualized to be felt and appreciated. The deathbed is a stage around which an audience clusters; the dying child is the star.

In 1866 Cameron's photographs came out of a heightened sense of life and death, of transience and permanence. As her domestic world changed – children left home, grandchildren appeared, friends and relations died, and the family finances teetered on the edge of catastrophe – she invested more and more of her emotional energy in her work, especially the new life-sized heads that would become something of her signature. That winter she again entered the photographic society competition in Berlin and this time gained a gold medal. Over the summer she exhibited in nearby Southampton at the Hartley Institution and won a silver medal and good reviews there too. In December she again rented the French Gallery for a one-woman show. All this at a time when the family was "penniless" and she was undoubtedly under pressure to give up her expensive "hobby."

The life-sized heads that Cameron produced out of her close contact with death in 1866 paved the way for what art historians once agreed were the best works of her career. Gernsheim, in his ground-breaking monograph on Cameron, argued that in 1867–70 she was at the height of her powers, and life-sized heads like *The Mountain Nymph Sweet Liberty* and May Prinsep as Beatrice are among those few he calls "masterpieces."[120] The life-sized heads of women and children paved the way for the bold, experimental portraits of famous men in the next few years, creating a pantheon of "immortal heads" out of Cameron's fear of death and longing for permanence.

CHAPTER 8

Kings and Beggars, Heroes and Heroines

O NE SPRING DAY in 1867 a young gentleman knocked on the door at Dimbola. Though unknown to the family, he had been to one of Cameron's exhibits in London in November of 1865 and there he had spotted Mary Ryan working as a gallery assistant. He had been much struck by her appearance and by the photographs as well. He had bought all the photographs in which she appeared, asked her to write up a bill, and left the exhibition.[1]

Mary Ryan had a colorful history.[2] Some time around 1859, when the Camerons were still living in a suburb of London, Julia Margaret had been approached by an Irish woman who was begging with her daughter on the street. Cameron took the two in, found the woman a job, and – struck perhaps by the beauty of the child – took over the child's upbringing. As many Dickens novels demonstrate, such arrangements were not all that unusual in the nineteenth century. Parents were less possessive about their children than they are now, and they would frequently lend them to others if they believed that the child would benefit. In this case, Mrs. Ryan and Mrs. Cameron probably believed that the arrangement was to Mary's advantage, although there is some evidence that Mrs. Ryan tried to reclaim Mary later on and was rebuffed. It is also uncertain what Cameron's original intentions were toward the girl: some accounts, including Cameron's own, describe Mary Ryan as a member of the family who unfortunately had to become a maid when money ran short. Others imply that she was always a maid, who happened to be educated with Cameron's own children.

It is clear, at least, that Cameron took Ryan with her when the family moved to the Isle of Wight in 1860. Some of Cameron's friends worried about the girl's future: Henry Taylor noted that she loved books and wondered what use it would be to a servant girl to read. He suggested that Cameron's generosity would only make the girl unhappy with her station in life. In 1861 he wrote to a friend,

Mrs. Cameron sees, I think, that these are rather puzzling questions; and finding
no satisfactory answer to them at present, is disposed to let time solve them, and
guard herself against petting the beggar more than she can help. The manners
and customs of her and her race (for her sisters are like her in some things) have
more of hope than of reason in them, and if foreseeing difficulties, they always
expect to be able to deal with them as they arise.

Taylor later noted that over the years Ryan was sometimes "rather naughty, and
revolts of the household and no small difficulties occurred from time to time, but
none were suffered to prevail."[3] In 1863, when Rejlander photographed both
Tennyson's and Cameron's households, the domestic tableaux [see figure] clearly
show Ryan as one of several maids drawing water and doing other outdoor chores
where the light was plentiful enough for photography. The middle-class ladies in the
photographs – including Cameron herself – all appear in dark, ruffled dresses. Ryan,
like the other maids, is dressed in a simple white dress and apron. Her sleeves are
rolled up to show capable arms. Her hair is coiled neatly and covered by a white ker-
chief. Her smile shows through the fixed poses of mid-Victorian photography. Though
her education may have placed her in a limbo state between the working and middle
classes, her daily duties and her costume identify her clearly as a servant.[4] Like
Henry Taylor, many of Cameron's neighbors must have shaken their heads, eyed the
lovely girl, and asked themselves that most Victorian question: "What will become of
her?"

Once Cameron had taken up photography late in 1863, Mary Ryan was one of her
favorite models. Cameron's 1865 exhibit included photographs of Ryan posing as
Queen Esther fainting before King Ahasuerus, from a story in the Bible about a
Jewish heroine pleading for her people, and as Miranda in a photograph entitled
Prospero and Miranda. While her fellow servant Mary Hillier specialized in Madonnas
and religious portraits, Mary Ryan usually played characters from literature or art.
Mary Hillier had a full, round face and a solemn, impassive expression that seemed
suited to sacred subjects. Mary Ryan, on the other hand, looked like the girl next
door: with her button nose and ready smile she was better suited for ingénue roles
like Shakespeare's Miranda. Both Marys may also have served as photographic
assistants to Cameron.

Perhaps it was Mary Ryan herself who opened the door at Dimbola in 1867 to discover the young gentleman from the gallery in London. Helmut Gernsheim, Cameron's
first biographer, tells the story with relish.[5] "The wildly romantic young man with long
hair" was brought into the drawing room, where he announced: "I have come to ask
for the hand of your housemaid. I saw her at your exhibition and I have all the time
kept the bill she wrote out for me next to my heart." He had waited until he had a

secure post in the Indian civil service and was "in no way deterred" by Ryan's inferior class. According to Gernsheim, Cameron carefully obtained permission from the couple's parents and sponsored the wedding in August at her own home.

The young gentleman turned out to be Henry Stedman Cotton, the son and grandson of East India Company nabobs. His family, in other words, had much in common with Cameron's and their social status was well above that of Mary Ryan. Emily Tennyson described him rather ominously soon after she must have met him, in mid-April:

> rather a handsome face with hair that is reddish, the eyes of an enemy more than of a friend, his face freckled, middle height. Very considerable ability, but a Comtiste, believing nothing that cannot be proved from experience. It was his worship of Nature that made him [decide to] marry Mary Ryan. He saw that photograph of her as Cordelia kneeling before Mr. Henry Taylor as King Lear at Mrs. Cameron's photographic gallery and thereupon decided to make her his wife.[6]

Cameron spent the month of July photographing Ryan and Cotton in romantic poses: in one, they model as *Romeo and Juliet* [see figure]. Ryan looks as if she is pulling away from Cotton's embrace, but this visual evidence of unease (if it is that) is never backed up with any textual evidence that Ryan felt anything other than pleased at her supreme good fortune. Cameron photographed them as a couple from Robert Browning's poem "Sordello." She also photographed Cotton as King Cophetua, from a poem by Tennyson about a king who spies a virtuous beggar maid and makes her his queen. Cameron eventually made much use of this comparison in both her photographs and her writing.

Cameron was clearly delighted by Ryan's good fortune in obtaining such a match. She was not a snob and she was an inveterate matchmaker, so this union must have charmed her. Indeed, her treatment of her maids was one of the many ways in which she flouted Victorian conventions, often just barely staying within certain uncrossable boundaries. Wilfred Ward, who lived on the Isle of Wight as a child in the 1860s, reminisced many years later that Cameron often took the "two Marys" into society with her, and once she even brought them as guests to the annual Cowes Regatta, the yacht race that was a popular social event for Victorian aristocrats. He noted that "the result was most embarrassing to Mrs. Cameron, as some of the more susceptible young men of the party paid them attentions which made the duties of a chaperon very onerous."[7] Emily Tennyson noted in a letter to Alfred once that their son Hallam had lifted his hat to a carriage full of women to discover that the "ladies" were only "Cameronian maids" who had borrowed the carriage to have tea with the soldiers at the local fort.[8] On the other hand, Cameron could be quite a stickler for the distinctions of rank. In a letter from 1866 Henry Taylor related a comic account of accompanying Cameron and two unidentified women, one a maid and the other a model, to London. Both model and maid traveled second-class, while Cameron and Taylor traveled first-class. Upon arrival in London, Cameron asked the model to climb onto the top of the carriage and ride outside like servants did. The model demurred. Taylor notes Cameron's response:

> Pretensions put down swiftly and strongly. Model ducks under and mounts up. Arrival – model lectured on difference of ranks and introduced to the Madonna and the Beggar-maid as models who were humble and knew their place – Model apologizes . . .[9]

It is interesting that even in 1866, well before the appearance of Cotton as King Cophetua, Mary Ryan was already known as the "Beggar-maid."

The wedding was set to take place on August 1 in the local church in Freshwater, with Mary's mother in attendance and Julia and Charles Cameron as witnesses. Adolphus Liddell, a cousin of Alice Liddell of *Alice in Wonderland* fame, attended the wedding dinner the evening before and was confounded by the mixture of upper and lower classes: "I sat between the two maids," he wrote later in his autobiography, "and I don't think I ever felt more shy, or had greater difficulty in making conversation."[10] Ryan asked Kate Shepherd, another maid in Cameron's home, to be her bridesmaid. The Tennysons attended, and lent their carriage to take the bride to church and later bear the married couple away to begin their new life together. The laureate's youngest son, Lionel, donned a gray suit and white gloves and acted as a page.[11]

On the wedding day the respectable young bridegroom suddenly noticed Kate Shepherd and rushed over to her with the words: "It is you I want to marry." Luckily, Cameron got the distracting bridesmaid out of the way, the ceremony continued, and Ryan easily "adapted herself to her new station" as wife of the future Sir Henry Cotton. Indeed, the story has a little-known conclusion: Cameron's great-niece Laura Gurney Troubridge retold the tale in her autobiography, claiming Watts told her that

> On their return from their honeymoon, Mr. and Mrs. C[otton] paid a visit to Aunt Julia, who arranged a small dinner party for them, and the party were, of course, waited on by Mrs. C's former fellow-servants. When the bride, attired in her smart satins and laces, came into the hall, she kissed each of her former associates, as a tribute to their friendship and work together, and, that duty done, she took no further notice of them, bearing herself in all respects as her husband's wife and the equal of anybody there.

This story was told approvingly by both Troubridge and Watts as evidence of "what a true lady she was in her mind and spirit."[12] Ryan's role-playing began in costume (posing as a maid, as a beggar girl, as a Shakespearean heroine) and it ended in costume (the satins and laces of a lady); her exit from the Freshwater stage was perceived as triumphant.

The couple left England for India on September 23. Though Gernsheim corresponded with some of their grandchildren and Cotton himself wrote an autobiography, Mary Ryan's response to her own romantic story is entirely absent.[13] There is some evidence that this unconventional marriage conquered more obstacles than just an indecisive bridegroom: Mrs. Ryan, for one, appears to have doubted whether the marriage would make her daughter happy[14] and Henry Cotton's parents seem to have been opposed to it as well. One traveler to the Isle of Wight as late as 1870 was regaled with island gossip about the wedding: the clergy of the island reportedly refused to conduct the service, even though Cotton was of age, because of his parents' disapproval. A clergyman had to be "imported" from the mainland for the ceremony, and many islanders condemned the local clergy for siding with the parents over the romantic couple.[15] Indeed, the story has been a famous part of Cameron lore from early on: even in its obituary for Cameron *The Times* of Ceylon retold the story of the maid who "used to dust the flour from her arms [so] that she might meet her suitor in the library."[16]

At the wedding Mrs. Ryan is supposed to have asked Mr. Cameron if he wasn't disappointed that Mary wasn't marrying his son Charlie. The story provides no answer for Mr. Cameron, but one can easily guess that, quite on the contrary, he may have been much relieved that Mary had made such a good match without the sacrifice of one of his sons. The Camerons' democratic impulses may have stopped short at that degree of cross-class intimacy. Indeed, one wonders how parlormaids chosen for their beauty and five grown sons shared one house without incident. In any case, Charlie Hay never did marry.

Cameron herself gives Ryan and Cotton's story a great deal of attention in *Annals of My Glass House*. Characteristically, she attributes the success of the marriage to her photography.

> Entirely out of the Prospero and Miranda picture sprung a marriage which has, I hope, cemented the welfare and well-being of a real King Cophetua who, in the Miranda, saw the prize which has proved a jewel in that monarch's crown. The sight of the picture caused the resolve to be uttered which, after 18 months of constancy, was matured by personal knowledge, then fulfilled, producing one of the prettiest idylls of real life that can be conceived, and what is of far more importance, a marriage of bliss with children worthy of being photographed, as their mother had been, for their beauty . . .[17]

Cameron wrote this autobiographical fragment in 1874, the same year that she produced her *Idylls of the King*, which included a photograph depicting Tennyson's King Cophetua and the Beggar Maid.[18] Her description of the romance and marriage blurs the boundaries between the different stories she photographed and even between the models and the characters they portrayed. It is clear from the photographs that she took of the couple in 1867 that she enjoyed the merging of their artistic and real-life roles when she chose to photograph them as Romeo and Juliet, or Cotton as King Cophetua. This was typical of a punning, or literal-minded, tendency in her art; similarly, she relished posing Mary Hillier as Mary the Madonna, or a girl named Magdalene as Tennyson's Maud because Maud was a Victorian nickname for Magdalene. Mary Ryan was clearly destined to play the beggar maid. In Ryan's case, however, Cameron seems to have eagerly endorsed the idea that her photography had created a reality instead of merely reflecting one.

Cameron's words in the autobiography make this explicit. "Entirely out of the Prospero and Miranda picture sprung a marriage . . ." she writes, claiming all credit for the marriage of Cotton and Ryan. She does not in fact name the couple in her account, but continues to call them by a confused set of character names: Cotton is always King Cophetua, from Tennyson's poem, and Ryan is alternately the beggar maid or Miranda. The odd sentence that jumbles the characters to claim that the "real King Cophetua" found his prize in "Miranda" is not as odd as it first appears: Tennyson himself cites Shakespeare's *Romeo and Juliet* as the source for his poem. *Romeo and Juliet* includes the line ". . . Cupid, he that shot so trim,/When King Cophetua loved the beggar-maid." Both Shakespeare and Tennyson got the original story of King Cophetua from an old English ballad, which Tennyson knew through *Percy's Reliques*, a seventeenth-century anthology of poetry. Cameron would likely have known these overlapping sources from her familiarity with the works of Tennyson and Shakespeare, so her jumbling of romantic couples from both sources was actually rather canny. For Cameron and her knowing circle of poets and authors, it might have been something of a private joke.

The King Cophetua of Shakespeare and Percy was one of Cupid's hapless victims. In Percy's ballad, he is an African king who rejected "nature's lawes" and "cared not for women-kinde."[19] He is rebuked, and his desire redirected, by Cupid's arrow, which he deeply resents, though the poem insists that he and the beggar maid live happily ever after. Tennyson omits this context and distills the lengthy ballad into sixteen succinct lines of iambic tetrameter. Cameron might have enjoyed the Cupid background, though, with its parallels to her role in "shooting" photographs of her own hapless victims and her insistence on taking the credit for the match herself. Indeed, in 1870 Cameron composed a photograph entitled *Cupid's Pencil of Light*, which represents Cupid as a photographer, complete with a literal pencil that "draws" on a glowing white page, instead of as a matchmaker armed with an arrow.[20]

Both Tennyson and Cameron omit the African origins of King Cophetua when they update Percy's ballad. Yet colonial locations are key to romantic myths, as seen in

Cameron's early exposure to Romantic literature as well. Though England's class structures were changing with industrialization and political reform, society at home was still quite rule-bound and it was far easier to embrace cross-class and inter-racial relationships when they occurred "elsewhere." Love could conquer all over there, but here social differences mattered intensely. It was in fact for his administrative service in India that Cotton was eventually knighted, and Ryan literally became "Lady Cotton."[21] Yet Cameron's account of the story privileges photography as the agency of this transformation: the romance began with Cameron's photograph and it ends with the creation of children "worthy of being photographed." For Cameron, the emphasis is always on the photography: it is photography that confers value and status, and photography that transforms Ryan into a lady; the class relations and the economics of empire are submerged in the literary allusions.

Cameron's photograph *King Cophetua and the Beggar Maid*, included in the second volume of her collaborative edition of *Idylls of the King* but probably taken earlier, is a curiously literal visualization of the story and of Tennyson's poem. Depending on the date it was taken, it may or may not have been a reference to Cotton and Ryan's real-life marriage. Here is the text of Tennyson's poem, entitled "The Beggar Maid":

> Her arms across her breast she laid;
> She was more fair than words can say:
> Barefooted came the beggar maid
> Before the King Cophetua.
> In robe and crown the king stept down,
> To meet and greet her on her way;
> 'It is no wonder,' said the lords,
> 'She is more beautiful than day.'
>
> As shines the moon in clouded skies,
> She in her poor attire was seen:
> One praised her ankles, one her eyes,
> So sweet a face, such angel grace,
> In all that land had never been:
> Cophetua sware a royal oath:
> 'This beggar maid shall be my queen!'

In her photograph Cameron duly visualized every detail about the king and the beggar maid: the crossed arms; the robe and crown; even the moon itself. With props and gesture she attempts not to portray the characters as much as tell the plot itself. The photograph is taken from a low viewpoint[22] and attempts to catch King

Cophetua in the very act of stepping off the platform. The class levels have been literalized, as they were in Tennyson's poem: the king is actually standing above the beggar girl. The Pre-Raphaelite painter Edward Burne-Jones later painted another version of this encounter, and he placed the king in the center of the composition, looking up at the standing beggar girl, who was similarly attired and posed.

Cameron's representation of the beggar girl is ambivalent: the girl wears revealing clothes, yet she covers herself modestly. As other scholars have noted in derision, the scene looks extremely posed: the woman, for example, is carefully situated so that she can be viewed equally well by the "King" and by the viewer of the photograph, although she herself stares vacantly into space. The backdrop to the photograph looks remarkably like a stage set: the models are enclosed within makeshift walls, curtains frame them, and a spotlight is fixed on them. Art historians have persuasively argued that Cameron's explicit theatricality in images like this one may have been an attempt to balance the competing demands of photography's realism with an imaginary subject.[23] Without these theatrical cues, Victorian critics and viewers could be confused as to how to read an ostensibly "truthful" image of an entirely imaginary scene. Often these "artificial" photographs were more admired by the Victorians than they are by critics today.

By the middle of the nineteenth century, class distinctions in England were both more fluid than ever and more fervently upheld. Cameron was viewed as eccentric for bringing her maids to social events, but she was not ostracized. Cotton and Ryan's marriage, while unconventional, was not insupportable. Such cross-class marriages were hardly unheard of, especially in Cameron's bohemian circle. The Pre-Raphaelite artists whom she knew from Little Holland House were famous for discovering beautiful shop girls, painting them obsessively, and then marrying them. Dante Gabriel Rossetti's marriage to the working-class model and artist Elizabeth Siddall had ended tragically with her death in 1862. William Morris and Ford Madox Brown had also married working-class women who modeled for them.

But the most interesting parallel of a cross-class marriage during this period is undoubtedly the secret relationship between the poet Arthur Munby and Hannah Cullwick, a maidservant. Munby was a good friend of Rossetti's and a gentleman who moved in the same circles as Cameron, though there is no known evidence of any meeting between them. He was obsessed with working-class women: he sought them out for conversations, flirtations, and also for photographic sittings. His personal papers at Trinity College, Cambridge include boxes full of photographs of Victorian working-class women that he had commissioned. During the 1860s, he maintained a complicated relationship with a maid-of-all-work, Hannah Cullwick, whom he eventually secretly married in 1873, though for years they continued to pretend that she was his maid. Like Ryan, Cullwick often posed for photographs, delighting Munby by her ability to appear as a lady as well as "in her dirt." She was photographed in other poses and roles as well – as a slave, as a man, and as a rural peasant. "Lady" and "maid" seem to have been simply other performances that she played for Munby, though she much preferred "maid." Perhaps Cullwick intuited what Cameron's models learned by experience – that working-class women had a greater range of roles to play than their "respectable" sisters.[24]

The Cinderella stories of upward mobility through romance were intimately connected with evolving cultural attitudes. Between 1866 and 1868, Matthew Arnold reacted to growing agitation for political reform by publishing the widely read articles that were collected as *Culture and Anarchy*. He championed the role of education and culture, especially the arts and humanities, in reforming society. Victorians increasingly viewed art and literature not just as luxuries in life, but as a crucial part of social policy. Arnold's advocacy of culture as a humanizing influence, especially for the working classes, was intended to be an explicit alternative to extending the vote. In the acrimonious debates over the 1867 Reform Act, influential intellectuals like Arnold and George Eliot argued that the working classes must first prove themselves worthy of the vote – through self-improvement and immersion in culture – before it should be granted. Political power hinged on first having cultural authority. Others, like John Stuart Mill, believed that the act of voting itself improved citizenship, and Mill worked assiduously to extend the vote to women as well. In both art and politics the very nature of class was in question: was class an essential identity that was fixed forever, perhaps by divine law? If so, then the working classes were fundamentally "different" and deserved to be governed by their betters. But if class (and, Mill would add, gender) was a matter of circumstances, of playing different roles at different times, then art and politics could also create new roles and characters for people. Politics had the power to transform a factory worker into a voter, perhaps one of those who would go on to found the new Labour Party in Britain by the end of the century. Art had the power to transform maidservants into ladies and queens.

Cameron's position in the political dramas surrounding the Second Reform Act is hard to judge. She knew both Benjamin Disraeli and William Gladstone, respectively the Conservative and Liberal Party leaders, from the time they both spent at her sister's salon at Little Holland House. But she may well have been more influenced by her friend Thomas Carlyle's vehement opposition to reform. Cameron had been friends with Carlyle and his vivacious wife, Jane Welsh Carlyle, since the move from India to England. As usual, Cameron had treated the curmudgeonly critic with fearless aplomb: she once sent the famous agnostic a prayerbook, to which the undaunted Carlyle responded: "Either the Devil or Julia Cameron must have sent me this!"[25] Both Carlyles treated her with the resigned affection and exasperation often aroused by Cameron's more outrageous stunts. Jane Carlyle dramatizes one of Cameron's visits to their Chelsea home in a letter from 1864 thus:

> An *inburst* of Mrs. Cameron and Mr. Watts (the Artist), the former hardly to be restrained from forcing her way into Mr C's bedroom while he was changing his trousers!! – I told *her* . . . 'It is a dangerous affair, rather, that you are there entering on, Mam!'[26]

Thomas Carlyle probably had greater patience for Charles Hay Cameron, a fellow Scot and scholar. In a letter from 1851 he describes a dinner party that he had attended reluctantly at a mutual friend's home: "Cameron there (husband of Mrs Cn) . . . a passabler evening than was hoped. Cameron has snow-white hair, a sleek small red face, lively little black eyes, and no *chin* to speak of; seems to be of Scotch breed or birth: may the Heavens be good to him, poor little fellow!"[27]

By the 1860s, Carlyle was the sage of Chelsea, and enjoying one of the high points in his reputation. In 1866 the stonemason's son had made a triumphant return to Scotland, where he was offered an honorary degree from the University of Edinburgh. During that trip, however, Jane Carlyle died suddenly, and a grief-stricken Thomas spent the next year reading her diaries and letters and mourning her. Jane's writings told her side of the story of their marriage, and Thomas found it eye-opening. Filled with remorse for having taken her for granted, he resolved to publish a reminiscence that would display her wit and talent to the world. From that book was born the dominant story of the Carlyles' marriage: the brilliant heiress had sacrificed herself to become the handmaiden to her husband's genius. Day in and day out Jane battled noise and tiresome visitors and all the tedious details of running a thrifty Victorian home so that Thomas could write about Frederick the Great's battles and read his drafts aloud to her in the evening.

Like George Eliot's Dorothea Brooke, many intellectual Victorian women sought partnerships with scholarly husbands. Some envisioned translating, transcribing, and cataloguing, content to be uncredited collaborators. Even this modest ambition was often dashed. Instead, the reality was often closer to that of Emily Tennyson and Jane Carlyle: answering fan mail; arranging a household routine around the precious work; and soothing the fragile egos that were hidden from public view. Cameron's niece Julia Jackson would take on this mantle in her second marriage to Leslie Stephen. After Julia Stephen's death, Leslie Stephen tried to push his daughters Vanessa and Virginia into a similar role, but they rebelled against the life of self-sacrifice that their mother had chosen.

In the spring and summer of 1867, while Cameron was matchmaking, a penitent Carlyle was brooding about Jane and ranting about reform. In August he published "Shooting Niagara – And After?," his most virulent attack on the efforts to extend the franchise. The American metaphor was carefully chosen: Carlyle believed that the United States had already shot the rapids and was descending into the abyss of unfettered democracy, where he feared England would soon end up as well. In the 1860s Carlyle and his former friend John Stuart Mill represented two diametrically opposed Victorian views: Mill advocated a "liberal" conception of human nature as molded by changeable human laws and history; Carlyle was equally ardent in defending the "conservative" position that universal laws fixed human nature in its essential character in all times and places. Carlyle's politics were often hard to predict over the course of a long career, but he always insisted on the immutable division between masters and servants, and work as the goal of life. In context, this meant that the imperial English were born to rule the world and the governed classes should just follow orders. "Shooting Niagara – And After?" offers a vivid portrait of an England en route to ruination, but it holds out a shred of hope that "men of genius" and other natural aristocrats might yet grab the rudder.[28]

Men of genius, that is, like Carlyle himself. Carlyle had prophetically lectured in 1840 on the hero as man of letters, and had then become one himself. "In the true Literary Man," he lectured, "there is thus ever, acknowledged or not by the world, a sacredness: he is the light of the world, the world's Priest."[29] The secular spirit of the age had turned the Victorians' immense tendency to worship toward the gifted men and women in their midst. The Romantic poets had started this hero worship of writers and artists by declaring the poet "the unacknowledged legislator of the world," in Shelley's phrase. The Victorians, plagued by doubts about God's existence, followed up by pouring their faith into charismatic preachers, poets, and politicians, creating a new cult of celebrity. This suited Carlyle perfectly: he believed passionately that "Universal History, the history of what man has accomplished in this world, is at bottom the History of the Great Men who have worked here,"[30] and few Victorians were more personally charismatic than he.

By temperament and by profession, Cameron was perfectly positioned to make hay of this hero worship. She had a strong urge to worship within her, and her portraits of John Herschel, Henry Taylor, and Alfred Tennyson were some of the results. Cameron's now-famous portraits of those Victorian "men of genius" were much on her mind in 1867, when several were completed and exhibited. On April 4 Cameron had packed up a cartload of photographic equipment and chemicals and descended on Collingwood, the home of John Herschel. She had been eager to photograph her old friend since she first took up photography, but the ailing septuagenarian did not often leave home. So during that busy and productive spring Cameron went to him, bringing along Mary Ryan as an assistant. She wrote to Lady Herschel asking for a dark room with one window that she would herself cover with yellow calico. She promised to be no trouble.[31]

In his diary Herschel described two "intense" and "energetic" days of photography on April 5 and 6, and then on April 8 he noted with seeming relief that Cameron and Ryan had finally left, with photographs in their blackened hands.[32] The results were worth the effort: Cameron's portraits of Herschel have been justly acclaimed as among her best work [see figure]. It is said that Cameron fluffed up Herschel's snowy hair to achieve the effect of the aureole around the astronomer's head, and she also emphasized his rheumy, far-sighted gaze. The close-up version of the three Herschel images that she took in that sitting reveals that she adapted her new work on life-sized heads into a signature style for photographing "great men." Like the Carlyle portrait taken a few months later, the photograph is sharply bisected by extreme shadow and bright light. It features a disembodied head leaning into the viewer in dramatic close-up. The compositions often entail a significant asymmetry – here, one eye appears slightly smaller than the other. Years later, in her autobiographical fragment, she would refer back to those photographs and the combination of love, reverence, and genius that created them. Herschel, she wrote, "was to me as a Teacher and a High Priest. From my earliest girlhood I had loved and honoured him, and it was after a friendship of 31 years' duration that the high task of giving his portrait to the nation was allotted me."[33] The importance of national pride in Cameron's portraits of great men shouldn't be underestimated: many reviewers and friends often commented that preserving the likeness of eminent Englishmen was one of the most important features of Cameron's work.

As soon as she returned home, Cameron wrote to Herschel in haste enclosing the prints. While the postman sat in the kitchen awaiting the letter, she breathlessly thanked him for the sitting and exclaimed over new studies that she had done of her niece Julia Jackson and her sister Virginia Somers. By April 20, she had word back from Herschel that he and his family loved the photographs. Her relief and pleasure were palpable. Herschel was engaged in his translations of *The Iliad* and she had taken away some new verses to read and share with friends. She ended her letter with praise of her own and yet another request, more veiled this time:

> I wish <u>you</u> could in a special metre write a Divine Poem on Photography then indeed it would be lifted to the heights of Song + what the sun does for us in yielding to us in one Instant of Time the imperishable Treasure of a faithful Portrait deserves your sweet Muse's sweetest serious words.[34]

Herschel's praise for his portraits may have emboldened her; on one surviving copy of the portrait he inscribed: "The one of the old Paterfamilias with his black cap on is, I think, the climax of Photographic Art and beats hollow everything I ever liked in photography before."[35] The almost-profile portrait that Herschel aptly calls "Paterfamilias" is a perfectly focused homage to Renaissance portraiture and the style of photography made popular by David Wilkie Wynfield. Here Cameron proves that she can produce sharply focused detail and varieties of texture as well as lighting: wrinkled skin, fluffy hair, stubbly chin, and swathes of plush black velvet all evoke the painstaking *trompe l'oeil* effects of a portrait by Hans Holbein, another English artist best known for representing the nation's "great men." Herschel may have come to regret his praise for the images because Cameron took to sending him blank mounts to sign so that she could sell the works with his "genuine Autograph."[36]

During this astonishingly creative period, Cameron moved back and forth between heroic portraits and narrative allegories. In contrast to the way that museums and art historians have typically divided her work into the portraits of men and the poetic compositions of women, Cameron in fact always worked on both genres simultaneously. Her range and versatility are especially apparent in the recently published complete catalogue of her work. Indeed, many of her best-known works from both genres come from this short stretch in 1867, when she worked at the height of her energies and powers. When she returned from Collingwood in early April, she threw herself into a new series of portraits of her favorite niece and model Julia Jackson, who was soon to be married. Jackson, who had refused proposals from the artists William Holman Hunt and Thomas Woolner, was engaged to a young barrister named Herbert Duckworth. The wedding was set for May and Cameron spent April obsessively photographing the soon-to-be-bride, scribbling "My Favorite Picture of all my Works. My niece Julia" under one half-profile and "Mrs. Herbert Duckworth" under many others.

Cameron may have been consciously experimenting with different ways of representing women's identities in these pictures: the photographs labeled "Julia Jackson" or "my niece" are soft-focus close-ups of a disheveled head looming out of the darkness. The photographs prematurely named *Mrs. Herbert Duckworth* show her model with carefully combed and pinned hair, still starkly lit but looking much more respectable in her lace-trimmed clothing. The profile version of *Mrs. Herbert Duckworth* [see figure] is a masterpiece of composition that more than equals Cameron's celebrated portraits of "great men." As in those portraits, the light hits the face from a dramatic right angle, but here Jackson's face turns toward it, so the light etches the curves and angles of her profile. Cameron cropped and cut the photograph into an oval shape, which emphasizes the semicircular rings of lace and trim at Jackson's collar and the sharp line of sinew running from her neckline to her crescent-shaped ear. Jackson is so beautiful that her face dominates the picture, but in fact the center of the composition is her half-shadowed ear and her turned neck. It is an audacious way to frame a portrait.

Cameron worked feverishly that spring and summer, documenting both private life (through the photographs taken around Julia Jackson and Mary Ryan's marriages) and public events. She touched on political events for perhaps the first time in her artistic career, through her portraits of men in the news like Thomas Carlyle and Edward John Eyre. On June 10, 1867 the poet William Allingham met Cameron on the train leaving London for the Isle of Wight. He described the scene in his diary:

> Down train comes in with Mrs. Cameron, queenly in a carriage by herself sur-
> rounded by photographs. We go to Lymington together, she talking all the time.
> 'I want to do a large photograph of Tennyson, and he objects! Says I make bags
> under his eyes – and Carlyle refuses to give me a sitting, he says it's a kind of
> *Inferno*! The *greatest* men of the age (with strong emphasis), Sir John Herschel,
> Henry Taylor, Watts say I have *immortalised* them – and these other men object!!
> What is one to do – Hm?'
>
> This is a kind of interrogative interjection she often uses, but seldom waits
> for reply. I saw her off in the Steamer, talking to the last.[37]

Despite her complaints, Cameron had in fact just finished taking her famous portrait of Carlyle: it was probably on the seat beside her. Cameron had registered three por-traits of Carlyle for copyright at the Public Record Office in Kew on June 8,[38] and she had probably taken them at Little Holland House during that trip to London. In com-plaining to Allingham, she probably meant to convey her own heroic efforts in persuading such men to sit for her – but in reality she was rarely denied.

The sitting with Carlyle may indeed have been an "inferno" when one imagines the two strong-willed personalities trapped in close quarters for the long exposures. Cameron knew the portraits were magnificent, especially the one in full face where Carlyle's craggy head pushes toward the viewer out of the darkness [see figure]. As always, her composition was driven by the sitter's personality, and here Cameron had a forceful presence that matched her own new skills with light and shadow. Cameron gave the portrait a prominent place in her autobiography, writing of it that

> when I have had such men before my camera my whole soul has endeav-
> oured to do its duty towards them in recording faithfully the greatness of the
> inner as well as the features of the outer man. The photograph thus taken has
> been almost the embodiment of a prayer.[39]

As with the gift of the prayerbook earlier, Cameron's association of Carlyle with reli-gion may have more to do with her own devotion to his genius than with any explicit hopes of calling him back to the Church.

Carlyle seemed a little disturbed by the vision of himself that he saw. "It is as if sud-denly the picture began to speak, terrifically ugly and woe-begone, but has something of a likeness – my candid opinion," he wrote to Cameron on June 9.[40] The photograph is radical. The face that emerges from extreme darkness is blurred with movement and half-effaced with shadows. The same elements that often spoiled nineteenth-century portraits – lack of light, the sitter's motion – are made into advantages peculiarly appropriate to this personality. Carlyle was a man in motion – he and his writing burst with the same energy that is starkly visible in this portrait. Lytton Strachey was one of many who described Carlyle's writing in terms that could be used for the portrait as well: "There are vivid flashes and phrases – visions thrown up out of the darkness of the past by the bull's-eye of a stylistic imagination."[41]

Carlyle was also a man of blacks and whites, with a Manichean view of the world as divided into pure good and pure evil. By limiting the light in the photograph from one angle only, Cameron highlights the shock of white hair and eliminates nearly all gray tones. The extreme lighting also produces one of the strangest effects in portrait photography: Carlyle's right eye is so deep in shadow as to be entirely without form. To produce and display a portrait like this required a bold self-assurance in the strength of both her own talent and Carlyle's genius. For a woman photographer who had been accused of being technically inept, the portrait was like a manifesto – or a nose-thumbing at the photographic establishment.

Cameron seemed sure of the effect the portrait would produce and exhibited it right away. By the middle of June, it was on display at Colnaghi's, where she had a rotating group of photographs available for viewing and purchase. She was right about the photograph. The gossip column of the *Athenaeum* wrote about the Colnaghi portraits on June 22, gushing about the Carlyle set that "the rugged, masculine look of these perfect pictures, the powerful and yet venerable air of the heads, are beyond praise."[42] The anonymous critic, perhaps one of Cameron's friends, singled out several portraits of great men, including portraits of Tennyson, Herschel, and the artist Val Prinsep, Cameron's nephew. As usual, the *Athenaeum* was interested first in the artistic value of the photographs, which it praised highly, but it was also concerned about preserving the likenesses of England's elite, another aspect of Cameron's work of which it approved. In describing the blurred and half-effaced portrait of Carlyle as "like" him, the critic must have meant what Cameron ultimately intended too: that it represented the inner greatness as well as the outer features. Interestingly, here, as elsewhere, critics commented on how well Cameron's photographs resembled the sitters, as if they knew them personally. Perhaps they did: bourgeois British society was small and the cultural elite was even smaller.

The *Athenaeum* critic emphasized the portrait's "masculinity" and it is not coincidental that the "great men" that Cameron and Carlyle believed in were indeed men. Did "great men" necessitate supportive, inferior women? Cameron, who knew firsthand how hard the wives of geniuses worked to protect their husbands' time, health, and egos, accepted that supporting role as a given – it was implicit in her stated worldview that men lived for action and women lived for love. Carlyle, still coming to terms with Jane's absence, was perhaps for the first time realizing the extent to which his public reputation was produced by Jane as much as by his own heroic efforts with writing. Her wit, her support, and her faith in him enabled him to work and helped confirm his brilliance for the public.

Yet, like many extraordinarily gifted people, Cameron had a distinctive ability to believe one thing sincerely and completely while enacting something entirely different in her own life. Yes, on the surface, she too looked like a dutiful wife who managed a home and fussed over her ailing husband. But in her work she was able to generalize the woman's supposed duty to enable and confirm masculine "genius" and she made that duty a defining project of her photographic career. In other words, as a photographer she was able to assist in the production of many "geniuses" – she enabled and confirmed them in portraits that hang in the National Portrait Gallery today as an English pantheon. With Carlyle, especially, the magnificent portrait was a collaboration: Carlyle, grieving for Jane and newly aware of the role of the sacrificing wife, embodying his own theories of hero worship for Cameron, already the professional midwife for England's geniuses. Carlyle did for Cameron what he was posthumously trying to do for Jane: he helped her make a name for herself. And Cameron could do for Carlyle and her other sitters what she was supposed to do primarily for her husband: support and honor them. Cameron's professional work, at first glance so at odds with her traditional gender attitudes, was in the portraits of "great men" cannily aligned with them. Paradoxically, playing handmaiden to genius turned out to be the best possible means of proving and revealing her own genius. Judging by her letters and diaries, perhaps this was true of Jane Welsh Carlyle as well.[43]

Cameron's newest portraits of celebrities were featured prominently in her exhibitions. She exhibited her work at the Universal Exhibition in Paris in 1867, where critics found her work unique in characterization and improved in technique.[44] In addition to the portraits of Carlyle and Herschel, she produced portraits of Tennyson, Longfellow (who visited Tennyson in the summer of 1868), and Darwin (who rented a house from Cameron that same summer). She also sought sittings with Ruskin and Dante Gabriel Rossetti during these years, but they refused her. When Ruskin and Cameron met at their mutual friend Henry Acland's home in Oxford Cameron insisted that he look through her portfolio of celebrity portraits, but Ruskin was not impressed.[45] He wrote her one letter that has survived in which he scolds her in patronizing language: "As for photography, you have only taken it up so eagerly because you have not known what Watts ought long ago to have explained to you that it has nothing in common with *art*."[46]

The obvious gap in the pantheon, of course, was George Eliot, who was already more than just another successful novelist: she was acclaimed as the moral voice of England. By the late 1860s, Eliot was a sage as renowned as Carlyle, and hostess of her own salon at her home outside London. Cameron knew of Eliot and sent her some photographs in January 1871 that Eliot graciously praised in characteristic language:

> My dear Mrs Cameron
> The love which you have so prettily inscribed on the beautiful presents which you have sent me, is the more precious because it is given for the sake of my books. They are certainly the best part of me, save only in the power which my fleshly self has of returning love for love and being grateful for all goodness . . .
>
> I thank you with all my heart. Wise people are teaching us to be sceptical about some sorts of 'charity' but this of cheering others by proofs of sympathy will never, I think, be shown to be harmful. At least, you have done me good . . .[47]

Surprisingly, Cameron seems never to have solicited Eliot for a portrait, and one can only wonder whether the prospect of representing a woman as a "great man" was too puzzling a problem. Like Cameron, Eliot was also often described as plain, or even ugly. For both women, their immense talents were set against their problematic lack of beauty. If Eliot could be represented neither as a great man nor as a beauty, then Cameron may have literally had trouble envisioning her. To display the laureate's leonine head in a shop window would only confirm his stature, but what to make of Mary Anne Evans' features above the name "George Eliot"? Although the public knew that Eliot was a woman, a photograph would explode the polite fiction of her identity.

Cameron's portrait of Annie Thackeray [see figure] may be instructive here: Thackeray was becoming a celebrated novelist herself, and Cameron's photograph of her dear friend, also made around 1867, was one of her few formal portraits. However, the difference in treatment between the impressionistic, emotional portraits of great men and this sedate, conventional portrait of Thackeray makes it clear that Cameron did not place her friend in the pantheon, although she admired Thackeray's well-received work enough to base a photograph on one of her stories.[48] Thackeray's portrait seems designed to refute Cameron's critics: it is perfectly focused in every detail, with nary a splotch or a streak. She is not a bold face coming out of the dark; she is a lady in pearls sitting in a standard three-quarter-length pose with all the requisite emblems of respectable femininity – ruffled dress, flower wreaths, pinned-up hair. It is an unusual example in Cameron's work of a studio-like portrait and it demonstrates that she was perfectly capable of producing portraits in that format if she so wished. Although she isn't known for this style of portraiture, she did produce other photographs of women in contemporary dress, including one set of Sara

Prinsep's niece May engaged in typical "feminine" activities, such as writing a letter or looking into a mirror.

There was another Victorian who did make it into the pantheon of great men in the spring and summer of 1867, and he was a telling choice. He was Edward John Eyre, colonial governor of Jamaica and explorer of the Australian outback, whom Cameron photographed on June 4, 1867, probably at Little Holland House when she photographed Carlyle. Eyre was in London defending himself against a parliamentary inquiry into his conduct during a bloody rebellion that had occurred in Jamaica in October 1865. Cameron's portrait of Eyre duplicates the style of her portrait of Carlyle: the lighting comes from the same angle and seems to highlight every gray hair in Eyre's beard; the rest of the photograph is almost entirely black, save for a hint of collar and necktie. It reveals a man much burdened, his eyes downcast and his face deeply lined. Eyre had reason to be worried.

Jamaica had become an English colony in the seventeenth century and it retained a certain degree of self-government. It had an elected assembly, which held a great deal of power over budgetary appropriations, and an appointed council to advise the Governor, who was selected by the Colonial Office in London. For over a hundred years Jamaican colonists had prospered under a plantation economy – slaves were imported and sugar was exported – but the abolition of slavery, the coming of free trade, and global changes in the supply of sugar had wreaked havoc on the economy. Profits were down, unemployment was rampant, and droughts made bad conditions worse. By the 1860s, the island was populated by 13,000 embittered white planters and over 400,000 black and mixed-race laborers struggling for survival. After months of rumor and grumblings, a rebellion broke out in Morant Bay and some thirty white citizens were killed. Governor Eyre's retaliation was swift and fierce: he sent hundreds of troops into the area and declared martial law there. The British shot or flogged every black man who fled before them and torched houses indiscriminately. They took prisoners and hanged them. One month later, 1,000 homes had been burnt down and 500 Jamaican blacks had been killed by the avenging British.

The rebellion appeared to have been isolated to Morant Bay, but Governor Eyre suspected that George William Gordon of Kingston may have been behind it. Gordon was a wealthy biracial plantation owner who had converted to Baptism and been elected to the Jamaican Assembly. He was a vocal critic of Eyre and the colonial magistrates, and therefore simultaneously admired by Jamaican blacks and hated by the white plantation owners. Back in Kingston, Eyre charged Gordon with conspiracy in the revolt and Gordon turned himself in for trial. But there was no trial: Eyre decided to extradite Gordon to the Morant Bay area that was still under martial law and summarily court-martial him. Gordon was convicted and hanged within five days, without ever being allowed to speak a word in his own defense.[49]

Back in England, news trickled in through the mail packets and the English public was torn between relief that Morant Bay hadn't turned into another Cawnpore and horror at the brutal reprisals. The nonconformist religious groups that had first spearheaded the anti-slavery campaigns now took up the cause of justice for Jamaica's emancipated blacks. They called for the speedy dismissal of Governor Eyre. Aghast at the execution of Gordon, some called for Eyre's prosecution for murder. For the three years that the parliamentary inquiry and trials were conducted, the Governor Eyre controversy was headline news. Partisanship for and against Eyre broke up friendships and brought down political careers. It aroused passionate feelings about the competing claims of nationalism, order, justice, authority, and the law, all of which were already in play due to the riots and demonstrations over the Reform Act.

Was Eyre a hero or a villain? When Cameron took his portrait alongside Carlyle's in June of 1867 she was almost certainly casting her vote for Eyre as hero. Carlyle had been an early supporter of Eyre's and he headed the Eyre Defense Fund in its early years. Tennyson, Ruskin, and Dickens also came out for Eyre, as did Cameron's brother-in-law Thoby Prinsep. Lined up against these Victorian heavyweights were the anti-Eyre Jamaica Committee and the formidable powers of John Stuart Mill. While the Eyre Defense Fund favored writers and thinkers, the Jamaica Committee included several prominent scientists, including Darwin and his "bulldog," Thomas Henry Huxley. Mill and Huxley both felt that Eyre's conduct and the public reaction demonstrated the imprudence of putting too much trust and authority into the hands of powerful leaders. When Mill had heard Carlyle lecturing on hero worship in the 1840s, he had impulsively stood up in the auditorium and shouted, "No! No!"[50] The Eyre controversy, which saw the two men square off as leaders of opposite camps, highlighted the fundamental differences in their worldviews: Carlyle was the gloomy prophet who argued that civilization depended on the orderly obedience of the masses to their leaders; Mill was the rational philosopher who argued that justice demanded all people be subject to the same neutral laws.

For Carlyle, the interpretation of the Eyre controversy was easy: Eyre had been a heroic explorer of Australia and by all accounts was a competent leader. Therefore, his character thus established, it was his job to keep order and it behoved the Jamaicans to obey him. As Carlyle had written earlier about heroes:

> Find in any country the Ablest Man that exists there; raise him to the supreme place, and loyally reverence him: you have a perfect government for that country; no ballot-box, parliamentary eloquence, voting, constitution-building, or other machinery can improve it a whit. It is in the perfect state: an ideal country. The Ablest Man . . . what he tells us to do must be precisely the wisest, fittest,

that we could anywhere or anyhow learn; – the thing which it will in all ways behove us, with right loyal thankfulness, and nothing doubting, to do![51]

It was Huxley, the great communicator, who best articulated the Jamaica Committee's opposition to this view of Eyre-as-hero. Writing to his friend Charles Kingsley, who had defended Eyre, he argued:

> He [Eyre] is as much responsible for Gordon's death as if he had shot him through the head with his own hand. I daresay he did all this with the best of motives, and in a heroic vein. But if English law will not declare that heroes have no more right to kill people in this fashion than other folk, I shall take an early opportunity of migrating to Texas or some other quiet place where there is less hero-worship and more respect for justice . . . . The hero-worshippers who believe that the world is to be governed by its great men, who are to lead the little ones, justly if they can; but if not, unjustly drive or kick them the right way, will sympathise with Mr. Eyre.
>
> The other sect (to which I belong) who look upon hero-worship as no better than any other idolatry, and upon the attitude of mind of the hero-worshipper as essentially immoral; who think it is better for a man to go wrong in freedom than to go right in chains; who look upon the observance of inflexible justice as between man and man as of far greater importance than even the preservation of social order, will believe that Mr. Eyre has committed one of the greatest crimes of which a person in authority can be guilty . . .[52]

Defenders of Eyre ranged from extremists who refused to believe that Jamaican blacks deserved the same civil rights as Englishmen, to moderates who deplored the violence but condemned the persecution of a government employee who was just doing his job. Cameron is likely to have believed, with Tennyson, that the facts of what happened in Jamaica were uncertain but that in the absence of certainty the claims of empire and social order trumped civil rights.[53] Henry Taylor, who worked in the Colonial Office while it was struggling to manage this crisis, also held that "the stumbling block of law should not be intruded upon the minds of men at the moment when they are suddenly charged with the rescue of a community from imminent destruction." He too weighed "what lawlessness was justifiable" and decided in favor of Eyre.[54] In 1866 Cameron was much concerned that Taylor's anxieties about the Jamaica crisis would ruin his health.[55]

It would be interesting to know for sure where Charles Hay Cameron stood in this debate: with the utilitarians and lawyers against Eyre, or with the authors and artists among his friends and family in Eyre's favor? Charles Hay, after all, had specialized in colonial law and had been known to hold progressive views on the rights of colonial subjects. Benjamin Jowett once reported to his friend Florence Nightingale that he had been talking to Charles Hay, who was "very much disposed to doubt whether the English have given India any sufficient compensation for the extinction of nationality & the loss of their natural leaders."[56] Needless to say, this was not a typical view among the British in India, and Charles Hay must have adopted it after his retirement. Charles Hay had been a colleague of John Stuart Mill's in the 1830s and 1840s when both men were members of the Political Economy Club. Unfortunately, no evidence of Charles Hay's views about Eyre has survived. Public opinion, however, agreed with Taylor, Tennyson, and (probably) Julia Margaret: in 1867 and 1868 the Jamaica Committee tried to prosecute both Eyre and a few of his officers on various charges, but each trial ended in acquittal. In the late 1860s the British public was facing great changes: reform was coming, with its threat to long-standing class assumptions and power relationships, and the Empire was growing more and more central to the national economy and identity. In identifying with the scared white citizens of Jamaica, the middle-class British at home were really defending their own way of life, which they believed was equally threatened.

When Cameron photographed Eyre and Carlyle, all of this complicated political background was shadowed in the darkness behind their haloed heads. Clearly, her choice of sitters and her "heroic" style of portraiture were in some sense political. But, just as clearly, her politics may have been somewhat artistic: a portrait photographer can do a great deal more with a theory of hero worship than with a liberal theory of equality. Cameron's portraits of Eyre and Carlyle may also have been driven at least in part by market forces: their prominence in the news of the time may have indicated the potential for greater sales. Cameron's politics were complicated, and mostly implicit. She never had any known association with the organized feminist campaigns of her day, and there were many.[57] Like Carlyle, she believed that greatness and genius were the main forces of history and progress. Like him, she believed that people, especially men, had fixed inner natures that were heroic . . . or not, brilliant . . . or not. And yet she believed that people, especially women, could also play roles, and that art could transform their characters in ways in which the vote never would. She believed that class mattered a great deal, but also that it could be transcended through art.

In May of 1867, when Julia Jackson married Herbert Duckworth and Henry Cotton courted Mary Ryan, John Stuart Mill's proposal to revise the Reform Bill to enable some qualified women to vote was defeated by 176 to 73 votes. In July, while Cameron was busy photographing Cotton and Ryan as romantic characters, Parliament was divided over the historic bill to extend the vote to parts of the working classes. The bill was passed on August 15, two weeks after Cotton and Ryan's wedding. Cameron's role in their relationship demonstrated that her interest in class relations would be played out in both her life and her work. And photography had the important added role of transforming Cameron herself – until recently an eccentric hostess and mother of six – into an artist at the same time that it transformed her models into muses, heroines, and ladies.

At the end of *Parallel Lives*, her book about five Victorian marriages, Phyllis Rose examines the Eyre case to show the interconnections of power relations within the state and within the home. As she observes, "the men who backed Eyre mostly tended to uphold strong male authority within the family and to expect submissiveness from wives."[58] She called them "romantic authoritarians," a term that is equally apt in describing Cameron's politics, domestic and otherwise. Both political and domestic unions of course depend on carefully calibrated hierarchies and differences. These differences can be eroticized, as they were by Arthur Munby and Hannah Cullwick, or romanticized, as Cameron did with Cotton and Ryan; they can be celebrated as good, by people like Carlyle, or condemned as bad, by people like Mill. The Camerons seem to have settled into a contented routine that served them well over decades: Julia fussed over Charles's health and led her own public life; Charles retreated to his own world of books but still made important decisions for the family.

Mary Ryan and Henry Cotton's marriage was emblematic for Cameron and her circle. It justified Cameron's faith in the transformative powers of photography and it also confirmed her assumption that marriages ought to be based on inequality and difference. Cameron and her sisters were famous matchmakers, as the fiasco between Ellen Terry and G. F. Watts had shown, and they had a penchant for promoting marriages that were like their own, with older husbands joined to much younger wives. In Ryan and Cotton's case, the couple's social and economic inequality clearly added appeal to the union. In contrast to John Stuart Mill's ideal of the companionable marriage between equals, Cameron and her circle seem to have believed that marital success was best based on a division of powers that eased the way toward a division of roles and spheres. Typically, of course, that meant that men should seek out women of less experience, intelligence, wealth, social standing, or talent than themselves. Coventry Patmore's 1850s poem cycle *The Angel in the House* dramatized this Victorian ideal of the perfect marriage as the union of a gifted man and a supportive, less able woman. The poem was a Victorian bestseller. Cameron photographed an illustration from the poem: a close-up head of a demure young woman framed in soft, fuzzy fur. Patmore himself seems to have espoused this view of marriage in his own life as well: he once wrote "the incomparable happiness of love between the sexes is similarly founded upon their inequality . . . . In the mutual worship of lovers there is always a tacit understanding of something of a King Cophetua and the Beggar-Maid relationship."[59]

But to their credit, Cameron and her friends often favored a more interesting con- jugal blend of status and abilities, rather than merely stacking all the decks in favor of the husband. In Cameron's own marriage, age may have been on Charles Hay's side but genius and talent turned out to be harder to assign. In Ryan's case as well, Cameron and her sisters may have felt that Ryan's great beauty partly offset her new husband's greater standing, wealth, and connections. In 1877 Annie Thackeray sur- prised her circle by marrying Richmond Ritchie, a second cousin sixteen years younger than herself. There was some gossip about them, but everyone seems to have mostly taken the news in their stride, and the marriage endured. The Tennysons' mar- riage was divided along conventional lines and Emily got little public credit for her role in Tennyson's genius, and yet many of their friends privately saw, understood, and valued Emily's talents, as Cameron did. Jowett wrote to Hallam Tennyson around the time of his mother's death that "Mrs Cameron . . . used to say to me that, though unknown, 'she was as great as he was.'"[60]

Cameron spent the summer of 1868 at Freshwater: she had rented a cottage to Charles Darwin and his family and photographed both him and one of his guests, the botanist Joseph Hooker. The Darwins' brief correspondence with Cameron is amus- ingly dominated by talk of terms and gardeners. After the visit, Darwin wrote to Hooker that "Mrs. Cameron has been jollier + kinder than ever + she seemed so pleased when I told her that you had been pleased with her – Your Photograph looks grand."[61] William Allingham visited Freshwater during the same week of August and recounts the conversations between Tennyson, Hooker, and Charles's visiting brother Erasmus. Charles he described as "tall, yellow, sickly, very quiet. He has his meals at his own times, sees people or not as he chooses, has invalid's privileges in full, a great help to a studious man." But Hooker and Tennyson were sociable, and as usual talk turned to religion, with Tennyson hoping for "an assurance of immortality."[62] Tennyson was still working on pieces of *Idylls of the King*.

Another of the guests that week was Captain Speedy and his charge, Prince Alámayou of Abyssinia (now Ethiopia).[63] The prince was the seven-year-old son of King Theodore II of Abyssinia, who had been an English ally in Africa for the past decade. However, Theodore had become disillusioned with the English in the early 1860s, and he began to show his displeasure by jailing Europeans and British citizens, including the British Consul, and holding them hostage (though in relative comfort) at a fortress in Magdala. By December of 1867, British hawks convinced Parliament to declare war on Abyssinia and another colonial debacle ensued. General Robert Napier invaded with a large troop of Indian forces, rescued a handful of British citi- zens, and routed the Abyssinians with superior weaponry at a cost of nine million pounds.[64] In the aftermath King Theodore committed suicide and his orphaned son was brought to England in the charge of a Captain Tristram Speedy, who knew

Amharic and had served on both sides in the Abyssinian War. Alámayou was brought to the Isle of Wight to meet Queen Victoria at Osborne on July 14 and he and Captain Speedy stayed on in Freshwater as the guests of another Mrs. Cotton. Perhaps Speedy had some connection already with these Freshwater Cottons, because within ten days he was engaged to their daughter, nicknamed "Tiny."[65] The Abyssinian party first visited with Cameron and Tennyson on July 18 and came again in August. Darwin ventured downstairs long enough to interrogate Speedy on Abyssinian habits and customs. His assistance was acknowledged in Darwin's *On the Expression of Emotion in Man and Animals*, which was published in 1872 and included photographic illustrations by Cameron's friend Rejlander. It is hard to imagine that Darwin did not have similar conversations on facial expressions and the use of photographs with Cameron.

In the meantime, Cameron took advantage of her opportunity and made thirteen photographs of Prince Déjatch Alámayou [see figure], Captain Speedy, and Casa, an Abyssinian attendant and translator.[66] As scholars Jeff Rosen and Panthea Reid have noted, Cameron had extensive ties to the Colonial Office, which had defended Eyre and deposed King Theodore. Indeed, she took and copyrighted a portrait of the Abyssinian diplomat William Gifford Palgrave that June, and later in the summer she also photographed General Napier, who was rewarded for his work with the title Lord Napier of Magdala. She may have been eager for sales while the Abyssinian War was still in the news: she registered the Palgrave and Abyssinian portraits within days of taking them, though in August she neglected to register later photographs of Napier and the Abyssinian group at all.[67] There was certainly a strong concern in England for the orphaned child and also talk about the commercial possibilities of the war. One newspaper had suggested that the heavy costs of the war be offset by income from the display of King Theodore.[68] The press was filled with illustrations of the battles and the protagonists, feeding the public's appetite for the "exotic."[69]

Speedy adopted a paternal and protective role with the boy, at least in public. He told Emily Tennyson that the prince was so traumatized by the events of the war he could only sleep in Speedy's arms.[70] The British liked to imagine Alámayou as a little Englishman: he was photographed by another Isle of Wight portraitist in a Western suit, and Allingham wrote down the prince's efforts at mimicking the conversation and gestures of the English – though it was unclear whether the prince was mocking them or trying to fit in.[71] Allingham was there when Cameron photographed Alámayou again on August 21 and he described the scene thus:

> Mrs. Cameron's: Captain Speedy opens the door. Little Alamayu, pretty boy, we make friends and have romps, he rides on my knee, shows his toys. His Abyssinian attendant. They dress to be photographed by Mrs. C, the Prince in

---

a little purple shirt and a necklace, Captain Speedy in a lion-skin tippet, with a huge Abyssinian sword of reaping-hook shape ('point goes into your skull'). Photographing room–Speedy grumbles a little, Mrs. C poses them. Photograph of Mrs. Tennyson's maid as 'Desdemona.'[72]

As Panthea Reid points out, despite Cameron's pro-colonialist politics, her photograph is less racist than other contemporary illustrations. Cameron defies expectations by dressing Speedy in African garb and emphasizing the personal connection between the prince and his attendants.[73] In some of the images the three are grouped closely together, looking at and touching each other. Emotionally, Cameron seems interested in the pathos of these people, though of course that impulse can be sentimentalizing and objectifying too. But within the terms of her own culture, sentiment was a way of emphasizing the similarities between peoples, not the differences. In one exception, which has been called *Spear or Spare*, Speedy does enact a scene of violent subjugation, holding a spear over Casa's neck, but again the theatricality of the composition mitigates its violence: it is clearly framed by curtains and posed for a long exposure. Casa holds the same ornamental shield that Cameron would later use as a prop for Elaine in *Idylls of the King*.

The Abyssinian series is interesting in part because it breaks down the conventional categories for Cameron's art. They are neither portraits of family, friends, or celebrities (though they are driven by the marketplace), nor narrative or allegorical tableaux (though they do illustrate scenes). They dissolve the usual division between Cameron's "English" work with "British" models and her later, brief, Sri Lankan work with "native" sitters. Alámayou is neither British nor "native," neither working-class nor aristocrat in the English class structure. Though a child, he is not photographed like Cameron's other child sitters either, with a tousled, "natural" look or a soft-focus close-up. He was a child deprived of his childhood, and Cameron had to figure out a new way to represent him. For better and worse he was placed in a category of his own: child, prince, African – and that is part of the pathos that Cameron seems to draw like a cloak around him. That pathos would find poetic closure in a few years: Alámayou died of pleurisy in 1879 while attending the Royal Military Academy.

During these years that Cameron was working so productively and successfully, the family was still struggling with ongoing questions: how to settle their sons in life, and how to keep afloat financially. In 1867 the challenge was getting eighteen-year-old Charlie Hay, the fourth son, out of the house. With Eugene in the West Indies, Ewen a coffee-planter in Ceylon, and Hardinge at Oxford, it was now necessary to establish Charlie in some sort of career, though money was tight as always. With their financial troubles temporarily eased by Overstone and Norman's last loan, the Camerons decided to send Charlie Hay to Bombay in the hopes of his landing on his feet in the time-honored tradition of younger sons in the colonies. Charles Henry Cameron, Charles Hay's son from before his marriage to Julia Margaret, had settled in Bombay, and the Camerons may have trusted to him and other friends there to "do something" for the young man. Lord Overstone again stepped in to assist the family, sending his godson 100 pounds and a gold watch as a parting present. Cameron sent Overstone a twenty-page letter of thanks that November, effusing over his generosity and her boy's merits: he was musical; he was sensible. Again, separations proved difficult for Cameron, and the letter shows what an emotional time it was:

> For 18 years of his young life this Boy has only been one year separated from me and whenever I feel that next week this very day week I must part with him for years perhaps forever I feel as if my courage would fail, and as if I never never could let him go in all his youth + brightness as he now is to those Tropical regions where the arrows of death fly so swiftly and so surely —[74]

The letter quickly segues into a discussion of photography, which was all absorbing in 1867. After her intense flurry of creative work in the spring and summer, Cameron had been ill in the fall of 1867 and was just now getting her energy back. Her husband too had had a relapse of some sort and she had nursed him as well. She notes that she is busy photographing Charlie Hay but it is a poignant task: "I sometimes think," she wrote, "that Portraits only give pleasure to happy hearts. To the bereaved they seem all too painful." Overstone was suspicious of Cameron's photography. In a letter he wrote to their old friend George Warde Norman on November 8, he asks for Norman's opinion about Charlie Hay's relocation to Bombay and worries about Julia Margaret: "I fear she is at Photography again a charmer who I thought had been finally dismissed."[75] Cameron's letter of thanks for the gift confirmed those suspicions, and he must have worried that Julia Margaret's work was again overtaxing the family finances.

Cameron had been aware of Overstone's disapproval from the outset — hence her gift of an album to him — and she again took pains to point out her successes in her art. Ruefully, she wrote: "I am anxious that you should see to what point I have now been able to bring Photography. Our English artists tell me that I can go no farther in excellence, so I suppose I must suppress my ambition and stop — but it is an art full of mystery and beauty . . . ."[76] Such frank talk about ambition is unusual from a Victorian woman; Cameron seems to be reluctantly agreeing with Overstone's presumed advice to give up photography. And yet the wording is deliberately ambiguous, and it is doubtful that she ever seriously considered giving up her art, despite the expense. To allay Overstone's fears, though, she went out of her way to point out how well Ewen was now managing their coffee estates at Rathoongodde, bringing in £1,000 to £1,500 net profit each year from land that had only yielded thousands of pounds of debt when agents managed it. She also included more recent photographic work with the letter.

In response to the gift from his godfather, Charlie Hay wrote one of those stiff little notes that punctuate the family's surviving archive. Time and again the Cameron boys were called upon to write dutiful letters of gratitude for the support and advice that their well-connected elders provided for them. Charlie Hay thanks Lord Overstone for the watch and concludes succinctly: "I hope you will hear that I am getting on well in Bombay. It will not be for the want of trying if I don't. I remain ever, Your grateful and affectionate godson."[77] By December, Lord Overstone was informed that Hardinge, the third son, had received an offer of a clerkship from the Colonial Governor of Ceylon. Overstone approved, and Hardinge too was duly sent a gift of 100 pounds and a gold watch. Another, more fulsome, letter from Hardinge was the result. Hardinge showed his early promise as a diplomat, thanking Overstone warmly but adding that he already owned a fine watch – could he have an alternative present instead? In a wordier variant of Charlie Hay's conclusion, Hardinge wrote: "I trust that some day you have the satisfaction of hearing that I am bearing honorably the name which my Father has made honorable before me."[78]

Cameron naturally spent that year again trying to drum up sales. She put on another one-woman show in January–February 1868 at the German Gallery on Bond Street. She displayed over 180 images and garnered good reviews from the London *Standard*, the *Morning Post*, and the *Art Journal*, which she excerpted and had printed up as a pamphlet for publicity purposes. William Allingham attended on February 4, noting that the gallery was now in charge of a new maid and model, Kate Shepherd (perhaps explaining her earlier confusion with Mary Ryan). Despite his mixed feelings about Cameron, Allingham was loyal to her and "blew the trumpet" for her show in the *Pall Mall Gazette*.[79] The *Photographic News* again sneered that "one portrait of the Poet Laureate [the "Dirty Monk"] presents him in a guise which would be sufficient to convict him, if he were charged as a rogue and a vagabond, before any bench of magistrates in the Kingdom."[80] A printed catalogue from that exhibit has survived, giving a good sense of Cameron's pricing and sales process. Art historian Sylvia Wolf has analyzed it carefully, and she notes that surprisingly the celebrity portraits do not necessarily fetch the highest prices. The most expensive photographs on Cameron's list were an autographed portrait of Alfred Tennyson and two portraits of Julia Jackson (*Mrs. Herbert Duckworth*). By this point in her career, Cameron was at home in her marketplace, even if she did continue to annotate new additions to her catalogue by hand. She also provided her customers with a choice of brown or grey toning and options for ordering sold-out prints.[81]

She gloated to Henry Cole in a letter from the spring that she had recently made two big sales: Daniel Gurney (her niece Alice Prinsep's father-in-law)[82] had bought twenty-four photographs for just over £12 and Michael Spartali, an Anglo-Greek diplomat, bought forty photographs of his daughter Marie for 20 guineas. "I am likely now to acquire fortune as well as fame for as I told you & you gave me entire sympathy a woman with sons to educate cannot live on fame alone!" she wrote, ever hopeful.[83] Nonetheless, she continued to give away at least as much work as she sold (though at a slower pace), including new albums to Watts in 1868 and Julia and Charles Norman in September 1869. The latter contained seventy-five images and was grandiosely (but not inaccurately) inscribed: "To the givers of my Camera I dedicate & give these works of this camera, with all gratitude for the inexhaustible pleasure to me, & to hundreds, which has resulted from the gift." That same month she gave an album originally containing fifty-one photographs to Henry Taylor's son Aubrey.[84]

Cameron also worried about damage to her precious but fragile glass negatives. At least once she noted on a print that the price was higher because the negative had broken.[85] She complained bitterly in a letter to Cole in June 1869 that she had recently lost over forty-five negatives due to cracked lines that appeared in the collodion over time.[86] Her earliest works, she explained, were intact, so she attributed the problem to a change in collodion manufacture. On May 11 she had attended the Photographic Society of London's monthly meeting to ask for advice about why this occurred and how to stop it, bringing her damaged work with her. The eminent gentlemen all gave her different explanations: Mr. Blanchard thought the problem was the sea air on the Isle of Wight; Mr. Dallmeyer, the lens maker, recommended more baths and rinsing of her glass plates; Mr. Thomas, Mr. Eliot, and Mr. Hooper agreed that wrapping the negatives in paper would protect them.[87] Cameron left unimpressed, and determined to print as much as she could while her negatives were intact and also to pursue engravings of her most successful works.

That fall Cameron parted with two sons but gained a new daughter-in-law. Ewen [see figure] had taken over his father's coffee plantations in Ceylon, but he found his bride in a local young woman named Annie Chinery, whose father was a doctor in Lymington, across the Solent from the Isle of Wight. Cameron too fell in love with this daughter-in-law and took many portraits of "our Birdie," as she was sometimes called. As with Jackson, Cameron took several photographs of Annie right before her wedding on November 18. Titled *My Ewen's Bride (God's Gift to Us)* and *The Bride*, they say more about Cameron's ability to project intense emotions into her work than anything about the real Annie Chinery. *The Bride* [see figure] is an extraordinary work and another example of how Cameron made the problems of early photographic technique into triumphant virtues. The wet collodion that coated each of Cameron's glass negatives was easily smeared and here the streaks turn the wedding veil into a diaphanous cloud. The result is a perfect illusion of bridal innocence and allure, though the reality seems to have been quite different. Annie Chinery Cameron

rejected Cameron's maternal advances and kept her distance, emotionally and physically. The couple left for Ceylon shortly after the wedding: they may have been
among the first passengers through the Suez Canal, which had opened that month.
They took Charlie Hay with them to start him in coffee planting too. The Bombay plan
had either been abandoned or unsuccessful.

A few months after the wedding, Cameron wrote to Herschel giving a demonstration of her intense investment in this daughter-in-law. Perhaps it was because the
circumstances of Eugene's wedding were so bitterly unsatisfactory after the high
hopes of his match with an old friend's daughter that Cameron turned to Annie
Chinery so eagerly. Cameron was always on the lookout for daughter figures,
especially since childbearing and ill health had weakened her intimacy with her own
daughter Juley. She wrote Herschel that she had loved Annie from the moment she
saw her and instantly wanted her for Ewen. Within two months, she crowed, they
were married, and she encloses Annie's portrait for Herschel with the caveat that her
coloring was the most marked feature of her beauty. She felt compelled to add a
verbal description to the visual image enclosed:

> Her brow is smooth white + as you see very lofty. Her hair golden brown–so
> brown + yet so richly burnished with gold–her skin very fine + enamelled but
> decidedly dark . . . a carnation rich red colour – bright hazel eyes very soft +
> liquid with a sweeping fringe of very dark lashes + dark eyebrows very finely
> chiselled nose, + the most exquisite mouth (of this you can see the record) a
> very slender figure with roundness + embonpoint height 5 foot 7 + fairy hands
> + feet . . .[88]

Cameron's correspondence does not contain many such passages, and judging by
the surviving letters, Annie's suitor could not have waxed so eloquently as his mother
did upon his fiancée's beauty. Descriptions like this force one to reconsider what
Cameron meant when she said in her autobiography that she "longed to arrest all
beauty." Her passionate attention to Annie's appearance, evident too in the photographs she took, reveal a sensual love of the human form that must have predated
any photographic ambitions, and perhaps contributed to them.

Cameron proceeds in the letter to Herschel to praise Annie's character and she
calls her her father's "Ewe Lamb," perhaps another pun on Ewen's name. On the
voyage to Ceylon Ewen fell overboard, and Cameron vividly depicts the manifold
dangers of his brush with death from the account in Annie's letter. Annie seems to
have maintained a courteous and impassive response to Cameron's fervor: when
Cameron exclaimed that she loved her enough to lay down her life for her, Annie
smiled and murmured, "I hope Mummie that won't be required of you." Cameron was
forced to acknowledge that "I should like her to love me as she does her own Parents

perhaps that is expecting too much."[89] Annie returned frequently for extended stays without her husband, perhaps because their marriage did not turn out to be as picture-perfect as Cameron had hoped.

A few decades after these events, Henry James – yet another member of Cameron's outer circle through his later friendship with Leslie and Julia Stephen – wrote a story called *The Real Thing*, in which a well-born couple who have fallen on hard times apply to an artist to sit as professional models. The artist realizes immediately that they are amateurs, but he is amused by their confident assumption that they can sit for portraits of gentry simply because they are themselves "the real thing." The artist hires them, but gradually discovers that they won't do at all. Of the lady, James's narrator says,

> do what I would with it my drawing looked like a photograph or a copy of a photograph. Her figure had no variety of expression – she herself had no sense of variety. You may say that this was my business, was only a question of placing her. I placed her in every conceivable position, but she managed to obliterate their differences. She was always a lady certainly, and into the bargain always the same lady. She was the real thing, but always the same thing.[90]

By the end, the artist finds himself using his servants for models and these respectable models as servants. Art, James seems to argue, is essentially transformative, if that isn't an oxymoron. If art cannot transfigure one thing into something else then, like photography, it is merely imitation. Cameron would have vigorously opposed the slur on photography, but she too believed in the infinite powers of art to transform and improve reality.

In the nineteenth century advocates of photography as an art had to battle constantly with such slurs. One Victorian photography critic, writing in 1864 about a different photographer's work, critiqued photography in the same terms as James would later:

> You may find some wonderful young woman, and wrap her up artfully in a blanket, and pose her voluptuously, and arrange daintily her taper fingers, and call her "Summer," but it won't do . . . The lady isn't Summer; there is strong evidence somewhere that she is Miss Jane Brown or Sophia Smith, and the drapery is a blanket, and all the rest of the thing as it *was* and not what you wish it to *appear* to be. Photography is too truthful – all your dodges are found out – you are an impostor, a mere conjuror, and no true artist at all.[91]

In the face of such attacks, with her devotion to photography as an art form and her belief in its ability to reveal essential characters even when her models are acting

---

roles, one can see why Cameron was so enthusiastic about Henry Cotton's engagement to Mary Ryan. With that proposal she could beat back such critics: "See," one can hear her cry, "that maid is a Miranda, and a bride worthy of a nobleman. Why, she lives in India now as Lady Cotton. Anyone can see her virtuous nature. King Cophetua did. My photographs revealed who she really was." Like Carlyle, Cameron may have believed that heroes were born and not made, but women seemed to have more powers to invent themselves, as Cameron herself had demonstrated. In the 1870s those assumptions would be put to the test, as the charmed circle at Freshwater began to unravel.

CHAPTER 9

The Fall of Camelot

B Y THE BEGINNING of the 1870s, the intimate circle around Tennyson at Freshwater was no longer a well-kept secret. Tourists came to the island expressly to get a glimpse of the laureate, much to his simultaneous pleasure and chagrin. Stories abound of Cameron mediating between Tennyson and his fans, encouraging him to notice them and then smoothing his ruffled feathers. In her first surviving letter from that year, Cameron used Tennyson's fame and her voluminous correspondence to argue with the postal service that the local postman be appointed to Freshwater.[1] His celebrity suited her purposes too – it brought her sitters and sometimes even buyers. He grumbled that innkeepers charged him double because they recognized him from her portraits, but everyone around him knew that he loved and needed the attention.

One reason for Tennyson's pinnacle of popularity in that decade was the on-going publication of his *Idylls of the King*. The idea of an Arthurian tale was long considered, and much delayed, since his first poem on the subject, "Morte d'Arthur," in 1842. He wrote and published four books of the series, "Enid," "Elaine," "Vivien," and "Guinevere," in 1859, and ten years later, in December 1869, he released another four: "The Coming of Arthur," "Pelleas and Ettarre," "The Holy Grail," and "The Passing of Arthur." Though still incomplete, the works were enormously popular and profitable. In the 1870s Tennyson and Cameron's circle basked in the reflected light of that success: fifty years later, Cameron's great-niece Laura Gurney Troubridge wrote:

> Nothing brings back those long-ago days like the thought of those little green volumes and the feelings they once aroused; yet how impossible to-day to recover the rapture with which one entered that fairyland of marvellous, impossible people, those knights in armour, with their lofty ideals, their tournaments and jousts . . .[2]

Annie Thackeray remembered "a succession of romantic figures" coming to visit and nights when a "whole company of lads and lasses went streaming away across the fields and downs, past silvery sheep-folds to the very cliffs hanging over the sea." She called Tennyson "King Alfred."[3]

For Cameron, however, the new decade was fraught with challenges. Her sons were gradually establishing themselves, but Henry Herschel Hay's future was in doubt and the family finances remained precarious. In the letter to Herschel that winter in which she extolled Annie Chinery Cameron, she also complained about her youngest son and the status of her career. Henry [see figure] was "a first rate actor" and a young man of great promise. "But for mental somnolence," she wrote in exasperation, "he would be perfect."[4] He was lazy and he made no effort at anything but acting and athletics, so the Camerons had sent the eighteen-year-old, at considerable expense, to a tutor to prepare him for admission to Oxford in a few months. In an interesting aside, Cameron told Herschel that if she could photograph "professionally," she could earn enough to help her sons establish themselves in careers. She often resolved to do so, but she feared the loss of liberty in choosing her sitters. Her photographic career had now broken even, she wrote, since she had sales totaling 1,700 pounds.[5]

Clearly, Cameron's definition of being a "professional" photographer had little to do with the money made from her work and even less to do with its quality. Her definition depended on her sense of her own independence, or lack thereof. She used "professional" as we would today use "commercial" – to describe a person whose services were available in a marketplace for any and all comers. It is known that Cameron protected her artistic choice of sitters carefully: in her autobiography she reproduced a note from a Miss Lydia Louisa Summerhouse Donkins, who requested a sitting and promised to arrive with her dress unwrinkled. Cameron scornfully declined, saying that she was not "a professional photographer" and adding that if she were, she would much prefer the dress crumpled. "I have more than once regretted that I could not produce the likeness of this individual with her letter affixed thereto," she wrote indignantly.[6] In another letter from the same period she crowed that in all her career she had photographed for three reasons only: "great beauty – great celebrity – and great friendship so I have kept my Portfolio choice."[7] Choice, in both its senses, was clearly paramount and that is what her self-proclaimed "amateur" status allowed her. Despite the importance of her new career, Cameron listed herself as "Wife," with no given profession, in both the 1861 and 1871 national censuses.[8]

In a sense, Cameron was facing the same career dilemma as her sons. How was an upper-middle-class person with good connections but no capital to earn a living within the narrow range of possible careers? Both Julia Margaret and Henry Herschel Hay had talents, but it was difficult for either one to exploit them without jeopardizing their class status, or, in Cameron's case, her creative independence. It is remarkable how much of this burden to settle her sons and support the family fell on Cameron herself: Charles Hay seems to have gone into a near-permanent retreat.

More than ever it is Julia Margaret who forwards bills to Hardinge, corresponds with lawyers, and generally manages plans for the family. In the letter to Herschel Julia Margaret wryly notes that Charles Hay is merrier than usual and seems carefree in the face of all these looming decisions. The only thing that he worried about more than she did was the loans: Charles Hay had inherited debts from his father and feared leaving such a legacy for his sons. Julia Margaret, on the other hand, once wrote Annie Thackeray blithely: "I myself never felt humiliated at the idea of receiving charities, for I always feel about friendship and love that what it is good to give it is also good to take."[9] Generosity gave her such pleasure that it was only fair for her to provide others with the same opportunity for benevolence. Reading between the lines of Cameron's letter to Herschel, it sounds as if the Camerons already knew in 1870 that they would soon end up following their older sons to Ceylon. Cameron missed the elder boys terribly, but first there was Henry Herschel Hay to sort out.[10]

Herschel took his role as godparent seriously and sat down that winter to write the young man a few well-intentioned letters. Acting was all very well, he declared, but it suffered from the evils of instant gratification: one must compensate by pursuing tasks that do not result in applause. "A good hard day's work at Algebra or Geometry or a stiff chorus or two of Aeschylus would be a capital and healthy corrective after a brilliant evening of private theatricals," he urged his godson.[11] Henry wrote back promptly and dutifully, listing the classical works he was reading but admitting that he was not following his godparent's advice at that very moment but instead indulging in the pleasure of writing to him. In another undated letter he may have lost some more ground by admitting: "I don't think there is much danger of my exceeding either in athletics or theatricals."[12] He was young and meant well, but his elders were unimpressed. Even his devoted mother kept up a constant refrain in her letters about his indolence. Emily Tennyson went further, deeming him a bad influence on her son Lionel. Lionel and Henry were close friends, but Emily tried to keep them apart as much as possible.[13]

In September came the shocking news of Julia Jackson Duckworth's sudden bereavement. Jackson had married the barrister Herbert Duckworth in 1867 and bore two children, George and Stella, in quick succession. She was pregnant with her third child when Herbert suffered a stroke and died on September 19. Their son Gerald was born soon afterwards. Julia went numb with grief and described her life as a "shipwreck."[14] She went into a decade-long depression and worried her family by candidly expressing her desire for death.[15] She later acknowledged that in those awful months she lost her faith in God. It was their common loss and their common atheism that later brought her together with Leslie Stephen. Cameron rarely photographed Julia Duckworth after her marriage, but a few photographs exist of her in deep mourning with her children in the garden of her mother's home in Kent.

Cameron continued to exhibit at the annual Photographic Society shows in London, but her registration of new photographs for copyright was slowing down,[16] perhaps because of her promises to economize by not producing new work and instead reprinting from older negatives. The deterioration of many of her older negatives made that project more pressing too. Still, her reputation was growing. In December 1870 she made a visit to Oxford and she found herself something of a celebrity. Emily Tennyson reported to her husband how uncharacteristically flustered Cameron became as she was flooded with invitations and attention. Dean Henry Liddell, the classicist father of Lewis Carroll's Alice, threw a party for her that was attended by some three hundred people. The rooms were all adorned with her work.[17] It must have been a treat for her to encounter a little hero worship of her own. Perhaps Charles Dodgson attended the party; he was still a tutor at Christ Church College alongside Liddell. Dodgson had recently fallen out with the Tennysons over an unpublished manuscript that he had in his possession. Emily had written Dodgson coldly that "a gentleman" would understand that the laureate did not want his unpublished work in circulation.[18] Dodgson took umbrage and severed all contact. Cameron, however, kept in touch with the maturing Alice Liddell and photographed her in 1872 as "Pomona" and "Alethea", comparing her to a Roman goddess and a Greek word ("truth") that her father would have known well.

Despite Cameron's growing fame, acquired with so much stubborn perseverance, the family was still barely afloat financially. Cameron began to turn to Hardinge, now in Ceylon clerking for Governor Hercules Robinson, for help with the bills and budgeting. In October 1871 she sent him a long letter in which she again considers selling Rathoongodde, given over to Ewen at his marriage, in order to raise money for the other sons and settle some debts. The end of the letter concludes with various accounts, which imply that the Camerons were borrowing heavily again from their old friends: another 500 pounds from Lord Overstone and, surprisingly, £112 from the widowed Julia Duckworth. Though incomplete, the bills provide a window into the daily life of the household. The Camerons were able to live largely on credit, for the Victorian practice of running accounts with local providers meant that they only settled up their bills infrequently, when they grew large. For example, they ran up large regular bills for coal, meat, wine, and farm produce, including dairy goods. That fall they were also paying a builder and an ironmonger, perhaps because earlier that year Cameron had completed a major renovation of her Freshwater house by adding a tower of her own design to join two adjacent houses.[19]

Cameron was also paying considerable amounts for photo mounts at a time when her prints were selling for around 16 shillings a piece. Contrary to her reputation as a careless housekeeper, she seems to have always been in charge of the domestic accounts and she knew what everything cost. Micawber-like, she simply persisted in

Julia Margaret Cameron, *Vivien and Merlin*, September 1874.

———

Charles Hay modeled for Merlin in Cameron's *Idylls of the King* photographs;
in this scene he is immobilized and blinded by the enchantress Vivien.

Julia Margaret Cameron, *King Arthur*, 1874.

———

This solo portrait of King Arthur, modeled by William Warder, a porter at Yarmouth,
is taken from a low viewpoint that may refer to Guinevere's position at
his feet in their farewell scene.

Julia Margaret Cameron, *'So Like a Shatter'd Column Lay the King'*, 1875.

An illustration of King Arthur's disappearance into the mists of Avalon, Cameron's photograph
has been mocked for its obvious theatricality.

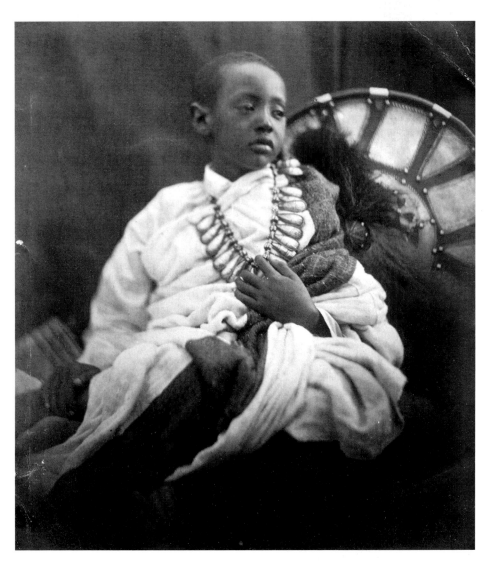

Julia Margaret Cameron, *Dêjatch Alâmayou*, 1868.

────────

The Ethiopian prince Alámayou came to England after his father's death in the
Abyssinian War, and Cameron photographed him and his companions
in the summer of 1868.

Julia Margaret Cameron, *Marianne North*, 1876.

Cameron took several portraits of the botanical artist Marianne North
when she visited Ceylon.

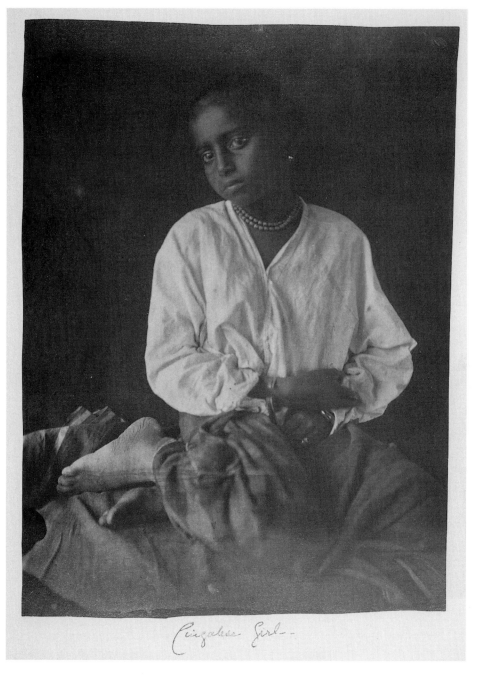

Cingalese Girl

Julia Margaret Cameron, *Cingalese Girl*, 1875–78.

—————

Some of Cameron's Ceylonese photographs, like this one, share the deep,
shadowed backgrounds of her work in England.

This example of Cameron's Ceylonese photographs resembles contemporaneous "ethnic" studies
in which local peoples are positioned against walls and
photographed in a "documentary" style.

Julia Margaret Cameron, British, 1815–1879, Ceylon (two natives, one with vase over head), c.1875,
albumen print from wet collodion negative, 27.5 x 22.8 cm,
Harriott A. Fox Fund, 1970.843, image © The Art Institute of Chicago.

This photograph shares iconographic and formal qualities with
Cameron's English photographs of Madonnas.

Julia Margaret Cameron, British, 1815–1879, Ceylon (unidentified girl with drape over head), c.1875,
albumen print from wet collodion negative, 25.5 x 19.3 cm,
Harriott A. Fox Fund, 1970.841, image © The Art Institute of Chicago.

always believing that funds would turn up. They did, but only because her friends continued to bail them out. In the accounts she sends to Hardinge she reveals that the £612 that she has already borrowed has been put down as partial payment for the largest bills but that they still owe over £800 more, before they even begin to cover their ongoing living expenses. Indeed, around this time Cameron mentions in a letter that their income was reduced from 10,000 pounds a year (in their heyday in Calcutta) to just 800 pounds a year.[20] So even after borrowing heavily they still had debts equivalent to their entire year's income. They were in serious arrears, and in the letter Cameron hopes for several hundred pounds from her sons, though it is unclear how the young men had acquired any capital. Henry had already turned his money over, and Cameron was confident that Hardinge would too. Though Eugene returned to England regularly during his employment in the West Indies, he rarely appears in family correspondence: only his son Archibald seems to have visited Freshwater. Ewen and Annie Cameron were fortunate to receive a generous settlement from his parents when they married, and it was uncertain how they would react to the proposed sale of Rathoongodde and the need to help Charles Hay and Julia Margaret out of debt. Charlie Hay had already refused to part with any of his money, much to his mother's indignation.[21] Far from earning money to provide for the boys, Cameron was reduced to borrowing from them.

Charlie Hay had been sent to Ceylon to manage an estate when Ewen and Annie settled there after their marriage late in 1869. But he had come home ignominiously about a year later with a reputation for "brandy drinking and smoking and in-action"[22] (according to his mother) and an infection that had spread from a tooth abcess into his jawbone. He must have been in considerable pain. For about two years he hung around the house resisting all of Cameron's efforts to reform his character and restore his health. By the fall of 1871, she seems to have almost given up on him, reserving her hopes for Henry's transformation instead. Both young men were infuriatingly idle and committed only to billiards. Charlie Hay kept late hours and scorned basic hygiene. Cameron complained to Hardinge about

> the drugged condition of self-administered opium for tooth ache in which I found Charlie and . . . the unspeakable neglect of himself which followed for weeks afterwards when no earthly persuasion of mine or Drs. could induce him *even* to rinse or gargle his mouth when pus flowed unceasingly mixing with all his food & even making himself & his whole rooms almost intolerable . . .[23]

These were the sons Cameron struggled to place in satisfactory employment. She had connections but she could not work miracles. "Charlie," she noted bitterly, "is full of the idea he can be made a Queen[']s Messenger or House Messenger with the touch of my wand for the asking."[24] The family was making a long, slow, and still difficult transition from the aristocracy to the middle classes.

225

Henry's future was still in doubt too. He had indeed gone up to Oxford in January 1871, but he was home again in the fall. Either the Camerons ran out of money to pay tuition (as had happened with Hardinge), or Henry was still not applying himself to his studies. The newest plan was to try to train him as a land agent, since he had declared a preference for outdoor work. Cameron agreed that with their "interest" they might be able to place him with one of their aristocratic friends, but he must first apprentice himself and learn surveying and book-keeping. His situation was remarkably like Fred Vincy's in *Middlemarch*, but without the love and hard-working example of a Mary Garth to steady him. Meanwhile, Cameron was scouting for potential brides for Hardinge. One of her favorite candidates was Annie Thackeray's second cousin Emily Ritchie, known as Pinkie. Cameron wrote to Pinkie in the fall of 1871, chastising her for not coming to the Isle of Wight to see some of their theatricals and praising Hardinge to her. Henry and Hardinge, she claimed, as she often did, were the two of her sons with the greatest potential:

> Hardinge has the heroic in him developed and fulfilled[.] Henry has it I believe but it is unfulfilled yet. Still I have great faith in Henry too + great hopes for him notwithstanding his <u>rooted mental</u> idleness. I hope he will as Har has done nail himself yet to the mast of duty.[25]

Hardinge came home from Ceylon for a brief visit in November, which Cameron commemorated by donating several of her portraits of great men to the Brockenhurst train station in which she first saw him again after an absence of four years.[26] In the letter quoted above she told Pinkie Ritchie that she considered returning with him to Ceylon in December, but she decided to stay and try to make something of Henry first.

There is little mention of Cameron's work in the letters that survive from the first years of the 1870s. She continued to send Watts photographs to critique. She exhibited her work in London and Vienna and she again rented Colnaghi's gallery for a one-woman show in January 1873. She sold twenty photographs to the American publisher James T. Fields for 10 pounds, a considerable discount on Colnaghi's prices.[27] Fields and his wife Annie had visited Tennyson at Freshwater in the spring of 1869, when Cameron had photographed some of their party. She sent a portfolio of work to Victor Hugo, in exile on the Channel Islands, and received effusive thanks in reply.[28] Cameron also continued to give her work away to friends and family members: in the early 1870s she gave out several bound books filled with reduced-size copies of her photographs. Curator Philippa Wright, who has written the only extensive study of these miniature albums, calls them "portable galleries" and believes that Cameron probably intended them to generate interest in her full-size work. These books were filled with cabinet- and *carte de visite*-sized photographs and they were less customized than her full-scale presentation albums. Cameron gave away nine known miniature albums between 1869 and 1875, including two to Hardinge, and presented copies of a miniature edition of her *Idylls of the King* to friends in 1875.[29] It was probably during these years that Emily Tennyson wrote to Cameron admonishing her for her spendthrift habits: "I do not mean to let you ruin yourself by giving the photographs away . . . . I feel bound to point with a solemn finger to those stalwart boys of yours saying 'Remember.' I see that I shall have to set up a shop for the sale of photographs myself all for your benefit."[30]

In fact, Cameron *was* thinking of her sons. In October 1872 the industrious Hardinge got an important promotion and a new boss when Sir William Gregory took over as Governor of Ceylon. The new appointment was a mixed blessing, for it sent Hardinge to Aharadanapura, which Cameron considered unhealthy.[31] After a brief internal debate, she took matters into her own hands and sent Gregory an eighteen-page letter begging him to take care of her son's health. Hardinge had previously vetoed any intervention in his career, but Cameron could not resist. In this surprisingly intimate letter Cameron claims that at Freshwater Tennyson "is the Sun of the Earth and I am the Priestess of the Sun of the Heavens so that my works must sometimes even surpass his –," adding rather confusingly, with heavy underlining, "not thanks to me –."[32] Cameron loved the Priestess of the Sun metaphor and used it both to claim authority and prestige and also to counter those critics (especially early in photography's history) who felt that photographs were made entirely by the sun, without any human agency. Perhaps here, once again, the metaphor allows her to dodge responsibility for what Victorian readers would have found an audacious boast: after all, she still implies that the sun is the primary agent and she is merely its anointed servant. Her puzzling postscript to the sentence becomes the safety valve for her ambitious claims. Cameron also confided in Gregory her oft-repeated opinion that Emily was the superior of the two Tennysons. Though it was her candid feeling, it was a telling confession that revealed something of her ambivalent feelings of adoration and envy of the poet.

Cameron also told Gregory about Henry and his genius for acting, noting that "it has required all my firmness to prevent his becoming a Professional Actor. It is a Gift born to him but I would rather he followed his Brother Hardinge's example + was harnessed to a life of official work and severe duty."[33] Cameron herself pursued amateur theatricals with gusto in those years; Emily Tennyson's journals are full of references to her rehearsals and shows. Was it any wonder, then, that Henry revived the notion of a theatrical career? In February 1873 Emily Tennyson had a frank conversation with Cameron, advising that Henry had not the energy to make his way as a professional actor nor to resist being brought down by his associates. By March, however, she was willing to talk to Alfred about supporting Henry during one last try at a stage career.[34] Cameron had somehow managed to resist Emily's advice and even turn it around. Indeed, she told Gregory that spring: "I abhor the [theatrical] life in its dark side of temptation[,] struggle[,] + indignity when a youth of talent must bear the kicks of an illiterate Stage Manager. But Henry is singularly pure + temperate + hopeful very like Hardinge in outward feature + inner nature."[35] It must have been around this time that Henry wrote to his brother Charlie Hay wondering if Ellen Terry could be prevailed upon to help him land a position in a good acting company.[36] Apparently, Henry did have some success, but it must not have been enough, for he had run out of options by the fall. Despite his mother's despair at parting from him and his own disappointed hopes, the plan was to send him to his brothers in Ceylon that autumn.

Emily Tennyson noted that Henry "soothes and manages" his mother beautifully, whereas "Charlie is such a sorrow to her."[37] It was a difficult winter. Cameron's sister Louisa Bayley died in March; though Cameron does not seem to have been especially close to her, she had recently written to Gregory that "we sisters all live very much in each other."[38] A few months before, Charlie Hay finally had surgery to remove his decayed jawbone and his mother nursed him through a long convalescence. Emily wrote to Edward Lear that "poor Mrs. Cameron" was ill from fatigue and worry about her sons. "But for this," she wrote,

> I believe she and Mr. Cameron would have been off to Ceylon with their son Henry. It seems so impossible for her to part from this last son who is a comfort to her and his best hope of work is in Ceylon though his inclination leads him to try the English stage. Imagine, in our London theatre almost all the actors are gentlemen and I have heard of two ladies going on the stage . . .[39]

By April, Cameron was feeling better and Charlie Hay too was well enough to consider returning to Ceylon. He left England again about a year later. Cameron wrote Hardinge complaining of her estrangement from Charlie Hay, whose lifestyle she still deplored, and arguing that he really was strong enough to return to some proper work. Her attachment to her sons was very physical: she spoke of her distance from Charlie Hay as literally an inability to "caress" him and her longing for Hardinge as a need to have him in her arms.[40] This physical yearning clearly intensified her depressions in their absence, and fed the decision to rejoin them in Ceylon.

In the same letter Cameron urges Hardinge to consider marrying and insists that he obtain a year's leave to England to look for a suitable wife. She implies that his life in Ceylon may include sexual partners but writes frankly that

> a less holy tie is to be lamented under the best of circumstances and a life that has not known the purer sanctifying influences of love filtering lust is a life that has not yet had developed in it the God as <u>exalting</u> and intensifying the

human nature and animal side of man and woman which animal side I do not at all despise. It is the rich soil that bears the golden fruit but if good seed is not sown in that soil it then degenerates into a dung heap does it not? Who would so intensely enjoy happy married life as you would my treasure[?]

This vision of a divinely (and maternally) sanctioned sexuality was in sharp contrast to her description of Charlie Hay, whose "kisses are sold to every wanton woman or rather given to her with money."[41] Hardinge in those years reached an apotheosis as favored son. Cameron searched his letters closely for evidence of a "Nimue," the sorceress renamed Vivien in Tennyson's *Idylls*, but he remained her (relatively) chaste and parfit knight.[42] He was reliable, securely settled, and devoted to his parents. He did eventually marry but not until after his mother's death.

That Easter saw another extended house party at Freshwater. Tennyson was in his element, walking the downs with a parade of maidens, reciting poetry, and waltzing solemnly in the evening balls. Annie Thackeray came. Her sister Minnie and Minnie's husband Leslie Stephen came, as well as Leslie's brother Fitzjames, who had finished a term in Charles Hay's old job of legal member for the Council of India. Blanche Warre Cornish, born a Ritchie and one of Annie Thackeray's second cousins and friends, came fresh from the publication of a novel. Her sister Pinkie came, still unmarried and singled out by Cameron for her "Har." Cameron's matchmaking for Hardinge had become so obvious that her friends teased her about the "string of pearls" she would set before him and Hardinge himself joked about the various candidate "Pearls." Cameron was equally hopeful that Browning might be brought to marry again, and thought she saw signs of an attachment to Annie Thackeray. She failed in both efforts at matchmaking.[43]

It had been a difficult few years, marked by illnesses and great uncertainty about the future of the family. Sara Prinsep and her husband were losing the lease to Little Holland House, their home for over twenty-five years. In 1873 they decided to move to Freshwater too: Thoby Prinsep bought land and Watts began to build a house, called the Briary. That fall they had begun construction. Meanwhile, Henry Herschel Hay was making plans to give up acting and join his brothers in Ceylon in November when a greater blow fell. In October, Julia Norman died of complications from childbirth. She had been ill for several years through miscarriages and confinements and she succumbed to blood poisoning in this last, sixth birth. After decades of anxiety about separations from her children, hoarding tokens and warning against every possible risk, Cameron had lost her only daughter. Few photographs, and even fewer letters, survive from that terrible autumn, but in January Cameron responded to Sir William Gregory's condolences with resignation and even reserve. She pities poor Charlie Norman and describes Juley's patience in suffering much as if it were a sentimental tale or an allegorical portrait, but comes to a surprising conclusion:

> I try to arise + be hopeful–and the prospect of my Son Hardinge's return to me is indeed like the rising of the Sun after a long dark night because the departure of my Benjamin of my youngest Son Henry Herschel Hay I felt even more acutely than I did my Daughter's death. This might seem to some unnatural but it was natural to me –even much as I cherished my daughter my youngest son had kept so close to me thro' all my severest trials.[44]

In the rest of the seventeen-some pages of the letter Cameron resolutely mentions only Henry, Hardinge, and her friend Lady Elcho's recent loss of her son. She counted up Henry's sacrifices for her sake, including the last, hard, sacrifice of his acting career, and described him as a nurse and comfort to her. Perhaps, implicitly, she felt that Juley was already lost to her, absorbed in her growing family and worn down by illness. Perhaps Juley had wanted to keep her distance from these insolvent parents who involved her husband in embarrassing negotiations over money. Certainly Julia and Charlie Norman were never mentioned as Freshwater guests, though they kept up with the Camerons through visits in London.[45] Perhaps this is why Cameron invested so heavily in surrogate daughters, especially Ewen's Annie, and in attempting to fashion her sons into heroes.

Despite her manic anxiety in anticipating crises, Cameron was always rather stoic once disaster struck. She turned with determination to work and banished grief and self-pity. She had another show at Colnaghi's opening that November and she must have turned to the preparations with relief. Her family, however, was shocked that she intended to go ahead with the exhibit so soon after her bereavement. Maria Jackson wrote to her daughter Julia about her sister Julia Margaret in the strongest terms:

> I can not understand her doing such a thing at such a time–She is evidently bent upon carrying it out & therefore has not mentioned it to any of us for she knows what we must feel. It grieves me so I can scarcely bear to mention it. It was very good of you to write & remonstrate. I have not yet–& I know it will be no good when I do. Had I known when she contemplated it I might have prevented it but who could have supposed that now she w[oul]d have carried out such a scheme.[46]

Maria expected that Charlie and others would be offended and she did write her sister a letter of protest. But she was right in her judgment of Julia Margaret's character: the show went on and any other signs of family strife were lost or destroyed.

Emily Tennyson's friend Mary Brotherton, another Isle of Wight neighbor, wrote astutely about Cameron and her show to one of Tennyson's brothers:

> I fear it is not a successful speculation–as to money. She is not likely to make money as a photographer, or indeed in any way. She is too orientally magnificent and generous in her ideas. I wish the Laureate would let her make another study of him–it would be of use to her financially, no doubt, but he objects to her portraits–which are full of power but hardly as flattering as a man once so handsome as the Laureate may wish his likeness to be. Nevertheless I would rather, were I him, go down to posterity in one of Mrs. Cameron's grand Rembrandtesque photos, than in the 'glorified-footman,' dying duck Mayall vulgarities which he, strange to say, prefers . . .[47]

Brotherton was on to something. At this stage, Cameron and Tennyson's relationship, though close, was particularly competitive. In her unfinished autobiography, written some time in 1874, Cameron wrestles too with Tennyson's preference for Mayall's portrait over hers and scorns the comparison.[48] The *Idylls of the King* was phenomenally successful just when Cameron desperately needed success to justify her career. And unlike Taylor and Watts, Tennyson actually made a lot of money from his art, which Cameron must have envied and resented too. Her work was recognized and admired but it barely broke even. The move to Ceylon seemed more and more inevitable, but it would end her career as she had known it. For his part, Tennyson was very fond of Cameron and wanted to help her, but he balked at additional portraits. They injured his vanity and increased his celebrity. He had to think of another way to support Cameron's work.

This, then, was the background to their collaboration on a photographic edition of the *Idylls of the King* the following year.[49] In 1874 the *Idylls* were not yet complete: Tennyson had written all twelve books, but they would not be published in their current form until 1885.[50] As Cameron told the story in letters to her old friend Sir Edward Ryan, now retired from the Supreme Court of India, some time around the end of August Tennyson approached her with the question

> "Will you think it a trouble to illuminate my 'Idylls' for me?" I answered laughing "Now <u>you</u> know Alfred that <u>I</u> know that it is immortality to me to be bound up with you that altho' I bully you I have a corner of worship for you in my heart" – and so <u>I consented</u>.[51]

It was very important to Cameron that the idea for this project came from Tennyson himself. She mentioned that fact several times in her five letters that month to Ryan and in a letter earlier that fall to the poet's brother Charles Tennyson Turner. But, as she explained in that first letter to Ryan, Tennyson originally proposed that she provide only two photographs for a small illustrated "people's edition" of the poem; the illustrations themselves would be reduced woodcuts from her large photographs. Cameron was disappointed when she saw them and decided to bring out a full-sized edition of the photographs as a gift book. This idea she variously claimed as her own or as Alfred's, but it was an entirely different matter financially: she bore the expense of the two volumes and it was no longer an edition of the complete poem. Cameron claimed that even the smaller edition of woodcuts was undertaken for "friendship," but if so, she lost a golden opportunity, because she knew how profitable Gustave Doré's illustrated *Idylls* was.[52] Eventually, she produced two volumes of twelve original photographs each, dedicated by permission to Queen Victoria's eldest daughter, the Crown Princess of Germany. Cameron's *Idylls* also included a prefatory poem, written by Charles Tennyson Turner, that reinforced Cameron's favorite attributes: her love of beauty and her mastery of the powers of the sun.[53]

Illustrating Tennyson's work was risky because he was famously hard to please. In 1857 Tennyson had complained about the liberties that several Pre-Raphaelite artists had taken in illustrating an edition of his poems. He had wanted an exact literal correspondence between the scene described in the poem and the accompanying illustration.[54] At the time, Ruskin had recounted a dispute between Tennyson, Watts, and himself in which Tennyson insisted that painters should serve his words and Ruskin and Watts retorted that "the poet *must* be content to have his painter in partnership – not a slave . . . ."[55] Like Watts, Cameron, of course, believed in the "idealizing" function of art and would have resisted a subservient role. Tennyson seems not to have seen Cameron's book until it was finished and he seems to have been satisfied with it: at least, Cameron noted in a letter that "our great Laureate Alfred Tennyson himself is very much pleased with this ideal representation of his Idylls . . . ."[56] Cameron managed to satisfy him by doing in her work what she had always done in her friendship with him: she admired him frankly but refused to be intimidated. Still, the stage was set for a power struggle.

Cameron took care to ally herself closely to Tennyson throughout the project, perhaps in order to please him and ease his suspicions about illustrators. When Cameron wrote to Edward Ryan that fall, she emphasized Tennyson's approval: he suggested it; he approved of the photographs; the hollow oak used in the Merlin photograph even came from his grounds. When Tennyson balked at the quotation Cameron had chosen to use under his portrait, Cameron telegraphed Ryan to make sure that the censored passage was not mentioned in any forthcoming review.[57] Similarly, she wrote to Ryan that Alfred believed his King Arthur was the "'the principle of conscience moving among his knights' and certainly my King Arthur has eyes that search into one . . . ."[58] She wanted to associate herself with the laureate to promote her sales and she wanted Ryan to arrange for her book to be reviewed in the London *Times*.

Cameron worked very hard on those photographs that fall. In order to achieve the twelve successes in the first volume (besides the frontispiece portrait of Tennyson himself as the "Dirty Monk"), she told Ryan (in various letters) that she had made between 180 and 245 photographs. Whatever the total figure, the work was daunting. She threw herself into finding models (and hiring some for perhaps the first time in her career), renting armor, and arranging props.[59] She was especially careful about her choice of models, and may have tried out different versions of different characters until she found one that fitted her vision. The first volume, probably published on December 15, comprises photographs of Gareth and Lynette, Enid, Merlin and Vivien, Elaine, Galahad and the Pale Nun, the Little Novice and Guinevere, and King Arthur, with a few variations from copy to copy. Cameron quickly determined to use one of her favorite models, Thoby Prinsep's niece May, for Elaine and her own husband as Merlin. Although Charles Hay had posed before for portraits, he was very rarely used in character parts, so his role as the aging magician seems to have been significant to Cameron. There is a hint in her letter to Edward Ryan that Charles Hay, like Merlin, was susceptible to the temptations of younger women.[60] She also kept to her own precedent by using May Prinsep and her fiancé Andrew Hichens for the photograph of the courting couple Gareth and Lynette.[61] Enid was modeled by a regular sitter, Emily Peacock, perhaps another Freshwater guest. For the other models, however, she searched long and hard.

Lancelot, in particular, was a problem. After all, he had to be persuasive as both a legendary knight and an adulterer. Cameron allegedly proposed Cardinal Vaughan, much to his embarrassment.[62] In December Cameron desperately wrote to Edward Ryan wondering if she could get John Everett Millais or Colonel Loyd Lindsay to sit for her or if she should advertise. The situation was so critical that Cameron sent Ryan a sample book with a blank page for the tenth photograph of Lancelot and Guinevere.[63] In the end, Lancelot may have been one of the models she acknowledged hiring; he has been identified only as Mr. Read in the copyright registration for the photograph a few days later. According to the copyright registers, a Mr. Coxhead, perhaps another hired model, posed for Sir Galahad. Cameron's Arthur was found in a local porter at Yarmouth Pier named William Warder.[64] Guinevere was modeled by a Mrs. Hardinge, perhaps a sister-in-law of Cameron's old friend.[65]

Although Merlin was obviously modeled by Charles Hay Cameron, Vivien was modeled by a visitor to the Isle of Wight, Agnes Mangles.[66] Cameron, who famously enlisted friends, family, and servants as models, may have had qualms about identifying members of her household with morally ambiguous women. Coincidentally, Mangles later wrote an anonymous reminiscence of Cameron in which she describes how she was visiting the Isle of Wight when Cameron recruited her as a sitter and how she resisted modeling for the "masculine" character of Zenobia and the "objectionable" character of Vivien.[67] Her description of sitting for Cameron, like others, portrays it as physically arduous and time-consuming: the poses are hard to hold and Charles Hay kept laughing in the middle of the exposures. Interestingly, though, the author/model calls herself a "lady amateur" and reveals that she herself took up photography later on.[68]

Tennyson's poem plays out a theme with variations on the questions of the visibility of truth and the appearance of good and evil. The term "idylls" itself implied a series of brief, pictorial sketches.[69] As art historian Carol Armstrong notes about Gareth and Lynette in her study of Cameron's illustrations for the poem, many of the plots revolve around blindness and sight, disguise and costume.[70] Gareth, dressed as a kitchen boy, tries to impress the lady Lynette. Geraint tests his wife Enid's virtue by forcing her to put on the maid's dress he first saw her in and obey his every word. Merlin is fooled by the "lissome" Vivien's beauty and tells her the charm that she uses to blind him. Elaine falls in love with the disguised Lancelot and wastes away. Galahad is the only knight to see a vision of the Holy Grail. Arthur is unable to see the adultery occurring under his very eyes between his wife and best friend. The twelve books also consistently present power struggles, usually between men and women. Cameron's *Idylls* are true to this dramatic conflict, but she asserts her own interpretation. As Armstrong points out, Cameron's photographic illustrations insistently exclude, immobilize, and disarm the powerful male characters in favor of the females.[71] Gareth is photographed asleep. "Geraint and Enid" is illustrated solely by two portraits of Enid. Merlin is photographed ensnared and blinded. Armstrong notes that when Vivien triumphs over Merlin she crows, "I have made his glory mine" – a claim that Cameron could echo in her assertion of authority over Tennyson's text.[72] By reducing his poem cycle into short captions for her photographs, written out in her own handwriting, she took over his work and made it her own.

The *Vivien and Merlin* photographs [see figure] are particularly interesting, in part because of Charles Hay's choice as model and in part because Vivien is a rare example of an evil female character in Cameron's world of women. Tennyson based his *Idylls* on Sir Thomas Malory's medieval epic and Cameron's friend Lady Charlotte Guest's more recent translation of the Welsh fable, *The Mabinogion*. But he substantially changed the character of Merlin's temptress, making her the pursuer instead of the pursued.[73] It was supposedly Edward Burne-Jones (who was working on his famous painting *The Beguiling of Merlin* at around the same time as Cameron was producing her *Idylls*) who insisted that Tennyson change the character's name from Nimue to Vivien, where the hint of French spelling could signify immorality to Victorian Britons. The charm that Vivien casts on Merlin has a certain poetic justice to it. Merlin asserts that it was first used by an Eastern king to control the "magnet-like" ("Merlin and Vivien," l. 571) effects of his wife's beauty.

When Cameron photographs Vivien casting such a spell on Merlin she is signaling Vivien's depravity but also asserting a woman's control over who and what is seen. With this image, Cameron implicitly asserts her power over a patriarchal Charles Hay, much as Vivien does over Merlin.[74] In addition, Cameron's title for the photograph, *Vivien and Merlin*, reverses the priority that Tennyson has given to Merlin over Vivien, and Cameron's composition places Vivien so much in the foreground that she appears much larger than Merlin. Whereas for Tennyson Vivien's spell can signal her evil and Merlin's weakness, for a female photographer, controlling who and what is seen is a positive sign of artistry and professionalism. The close identification of Vivien and Cameron, or the "harlot" and the artist, is further underscored by the "waving hands" in the poem and the moving hands in the photograph. Just as Vivien's gesture reveals her vice, Cameron's handiwork and handwriting reveals her artistry. Thus, even if Vivien's association with the photographer is empowering, the photographer's association with Vivien tends to perpetuate the Victorian characterization of women artists as disreputable.

There is another, more sympathetic, figure of the woman artist in Cameron's *Idylls*, though she is not an easier role model. She is Elaine, prefigured in Tennyson's earlier poem "The Lady of Shalott," another innocent young woman who loved too much. Like Ophelia, she ends up in a watery grave. But in the meantime the Lady of Shalott wove her story into an exquisite tapestry and Elaine embroidered a shield cover for Lancelot with his emblems and her own designs. It is an important part of the moral of those stories that these creative women are forced to choose between art and love; the implication seems to be that women artists must suffer for their art. As Armstrong notes too, Elaine's embroidery is central to Cameron's representation of her in the two photographs of Elaine that she included in the first volume of the *Idylls*. Cameron actually scratched the negative to make Elaine's embroidered bird more visible, and in the second image she poses Elaine to gaze sadly at her own hands and the empty shield cover on her lap.[75]

Like Elaine and Enid, Guinevere earned herself several photographs out of the twelve in Cameron's first volume. In various surviving copies she is shown standing alone, in a seated portrait with Lancelot, and in a double portrait with the Little Novice who soothes her after her retreat from Camelot to a convent in Glastonbury. There is an anecdote that the model for Guinevere was found exhausted after a long day of sitting and complained that she had spent the day on the floor clutching Arthur's feet in a representation of their famous farewell, where Guinevere prostrates herself to ask her husband's forgiveness. It is the culminating moment of her shame and Cameron clearly decided not to use the photograph.[76] However, the final images of the volume comprise two head-and-shoulders portraits of Arthur [see figure], both taken from a very low viewpoint, which may suggest Guinevere's point of view without implicating her in the scene of her humiliation.[77]

A year earlier, well before the collaborative *Idylls* were thought of, Cameron revealed her own opinion of that famous scene in a letter to Sir William Gregory:

> I do not see why coldness should belong to perfectness, + I for one think King Arthur very imperfect – 'The frailty of a Man' + the 'Security of a God' describes the perfect man but King Arthur seems to have had no frailty but that of self righteousness + certainly his neglect of his lovely young Wife ought to have brought on self reproach instead of the morbid harangue of his farewell. I know what a heretic I am + that the Nation (like Gladstone) think this the finest thing in the English language – I wholly differ + I have always told Alfred Tennyson so + I believe he half thinks I am right for when I say to him Silence would have been so much nobler than this pitching in rhetorically to a poor fallen woman – he only answers me Bah – but how do you express Silence?[78]

Although the collaborative *Idylls* may well have been Tennyson's idea, this was a woman who was ready with her own interpretation of the poem.

In the same letter Cameron makes one of her frequent comparisons of her son Henry to Arthur's purest knight, Sir Galahad. And again, a year later in her letter to Ryan, Henry is "such a principled young creature. He is the one Sir Galahad in the family."[79] Henry had left for Ceylon after his sister's death the year before and reports of his progress as a coffee planter were good. As Cameron was publishing and promoting the *Idylls* that winter, Ewen was home with them, Hardinge was awaiting his next leave in England, and even Charlie Hay was earning good notices from his mother. The appeals to Overstone continued, though: 100 pounds for Eugene's debts in 1870; another 50 pounds for Charlie Hay in 1872; and then a long letter of petition from Charlie Hay in 1874 when he requested a loan of 5,000 pounds to buy property in Ceylon. He had only been sole manager of an estate for eight months before he made his appeal.[80] Charles Norman, always a careful mediator between his family-by-marriage and their lenders, advised Lord Overstone to let the young man prove himself before extending such a great sum. The following year Overstone did extend a 7,000-pound mortgage jointly to Charlie Hay and Henry at a 5 per cent interest rate. The brothers bought an estate called Lippakelle and put their hopes in growing cinchona, a South American tree from which quinine was derived. A few months afterwards, Henry Herschel Hay wrote to Charlie Norman asking to transfer Overstone's mortgage from primary lien on the estate to a secondary one so that he and his brothers could raise more money to buy two other estates. Norman, Overstone, and the land agent they consulted felt the brothers were overextended and telegrammed Henry Herschel Hay that the request was denied.[81] The brothers repaid the original mortgage in 1878.[82]

Both Cameron and Tennyson had sons newly independent at the time of the *Idylls*: Cameron's youngest, Henry, was almost twenty-three years old and Tennyson's youngest, Lionel, was twenty. Both parents were still engaged in the difficult process of setting their sons up properly as adults. In Cameron's case, the situation was complicated by the family's socioeconomic decline. In Tennyson's case, the problem was the reverse: his genius, his reputation, and his wealth set a very high standard for his sons. In 1883 he would accept a baronetcy, in part in order to bequeath it to Hallam.[83] Hallam and Lionel had every advantage: what were they going to make of themselves? It is worth, then, shifting gears and thinking about Cameron and Tennyson's work on the *Idylls* as not only preoccupied with the role of women in culture and society but also the problem of male succession. After all, the adultery that brings about the fall of Camelot was historically dangerous because of its threat to inheritance and succession. In his final speech to her, King Arthur blames Guinevere for bringing moral contagion to his Round Table and he cries: "Well is it that no child is born of thee" ("Guinevere," l. 421), but presumably the struggle for control over his kingdom would have been very different if there had been a son.[84] The shape of the poem is circular, like the round table, in the return of Excalibur to the Lady of the Lake and the insistence on cycles, as "the old order changeth, yielding place to new" ("Passing of Arthur," l. 408). In Cameron's and Tennyson's situations, there was nothing as momentous as a civilization at stake, but they took seriously their roles as parents and scrutinized their sons' characters and prospects for signs of good and evil. They wanted their sons to turn out like ideal knights – good, true, chaste, valiant – and Cameron, at least, sized up her sons against this standard quite explicitly. They jockeyed in her favor according to their resemblance to this ideal, and she held for a long time to her cherished image of her "Benjamin," Henry.

In their conscious adoption of a chivalrous ideal for men, Cameron and Tennyson were hardly alone. The Arthurian revival was in full swing in Victorian art and literature by mid-century, as other scholars have documented.[85] Watts painted many Arthurian scenes, including a Galahad modeled on Sara Prinsep's son Arthur.[86] The public schools were full of explicit references to a knightly model, from the Arthurian designs for their stained-glass windows to the very notion of honor as the ultimate good. Although many factors contributed to these trends, Tennyson was often blamed and credited. As one mid-century schoolboy reminisced later,

> Whatever might be felt about them now, these *Idylls* had an immense influence upon us as boys at the time. The contrasted knightly types, Galahad, Percivale, Lancelot, Bors, the sage Merlin, above all King Arthur himself, were very much to us. Side by side with Homer and Greek history, they gave us our standards. We saw them in our Head, in our Masters, and in our comrades.[87]

In the 1880s some of the aristocratic British youths who had grown up with these ideals, though married, began conducting passionate, Platonic relationships based on the terms of courtly romance. Some of the members of this so-called "Souls" clique were the children of Cameron and Tennyson's close friends.[88] Tennyson, so wedded to fidelity, would have been aghast that his work could have such consequences. Indeed, he had been accused of encouraging immorality once already, when Robert Buchanan included him in his notorious critique of "The Fleshly School of Poetry" in 1871. In charging that contemporary poetry revealed a licentious interest in bodies and sensuality, Buchanan singled out Dante Gabriel Rossetti, Algernon Swinburne, and Charles Baudelaire for blame, but he included Tennyson's Vivien and Maud as well.[89]

The Tennysons may not have worried as much about their sons' characters as the Camerons did – Hallam and Lionel Tennyson were both at Cambridge in 1874 and doing well – but they faced a similar professional problem in Lionel's interest in acting and singing.[90] It was one reason why Emily wanted to keep Henry Herschel Hay away from her son. That year Emily Tennyson suffered some kind of a gradual collapse, due (people assumed) to overwork in her management of her household and her husband's career. Hallam took over his mother's role as secretary to his father for the first time. In fact, with brief exceptions, he devoted the rest of his life to his father's work. It was a sacred Tennyson family truth that Hallam had sacrificed his own prospects out of duty and devotion, but Ann Thwaite, Emily's biographer, finds the story more complicated. Certainly Emily and Alfred were gratified all their lives by the proximity and steadfast loyalty of this heroic son, but Thwaite suggests that Hallam's role in the family evolved over time and he didn't so much as decide to sacrifice himself as drift into a convenient and safe harbor.[91] He secured the role of the good son, much as Hardinge did, whereas Lionel, who eventually obtained a civil service job and died young returning from India in 1886, was cast as the erring son. After his tragic early death, Lionel inspired a heady mix of guilt, regret, and adoration from his parents, who then clung the more tightly to Hallam. All this was still in the future at the beginning of 1875, but already Tennyson felt depressed over his sons' absences and Cameron was planning reunions with hers: first Hardinge's return to England and then her own move to join them in Ceylon.

In May Cameron published a second volume of photographic illustrations to the *Idylls*, though this time the scenes were drawn from a broad range of Tennyson's work. She included three photographs based on "The May Queen," three from *The Princess*, three from the *Idylls of the King*, and one each from "Mariana," "The Beggar Maid," and *Maud*. The second volume seems to circle back on Cameron's and Tennyson's careers: she returns to poems she has photographed before, like "The May Queen" and "The Beggar Maid." Models and props from the first volume of the *Idylls* show up again in new guises:[92] Elaine's carved chair becomes a support for Mariana's weariness, for example. "The May Queen" also refers back to Cameron's earliest project, her translation of *Leonora*, in its theme of a mother's loss of her daughter. This time she used Emily Peacock (formerly the model for Enid), introduced Lionel Tennyson as the May Queen's lover, and punned on her book's May 1 publication date. Elaine reappears, this time on her death bier. Mary Hillier makes a brief appearance in the final photograph as Maud. Could Cameron have already known that this would be the last major project of her photographic career? In revisiting so many former subjects, she seems to have been preparing a farewell.

When the first volume of the *Idylls* came out, Cameron had begged Edward Ryan to use his influence at the London *Times* and place a review of her work in time to drum up Christmas sales. The book was not reviewed until January, however, and only two pieces appeared. The reviewer in the *Morning Post* sounded suspiciously knowledgeable about Cameron's working methods: either he or she knew Cameron personally or was provided with details by a mutual friend.[93] It was an enthusiastic and flattering critique of the work, dwelling on the sentiment of each illustration and the skill of the models. The critic goes out of his or her way to point out the importance of a close fit between model and character:

> [Sitters] must be no mere models in the ordinary acceptation of the word, but men and women of peculiar types, combining with fine *physique* high mental culture as well, and abundantly imbued with the poetic spirit of the themes they cooperate in illustrating. They must be people who understand the significance of action and gesture, and the import of dramatic expression. In this regard Mrs. Cameron has been particularly fortunate, the representatives of her *dramatis personae* being evidently individuals who, thus highly qualified, partake her inspiration and lend themselves to the realisation of her poetic conceptions.[94]

Again, both Cameron and Tennyson's works lent themselves to typological readings. The sitters must somehow match the characters, who in turn represented particular ideas. It was a universalizing theory that tended to favor similarities over differences. Other Victorian viewers made similar connections between character and model: the publisher C. Kegan Paul wrote to Cameron that "Merlin is grand, the Vivien not quite Vivien, but then she is too good to be so."[95] Cameron herself wrote of her model that "she is not wicked eno' for she is a sweet girl . . . ."[96]

Despite good reviews and Cameron's best efforts at publicity, the work seems to have failed commercially.[97] This must be at least in part due to the enormous expense of the edition. Although books illustrated with original photographs were not unheard of at the time, they were extremely expensive to produce.[98] In the 1880s the invention of halftone reproduction would make it affordable to reproduce a single photograph in multiple copies of books and newspapers.[99] In 1874, however, producing Cameron's edition of the *Idylls* actually necessitated printing up multiple photographs from each unique negative and then pasting each original photograph into a printed book. Helmut Gernsheim estimated that production costs pushed such photographic books to an average price of 30 shillings a volume, which was about equal to the price of a three-decker novel and about ten times the average weekly salary of a housemaid.[100] The *Idylls* sold for 6 guineas a volume, or four times that average price, but even this outrageous sum barely covered Cameron's production costs.[101]

In addition, in her pursuit of commercial success and "high art" Cameron wanted it both ways. She may have wished for Alfred's "mountain heap of profits,"[102] but she scorned small, cheap popular editions and went out of her way to signal that her book was a work of art, not a commodity.[103] Besides the original photographs, much of the text in the book was reproduced from lithographed handwriting, lending it the air of a personal album, much like the gift albums Cameron presented to friends in the 1860s. Although the amount and placement of handwriting varies from copy to copy, this variation makes each book seem even more unique. Handwriting obviously adds value to the mechanical reproduction, and it was sometimes difficult for Cameron's sitters to keep up with demands for their autographs. Gernsheim notes that in periods of great demand Cameron actually forged Tennyson's signature, just as her maids would forge Cameron's copyright statement when time was short.[104] The use of handwriting also serves the function of reasserting Cameron's claims for photography as an art form. She again insists on the intervention of the artist's hand between the mechanical camera and the art image. The handwriting is the mark of the artist's unique personality, just as it is the mark of the art object's unique value.

Mike Weaver has argued that Cameron's photographs find their meaning exactly in the gap between "idealist fiction and realist fact:" Cameron transforms her "actual models" into "ideal subjects."[105] However, Cameron's work, and its context in Victorian aesthetic debates about photography and art, reveals the instability of such distinctions: although Victorians used these terms and struggled to keep them separate, there was little consensus on the definitions of "realism" and "idealism" and in practice their opposition often collapsed. Early-twentieth-century art critics judged the collaborative *Idylls of the King* a "failure" precisely because of this blurring of categories. Helmut Gernsheim expressed a fairly typical critical view of Cameron's *Idylls*:

> *We* believe that in them Mrs. Cameron attempted the impossible, something photography cannot and should not be made to do, something which is much better left to the able illustrator with pen and pencil – such as Gustave Doré, who also illustrated the *Idylls*. For despite the singular artistry with which Mrs.

Cameron arranged her groups to bring the characters represented into the pure region of ideality, her compositions persist in producing a realistic effect which can only be termed incongruous. We have come to realize that photography is a most difficult medium to express imaginative subjects and that most attempts to illustrate the unreal by a medium whose main contribution to art lies in its realism are doomed to failure.[106]

What this judgment elides is the historical and aesthetic context of Cameron's work, which complicated those very distinctions that Gernsheim believed were natural and universal. Victorian critics grappled earnestly with the definitions of the real and the ideal and the appropriate boundaries of each term. They often concluded, like Patmore in his 1866 review, that Cameron's photographs challenged their assumptions.

When David Wilkie Wynfield started photographing artists in costume in 1863, art critics loved it. But by the 1870s, costumed portraits were looking too . . . theatrical, and there was a backlash against them.[107] Photography historian Malcolm Daniel has noted that Rejlander explicitly compared his photographs to professional theater and Shakespeare, but a generation later his colleague P. H. Emerson derided Rejlander's work by comparing it to amateur theatricals.[108] There was Theater, and there was theater, and photographers tried to navigate between the professional and the amateur kinds, hoping to claim the prestige of the former and the popularity of the latter. By the late 1860s, Cameron's portraits had turned toward only the vaguest suggestion of costume, but her photographs for the *Idylls of the King* probably suffered critically and commercially from the backlash against theatricality and they have never quite rebounded.

Inevitably, the indiscriminate mingling of the real and the ideal, which has so infuriated modernist viewers of Cameron's work, leads to accusations of theatricality. The more obvious the artifice – like Cameron's fog-filled boat and the scratchings that were supposed to decorate Elaine's shield-cover – the more parodic the effect. Charles Hay Cameron observed this in his early *Essay On the Sublime and the Beautiful*: the "incongruous mixture of the vulgar with the sublime is a sort of natural parody." Once the viewer is aware of the artifice in art the effect is ruined, he reasoned.[109] Tennyson himself was not immune to this charge: in another example of how far theatricality had fallen out of favour just as the theater itself had risen to respectability, Gerard Manley Hopkins complained about Tennyson and his famous poem:

> He should have called them *Charades from the Middle Ages* . . . . Each scene is a triumph of language and of bright picturesque, but just like a charade– where real lace and good silks and real jewelry are used, because the actors are private persons and wealthy, but it is acting all the same . . .[110]

241

Again, it is the blurring of boundaries – the real and the pretend; the true and the false – that bothered Hopkins. The next generation called that suspension of disbelief hypocrisy. The Victorians practiced a kind of doublethink that lends itself easily (post-Freud) to charges of repression and denial. It is a cliché by now that the earnest, sentimental Victorians were followed by the sarcastic Edwardians and the ironic modernists. The postmodernists rediscovered theatricality as high camp, but they didn't know what to make of theatricality that was meant sincerely and didactically. The pendulum seems to be swinging back toward an appreciation of the complexity of art like Cameron's and the context from which it emerged.[111]

Tennyson's *Idylls of the King* are often read through the lens of nationalism. At the end of the Napoleonic Wars, and with its early embrace of industrialization, Great Britain was a global force to be reckoned with for decades. But by mid-century, embarrassing military "victories" like those in the Crimea and Abyssinia and colonial revolts like those in Jamaica and India made that power seem more precarious. The Unification of Italy might be cause for celebration in Britain, but the Unification of the German states, and the rise of Prussia, was cause for alarm. The Franco-Prussian War in 1871 had demonstrated just how powerful Prussia had become. It was a good time to contemplate the rise and fall of empires, and that is one of the subtexts of Tennyson's poem – and one reason for its popularity.

The poem also lends itself to a more domestic reading, though, and that is what Cameron emphasized in her illustrations. She preferred portraits of the female characters and chose scenes of love and faith. She leaned in sympathy toward the flawed, suffering Lancelot and Guinevere and away from the perfect, impassive Arthur, in a pattern of readerly identification that traces its roots at least back to Milton's charismatic Lucifer. Fallen heroes usually upstage their more righteous comrades. Prodigal sons are loved more than their honorable brothers. The *Idylls of the King*, as Cameron interpreted it, was a romance in which men and women struggled to find and hold onto their true characters and their true loves in a twilight world. It dramatized the poignant banality of the first and last human truth: everything comes to an end. Cameron and Tennyson felt that themselves, as they aged and as they looked around at their charmed life in Freshwater and thought, "This too is passing . . . ." Little Holland House was no more; the boys were grown and departed; the girls were married and mothers themselves. The last line of "The Passing of Arthur" reads: "And the new sun rose bringing the new year." The cycles of growth and decay that Tennyson traced so often included both suns and sons.

In her *Idylls*, Cameron was photographing a ghost world in more ways than one. Her last photograph for the second volume shows the dying King Arthur, surrounded by attendants, floating to his death on a makeshift boat [see figure]. In composition it closely resembles Daniel Maclise's take on the same scene in the 1857 Moxon Tennyson, illustrated by Pre-Raphaelite artists. It is one of the last photographs of Cameron's English career and it harks back to her first creative project: her translation of *Leonora* in 1847, also illustrated by Maclise.[112] It is an image that presages the Camerons' departure from England in a few short months.

CHAPTER 10

Eden

O N OCTOBER 21, 1875 a strange crowd gathered before the steamer *Pekin* departing from Southampton.[1] Amid the parting friends and the piles of luggage were a cow and two coffins. Julia Margaret Cameron, exhausted and emotional, expected that she would never again see the friends and relatives assembled there to see them off, so she packed coffins to prepare for their deaths in Ceylon. She was sixty years old. Charles Hay, now eighty years old, wandered around leaning on an ivory cane and holding a pink rose given to him earlier that morning by Emily Tennyson when he went to say goodbye to her.[2] The Camerons were travelling with Hardinge, returning to his civil service job in Ceylon, Julia Margaret's great-niece and adopted daughter Mary Clogstoun, and their maid Ellen Ottingham. Called "Little E," Ottingham had been in faithful service with the family since Henry's birth, though she seems never to have been photographed. Charles Henry Cameron, introduced to Annie Thackeray by Julia Margaret as her "stepson," was there too to see them off. Julia Margaret's sisters provided gifts for the long voyage: Maria Jackson gave them tea and Virginia Somers sent the cow for fresh milk. They would travel through the Suez Canal for the first time, which would shorten the trip by about two weeks. Somewhere among all the boxes must have been Julia Margaret's heavy camera and some of her favorite prints. The Camerons had run out of cash and on their way to Southampton Julia Margaret tipped porters with her photographs.

The Camerons' decision to leave England is often described as sudden, but it was long in preparation. While they may have decided impulsively to take advantage of Hardinge's help by accompanying him on his return, they had considered this step for at least a decade and they had almost committed to it before. As early as 1870 Cameron had written to Herschel that she hoped to end her life in Ceylon with her boys.[3] In the summer of 1875 both Ewen and Hardinge were home in England and the Camerons proceeded to settle their legal and financial affairs.[4] In a flurry of telegrams they consulted lawyers, lenders, and the trustees of their settlement, the aging Thoby

Prinsep and now Charles Norman and perhaps their nephew-in-law, Herbert Fisher (the executor of their wills). Their old friend Edward Ryan, once a trustee, had recently died. As Ewen wrote their lawyer, 500 pounds was again "urgently wanted."[5]

Julia Margaret set about hastily dispersing all their belongings: everything was given away or sold to pay for their passages to Ceylon. Tennyson bought some of their books, which had already been carried back and forth across the Indian Ocean.[6] Annie Thackeray bought the lease to the cottage called The Porch, where she and her sister Minnie had first gone in their grief at their father's death when Cameron was just starting her photographic career.[7] Cameron was especially upset about leaving her gardens, where she had planted everything with her own hands.[8] In a letter to an unnamed recipient in which she details these grievous losses, she blames the difficulty on the debts that she ran up to improve the Freshwater houses. She does not mention her work as a factor in her decision or her situation. She was sick again, and recognized that all her life she was prone to collapses at every parting.[9]

The decision to move to Ceylon was certainly agreeable to Charles Hay, who got out of bed and walked down to the sea for the first time in twelve years when he heard the plan. But it seems clear, even from that anecdote, that the choice was indeed Julia Margaret's to make. Her career was extremely important to her, but so were her sons, and it was perhaps impossible to continue ignoring financial realities as they had been doing. With Cameron's *Idylls* unlikely to have made money, and with their expenses always outrunning their income, there must have been few options left. Now that Ewen, Hardinge, Charlie, and Henry all seemed to be permanently settled in Ceylon, the decision was straightforward, if difficult. When Cameron's great-niece Laura Gurney Troubridge asked Aunt Julia why she was moving, she replied simply, "Where your heart is, there is your treasure also."[10]

Certainly Charlie Norman and Lord Overstone approved this sensible step. Cameron wrote Overstone a long letter in September detailing their decision and Overstone wrote their old friend George Warde Norman in response that it was "less impulsive, and more reasonable and sensible than usual with her. I agree with you in thinking that under all the peculiar circumstances of their case they have decided wisely—."[11] Overstone and the Normans may have interpreted the decision as financial, but Cameron spoke about it only as an emotional decision or a medical one. To Overstone, she remarked on Charles Hay's failing health and the prospects of improvement in a warmer climate. She acknowledged that his life at Freshwater for the past twelve years (the exact term of her career) had been

> a stagnant sort of life—for he has kept entirely on his own Lawn, + not moved beyond it, getting much pleasure from his Shrubs + his Books, but not drinking at any of the usual Founts of Life for pleasure and Variety or new Inspiration.

Since the decision to move, however, he had astonished her and the neighbors by appearing again, like Rip Van Winkle, in their midst.[12] Charles Hay, for his part, wrote a typically terse but heartfelt farewell to his old friend Overstone: "perhaps you and I may not shake hands again, but I doubt not that both of us will preserve the affectionate memory of our long + cordial friendship, made more impressive, in my own case, by gratitude for much substantial help."[13] This was the only acknowledgment of their debt to him in either of their letters.

Cameron's remarkable blind spot about money was not quite as simple as it first appeared: she was not, for example, ignorant of basic accounting. It was she, like many Victorian wives, who managed the household budgets, and due to Charles Hay's ill health she had additional responsibilities for large expenses like the house and her sons' education.[14] Neither was she uninterested in money. She knew it mattered and she frankly wanted more, but she persisted in a sort of denial about her own financial position. Her money-making schemes always involved grand gestures and, inevitably, more outlays. She may not have been attached to material luxuries but she was blithely attached to a luxurious lifestyle that her income could not support. It may have been that her early experience of wealth as a member of the British elite in Calcutta had left her with an inalienable expectation of abundance. Money seemed to her to be easy to make and easy to spend. If someone admired something she owned, she gave it to them. If producing one volume of photographs was a good idea, why not two? Cameron's generous personality intensified her fixed sense of her own identity as a member of the upper class, even though she and Charles Hay could not keep up with their peers. It was a disastrous combination financially, but without it her photographic career would not have been the same.

In preparation for departure, Cameron had gone to London on October 18 to make her final entries into the copyright book, registering autotypes (carbon prints) of five of her portraits of famous men: Watts, Darwin, Herschel, Tennyson, and the violinist Joseph Joachim.[15] She had arranged for the Autotype Company of London to hold her negatives and reproduce them on demand. They took a heavy commission – probably 40 per cent – but their carbon prints had no silver salts in them and so they were not vulnerable to the gradual darkening of silver salt in light. Cameron may not have fully realized the costs involved; she wrote to Annie Thackeray early in November, from on board ship, that she would gladly pay a 25 per cent commission, but shortly afterward she wrote Blanche Cornish (Annie's second cousin) for help in extricating her from the arrangement. She had spent 2 guineas per negative to create autotypes of many of her most commercial photographs and she had counted on selling each carbon print for 7s. 6d. Whether the commission charged took away her profit or the company refused to sell the prints at that price is unclear, but Cameron dispatched Blanche and her husband to argue with them.[16] She did not entirely sever the arrangement, though, because she continued to order copies of her own autotypes from Ceylon, and some of her glass negatives were held by the Autotype Company until the Second World War, when they were destroyed by bombing, along with whatever correspondence might have survived.[17]

Although Cameron did not know it yet, Annie Thackeray and her family had suffered a terrible blow that month. Annie's sister Minnie, married to Leslie Stephen and expecting her second child, died very suddenly in London. The Stephens had returned from a trip abroad, where Minnie hadn't been feeling very well. Annie was out of town and their friend Julia Duckworth paid a call and left feeling that her own depressed spirits dampened the company. That night Minnie suffered fatal convulsions and the next day Leslie Stephen became a widower for the first time. The baby was stillborn. Annie received an ominous telegram and raced back to London but she was too late to see her sister.[18] It was the first in a series of blows that would nearly unman Leslie, and he would lean heavily on his first sister-in-law Annie through all of them. Soon it would become clear that his and Minnie's daughter Laura, a sweet child Cameron had admired at Freshwater, suffered a mental disability that kept her in institutions for most of her life.

Cameron would not learn any of this terrible news until well after her arrival in Ceylon. The voyage itself was uneventful. Cameron wrote to Emily Tennyson: "I need not tell you that amidst all this bustling world of 380 people, my husband sits in majesty like a being from another sphere, his white hair shining like the foam of the sea, and his white hands holding on each side his golden chain."[19] She described their stop in jewel-like Malta, where Charles Hay had lived a lifetime ago when his father was governor there and where he too had once hoped for an appointment. Charles Hay recalled throwing oranges in the fountain when he was boy and marveling when they were tossed up in the air by the water.[20] The passage through the Red Sea was unbearably hot and the Camerons suffered in their cabins with a locked porthole rather than sleep on the mattresses placed out in the saloon for overheated passengers.[21] They arrived in Ceylon on November 20 and Julia Margaret promptly fell seriously ill. She wrote later that she thought this illness had been the result of her heroic efforts to prepare for the move, as well as the anguish of partings.[22] She had recovered by January. Charles Hay continued his remarkable revival and began riding around on a pony, much to everyone's amazement.[23]

Ceylon in the 1870s was different to the Ceylon Charles Hay had legislated for and fallen in love with forty years earlier. Legend often compared the island to the Garden of Eden (hence the name of its highest mountain, Adam's Peak, which Christians believe to bear the mark of Adam's footprint), but it was rapidly being developed by Europeans. Partly as a result of the shift he had recommended to British property laws from traditional models of shared land use, the island had attracted speculators, who bought up formerly public lands and brought in new crops. Coffee was one of those imports in the 1840s and the Cameron sons were just a few of the young entre-preneurs trying to make their fortune in coffee. In the 1860s and early 1870s, however, the coffee crops suffered a blight that turned the more practical planters toward other crops. Tea cultivation was and still is popular. But the Camerons seem to have stuck with coffee and also dabbled in the newest import, cinchona. Native to South America, cinchona was the tree from which quinine, used for treating malaria, was derived. Under the direction of Cameron's one-time sitter, Sir Joseph Dalton Hooker, Director of the Royal Botanic Gardens, the British managed to export cinchona trees and cultivate them in their tropical colonies, especially India and Ceylon.[24] The Dutch also imported it into Indonesia, where it quickly became a major crop and export. There was a humanitarian argument for this – malaria was a devastating threat in those countries – but it dramatically affected global trade as Indonesia and India overtook South America in the production of quinine.

The Camerons' estates were located within the central mountainous district toward the south of the island. The largest communities nearby were Kandy and Nuwara Eliya, a well-known hill station where the British liked to retreat during hot weather. A new railway connected Colombo on the coast with Kandy in the interior. Ewen still owned and ran Rathoongodde, where he lived with his wife Annie, often known as Birdie or Topsy, and two children. He seems to have made the estate profitable. The Camerons' relationship with Topsy had deteriorated, though, and Julia Margaret's paeans to her daughter-in-law's perfection had turned into scoldings for her reluc-tance to share Ewen's money.[25] Charlie Hay and Henry Herschel Hay had been managing other people's estates and had just bought their own, called Lippakelle, near Nuwara Eliya. Hardinge still worked for Sir William Gregory, the Governor of Ceylon, but he was based in Kalutara, a seaside fishing village on the west coast, south of Colombo. He worked hard and travelling in Ceylon was difficult, so some-times Cameron did not see him for two months at a time. Julia Margaret and Charles Hay often stayed with Hardinge in Kalutara, but their own residence in Ceylon was a rented bungalow in the mountains near an area known as "Cameron's land."[26]

For Julia Margaret, life in Ceylon posed new threats to the health and well-being of her sons, even though they were gratifyingly close by. She made Henry promise not to go elephant-hunting until after she was dead. He was an avid sportsman and she worried about shooting parties: what if his companions were careless? To keep him from hunting, she encouraged Henry in his amateur theatricals.[27] When Hardinge, in his governmental duties, tried to stave off a flood, she admired his heroism but scolded him for standing for hours in muddy water.[28] Although Cameron still viewed Hardinge as a hero, Sir William Gregory nicknamed him "the Tortoise."[29] Cameron described her own life in Ceylon as "a most acceptable monotony": in a letter she wrote to Henry Taylor she rejoiced that

As for excitements–when our hens have hatched their chickens, or a cow has calved, the household is in a stir. And when the Tappal post boy brings in the daily post my heart beats a little more rapidly and then subsides, too thankful if it is all the same as yesterday . . . . On the day of the week that the English mail comes in there is an awakening. I jump up, seize hold of the brown tin box, hung by a leather strap over the shoulder of my little ebon Mercury–say to E. [their maid, Ellen Ottingham] rapidly, 'Give him a present,' and empty my box.[30]

On November 20, 1876, her first anniversary in Ceylon, Cameron began a short account of her life there. It described her continuing admiration for the beauty of the island and her sympathy with the "primitive simplicity of the Inhabitants." Mostly she emphasized the healthfulness of the climate, which had produced wonders in her husband especially.[31] By implying an audience, it appears that she was intending to publish this document, which would fit in with a subtle shift toward writing in her last years. In September 1875, just before she left England, she had written a poem entitled "On a Portrait," which was published in *Macmillan's Magazine* the following February.[32] The poem describes a lovely face shadowed with suffering and echoes Edgar Allan Poe's famous dictum that the most poetic subject in the world is the death of a beautiful woman. The combination of beauty and pain, so common in Cameron's photographs as well, evokes the image of Julia Duckworth and it is natural to read the poem as a description of one of Cameron's own portraits of her great-niece, as some scholars have done.[33]

Indeed, "On a Portrait" is hard to read otherwise than as Cameron speaking about one of her own works. Though the woman described in the poem is silenced with "a mouth where silence seems to gather strength/From lips so gently closed . . .," the poet/narrator is quite verbose, asking rhetorical questions and providing six stanzas of commentary on the portrait. While it is true that the poem's description offers a fetishized list of body parts – eyes/lids, mouth/lips, head/cheek – it is the narrator's commentary that directs the viewer/reader's eye across the face, thus adopting a role much like a photographer's. As one critic has rightly noted, the narrator seems to be reading a painting, not a photograph,[34] which could underscore Cameron's artistic mission to elevate photography to the status of painting. The poem concludes with a recognizable reference to Cameron's aesthetic:

> Genius and love have each fulfilled their part,
> And both unite with force and equal grace,
> Whilst all that we love best in classic art
> Is stamped for ever on the immortal face.

Although the last line leaves a rather violent impression, the sentiment is consistent with Cameron's obsession with representing and uniting the gendered spheres of love and genius. It was during her years in Ceylon that Cameron wrote to Henry Taylor her oft-quoted maxim that "men [are] great through genius, women through love–that which women are born for."[35] It echoes a line from the "Merlin and Vivien" book of Tennyson's *Idylls of the King*: "'Man dreams of Fame while woman wakes to love'" (l. 458).

Cameron also wrote an undated poem called "Farewell of the Body to the Soul" at around the same time: it too is written as if spoken by a narrator, in this case "the body" speaking to "the soul." Similar in form to "On a Portrait," it also shares its melancholy tone. The body says goodbye to the soul, which flies away liberated but sadder for the loss.[36] In her letters from Ceylon, Cameron occasionally cited bits of verse translations into French.[37] During the monsoon season, when 30 inches of rain fell in sheets for fifteen days so that the world outside looked like "white darkness," she wrote to Henry Taylor that she was reading a lot: all of Sophocles and a "Polyglot" book in English, German, French, and Italian.[38] Shortly before her departure, she and Taylor had experienced one of the few storms in their long friendship: Cameron had objected to his asking for the return of his letters to her so that he could use them in the autobiography he was preparing. Cameron protested that the letters were precious to her and she resented the possibility of private memories being made public. It seems that she felt, like Tennyson much earlier in their relationship, that autobiographies should leave private friendships alone. She even went so far as to promise Taylor that she would not write one of her own, which perhaps explains why the *Annals* were never finished. Cameron did make up with Taylor, and she received and read his two-volume autobiography in Ceylon with great pleasure.[39]

Cameron's acquaintance among the colonial civil service was wide, so friends and friends of friends often came through Ceylon to visit. Thoby Prinsep's niece Louisa, now married to William Bowden-Smith, seems to have lived or visited near Rathoongodde. The best description of Cameron's life in Ceylon, though, comes from Marianne North, the botanical artist who visited in 1877. North also provides the only contemporary account of Cameron's photographic practice in Ceylon. North was an articulate and canny observer of colonial society: she noted the claustrophobic expatriate culture in towns like Kandy and easily saw through the posturing of the striving Britons she ran across in her travels around the world. She traveled alone through Ceylon in 1876, visiting Sir William Gregory and painting the botanical gardens in Kandy. She had never met Cameron, but Cameron had heard of her trip and invited her to Kalutara, where she was living with Hardinge at the time, in a house overlooking the river with coconut, mango, and breadfruit trees all around.

North visited in January and described the chaotic scene: rabbits, squirrels, and mynah birds ran through the house while monkeys and a tame stag gathered around the outside. "The walls of the rooms," she continued,

> were covered with magnificent photographs; others were tumbling about the tables, chairs, and floors, with quantities of damp books, all untidy and picturesque; the lady herself with a lace veil on her head and flowing draperies.[40]

In her own way, North was as independent and outspoken as Cameron and they took to each other at once. Cameron resolved to photograph North [see figure], though she is not known to have photographed any of her own family or any other British friends while in Ceylon. In a letter to Sir William Gregory she complained that she had lost a chance to photograph him, but she never tried again.[41] She did take four of North, however, and North wrote frankly of the experience:

> She dressed me up in flowing draperies of cashmere wool, let down my hair, and made me stand with spiky cocoa-nut branches running into my head, the noonday sun's rays dodging my eyes between the leaves as the slight breeze moved them, and told me to look perfectly natural (with a thermometer standing at 96 degrees)![42]

The experience brought out North's sense of humor and she laughed over another portrait, equally unsuccessful to her mind, and the waste of twelve glass plates. She was amused that Cameron then tried to describe her guest in a letter to one of her sisters and used such terms as made North blush and compare it to a funeral oration. Clearly, she was charmed and she couldn't resist Cameron's more effusive gestures. When North complimented her on a shawl, Cameron took a pair of scissors, cut it in two, and gave one half to her. And when North came back in November, Cameron tried to give her the other half by flinging it after her carriage as she departed.[43]

North mentions in her memoir that Cameron took photographs of Ceylonese natives too, and as a whole the Ceylonese photographs demonstrate that Cameron had developed an entirely new style of photography, perhaps in adaptation to her new surroundings. Almost all of her Ceylonese photographs are taken out of doors, for example, which the climate and sunshine made possible. But, more strikingly, the photographs are taken from a greater distance and are closer to full-length. For the most part, the characteristic close-ups, dark shadows, and even the soft-focus are gone. There are no allegorical or literary illustrations; in fact, these images usually have no titles at all, and no copyright statements. The photographs have been rarely studied, and even less often exhibited.[44] When they are discussed, it is always assumed that Cameron's portraits from Ceylon are all of native people and so the interpretation breaks down along race and national lines: Cameron's work typically gets divided into English photographs (subcategories: famous men and fair women) and Ceylonese photographs (natives). Like the earlier portraits of Prince Alámayou, the two portraits of Marianne North are an important exception to this reading of Cameron's work.

Approximately twenty-six photographs taken by Cameron in Ceylon, including the four of North, are known to have survived.[45] There are too few to generalize from; in fact, they show a remarkable variety. Just as one discerns a consistent style, one finds the image that breaks that particular rule. They are mostly taken out of doors, with foliage as background, but *Cingalese Girl* [see figure] seems to be taken indoors with Cameron's "English-style" background of deep shadows. Two portraits of pairs of women holding vases on their heads are taken outdoors but against a plain wall [see figure]. Most of the photographs are taken from the middle distance and show their models looking straight at the camera, but at least one shows a native woman in strict profile. It has been argued that when Cameron positions her camera at a greater distance from her models in Ceylon, she is expressing her difference from them as a colonialist and a white woman.[46] It could follow, then, that her shift in composition toward half- or full-length figures instead of expressive faces reveals her colonialist assumption that non-European people be represented as bodies, not as full human beings. And yet two portraits of Marianne North share these same techniques – greater distance and full-length representation of the body – so Cameron's new style was not exclusively a response to native sitters.

It may, however, demonstrate that Cameron's emotional urgency in representing intimacy and lifelikeness was alleviated now that regular separations were not always on the horizon. The tolerance of motion in the English photographs, which revealed the sitter's vitality instead of the "deathlike" stillness she so deplored, and the extreme close-ups of her English work, were all perhaps partly motivated by Cameron's fears about loss and separations. These anxieties were less pressing now that she had settled in Ceylon. It was at least inevitable that in Ceylon photography would serve a different function in her life: she did continue to exhibit her work in London shows and in the 1876 Centennial Exhibition in Philadelphia, but as far as we know she only submitted her English works.[47] It is not thought that she ever exhibited or tried to sell her Ceylonese photographs, though there was a flourishing photographic business in Ceylon and a market in England for "ethnographic" portraits of colonial peoples. Now that Cameron no longer had the necessity (or the excuse) of pursuing photography to make money, why then did she continue? Clearly, she was driven by a strong creative impulse, which had sustained her through much discouragement and commercial failure, but how would she frame this pursuit rhetorically, now that she couldn't claim to do it to acquire capital for her sons' careers? Nor could she claim to immortalize great men for the nation. It may be that this lack of emotional urgency and practical necessity is what diminished her production in Ceylon. Other successful photographers in Colombo found a way to obtain all the necessary chemicals and equipment. What Cameron really needed in order to continue was a compelling project.

There is no question that she could have found one in Ceylon. But Cameron's surviving letters make few references to photography and the evidence suggests that she did not have a specific purpose in mind for those final photographs, since there is no text or context directing our interpretation of them. It is possible that the only photographic project she could envision pursuing in Ceylon would be an ethnographic one, like the popular studies describing racial and ethnic types from "exotic" locations. A few of the portraits of local Ceylonese models are strikingly similar to "documentary" photographs such as those published by the India Office in an eight-volume set entitled *The People of India: A Series of Photographic Illustrations, with Descriptive Letterpress, of the Races and Tribes of Hindustan*. The volumes were published between 1868 and 1875 and Cameron would have seen some of them at the Photographic Society of London, where they excited much interest. Collated from works by different photographers, the images include some of women posing closely together against a plain wall from a middle distance.[48] They look much like Cameron's two photographs of two women against a blank wall, holding vases [see figure].[49] The vases are typical props in ethnographic studies: they are an easy symbol for femininity and preindustrial handiwork.[50] Photographers in India often complained about the difficulty of getting native sitters to relax for the camera; in one telling anecdote, the well-known photographer Samuel Bourne wrote to the *Photographic Journal* in London that despite his coaxing his sitters persisted in standing "bolt upright, with their arms down as stiff as pokers, their chins turned up as if they were standing to have their throats cut."[51] Considering the unequal social relations between British photographer and Indian subject, it is not surprising the models looked uncomfortable.

As a woman photographer, Cameron may have had a significantly easier time working with native women, for there were religious and cultural taboos against contact with men outside their families. Her relationships with the native "coolies," as she called them, are hard to read through the historical distance and the sketchy surviving record. She may have toyed with the idea of photographing native women as "colonial subjects" for an ethnographic volume (as a few of the images suggest), but other examples of the Ceylonese photographs instead show a remarkable continuity with her English work, or even a recasting of that work into a new light. For example, the relatively close-up head of a Ceylonese girl [see figure] with her head covered in a shawl closely echoes the Madonna images that Mary Hillier had posed for ten years before. With her hair down, her head and body swathed in draped folds, and her direct, impassive gaze, she could be another religious or allegorical figure, except that there is no caption to direct our interpretation that way. Like *Cingalese Girl*, this photograph seems to be taken indoors and again uses Cameron's "English-style" deep black background and implies an intimacy with her subject, though it avoids the extreme close-up of some of Cameron's "life-size heads." In this Ceylonese portrait, and in the similar portraits of Mary Hillier as a swathed Madonna, the white drapery creates a dramatic contrast to the black background and the models' dark hair. Both images use lighting and composition to create studies in black and white, though one model is "white" and the other "black."[52]

Similarly, the portrait of North draped in a shawl (perhaps the one Cameron cut in half later on) reveals an otherwise unnoticed connection between her and the young, covered Ceylonese model, and between both of them and the canonical representation of Cameron herself taken by Henry Herschel Hay [see figure]. This in turn casts a new light on the whole pantheon of draped, swathed, and covered women in Cameron's oeuvre. Suddenly, one can read backwards and see them all as dressed in saris, as "Oriental" as Cameron and her sisters seemed when they tied their dresses with cords around their waists. One can also read forwards and see these Ceylonese women with their own insistent drapery as cousins to those figures from the Elgin Marbles. It is a typological interpretation that Cameron would have appreciated. It implies, however, that Cameron's vision emphasized the similarities among women over the differences between races, nations, and ethnicities. In this reading, Cameron's complete photographic works would reveal that gender trumps race, class, and nationality as the most essential attribute of humanity in her artistic vision. It is an intriguing speculation.[53] Cameron's representation of gender roles was certainly varied and diverse, though it includes consistent stylistic elements across race and class – as the panoply of draped and informally intimate portraits show. But, on the other hand, during her fifteen-year career, Cameron also demonstrated her deep belief in roles and identities as performances, so it is hard to generalize.

Cameron's attitudes toward the people she lived among were typical of the more liberal and open-minded colonialists of her time. She believed strongly in the "civilizing" mission of the British in their colonies, but she favored humanitarian improvement projects – hospitals, dams, bridges, and schools – over military or evangelical campaigns. Despite her own deeply held religious faith she seems to have had little to do with missionaries in the colonies. Cameron wrote to Sir William Gregory about his legacy as Governor-General of Ceylon and concluded: "I have seen a good deal of Governor Generals + Governors + I would rather have established Wells + Hospitals for Coolies than have annexed the Punjab." In tiny handwriting she appended between the lines: "also would I thank God as a God if I had arrested or mitigated a famine," which is precisely what she had tried to do decades before during the Irish famine.[54]

Of course the "progress" that she and Charles Hay advocated for Ceylon would and did change the traditional ways of life in Ceylon in more ways than they could possibly have realized. Did Charles Hay know, when he rewrote the legal code for the country, that he was legislating changes that would allow him to become for a time the largest landowner in Ceylon? Such self-interested capitalism was not part of the utilitarian ethic, though conflicts of interest are always rife in the gap between theories and practices. One vivid example of the tangled strands of assumptions and consequences is Cameron's description of the recent changes in Kalutara:

> The Bridge is as it were a monument to the Power of Europe flinging its iron embrace over the noble River–and in its solidity and stability proving itself a benefit to all, thro' all time . . . . The Hospital is half way completed + presents a grand face already, ensuring air + ventilation[,] cleanliness + comfort . . . . Opposite the Hospital the road is to be cleared of all huts + open to the delicious healthgiving Sea and next there is to be a clean + good Market + just beyond this the Station is to be built, so that next year the rail may steam more + more of civilization towards us + around us–But the improvement in the Irrigation of the whole district is the real golden change which marks the present Kalutara from the past Kalutara–and thank God not only the lands + pastures of the natives are improved but their actual minds + mental pastures seem to be becoming irrigated, + watered with little rills of perception as to the <u>benefit</u> of labor . . .[55]

Like most of her British contemporaries, Cameron believed that "Orientals" (a term she used to include Southeast Asians and Arabs) were fundamentally lazy, and her letters are filled with anecdotes of her finding what she was looking for in their behavior. The most telling example is later in the same letter to William Gregory, when she comments in an aside that it is no wonder that Christ's disciples could not watch with him for even one hour: they were Orientals. For Cameron, and many of her contemporaries, the colonial peoples she encountered did not inhabit the same time and place as Europeans: they were representatives of ancient races and cultures. In this racist but omnipresent discourse, "Oriental" cultures were static and unchanging. They did not evolve and they needed to be brought forcibly into a Westernized present. For Cameron, this colonialist ideology also suited her typological art: of course the Ceylonese woman covered in a shawl suggests a Madonna. After all, Mary was "Oriental." Important ethnic, religious, and historical differences are elided in this view, but that too suited Cameron's aesthetic of transcendence. The whole point of typology is to find and value similarities over differences.

It was in her last years in Ceylon that Cameron wrote most explicitly about the colonialist attitudes that had shaped her life and her role in the world. In that same long letter to Sir William Gregory she explained that, despite arguments to the contrary, she still believed that an innate sense of honor and virtue both justified and enabled the colonial officer's rule. That is, the British Empire was founded on moral superiority and it was the recognition of that moral superiority that subdued its subjects and inspired their loyalty and obedience. Civil service reform, she argued, by opening colonial posts to examination instead of patronage, favored intelligence instead of good breeding (what she also called "manners"), to the detriment of colonial governments. She and her husband had battled the reformers among their colleagues in the civil service, including Edward Ryan and, long ago, Charles Trevelyan, but her confidence in the British gentleman held firm. She cited a story that Trevelyan had told her: an Indian reported how a hill chief in the North West Frontier had asked him how a handful of Europeans could govern the whole of India and the Indian had answered, "Because Europeans never lie." This was clearly a story and a statement that was not examined closely, but it fueled Cameron's belief that inherited privilege and "gentlemanliness" were the best qualifications for colonial power. She concluded: "a native thro' all India would more frankly recognize the authority of a Prinsep than that of a Jones[,] Smith or Robinson."[56]

That these assumptions were self-serving is embarrassingly obvious. Cameron thought her own sons were indolent and her rhetoric on their "heroism" often transparently camouflaged her anxieties about their failure to meet her moral standards. By what right could they attain prestige and power comparable to their father's and uncles' except through old-fashioned patronage and class privilege? The Tennysons were caught in the same disorienting change of rules when it came to finding a career for their son Lionel. Lionel failed an examination for the civil service but was given a junior clerkship in the India Office thanks to a nomination from Lord Salisbury. Once upon a time that would have secured his future, but now nominees were not promoted as fast as those who entered by examination, and Lionel's career floundered.[57] Cameron repeated to Gregory a friend's joke that Hardinge was the "Earl of Kalutara," the "Viscount of Parradure," but the unease about their aristocratic past and the family's uncertain future in a meritocratic culture shone through. Ever attentive to Hardinge's career, she argued with Gregory about the colonial service's policy of making top appointments from outside the local area. She was appalled that the positions of Colonial Secretary and Auditor General for the island were opening up and that administrators already working on the island, like Hardinge, could not be promoted into them. This was not Gregory's decision, though, but a longstanding London policy that originated in Henry Taylor's Colonial Office. In recounting her and Charles Hay's arguments with Taylor on this subject, Cameron complained to Gregory that "Henry Taylor argued that men outside the service were less likely to be influenced by local interests (might almost have said corrupt motives) [–] such is not the stuff our men are made of!"[58] There was no arguing with such blind faith.

In 1878 the Camerons impulsively decided to revisit England. In April Julia Margaret wrote to her friend Pinkie Ritchie from on board the steamer *Poonah* to announce that they were off the coast of Malta and would soon be back in England for a whirlwind visit. Hardinge was ordered home for his health and his parents decided to accompany him for a month. Thirty-one-and-a-half days in England, Cameron wrote gleefully, and then they would return to their tropical home to finish their days. She knew that this would be the last trip, and it was. Henry had already returned to England to be best man at Lionel Tennyson's wedding on February 25 to Eleanor Locker, whom Cameron had photographed years before.[59] Ewen and Charlie Hay must have been at home in England too, because Cameron wrote of the pleasure of having her five sons together.[60] The few letters that survive from Eugene in that period (none to his parents) are dated from the Royal Arsenal at Woolwich, so he seems to have remained in his Royal Artillery commission but returned from the West Indies.

Much had changed since the Camerons' departure. Thoby Prinsep, long blind and ailing, had died in February. His granddaughter Laura Gurney Troubridge had been told that he could die at any moment, so when he fell asleep she would shake him anxiously, asking, "Are you dead, Grandpapa, are you dead?" He would wake up laughing, but when he really died, Sara Prinsep collapsed and the indomitable Julia Duckworth took over.[61] Cameron's old friend Jane Senior had also passed away. The next generation was marrying: besides Lionel, Annie Thackeray had surprised her friends and family by becoming engaged to her much younger second cousin Richmond Ritchie. They had married the year before, in August 1877, despite Leslie Stephen's disapproval. The wedding was quiet, with Lionel Tennyson as best man and Richmond's sister Pinkie attending. Leslie Stephen and Julia Duckworth stood up next to Annie; a gloomier pair would be hard to imagine. The relationships between these few close friends (and cousins) were already claustrophobic and destined to become more so. Richmond Ritchie had also just entered the India Office, by passing the examination, and he went on to enjoy the career that Lionel might have had, eventually being promoted to Permanent Under-Secretary of State for India and being knighted for his service.[62] The Ritchies and the Tennysons, married within six months of each other, were inextricably bound together: after Lionel's death in 1886, his widow Eleanor had an affair with Richmond that almost broke up the latter's marriage.[63]

With Annie no longer soothing his grief over Minnie, Leslie Stephen looked for comfort elsewhere and increasingly found it in his companion in bereavement, Julia Duckworth. The two married in March 1878. When Leslie was married to Minnie, Cameron had found him "grave" and "shy," but he warmed to her, as everyone did, and she took pride in the fact that he would recite poetry to her but no one else of the Freshwater party.[64] When Cameron heard the news of Leslie and Julia's engagement in Ceylon, she instantly wrote two ecstatic letters of congratulation to the couple, urging them to come to Ceylon for a honeymoon. But to her sister Maria the next day she wrote a longer and more ambivalent letter, hoping that Maria was pleased with the engagement but not sure that she was. While the sisters were clearly hoping that Julia would have another chance at happiness, they may also have worried about Leslie's acknowledged agnosticism and his seriousness. "Dear Leslie" was admittedly stern, Cameron admitted to her sister, but "he was not made of Iron or of Stone as those Gods of pure Intellect so often are."[65]

Cameron had supposedly hoped that her son-in-law Charles Norman would be persuaded to marry Julia Duckworth, thus keeping them both in the family and substituting one Julia for another. But Charlie Norman too had moved on: he was engaged to be married to Emily Mangles that June. Julia Margaret and Charles Hay were able to attend that wedding, though it must have stirred up painful memories. They were also in town for the birth of Annie and Richmond's first child, Hester, that month. Cameron was in raptures, and wrote to the new mother:

> Yes darling Annie God has blessed the day–That inestimable precious gift of yr little Hester will be one more of those glorious gifts which fill the soul of us poor Mortals with Gratitude. It is a trembling joy is it not[?] this sacred possession of children of one's own . . .[66]

Annie recorded in her journal, "In the evening the nurse said to me 'a strange looking lady appeared after the christening and threw a white Indian shawl over the baby.' I saw the white shawl, and knew it was my dear Mrs. Cameron."[67]

The Camerons should have returned to Ceylon in late June, if Julia Margaret's calculations were correct, but they seem to have extended their stay. Cameron gave Hallam Tennyson a book inscribed with the date July 9, 1878 and a Mr. and Mrs. Cameron appear in the Reverend Francis Kilvert's diaries as guests with the Taylors at a country party to Moccas castle and church, near the Welsh border, on July 10.[68] Emily Tennyson mentions that the Camerons were still around in the fall of 1878 and Cameron wrote Alfred a last letter dated October 15, 1878 just as she was leaving England once more.[69] The Camerons were back in Kalutara by the end of the year, but when Hardinge fell ill again they moved to Henry's bungalow, Glencairn, in the mountains. It was there that Cameron herself fell ill, probably with her old bronchial complaint. After a ten-day illness, she died on January 26. It has been told and retold that on her deathbed Cameron looked out of her window at the evening sky and uttered her last word: "Beautiful."[70] The source for this story could only have been one of her sons, perhaps Henry in a letter home, but the original reference hasn't surfaced. It is only too fitting a conclusion to a life spent, by her own claim, in the pursuit of beauty. Indeed, it was a novelist who made the most of this most theatrical of deathbed scenes: Virginia Woolf resuscitated the story in her 1926 essay.

Cameron's obituaries in Ceylon emphasized her well-known generosity and benevolence. Those in England paid tribute to her photographic gift in the same terms as always: her work was uneven but it had "force and vigor."[71] The *Photographic News* again rehearsed the old conflicts over focus and concluded rather tepidly that Cameron had exerted a good influence on other photographers. Interestingly, the reporter recounted that a mutual friend in Ceylon testified that she was also "a poetess of no mean order."[72] The ailing Charles Hay had outlived his wife after all, but not for long. He died on May 8, 1880, while his sons read to him from Homer. "I am happier than Priam," he is supposed to have said, "for I have all my sons around me."[73] Hardinge's new wife, Kitty, was there at the time and wrote to her mother in England what a fine, courtly old gentleman Charles Hay had been, never complaining and patient to the end. His sons, she said, felt their loss very much, but she found the funeral in Ceylon, with the sunshine and birds singing, much happier than funerals in England. As at Julia Margaret's funeral, two white bullocks pulled the body in a cart along mountain roads as far as they could and then it was carried by natives from the Rathoongodde estate to the burial grounds at St. Mary's Church in Bogawantalawa. This church had been consecrated in 1874, and the Camerons had helped commission and pay for its three stained-glass windows.[74] Now they are buried there beside each other, in fulfillment of Charles Hay's wish to remain on his beloved island for ever.

Emily Tennyson received the news of Julia Margaret's death with great sorrow. She wrote to her sister: "We are not likely to find one to take her place so loving and strong in her woman's way and so child-like in her faith."[75] Their faith was one of the strongest bonds of their long friendship and Emily wrote characteristically comforting words to the Cameron sons in Ceylon: "Our hearts ache to think of the void in his [Charles Hay's] and yours. God alone can make it bearable."[76] She noted that Eugene seemed to be feeling "much more hopeful about himself;" it is the first confirmation of a vague sense that something had gone wrong in Eugene's life, though he remained in some contact with old friends. The year before he had lunched with Lord Overstone and asked him and George Warde Norman to propose him for membership in the Athenaeum Club. Overstone had reluctantly agreed at the time, but he thought they were too old to place anyone on the twelve-year waiting list. Overstone wrote to Norman suggesting they decline after all, and two days later Eugene wrote him abruptly to cancel the requested favor:

> Dear Lord Overstone,
>
> I am troubled to hear that my request has been causing you + Mr. Norman correspondence + worry. No result could have been less desired by me than that. Pray think no more about it, or if you think only think that Charles Cameron's son was anxious to connect his name, however unworthy, with the band known in W. Kent of yore as "the philosophers."[77]

Eugene was proposed by other members; but before his name could come up, he died in a fire in 1885 on board a ship crossing the Atlantic.[78]

Of Cameron's other sons, only Ewen remained in Ceylon, where he died in 1889. Hardinge rose as far as he could in the Ceylonese civil service and retired in 1904 to return to England and complete his long-interrupted Oxford degree. He married twice but had no children. Charlie Hay made his way back to England as soon as his father died (if not before: he was not at his father's deathbed). He and Henry Herschel Hay paid back the mortgage on Lippakelle to Lord Overstone early in 1878, but they seem to have continued to own the estate and still had hopes for their cinchona crop. In October 1880 Charlie Hay wrote again to Lord Overstone from France, returning a letter that Overstone had written to his father in 1844 and admitting candidly that "I myself really don't know what to do –I have been trying hard to get employment in England and failed tho' I very nearly got something." He claimed that his health forbade his return to Ceylon; he was "very unhappy and unwell."[79] He must have been hoping that Overstone would come through, yet again, with some loan or favor, but Overstone's reply has not survived. Charlie Hay died in Germany in 1891.

Henry Herschel Hay eventually gave up on cinchona and returned to London to set up a photography studio. He had already taken the two striking photographs of his mother around 1874. He must also have collaborated with his mother on some of her work, because her autobiographical fragment refers to him as a photographer and some prints from 1873 bear evidence of collaboration.[80] His first copyrighted photographs were taken in April 1884 and registered on May 21. Unsurprisingly, they were portraits of Tennyson, taken at Farringford. Henry was listed as the proprietor of a studio on Oxford Street, but by October he had moved to a more permanent location at 70 Mortimer Street. Of the photographs he registered for copyright between 1884 and 1893, most seemed to continue the major themes and subjects of his mother's career. He took photographs of Watts and Ellen Terry; he photographed the famous actor Henry Irving in character as Becket (from a play written by Tennyson) and the American actress Mary Anderson in her roles from Shakespeare.[81] He occupied much the same place in his mother's circle as she once had: the extended family used him as their portraitist, and even Charles Dodgson, after giving up photography, brought his child sitters to Henry for portraits.[82] The Tennysons continued to support him by patronizing his studio. In 1889 Hallam arranged for him to take and publish a joint portrait of him and his parents, but no one was pleased with it and (perhaps not coincidentally) it strays the furthest from his mother's style.[83] Henry retained his interest in the theater too and played Humpty Dumpty and the Carpenter in productions of *Alice's Adventures in Wonderland* at the beginning of the twentieth century.[84]

Henry remained close to all the old circle and was present at Emily Tennyson's funeral, at Freshwater, in 1896. Alfred had died in 1892. Watts would be the only one of his generation of Freshwater friends to outlive the Victorian age and greet the twentieth century: he died in 1904. Hardinge and Henry Herschel Hay both died in 1911. By then, photography had turned into something more comparable to what it is today. In 1878 the dry-plate process made developing negatives much easier, cleaner, and faster. The invention of halftone printing in the 1880s enabled photographs to be easily reproduced in newspapers and books, which revolutionized publishing. When George Eastman invented the Brownie camera, hobbyists no longer had to develop their own negatives at all, and the snapshot was born. Suddenly, photographs were genuinely popular and commercial: they could be taken by anyone, anywhere, and they could be viewed by anyone, anywhere.

Of the personal legacy of Cameron and her sisters, the succeeding generation should have the last word. Laura Gurney Troubridge noted astutely that

> everything they did, said and thought mattered, according to them, and this conviction made them the centre of everything in their own circles . . . . Their vision, though sufficiently keen and piercing, was not wide. They seem to me now, these dear dead people, like grown-up children, with their superabundant energy, their untempered enthusiasms, their strangle-hold on life, their passionate loves and hates.[85]

About her great-aunt's photographs, for which she had modeled as a child, she wrote that the sitters would "learn more about their own faces than the looking-glass ever told them."[86] Like Cameron, she believed in the reality of an inner "truth" hidden beneath an outer "appearance." That very Victorian assumption would later inspire much of Freud's work. But in Cameron's day it was couched as worship, the humble, patient, ever-hopeful pursuit of meaning understood as something visible. It was an urgent desire to see clearly and face to face. Tennyson's "Crossing the Bar," supposedly composed during the twenty-minute crossing from the Isle of Wight to Lymington, makes a fitting epitaph to Cameron's life's work, as it also served at the funeral services for both Alfred and Emily:

> For tho' from out of bourne of Time and Place
> The flood may bear me far
> I hope to see my Pilot face to face
> When I have crossed the bar.

"Life Stand Still Here"

I F YOU HAD attended the original performance of *Freshwater*, you would have been bundled in scarves and clad in thick boots, for it would be January in London, and you would feel the damp cold.[1] You would be friends with the play's author, Virginia Woolf, or if you were family you would probably call her by her nickname, "Goat." You would know of Cameron's work because you would have been to Vanessa Bell's house and seen Cameron's portraits of Virginia and Vanessa's mother Julia Duckworth Stephen hanging on the walls, or you had heard the sisters talk about Great Aunt Julia, whom Woolf was going to include in her proposed history of English eccentrics. Family stories about Aunt Julia had circulated for years, and Woolf had even written them down in her introduction to her edition of Cameron's work, *Victorian Photographs of Famous Men and Fair Women*, which she had published with the art critic and fellow Bloomsbury group member Roger Fry nine years earlier. If you had a special invitation from Mrs. Clive Bell and Mrs. Leonard Woolf to attend *Freshwater: A Comedy*, you would show up at Vanessa Bell's studio in Bloomsbury the night of January 18, 1935, greet your friends and relations, and take a seat before a curtained stage at one end of the room. You would perhaps have brought a gift for the sixteen-year-old Angelica Bell, Vanessa's daughter and Virginia's niece, whose birthday the play honored, and who had a leading role. You would probably be a "genius" yourself.

For *Freshwater* was written, performed, and viewed by the inner circle of Bloomsbury, that now-mythic group of radical intellectuals, writers, and artists. Bloomsbury had begun at Cambridge, where Clive Bell, Leonard Woolf, Lytton Strachey, and Desmond MacCarthy, among others, had befriended Thoby and Adrian Stephen and, through them, their sisters Vanessa and Virginia, who would further cement the group's close ties through marriage. Woolf had drafted the play twelve years earlier in 1923 as a private theatrical, but had shelved it while she worked on other projects. Named, like Bloomsbury, after a community that had also fostered artists and authors, *Freshwater* was typical of Bloomsbury entertainments, which in turn evoked the amateur theatricals of the Victorians in Cameron's circle. One of the Victorian customs that the Bloomsbury set had not rejected was the tradition of assembling friends and family to produce plays, complete with costumes and musical accompaniment, for their own amusement or to benefit a favored cause. Within Bloomsbury, members took turns writing, directing, and acting in these plays, though Woolf was too shy to ever take a role herself. She cast *Freshwater*, though, assigning roles mostly to family members: her sister and brother, their children, and her own husband played the main characters. The audience of nearly eighty people included Vanessa's husband, the art critic Clive Bell, and his brother, who reportedly laughed so loud that it was hard to hear the dialogue. The evening was a rousing success.

Both the 1923 and 1935 versions of the play describe the break-up of the Freshwater circle. Both plays focus on the domestic chaos that surrounded the production of great art by Alfred Tennyson, G. F. Watts, and Cameron. The dialogue is filled with non sequiturs and the action is continually interrupted by artistic inspiration. The surreal dialogue and plot of the play relate to Woolf's experiments with a new, looser writing style in the 1920s, but on this occasion it also has its basis in the actual conditions at Freshwater, where people often dispensed with conventional language just as Woolf was trying to do in her writing. The poetic language (often literally quotations from Tennyson's work) and the comically exaggerated speeches are part of Bloomsbury's attempts to break with the dominant realisms of nineteenth-century art and literature, even though the play itself represents some of the major figures associated with Victorian culture in Watts, Tennyson, and Cameron. Woolf literally collapses time in the play as well, juxtaposing events that occurred between 1865 (the break-up of the Watts–Terry marriage) and 1884 (Tennyson's elevation to the peerage) within one afternoon. This contrast between nineteenth-century realism and twentieth-century modernism is more apparent in the 1935 revision of the play, which includes a number of ambivalent references to "fact" as the common denominator of Watts's, Tennyson's, and Cameron's arts.

The central character, who tries to understand and then interpret this crazy ménage, is the actress Ellen Terry. By the time of Woolf's writing, Terry was a theatrical legend: her career had spanned Victorian and Edwardian theater, and she had been immensely popular with both generations. For the Bloomsbury audience, her name would be as celebrated as those of Tennyson, Watts, and Cameron. Indeed, in the 1920s and 1930s the reputations of Tennyson and Watts were on the decline, and Cameron was little known outside photographic circles. In the play, Terry confesses herself disappointed by these stodgy Victorians: she complains that "I thought artists were such jolly people – always dressing up and hiring coaches and going for picnics and drinking champagne and eating oysters and kissing each other and – well, behaving like the Rossettis."[2] Instead she finds herself with a husband who "drinks a glass of hot water at nine and goes to bed in woollen socks each night at nine thirty sharp." Woolf, who had seen Terry perform in the early twentieth century, used the actress as a transitional figure between the Victorians in Freshwater and the modern Bloomsbury clique. It is Terry who spans the three generations, who feels out of place at Freshwater, and who literally flees to Bloomsbury at the end of the play. It is to Terry that Cameron bequeaths her camera, as Cameron sets sail for Ceylon and Terry moves toward modernism with the words: "Take my lens. I bequeath it to my descendants. See that it is always slightly out of focus."

Woolf's comedy gets at something often lost in the anecdotes about Cameron's eccentricities: her humor and wit. Cameron convincing Tennyson to head a parade of maidens down to the beach at Freshwater so that he can ceremonially wed the sea, like a Venetian Doge, is funny as well as batty. The Bloomsbury crew inherited that delight in the absurd, and Woolf was able to show the Freshwater bunch in a pose that Cameron never could: laughing.[3] The darker side of the play is visible in the vaguely sinister sexual appetite of the older male artists for the young girl-model, Ellen Terry. Again, this does not seem to be the way that Terry actually experienced her life with Watts, but it reflects a recurrent concern in Woolf's work with the human costs of art and genius. In *To the Lighthouse*, her semi-autobiographical portrait of her parents' marriage, Woolf portrays Mr. Ramsay, the character based on her father, as a brilliant philosopher who demanded constant sympathy and attention from his wife. The dilemma of the woman artist, torn between duty to her art and duty to her family, was a lifelong struggle for both Cameron and Woolf.

Freshwater may have a serious agenda, then, when read in this light. Despite Woolf's comic exaggerations about Aunt Julia's eccentricities, Cameron must have been an important role model as a woman who was an artist herself instead of being a supporting player to the men around her. To those who said "women can't write, women can't paint," as someone told her artist character Lily Briscoe in *To the Lighthouse*, Woolf could reply: But look at Aunt Julia; women can produce great art – women can devote themselves to their work without enslaving those around them, even though Cameron was just as demanding of her models as Watts. Though Woolf didn't play a role in the 1935 production, she did play out an identification with Cameron: by assigning the role of Cameron to her sister, the artist, and the role of Cameron's husband to her own husband, Leonard Woolf; by stage-managing her characters as completely and invisibly as Cameron posed her models in her photographs; and by producing her work from the bodies and personalities of her favorite friends and relatives.

Although the production of a piece of writing and the production of a photograph, especially over a gap of sixty years, require different conditions and abilities, both

Woolf and Cameron worked creatively from their domestic and social circles. The Bloomsbury theatricals came out of an inspired collaboration of artists, writers, and intellectuals who were also friends and family. Woolf's *To the Lighthouse* effected the same transfiguration of family history into radically modern novel. Cameron's photographs are a wonderfully sustained transformation of domestic circumstances into public culture. Woolf's and Cameron's shared interest in the domestic origins of creativity makes the play *Freshwater* seem inevitable: it was a self-conscious effort to pay homage to their common artistic goal of mediating the public and private worlds. Like Cameron's photographs, *Freshwater* can neither be understood simply as a private nor a public work of art: it is both and neither, or something in between.

When Woolf drafted the play in 1923, the Edwardian revolt against the Victorians was in full swing. Fellow Bloomsbury member Lytton Strachey had already published his bestselling *Eminent Victorians*, a series of biographical profiles that exploded the myths of Victorian morality. Woolf's play shares some of Strachey's ridiculing of Victorian values, but it also seems to have a secret sense of irony that, after all, those eccentric Victorians were really much like the eccentric Bloomsbury clan. When Virginia Woolf and Roger Fry published their selection of Cameron's work in 1926, Fry wrote in the introduction that Cameron's artistic circle

> cultivated the exotic and precious with all the energy and determination of a dominant class. With the admirable self-assurance which this position gave them they defied ribaldry and flouted common sense. They had the courage of their affectations; they openly admitted to being 'intense.'[4]

He could just as easily be talking about his Bloomsbury friends. If the Freshwater group walked about spouting poetry and allowing art to run amok in their homes, the Bloomsbury clan were just as famous for their unconventional domestic arrangements. If Cameron and her sisters set their own fashion by wearing loose clothes and draping themselves in shawls, so did Vanessa Bell and Virginia Woolf.

Virginia Somers and Sophia Dalrymple, the last of the legendary Pattle sisters, lived long enough for Virginia Woolf to form her own impressions of them. Sophia, she concluded was "the improper Monte Carlo Great Aunt." Indeed, Sophia did move to Monte Carlo and convert to Roman Catholicism late in her life.[5] "Aunt Virginia," her nineteen-year-old namesake mused, was "a large white form artistically grouped on the sofa." "I can never quite see Aunt V's surpassing charm or beauty," she wrote to a cousin. "The charm at any rate need not have vanished though the beauty has almost entirely. Save her great eyes, which are beautiful—and her enthusiasms and loud whispers and French manners, I think she was rather disappointing."[6] Woolf's verbal shrug was not just the response of a young woman to an aging elder; it was a response to her time and theirs. The charms and talents of the Pattle clan were of their day: they seized their moment with energy and drive, but also within certain limitations of their era. It would have been very difficult for any of them to choose to forego domesticity and motherhood as Woolf did, and it was perhaps being a mother that framed Julia Margaret's career more than any other factor. What does not seem to have changed in fifty years, though, was the feeling of being an outsider. Even Virginia and Vanessa Stephen, born on English soil into the cultural elite, felt as though they didn't fit in with their peers. Like the Pattles, they too found refuge in a clique of like-minded friends. Little Holland House, Freshwater, and Bloomsbury may have seemed exclusive, and peopled by England's elite, but they were born of a feeling of distance and alienation from the small, closed worlds of English society.

Yet the combination of identifying as an outsider while appearing like an insider has a powerful appeal for those who are truly offstage. For us, the continuing interest in Cameron's Freshwater circle and Woolf's Bloomsbury crowd arises at least in part from our own half-painful exclusion from its glow. Cameron's portraits of "famous men and fair women" and Woolf's play by and about Bloomsbury give us a tantalizing glimpse into a world that they are inside and we are definitely outside. The play's references to poetry and classics, to London geography, to Bloomsbury pets and in jokes that we scarcely understand all reinforce that sense of their inclusion and our exclusion from this elite society, though they tease us with a pleasurable glimpse through the window. We view Cameron's photographs and think she lived among an extraordinary group of beautiful and accomplished people, whom she recorded with a style all her own. We view Woolf's play, we read Bloomsbury memoirs, and we watch one Bloomsbury film after another with the fascinated sense that those gifted people were different from us and yet like us – they were privileged and creative but they had ordinary problems too. The intimacy that Cameron and Woolf's works evoke is real (they knew and loved the people they represented) and it gives us the half-pleasant, half-painful sensation of being inside and outside their magic circles. We can be honorary members of the club, but only until the curtain falls.

The historian Noel Annan wrote an influential article decades ago that first defined several prominent families as the "intellectual aristocracy" of England.[7] The intermarrying Stephens, Stracheys, and Darwins (among others) held a disproportionate amount of cultural power as academics, writers, scientists, and intellectuals from the nineteenth through to the early twentieth century. Annan emphasized the men's achievements, from the days when women were mostly excluded from academic appointments and many professional societies. Yet the central roles of Cameron and her sisters, as well as Virginia Woolf and Vanessa Bell among their daughters, nieces, and descendants, within this intellectual aristocracy confirm what one critic has called a "cultural matriarchy" as well.[8] Angelica Bell Garnett, the daughter and niece whose birthday provided the occasion for *Freshwater's* performance in 1935, wrote in her memoir that

> I had hung some photographs of my grandmother Julia Jackson, taken by my great-great-aunt Julia Margaret Cameron. As I looked at them I became conscious of an inheritance not only of genes but also of feelings and habits of mind which, like motes of dust spiralling downwards, settle on the most recent generation. Vanessa [her mother] shrank into a mere individual in a chain of women who, whether willingly or not, had learnt certain traits, certain attitudes from one another through the years.[9]

The creative work that came out of that distinguished lineage both confirmed and constructed its reality: that is, as Cameron and Woolf continued to draw on their family and friends as starting points for their creative work, those family circles seemed more and more interesting in their own right too. Their family fictions continue to enthrall us with their domestic roots and with their promise of intimacy with their extraordinary communities.

The Bloomsbury crew may well have looked back to the Freshwater circle as their forebears, not only as the literal ancestors of the Stephen siblings but also as their model for a privileged and relatively autonomous group of intellectuals. Indeed, the mythology of a creative circle of great talents is undoubtedly part of the enduring appeal of the play and Bloomsbury itself, regardless of changing aesthetic trends. In the 1980s the play was performed again in a postmodern context, starring the French writers Eugene Ionesco, Nathalie Sarraute, and Alain Robbe-Grillet. It seems that the play continues to attract new audiences and new generations of artists, despite its originally private function. It is this creative milieu that the directors of the Dimbola Trust want to resurrect in Cameron's house by making it a center for contemporary arts.

Perhaps surprisingly, Woolf was reportedly suspicious of photography as a medium. She wrote mockingly to her sister in 1920, shortly before drafting the play, that in photographs "absolute truth is obtained – no sentimental evasions – what they call facing facts."[10] She may have been responding to what Fry called the "too acute, too positive quality from which modern photography suffers."[11] She may, then, not have associated Cameron's idealizing, slightly out-of-focus photographs with the realism that she and her peers were rejecting. Lucio Ruotolo, the Woolf scholar who edited *Freshwater* for publication, has also argued that Woolf believed that photography oversimplifies the complex reality it represents. Vanessa Bell felt that Woolf had captured some elusive truth about their mother in her novel, but Bell also kept the Cameron portraits of their mother hanging on the walls of her house. She too identified with and drew on her great-aunt's work: in making her own portraits of her mother, she referred to Cameron's photographs.[12]

But if Woolf was aware of Cameron as a role model, why did this famous feminist and indefatigable defender of women's creativity represent her own great-aunt's extraordinary artistic achievements in such a lighthearted way? Every known reference to Cameron's work among Woolf's writings emphasizes Cameron's eccentricities without explicitly celebrating the work itself. It is true that Woolf felt particularly out of her depth with the visual arts: there was a clear line separating the writers and the artists of Bloomsbury. Though she must have valued Cameron's work, she may have been unable to write the sort of homage to Cameron that she did write for neglected nineteenth-century women writers. In the book she co-authored on Cameron, she left the critical assessment in the capable hands of her friend Roger Fry. But Woolf may also have wanted to dramatize Cameron's behavior, and the radicalness of being a creative woman, in order to make her own eccentricities and creative ambitions less threatening. Woolf herself was tormented by mental breakdowns and may have used the contrast with Cameron to make herself, her work, and her Bloomsbury circle seem relatively ordinary.

Like the actress Ellen Terry, Cameron too could play the madwoman when it served her purpose, but she was less adept at outrunning the legacy of the role. Whereas Terry could play Ophelia to rave reviews, Cameron has sometimes been caught in the net of her own admitted eccentricity and stumbled with critics. She too produced several Ophelias in 1867 and many other tragic heroines, perhaps as a way to harness the appeal of those characters without enacting those parts in real life. She did not submerge her model in a bathtub full of water, however, as Millais had: she took more large, close-up heads of women much like the others she photographed, with long, loose hair, staring eyes, and a symbolic flower pinned to her cloak to close it. Those sorry, soggy Ophelias are magnetic poles for women trying to decide whether to make art or be art: at best, women like Terry and Cameron played with their possibilities; at worst, women like Virginia Woolf were subsumed by them. Woolf's death by drowning is a potent part of her celebrity.

Woolf never met Cameron, who died in Ceylon several years before she born. But they shared creative gifts and a long family tradition of powerful women, in which Julia Jackson Duckworth Stephen played an important pivotal role and influence. The deaths that punctuated the Stephen family history realized all of Cameron's worst fears for her own family as losses piled on top of losses. A familarity with great love and great pain links the three generations. In Woolf's novel about her own childhood, *To the Lighthouse*, she compares the different creativities of her artist character, Lily Briscoe, and Mrs. Ramsay, a devoted housewife based on her mother, Julia Stephen:

The great revelation had never come. The great revelation perhaps never did come. Instead there were little daily miracles, illuminations, matches struck unexpectedly in the dark; here was one . . . . Mrs. Ramsay saying, 'Life stand still here'; Mrs. Ramsay making of the moment something permanent (as in another sphere Lily herself tried to make of the moment something permanent)– this was of the nature of revelation. In the midst of chaos there was shape; this eternal passing and flowing . . . was struck into stability. Life stand still here, Mrs. Ramsay said.[13]

Life stand still here – Cameron and Woolf said that too. All that elusive life and love could be pinned down as art. In the midst of chaos, there was shape – that was what Woolf heard in the voices in her head and what Cameron saw in those deep black shadows.

ENDNOTES

Abbreviations Used in Endnotes

Works

Cox and Ford	Julian Cox and Colin Ford, *Julia Margaret Cameron: The Complete Photographs* (Los Angeles: J. Paul Getty Museum, 2003).
ET Journal	James O. Hoge, ed., *Lady Tennyson's Journal* (Charlottesville, VA: U of Virginia P, 1981).
ET Letters	James O. Hoge, ed., *The Letters of Emily Lady Tennyson* (University Park: Penn State UP, 1974).
Ford	Colin Ford, *The Cameron Collection* (London: Van Nostrand Reinhold, 1975).
Gernsheim	Helmut Gernsheim, *Julia Margaret Cameron: Her Life and Photographic Work* (NY: Aperture, rev. edn. 1975).
Hill	Brian Hill, *Julia Margaret Cameron: A Victorian Family Portrait* (London: Peter Owen, 1973).
Hopkinson	Amanda Hopkinson, *Julia Margaret Cameron* (London: Virago Press, 1986).
JMC's Women	Sylvia Wolf, ed., *Julia Margaret Cameron's Women* (New Haven: Yale UP, 1998).
Lukitsh	Joanne Lukitsh, *Cameron: Her Work and Career* (Rochester: International Museum of Photography at George Eastman House, 1986).
Mia Album	*For My Best Beloved Sister Mia: An Album of Photographs by Julia Margaret Cameron* (Albuquerque: University of New Mexico Museum, 1994).
Orange and Beaumont	Sir Hugh Orange's "The Chevalier de l'Etang (1757–1840) and His Descendants the Pattles," revised, edited, and recast by John Beaumont (Julia Margaret Cameron Research Group, 2002). An abridged version was published in *The Virginia Woolf Bulletin* No. 7 (May 2001), No. 8 (September 2001), and No. 9 (January 2002).
Weaver	Julia Margaret Cameron, *The Whisper of the Muse*, essay by Mike Weaver (Malibu: J. Paul Getty Museum, 1986).
Woolf and Fry	Virginia Woolf and Roger Fry, intros., ed. Tristram Powell, *Victorian Photographs of Famous Men and Fair Women* (Boston: A&W Visual Library, rev. edn. 1973).

People

CHC	Charles Hay Cameron
CHC Jr.	Charles Hay Cameron, Jr.
CLN	Charles Loyd Norman
GFW	George Frederic Watts
HHC	Hardinge Hay Cameron
HHHC	Henry Herschel Hay Cameron
JFWH	John Frederick William Herschel
JHCN	Julia Hay Cameron (later Norman)
JMC	Julia Margaret Cameron
SLO	Samuel Loyd, Lord Overstone

Prologue: **Orlando in Los Angeles**

1. Virginia Woolf, *Orlando: A Biography* (San Diego, CA: Harvest/HBJ, 1928): p. 300. The epigraph is from pp. 266–7 and used by permission.
2. Curator Violet Hamilton is collecting and editing Cameron's letters for publication, which will be an enormous help to future scholarship.
3. Woolf and Fry, pp. 23–8.
4. See, for example, Lindsay Smith's "The Politics of Focus: Feminism and Photography Theory," in *New Feminist Discourses*, ed. Isobel Armstrong (London: Routledge, 1992): pp. 238–62 and her "Further Thoughts on 'The Politics of Focus,'" in *Gendered Territory*, ed. Dave Oliphant (Austin, TX: Harry Ransom Humanities Research Center, 1996): pp. 13–31. Sylvia Wolf's 1998–99 exhibition and catalogue, *Julia Margaret Cameron's Women*, also goes a long way toward questioning those gendered assumptions.
5. *Annals of My Glass House*, reprinted in Gernsheim, p. 182.
6. Unpublished letter from JMC to Samuel G. Ward, June 16, 1869, quoted by permission of Houghton Library, Harvard University, bMS Am 1465 (176).
7. *Ibid.*, p. 68.
8. This passage and the photographer's full story are told in Henry Mayhew, *London Labour and the London Poor* (1861), ed. and intro. Victor Neuberg (NY: Penguin Books, 1985): pp. 335–44.

Chapter 1: **The Empire's Children**

1. Hill, p. 29. I am greatly indebted to Hill and to Orange and Beaumont for details of the Pattle family history.
2. Note that I use the term "Anglo-Indian" to refer to anyone of British origin who had been born, lived, or worked in India. This was the standard usage in the early nineteenth century, when people of mixed race were known as "Eurasians." Only later in the Raj did the term "Anglo-Indian" become associated exclusively with those of mixed British and Indian ancestry, who formed a caste of their own. Similarly, I use "Ceylon" instead of "Sri Lanka" because it was the term in use in English at the time. I am indebted to Stephen Espie of Bangalore for helping to sort out these etymologies.
3. In 1818 Calcutta had several respected portrait painters accepting commissions from the British establishment there, but the Pattles clearly preferred to commission their portrait in Europe, even if James couldn't sit for it.

4. Orange and Beaumont, p. 2.

5. This family history is based on archival research published by G. Thomas as "The Mélange that was Julia Margaret Cameron" in *Photographic Journal* (July 1988): pp. 302–3.

6. There are many examples of the colonial British providing for their illegitimate (and often biracial) children in their wills. William Makepeace Thackeray, for instance, administered a legacy left to his illegitimate half-sister until her death in 1841. Gordon N. Ray, *Thackeray: The Uses of Adversity 1811–1846* (NY: McGraw-Hill, 1955): pp. 49, 64.

7. M. M. Kaye, ed., *The Golden Calm: An English Lady's Life in Moghul Delhi* (NY: Viking Press, 1980), pp. 114–15.

8. Hermann Kulke and Dietmar Rothermund, *The History of India*, revised and updated edn. (London: Routledge, 1990): p. 268. By then, China had outlawed the importation of opium but the English continued to smuggle it in.

9. Woolf and Fry, p. 13.

10. Ethel Smyth, *Impressions That Remained* (NY: Alfred A. Knopf, 1946): p. 476.

11. Orange and Beaumont, p. 20. Sara Pattle was baptized "Sarah," but as an adult she spelled her name "Sara."

12. Thackeray is one candidate for the honor of coining this name, but there are others. Virginia Woolf, for example, credits Henry Taylor; see Woolf and Fry, p. 14.

13. Orange and Beaumont, pp. 7, 21.

14. Ann Monsarrat, *An Uneasy Victorian: Thackeray the Man* (London: Cassell, 1980), pp. 10–14.

15. See, for example, Hill p. 28.

16. Gernsheim, p. 182.

17. J. H. Bernardin de St. Pierre, *Paul and Virginia*, trans. Helen Maria Williams (1796) (Oxford: Woodstock Books, 1989): p. 22.

18. Hill, p. 22, and Orange and Beaumont, p. 10. Orange and Beaumont also speculate that Madame Campan might have taken in the elder Pattle girls, Adeline and Julia Margaret, as private pupils around 1818; see note 18, p. 3.

19. Lynn Hunt makes these points in her reading of *Paul et Virginie* in *The Family Romance of the French Revolution*. She also notes that as fathers became more benevolent in late-eighteenth-century French literature, they also gradually disappeared altogether, resulting in a rash of novels about orphans and fatherless societies of which *Paul et Virginie* was one of the most popular (pp. 25, 27–32). She attributes the disappearance of fathers to political changes in the relationship of the French people to their king (Berkeley: University of California Press, 1992).

20. Bernardin de St. Pierre, pp. 24–5.

21. See also Julian Cox's reading of this photograph in *In Focus: Julia Margaret Cameron* (Los Angeles, The J. Paul Getty Museum, 1996): p. 18, and Cox and Ford, pp. 51–2.

22. Cameron scholar Colin Ford has written that the umbrella is in fact from India. Ford, p. 120.

23. All the information about Adeline and Colin Mackenzie's marriage comes from Colin's second wife, Helen Mackenzie, in *Storms and Sunshine of a Soldier's Life* (Edinburgh, David Douglas, 1884), vol. 1, pp. 29–30, 51.

24. Orange and Beaumont, p. 21. Much of the information about the Pattle family's movements in the 1830s comes from this invaluable essay.

25. The one letter that has survived is from Cameron to Maria Jackson, February 6, 1878, in the Berg Collection of the New York Public Library. Similarly, one image of Maria Jackson by Cameron is

now in the collection of the Art Institute of Chicago. Cameron makes a reference to photographing her sister Virginia in a letter dated April 10, 1867 (Royal Society, London, HS 5:165), but no print has been found.

26. Joanne Lukitsh, "Album Photographs on Museum Walls: The Mia Album" in *Mia Album,* p. 30.

27. Virginia Woolf, *To the Lighthouse* (San Diego: Harcourt Brace Jovanovich, 1927): p. 17.

Chapter 2: Double Stars

1. Thomas Pinney, ed., *The Letters of Thomas Babington Macaulay* (Cambridge: Cambridge UP, 1976): vol. 3, p. 87.

2. Elizabeth French Boyd, *Bloomsbury Heritage: Their Mothers and Their Aunts* (NY: Taplinger Publishing, 1976): p. 9.

3. Edgar F. Harden, *Selected Letters of William Makepeace Thackeray* (Hampshire: Macmillans, 1996): p. 27.

4. Boyd, pp. 10, 124.

5. It has often been noted, mostly by twentieth-century scholars, that Julia Margaret was the only "plain" sister. Critics have surmised that this is why Julia Margaret devoted herself to creating and documenting beauty in her photographic career. I haven't found evidence that her appearance mattered much to Julia Margaret or to her immediate contemporaries, but perhaps it enabled her to imagine a future as someone who did the looking, rather than someone who was looked at. As in the case of George Eliot, another famous Victorian woman of talent, accomplishments, and notorious "ugliness," it is also possible that public opinion grants women either genius or beauty but not both: society views them as mutually exclusive and perhaps even takes a little gleeful pleasure in grudgingly acknowledging a woman's talent and then mocking her appearance.

6. Nina Auerbach, *Ellen Terry: Player in Her Time* (NY: W. W. Norton & Co., 1987): p. 81.

7. Quoted in Gernsheim, p. 180.

8. These anecdotes are retold in Gernsheim, p. 42 and Woolf and Fry, p. 19.

9. Quoted in Quentin Bell, *Virginia Woolf: A Biography* (NY: Quality Paperback Book Club edition, 1972): vol. 2, p. 15. Bell's own opinion of the Pattles' beauty is on pages 19–20.

10. *Ibid.,* p. 17.

11. Wilfred Blunt, *'England's Michelangelo': A Biography of George Frederic Watts* (London: Hamish Hamilton, 1975): pp. 72–3.

12. Indira Ghose, ed., *Memsahibs Abroad: Writings by Women Travellers in Nineteenth Century India* (Delhi: Oxford UP, 1998): p. xii. According to the *Dictionary of National Biography*, which Leslie Stephen edited late in the century, Colin's religious fervor was still so strong that the Afghans called him "the English Mullah." *DNB*, 1st supplement, vol. XXII, p. 997.

13. The rumors about James Pattle are well summarized by Boyd, pp. 7–9, 146–7. Orange and Beaumont cite an 1841 dispute between Pattle and the Civil Service Annuity Fund (note 6, p. 3) and *The Report on the Public Meeting at Town Hall in Calcutta* on November 24, 1838 refers to a civil trial called *Pattle v. Patton* that was instigated by a senior civil servant, pp. 28–9.

14. Weaver, p. 26.

15. Mackenzie, pp. 53–6, 75.

16. John Pemble, ed., *Miss Fane in India* (Gloucester: Alan Sutton, 1985): p. 61. My thanks to John Beaumont for discovering and sharing this source with me. It is possible that the Captain Smyth

mentioned is the father of Ethel Smyth, author of *Impressions That Remained* and the source for Virginia Woolf's anecdotes about James Pattle. Ethel's father was John Hall Smyth, who had claimed to know James Pattle while serving on the Governor General's staff. Sir Charles Metcalfe was Governor-General of India in 1835–36. John Hall Smyth later served in the Indian Mutiny and rose to be a major-general. However, there were many other Smyths in India.

17. *Ibid.*, p. 99.

18. Ford, p. 6.

19. Gunther Buttman, *Shadow of the Telescope: A Biography of Sir John Herschel*, trans. B. E. J. Pagel (NY: Charles Scribners Sons, 1970): p. 120.

20. Some of this account of nineteenth-century Cape Town comes from Lady Duff Gordon's *Letters from the Cape* (London: Oxford UP, 1927). Though Lady Duff Gordon was in Cape Town in the 1860s, some of her descriptions are relevant to the earlier decades, and her experience as an upper-class Englishwoman going to the Cape for her health may have been similar to Cameron's.

21. Quoted in Larry J. Schaaf, *Out of the Shadows: Herschel, Talbot, and the Invention of Photography* (New Haven: Yale UP, 1992): p. 2.

22. Richard Adams Locke, "Great Astronomical Discoveries Lately Made by Sir John Herschel at the Cape of Good Hope," bound as a pamphlet in New York, 1835. All of the descriptions quoted come from pages 10–28. The original text of the "moon hoax" is available online at www. museumofhoaxes.com.

23. *Ibid.*, p. 28.

24. Edgar Allan Poe, *The Complete Tales and Poems of Edgar Allan Poe* (NY: Vintage Books, 1975): p. 39.

25. David S. Evans, Terence J. Deeming, Betty Hall Evans, Stephen Goldfarb, eds., *Herschel at the Cape: Diaries and Correspondence of Sir John Herschel, 1834–1838* (Austin, TX: University of Texas Press, 1969): pp. 236–7.

26. *Ibid.*, p. 282.

27. Unpublished letter from JMC to JFWH, January 15, 1851, Herschel Family box #MO133, Harry Ransom Humanities Research Center, University of Texas at Austin.

28. Unpublished letter from JMC to JFWH, May 24, 1847, Royal Society, London, HS 5:150.

29. Orange and Beaumont, p. 29.

30. See John Beaumont, "Charles Hay Cameron (1795–1880): Benthamite Jurist," (Freshwater, Isle of Wight: Julia Margaret Cameron Research Group, 2002): pp. 26–7. Much of the information about Charles Hay Cameron's life before meeting Julia Margaret has been drawn from this enormously useful essay. Among the Norman family papers deposited by descendants of the Camerons' daughter, Julia Norman, at Kent County archive is a letter addressed to "Dear Papa" and signed Ellen Cameron. It is dated September 25, 1837, before Charles Hay had married Julia Margaret, and seems to have been written by a girl about six or seven years old. U310, C111. There are other references to a daughter Ellen in unpublished letters from CHC to JMC, November 3–8, 1850, Research Library, The Getty Research Institute, Los Angeles (850858), box 1, folder 2. The children's mother, whoever she was, died in 1850.

31. Beaumont, p. 6.

32. *Ibid.*, pp. 4–6.

33. G. C. Mendis, ed., *The Colebrooke-Cameron Papers* (London: Oxford UP, 1956): vol. 1, pp. xii–xiii. See also Chandra Richard DeSilva, *Sri Lanka: A History* (NY: Advent Books, 1987): pp. 156–7.

34. There is one known reference to Charles Hay Cameron among Jeremy Bentham's correspondence. On October 18, 1831 Bentham wrote a letter of introduction for Charles Hay describing him as a "highly-esteemed friend of mine." John Beaumont informed me of this letter, which will be published with Bentham's complete correspondence by the Bentham Project, University College, London, in 2004.

35. Unpublished letter from CHC to JMC, November 8, 1850, Research Library, The Getty Research Institute, Los Angeles (850858), box 1, folder 2.

36. Charles Hay Cameron, *Two Essays: On the Sublime and Beautiful and On Duelling*, privately printed, London, 1835, p. 33.

37. *Ibid.*, p. 59.

38. Unpublished letter from JMC to JFWH, January 15, 1851, Herschel Family box #MO133, Harry Ransom Humanities Research Center, University of Texas at Austin.

39. Original punctuation and capitalization. Unpublished manuscript from the Research Library, The Getty Research Institute, Los Angeles (850858), box 1, folder 11.

40. Original italics. Quoted by Weaver, p. 29.

41. John Bird Sumner, *Evidence of Christianity derived from its Nature and Reception* (London: J. Hatchard and Son, 1824): p. 427.

42. Reprinted in Weaver, p. 62.

43. Quoted in Hill, p. 154.

44. Quoted in George Levine, *Darwin and the Novelists* (Cambridge: Harvard UP, 1988): pp. 24–5.

45. This paragraph paraphrases arguments made by Adrian Desmond and James Moore in *Darwin: The Life of a Tormented Evolutionist* (NY: W. W. Norton, 1991) in their discussion of Herschel's influence on Darwin's thought, especially pages 213–14.

46. *Ibid.*, pp. 184–85.

47. *Ibid.*, quoted on p. 215.

48. *Ibid.*, p. 485.

49. For more detail about the state of British science in the 1830s, see S. S. Schweber, "Scientists as Intellectuals: The Early Victorians" in James Paradis and Thomas Postlewait, eds., *Victorian Science and Victorian Values: Literary Perspectives* (NY: Annals of the New York Academy of Sciences, 1981).

50. This summary of photographic history draws on the second chapter of Beaumont Newhall's standard *The History of Photography*, revised edn. (NY: Museum of Modern Art and Little, Brown and Company, 1988). For a more recent account of photography's many origins, see the second chapter of Geoffrey Batchen's *Burning with Desire: The Conception of Photography* (Cambridge, MA: MIT Press, 1997).

51. See, for example, Jonathan Crary's account of the kaleidoscope, the phenakistiscope, the thaumatrope, and the better-known stereoscope in *Techniques of the Observer* (Cambridge: MIT Press, 1990): pp. 105–18.

52. Quoted in Newhall, p. 20.

53. Buttman, p. 132.

54. Crary, p. 13. See also John Tagg, "The Currency of the Photograph" in Victor Burgin, ed., *Thinking Photography* (London: Macmillan, 1982).

55. Quoted in Newhall, p. 16.

56. Unpublished letter from JFWH to JMC, June 16, 1839, Research Library, The Getty Research Institute, Los Angeles (850858), box 1, folder 12.

57. Original underlining. Unpublished letter from JFWH to JMC, August 18, 1846, Research Library, The Getty Research Institute, Los Angeles (850858), box 1, folder 12.

58. Letter from JMC to JFWH, December 31, 1864, reprinted in Ford, p. 141.

59. This is an example of what Mike Weaver has described as the dominance of analogies in Cameron's work, see Weaver, pp. 26, 37.

Chapter 3: Memsahib

1. There were many currencies in India in the nineteenth century. During the early decades the Company coined its own currency and so "Company rupees" were a fairly stable form of exchange in the Bengal region. Currency exchange was then usually pegged at 10 Company rupees to 1 British pound sterling. Thus, Charles Hay had in total settled approximately 10,000 pounds sterling on Julia Margaret. To put that number in perspective, Thomas Babington Macaulay's salary as Cameron's superior in 1837 was £10,000 per year and it was considered an exorbitant sum. Charles Hay's annual salary until his promotion into Macaulay's old position was more likely to be in the £1,000–2,000 range, judging from Sally Mitchell's estimates of typical Victorian incomes in her book *Daily Life in Victorian England* (Westport, CT: Greenwood Press, 1996): pp. 32–6.

2. This can be inferred from the will of her father, James Pattle, which was probated in July 1846 and bequeathed his fortune to his younger daughters, not out of lack of affection for his elder daughters, he insisted, but because Adeline, Sara, and Julia Margaret had been well provided for by his late brother. Public Record Office PROB 11/2309. Sara and Julia Margaret inherited £100 each to buy mourning rings for their father.

3. Quoted in Weaver, p. 62.

4. Unpublished letter from JMC to JFWH, May 24, 1847, Royal Society, London, HS 5:150.

5. Thomas Pinney, ed., *The Letters of Thomas Babington Macaulay* (Cambridge: Cambridge UP, 1976): vol. 3, p. 92.

6. Quoted in Indira Ghose, ed., *Memsahibs Abroad* (Delhi: Oxford UP, 1998): pp. 185–7.

7. See Margaret MacMillan's *Women of the Raj* (NY: Thames and Hudson, 1988): pp. 142–53 for these and other details about Anglo-Indian households.

8. *Ibid.*, pp. 69, 85–7.

9. Patrick Brantlinger, *Rule of Darkness: British Literature and Imperialism, 1830–1914* (Ithaca: Cornell UP, 1988): pp. 87–90.

10. MacMillan, pp. 8–9.

11. Edward W. Said, *Orientalism* (NY: Vintage Books, 1979): pp. 78–9, 214–15.

12. MacMillan, p. 147.

13. H. G. Keene, *A Servant of 'John Company'* (London: W. Thacker & Co., 1897): p. 80.

14. John Stuart Mill, *Autobiography*, ed. and intro. Jack Stillinger (Boston: Houghton Mifflin Co., 1969): pp. 85–6.

15. Raleigh Trevelyan, *The Golden Oriole* (NY: Simon & Schuster, 1987): pp. 212, 214.

16. Thomas Babington Macaulay, *Selected Writings*, ed. and intro. John Clive and Thomas Pinney (Chicago: U of Chicago P, 1972): pp. xviii–xix.

17. Hermann Kulke and Dietmar Rothermund, *A History of India* (London and NY: Routledge, 1990): p. 257.

18. Trevelyan, p. 217.

19. All the quotations from the "Minute on Indian Education" come from Macaulay's *Selected Writings, op. cit.*, pp. 237–51.
20. Trevelyan, p. 223.
21. See David Kopf, *British Orientalism and the Bengal Renaissance* (Berkeley: U of California P, 1969): pp. 246–7, and Eric Stokes, *The English Utilitarians and India* (London: Oxford UP, 1959): pp. 197–9 for discussions of these debates.
22. Quoted in Stokes, p. 196.
23. Emily Eden, *Miss Eden's Letters*, ed. Violet Dickinson (London: Macmillan & Co., 1919): p. 320.
24. There is occasional debate about Charles Hay Cameron's utilitarian colors, but Leslie Stephen, who ought to have known, described Charles Hay in the *Dictionary of National Biography* at century's end as "a disciple and ultimately the last disciple of Jeremy Bentham." Quoted in Stokes, p. 223. However, as one can see from Macaulay's own early experience criticizing utilitarianism, real people didn't fall easily into these ideological categories. Macaulay agreed with James Mill and David Ricardo on laissez-faire economics and British imperialism, but the Mills, father and son, disagreed with Macaulay on the imposition of the English language in India (Pinney, vol. 3, p. 150). Macaulay, Cameron, and Trevelyan agreed on judging actions and policies according to a utilitarian calculus of consequences, but Trevelyan was a fervent evangelical and neither Macaulay nor Cameron held strong religious views. Charles Hay does not seem to have provoked the same animosity as other utilitarians, however.
25. Pinney, vol. 3, p. 146.
26. Stokes, pp. 224–5.
27. Chandra Richard DeSilva, *Sri Lanka: A History* (NY: Advent Books, 1987): p. 156.
28. Quoted in G. C. Mendis, ed., *The Colebrooke-Cameron Papers* (London: Oxford UP, 1956): vol. 1, p. xlii.
29. Pinney, vol. 3, p. 162.
30. Trevelyan, p. 270.
31. Quoted in James Morris, *Heaven's Command* (San Diego, CA: Harcourt Brace & Company, 1973): p. 101. Original italics. Morris does not give a footnote for his source. For Morris's account of the First Afghan War, see pp. 86–112.
32. William Broadfoot, *The Career of Major George Broadfoot in Afghanistan and the Punjab* (London: John Murray, 1888): p. 103.
33. He was right to be concerned. According to the *DNB*, Lord Ellenborough denied honors to all who served in the Kabul disaster, regardless of their individual valor. Mackenzie was retroactively acknowledged for his service in 1853. *Ibid.*, p. 998.
34. Broadfoot, p. 120.
35. *Ibid.*, p. 199.
36. *Ibid.*, p. 200.
37. *Ibid.*, p. 200.
38. Unpublished letter from JMC to George Broadfoot, September 11, 1843, British Library, Add. 40127.
39. Eden, p. 268. Original underlining.
40. Unpublished letter from JMC to George Broadfoot, September 11, 1843, British Library, Add. 40127.

41. Unpublished letter from CHC to George Broadfoot, December 5, 1844, British Library, Add. 40127.

42. *Ibid.*, original underlining.

43. Unpublished letter from CHC to George Broadfoot, February 9, 1845, British Library, Add. 40127.

44. *Ibid.*

45. Typescript of *My Precious Worthing Journal* by Margaret Hay Cameron, May 1845–May 1847. The current whereabouts of the original manuscript are not known.

46. *Ibid.*

47. Transcript of an unpublished letter from JMC to her daughter Julia, April 7, 1845, Research Library, The Getty Research Institute, Los Angeles (850858), box 1, folder 8.

48. James Morris mentions that the first Irish relief fund came from Calcutta, *op. cit.*, p.160. His description of the Irish famine follows on pages 160–74.

49. J. W. Feakin, ed., *The Ewen Cameron Journal*, July 17, 1860 (Freshwater, Isle of Wight: Julia Margaret Cameron Research Group, 1999): n.p.

50. Unpublished letter from Henry Lord Hardinge to JMC, February 16, 1850, Bodleian Library, Oxford University, MS Eng lett c. 1 ff. 123–4.

51. See Charles Viscount Hardinge, *Viscount Hardinge* (Oxford: Clarendon Press, 1891): p. 166, and unpublished letter from JFWH to JMC, June 28, 1841, Research Library, The Getty Research Institute, Los Angeles (850858), box 1, folder 12. Julia Margaret did pass along to Hardinge a specimen of gun cotton that Herschel had sent to her. Gun cotton was later used in the wet collodion process that Julia Margaret utilized for her photographs (unpublished letter from JMC to JFWH, May 24, 1847, Royal Society, London, HS 5:150).

52. Unpublished letters from the Herschel family to JMC, June 28, 1841, Research Library, The Getty Research Institute, Los Angeles (850858), box 1, folder 12.

53. See Julian Cox's essay "'To . . . startle the eye with wonder & delight': The Photographs of Julia Margaret Cameron" in Cox and Ford, p. 42 and n. 6, p. 73. In one letter from Cameron to Herschel she stated that he had sent her calotypes in 1839, but Herschel's 1841 letter is the first known reference to his sending her samples. See unpublished letter from JMC to JFWH, October 23, [1866], Royal Society, London HS 5:173.

54. Ray Desmond, *Victorian India In Focus: A Selection of Early Photographs from the Collection in the India Office Library and Records* (London: Her Majesty's Stationery Office, 1982): p. 2. In the notes for his book on file at the India Office of the British Library Desmond included documentation of an article in *The Englishman* dated November 1, 1848 announcing the first calotype photographer in Calcutta. MS Eur D1132.

55. Antony Wild, *The East India Company: Trade and Conquest from 1600* (NY: The Lyons Press, 2000): p. 120.

56. In Margaret Hay Cameron's *My Precious Worthing Journal* there are references to the poem in 1845 and to Cameron's translation in 1846, so it seems to have originated around that time.

57. Gottfried Bürger, *Leonora*, trans. Julia Margaret Cameron (London: Longman, Brown, Green, and Longmans, 1847): p. vi. As Amanda Hopkinson also suggests, it is hard to imagine that Julia Margaret would not have seen either Taylor's or Scott's translations, since both had been published in the 1790s and Julia Margaret was an avid reader of Scott's work. See Hopkinson, pp. 45–7, for her perceptive discussion of Cameron's translation.

58. Charles Hay Cameron, *Two Essays On the Sublime and the Beautiful and On Duelling*, privately printed, London, 1835, p. 22.

59. Bürger., p. v.

60. *Ibid.*, p. vii. Also quoted in Hopkinson, p. 46.

61. *Ibid.*, p. vi.

62. *Ibid.*, stanza 65.

63. Reprinted in *The Norton Anthology of English Literature*, gen. ed. M. H. Abrams, 6th edn., vol. 2 (NY: Norton and Co., 1993): p. 387. All quotations from this essay come from this edition.

64. Unpublished letter from JMC to JFWH, May 24, 1847, Royal Society, London, HS 5:150.

65. Gernsheim published an excerpt of a review from *The Art-Union* (February 1847), see Gernsheim, p. 185. The anonymous critic agrees with Cameron's comment in the preface that her translation is perhaps less poetic but more faithful.

66. Charles W. Millard, "Julia Margaret Cameron and Alfred Tennyson's *Idylls of the King,*" *Harvard Library Bulletin* 21:2 (April 1973): p. 200.

67. From a letter to Henry Halford Vaughan, April 5, 1859, published in full in Mike Weaver, *Julia Margaret Cameron 1815–1879* (London: Herbert Press, 1984): p. 152.

68. Transcript of unpublished letter to CHC, August 11, 1848, Research Library, The Getty Research Institute, Los Angeles (850858), box 1, folder 4.

69. Pinney, vol. 3, p. 239.

70. *Ibid.*, p. 204.

71. *Report on Public Meeting Held at Town Hall in Calcutta* (November 24, 1838): pp. 28–9. Tagore was the grandfather of the Indian nationalist Rabindranath Tagore.

72. John Beaumont, "Charles Hay Cameron (1795–1880): Benthamite Jurist," (Freshwater, Isle of Wight: Julia Margaret Cameron Research Group, 2002): p. 18.

73. *A Letter from Sir Edward Ryan and Mr. Charles Hay Cameron to the Honorable The Court of Directors of the East India Company* (London: Eyre and Spottiswode, 1850): p. 9.

Chapter 4: Lion-Hunting in London

1. See John Beaumont, "Charles Hay Cameron (1795–1880): Benthamite Jurist," (Freshwater, Isle of Wight: Julia Margaret Cameron Research Group, 2002): p. 9.

2. Ismeth Raheem and Percy Colin Thomè, *Images of British Ceylon: Nineteenth Century Photography of Sri Lanka* (Singapore: Times Editions, 2000): p. 35. There are many variant spellings for the Sri Lankan place names around the Camerons' estates. I will use the Camerons' spellings for consistency with the quotations from their letters. Thus I use "Rathoongodde," not "Rahatungode" like Raheem and Thomè.

3. Unpublished letter from W. Clerihew to CHC, August 21, 1846, Research Library, The Getty Research Institute, Los Angeles (850858), box 1, folder 4.

4. Unpublished letter from CHC to JMC, November 8, 1850, Research Library, The Getty Research Institute, Los Angeles (850858), box 1, folder 2.

5. Beaumont, *op. cit.*, p. 27. The Camerons did keep up with Charles Henry, though, and he came with the family to dinner at the Tennysons' home on February 23, 1857, presumably while he was in England on some home leave. *ET Journal*, p. 85. This easy social interaction between the family and the illegitimate son is unusual and it is not clear how the Camerons presented him to the Tennysons. The editor of Emily's journals misidentifies Charles Henry as Charles Hay's brother and Anne Thackeray Ritchie once refers to him as Julia Margaret's "step-son," perhaps

inspiring the rumors of Charles Hay's earlier marriage [Anne Thackeray Ritchie, *From Friend to Friend* (NY: E. P. Dutton and Co., 1920): p. 31]. It was not typical for respectable Victorians to acknowledge illegitimate relatives publicly.

6. Winifred Gérin, *Anne Thackeray Ritchie* (Oxford: Oxford UP, 1981): p. 6.

7. Ritchie, p. 4.

8. Unpublished letter from JMC to JHCN, July 31, 1855, Kent County archive, U310, C75, #18.

9. The account of the meeting is quoted by Gernsheim, p. 18. Beaumont discovered that Charles Hay Cameron had met Taylor in England in the 1820s through mutual friends at the Colonial Office. This makes it even less likely that the meeting was entirely accidental, *op. cit.*, p. 19.

10. Unpublished letter from JMC to JFWH, November 1, 1849, Royal Society, London, HS 5: 151.

11. Henry Taylor, *Autobiography of Henry Taylor 1800–1875* (London: Longmans, Green and Co., 1885): vol. 2, p. 49.

12. Unpublished letter from JMC to JFWH, November 15, 1849, Royal Society, London, HS 5:152.

13. Henry Taylor, *Philip Van Artevelde* (Boston: James Monroe Co., 1835), p. xi. Charles Hay Cameron had made similar points about poetry being the most "intellectual" of the arts in his *Essay On the Sublime and the Beautiful*, also published in 1835.

14. Entry for Julia Margaret Cameron in Leslie Stephen and Sidney Lee, eds., *Dictionary of National Biography*. Signed "J.P.S." [Julia Prinsep Stephen] and based on "Personal knowledge." Reprinted in Diane F. Gillespie and Elizabeth Steele, eds., *Julia Duckworth Stephen: Stories for Children, Essays for Adults* (NY: Syracuse UP, 1987): pp. 214–15.

15. Laura Troubridge, *Memories and Reflections* (London: Heinemann, 1925): p. 20.

16. Caroline Dakers, *The Holland Park Circle: Artists and Victorian Society* (New Haven: Yale UP, 1999): pp. 72–80.

17. Wilfred Blunt, '*England's Michelangelo': A Biography of G. F. Watts* (London: Hamish Hamilton, 1975): p. 74.

18. Some women needed reassurance. Watts had to coax his friend Jeanie Nassau Senior into posing for him in the 1850s. Later the first female Inspector of Workhouses and Pauper Schools, Senior was also known among her friends for her luxuriant golden hair, which both Cameron and Watts rhapsodized about in letters to and about her. In assuring Senior that posing for him was quite proper, he begged to borrow only her hair, hand, or elbow; see Dakers, p. 34.

19. William Rothenstein, *Men and Memories* (London: Faber and Faber, 1931): vol. 1, p. 33.

20. See Dakers, pp. 10–11, 31, and figure 14.

21. A. G. C. Liddell, *Notes from the Life of an Ordinary Mortal* (London: John Murray, 1911): p. 253.

22. For an interesting discussion of the two versions of this photograph that makes some of the same points that I do, see the round-table discussion in Julian Cox, ed., *In Focus: Julia Margaret Cameron* (Los Angeles: J. Paul Getty Museum, 1996): pp. 117–20.

23. Mrs. Russell Barrington, *Reminiscences of G. F. Watts* (London: George Allen, 1905): pp. 100–1.

24. Charles L. Eastlake, *Hints on Household Taste* (1868) (NY: Dover Books, 1969): pp. 2–3.

25. William Morris's "Daisy" wallpaper was revealed during the renovations of Julia Margaret Cameron's home, Dimbola, when it was taken over by the Julia Margaret Cameron Trust and opened to the public.

26. Weaver, pp. 18–20. Cameron herself was a member of the Arundel Society, which was devoted to making inexpensive reproductions of European paintings available in England.

27. See William Michael Rossetti, "The Brotherhood in a Nutshell," *The Germ* (1850), reprinted in Derek Stanford, ed., *Pre-Raphaelite Writing* (London: J. M. Dent, 1973): pp. 15–17.

28. Mary S. Watts, *George Frederic Watts* (NY: Hodder and Stoughton, 1912): vol. 1, pp. 91–2.

29. Charles Dickens in *Household Words* (May 1856), reprinted in Stanford, *op. cit.*, p. 29.

30. John Ruskin, letter to *The Times* (May 13, 1851), reprinted in Stanford, *op. cit.*, pp. 32–5.

31. Georgiana Burne-Jones, *Memorials of Edward Burne-Jones* (NY: Macmillan, 1906): p. 159.

32. Quoted in Blunt, *op. cit.*, pp. 82–3.

33. Hill, p. 61.

34. Dakers, p. 28.

35. *Ibid.*, p. 28.

36. Kenneth O. Morgan, ed., *The Oxford History of Britain* (NY: Oxford UP, 1988): p. 521.

37. Blunt, *op. cit.*, pp. 84–7.

38. Mrs. Edward Twisleton, *The Letters of the Honorable Mrs. Edward Twisleton* (London: John Murray, 1928): pp. 303–4. Apparently the Twisletons had been good friends with Henry Halford Vaughan but broke with him and the Pattle sisters over his conduct toward one of Mrs. Twisleton's relatives. She commented in her book that he made an "unworthy marriage." In fact, he married Adeline Jackson, Cameron's niece.

39. Earl of Bessborough, ed., *Lady Charlotte Schreiber: Extracts from Her Journals 1853–1891* (London: John Murray, 1952): pp. 82–7, 107. The details of this short-lived engagement are told in Brian Thompson's *The Disastrous Mrs. Weldon: The Life, Loves, and Lawsuits of a Legendary Victorian* (NY: Broadway Books, 2002): pp. 62–71.

40. Daphne Du Maurier, *The Young George Du Maurier: A Selection of His Letters 1860–67* (NY: Doubleday, 1952): p. 113. Original italics.

41. Her daughter, Laura Troubridge, describes her mother's social life in *Memories and Reflections*, *op. cit.*, p. 10. Other gossip about Alice Prinsep Gurney is cited by George Meredith in C. L. Cline, ed., *The Letters of George Meredith* (Oxford: Oxford UP, 1970): p. 117.

42. For example, see Blunt, *op. cit.*, pp. 77, 80.

43. Hill, p. 50.

44. Kathleen Fitzpatrick, *Lady Henry Somerset* (Boston: Little, Brown, 1923): p. 24.

45. Gordon N. Ray, *The Letters and Private Papers of William Makepeace Thackeray* (Cambridge, Harvard UP, 1945): vol. 2, pp. 525–7.

46. "On a Good-Looking Young Lady," *Punch* 18 (June 8, 1850): pp. 223–4.

47. The account of the Thackeray–Taylor flap, including the quotations, comes from Ray, vol. 2, pp. 694–6.

48. *Ibid.*, vol. 3, p. 73.

49. Du Maurier, p. 119.

50. For example, Catherine Peters, *Thackeray: A Writer's Life*, revised edn. (Stroud: Sutton Publishing, 1999): p. 226.

51. *ET Journal*, p. 21.

52. *ET Journal*, pp. 28–9 and Cecil Y. Lang and Edgar F. Shannon, Jr., eds., *The Letters of Alfred Lord Tennyson* (Cambridge: Harvard UP, 1987): vol. II (1851–1870), p. 37.

53. Unpublished letter from CHC to JMC, November 8, 1850, Research Library, The Getty Research Institute, Los Angeles (850858), box 1, folder 2.

54. John W. Feakins, *The Coffee Estates of Old Ceylon, 1820–1880*, (Freshwater, Isle of Wight: Julia Margaret Cameron Research Group, n.d.).

55. Beaumont, *op. cit.*, p. 19.
56. Unpublished letter from CHC to JMC, December 16, 1850, Research Library, The Getty Research Institute, Los Angeles (850858), box 1, folder 2.
57. Unpublished letter from CHC to JHCN, January 22, 1851, Kent County archive, U310, C76 #2.
58. Unpublished letter from CHC to JMC, January 24, 1851, Research Library, The Getty Research Institute, Los Angeles (850858), box 1, folder 2.
59. Unpublished letter from JMC to JFWH, January 15, 1851, Herschel Family papers #M0133, Harry Ransom Humanities Research Center, University of Texas at Austin.
60. See Asa Briggs, *Victorian People* (Chicago: U of Chicago P, 1972): pp. 35–8.
61. Herbert Read quoted in Stanford, *op. cit.*, p. xxvi.
62. Ralph Nicholson Wornum, "The Exhibition as a Lesson in Taste," *The Crystal Palace Exhibition: Illustrated Catalogue, London 1851* (repr. NY: Dover Books, 1970): p. v.
63. Phyllis Rose, *Parallel Lives* (NY: Alfred A. Knopf, 1983): p. 78. See also Tim Hilton, *John Ruskin: The Early Years, 1819–1859* (New Haven: Yale UP, 1985): pp. 179–80.
64. Unpublished letter from JMC to JHCN, May 16, 1856, Kent County archive, U310, C75, #28.
65. Unpublished letter from JMC to JHCN, July 24, 1858, Kent County archive, U310, C75, #61.
66. Dakers, p. 23.
67. Blunt, p. 74.
68. Fitzpatrick, p. 11.
69. Fitzpatrick, pp. 70–1.
70. Watts, vol. 1, p. 129.
71. Du Maurier, *op. cit.*, pp. 113, 119, 126.
72. *Ibid.*, p. 127.
73. Fitzpatrick, pp. 17–18.
74. *Ibid.*, p. 15.
75. *Ibid.*, p. 36.
76. Alan Gregory, *Lord Somers: Something of the Life and Letters of Arthur, Sixth Baron Somers* (Victoria, Australia: Lord Somers Camp and Power House, 1987): p. 11.
77. Fitzpatrick, pp. 38–9. Original italics and punctuation.
78. *Ibid.*, p. 83.
79. Unpublished letter from JMC to JHCN, July 21, 1856, Kent County archive, U310, C75 #29.
80. Unpublished letter from JMC to JHCN, July 23, 1856, Kent County archive, U310, C75, #31.
81. Unpublished letter from JMC to JHCN, December 17, 1856, Kent County archive, U310, C75, #35. Original punctuation and underlining.
82. Unpublished letter from JMC to JHCN, December 20, 1856, Kent County archive, U310, C75, #36.
83. Watts, vol. 1, pp. 157–8.
84. *Ibid.*, vol. 1, p. 161.
85. James Morris, *Heaven's Command* (San Diego: Harcourt Brace, 1973): p. 223.
86. Unpublished letter from JMC to JHCN, July 31, 1857, Kent County archive, U310, C75, #53.
87. This new evidence and its interpretation is the subject of Joanne Lukitsh's important recent essay "Before 1864: Julia Margaret Cameron's Early Work in Photography" in Cox and Ford. My argument is greatly indebted to her examination of Cameron's early albums, which will also be discussed in more detail in Chapter 5. My thanks to her and Julian Cox for allowing me access to their essays before publication.

88. Roger Taylor and Edward Wakeling, *Lewis Carroll, Photographer: The Princeton University Library Albums* (Princeton: Princeton UP, 2002): pp. 47–50.

89. *Ibid.*, p. 50.

90. Lukitsh in Cox and Ford, pp. 95–8.

91. *Ibid.*, p. 96.

92. The summary of Norman and Cameron's relationship is based on Beaumont, *op. cit.*, pp. 2–5. The excerpt from Norman's autobiography is quoted by Beaumont, p. 3.

93. Unpublished letter from JMC to JHCN, September 29, 1857, Kent County archive, U310, C75, #57. Original underlining and punctuation.

94. Unpublished letter from JMC to JHCN, December 5, 1858, U310, C75, #64. Original underlining.

95. Taylor, *op. cit.*, vol. 2, pp. 251–2.

96. See Jan Marsh and Pamela Gerrish Nunn, *Pre-Raphaelite Women Artists* (London: Thames and Hudson, 1998): p. 72.

97. Reproduced in Joanne Lukitsh, *Julia Margaret Cameron: Her Work and Career* (Rochester: International Museum of Photography at George Eastman House, 1986): p. 45.

98. Gernsheim looks at several examples of Pre-Raphaelite influence on Cameron's photographs in his book; see pp. 77–8. A more detailed analysis of the influence of the Pre-Raphaelites on Cameron and Cameron on the Pre-Raphaelites can be found in Michael Bartram's *The Pre-Raphaelite Camera: Aspects of Victorian Photography* (Boston: Little, Brown and Co., 1985).

99. Lindsay Smith, *Victorian Photography, Painting and Poetry: The Enigma of Visibility in Ruskin, Morris, and the Pre-Raphaelites* (Cambridge: Cambridge UP, 1995): pp. 110–12.

Chapter 5: Idylls of Freshwater

1. J. W. Feakins, "The Ewen Cameron Journal" (Freshwater Bay, Isle of Wight: Julia Margaret Cameron Research Group, n.d.): p. 5.

2. Unpublished letter from JMC to JFWH, March 27, 1860, Royal Society, London, HS 5: 155.

3. Gernsheim, p. 23.

4. *Ibid.*, p. 23.

5. Unpublished letter from JMC to SLO, November 3, 1859, University of London Library, MS 804/1846. Original underlining.

6. *Ibid.*

7. *Ibid.*

8. Unpublished letter from CHC to SLO, October 2, 1859, University of London Library, MS 804/1844.

9. Unpublished letter from JMC to SLO, November 3, 1859, University of London Library, MS 804/1846.

10. Unpublished letter from JMC to JHCN, February 20, 1860, Kent County archive, U310 C75, #75.

11. *Ibid.*

12. Unpublished letter from JMC to JFWH, March 27, 1860, Royal Society, London, HS 5:155.

13. Anne Thackeray Ritchie, *From Friend to Friend* (NY: E. P. Dutton, 1920): pp. 28–9.

14. Unpublished letter from JMC to CHC, May 25, 1860, Heinz Archive & Library, National Portrait Gallery, London.

15. *Ibid.* Original punctuation and underlining.

16. D. P. O'Brien, ed., *The Correspondence of Lord Overstone*, 3 vols. (Cambridge: Cambridge UP, 1971): vol. 2, p. 920.

17. Unpublished letter from Henry Taylor to the Duke of Newcastle, Bodleian Library, Oxford University, MS Eng lett d. 12 (1860–75), f. 17.

18. O'Brien, vol. 3, p. 1045.

19. Feakins, *op. cit.* All of the quotations from Ewen's journal and the descriptions of his life in Ceylon come from this publication.

20. Unpublished letter from JMC to JHCN and CLN, July 18, 1860, Kent County archive, U310, C63, #5.

21. Feakins, *op. cit.*

22. Unpublished letter from CHC to JHCN, November 21, 1860, Kent County archive, U310, C75, #81.

23. Robert Bernard Martin, *Tennyson: The Unquiet Heart* (NY: Oxford UP, 1980): pp. 373–4. See also Hester Thackeray Fuller, *Three Freshwater Friends*, ed. Elizabeth Hutchings (repr. Newport, Isle of Wight: Hunnyhill Publications, 2000): p. 9.

24. Cecil Y. Lang and Edgar F. Shannon, Jr., eds., *The Letters of Alfred Lord Tennyson* (Cambridge: Harvard UP, 1987): vol. 2, p. 220.

25. *ET Journal,* p. 137.

26. *Ibid.*, p. 147.

27. *Ibid.*, pp. 62, 88–9, 142–3.

28. Unpublished letter from JMC to CHC, May 25, 1860, Heinz Archive & Library, National Portrait Gallery, London. Original underlining. Tennyson reportedly came up with that line while observing his grounds at Farringford and later used it in "Guinevere," just published in 1859. See Fuller, *Three Freshwater Friends,* p. 18.

29. H. T. Fuller and Violet Hammersley, eds., *Thackeray's Daughter* (Dublin: 1951): p. 112.

30. Unpublished letter from JMC to CHC, May 25, 1860. Heinz Archive & Library, National Portrait Gallery, London. Original underlining.

31. Gerhard Joseph makes an interesting argument about Tennyson's eyesight and his poetic vision compared to Cameron's "soft-focus" photographic vision in his *Tennyson and the Text: The Weaver's Shuttle* (Cambridge: Cambridge UP, 1992). He argues that both Cameron and Tennyson alternate between an aesthetics of close, clear vision and an aesthetics of far, hazy vision.

32. Unpublished letter from JMC to CHC, May 25, 1860. Heinz Archive & Library, National Portrait Gallery, London. Original underlining.

33. Martin, p. 423.

34. Reprinted in Gernsheim, p. 183.

35. *ET Journal*, p. 55.

36. Unpublished letter from JMC to J. T. Fields, October 22, 1859, Henry E. Huntington Library, San Marino, California, FI 880.

37. Unpublished letter, GFW to Emily Tennyson, October 13, 1858. On microfiche at the Watts Gallery, Guildford, and the Tate Gallery archive, London, vol. XII, fiche 34, G3–4. It is unclear whether this letter was mailed or not. Emily Tennyson voiced her hesitation about the portrait to Thomas Woolner in a letter dated March 23, 1859, *ET Letters*, pp. 132–3.

38. Unpublished letter from William Holman Hunt to JMC, November 22, 1859, Rosenbach Library, Philadelphia.

39. See the entries for Cameron's three youngest sons in the Charterhouse Register 1769–1872. My thanks to the archivist Mrs. Ann Wheeler for clarifying their attendance dates.

40. See Lukitsh in Cox and Ford, pp. 96–8.
41. The transcript of this letter is excerpted in Lang and Shannon, vol. 2, pp. 340–1. The original manuscript is at the Rosenbach Library, Philadelphia.
42. Quoted in Una Taylor, *Guests and Memories* (London: Oxford UP, 1924): p. 221. See also page 201 on Henry Taylor's perception of Tennyson's dual, gendered personality.
43. Tennyson and Swinburne are quoted in Christopher Ricks, *Tennyson* (NY: Macmillan Company, 1972): p. 218. In context, Swinburne's use of the term "bisexual" refers to a doubled sexual identity, not having sexual partners of both sexes. Tennyson himself was not self-conscious about any homoerotic elements in his poetry; by the 1890s, however, the poet's son Hallam was very concerned to omit or overexplain the more ambiguous passages in his father's writings.
44. Hill, p. 111. Cox and Ford's complete catalogue of Cameron's work, however, did not discover any extant print with that inscription on it.
45. Carol Armstrong, *Scenes in a Library: Reading the Photograph in the Book, 1843–1875* (Cambridge, MA: MIT Press, 1998): p. 368. Gerhard Joseph also makes this point in Chapter 4 of his *Tennyson and the Text: The Weaver's Shuttle, op. cit.*
46. Unpublished letter from JMC to GFW, December 3, 1860, Heinz Archive & Library, National Portrait Gallery, London. On microfiche at the Tate Gallery archive and the Watts Gallery, Guildford.
47. Henry Taylor, *The Autobiography of Henry Taylor*, 2 vols. (London: Longmans, Green, and Co., 1885): vol. 2, p. 197.
48. Unpublished letter from GFW to JMC, January 3, 1861. Typescript on microfiche at the Watts Gallery, Guildford, and the Tate Gallery archive.
49. Unpublished letter from JMC to GFW, December 3, 1860, Heinz Archive & Library, National Portrait Gallery, London. Original underlining.
50. H. Taylor, vol. 2, p. 193.
51. Fuller, *Three Freshwater Friends*, p. 36.
52. Brian Hinton, *Immortal Faces: Julia Margaret Cameron on the Isle of Wight* (Newport: Isle of Wight County Press, 1992): p. 2. The date comes from *ET Journal*, p. 151.
53. Hinton, pp. 6–27 *passim*.
54. Unpublished letter from JMC to JHCN, attributed to February 20, 1860, but clearly misdated because Charles Hay was not in England at that time. There are references to March winds and to the Cloughs, who visited Freshwater in March 1861, so I consider that the correct date. Kent County archive, U310 C75, #73.
55. V. C. Scott O'Connor, "Mrs. Cameron, Her Friends, and Her Photographs," *The Century Magazine*, 55:1 (November 1897): p. 9.
56. Unpublished letter from JMC to JHCN, August 11, 1861, Kent County archive, U310 C75, #85.
57. Martin, p. 535.
58. Quoted in Wendell V. Harris, *Arthur Hugh Clough* (NY: Twayne Publishers, Inc., 1970): p. 150.
59. The poem is reprinted in Mike Weaver, *Julia Margaret Cameron 1815–1879* (London: Herbert Press, 1984): p. 154.
60. Francis Turner Palgrave, *The Golden Treasury* (London: Macmillans, 1861).
61. She did photograph his brother William Gifford Palgrave, explorer and author of travel books. Tennyson also seems to have often felt that William was the more interesting of the two brothers; Martin, p. 433.

62. Unpublished letter from Thomas Woolner to JMC, December 30, 1859, Rosenbach Library, Philadelphia.

63. U. Taylor, p. 225.

64. Ritchie, p. 7.

65. Martin, p. 425.

66. H. Taylor, vol. 2, p. 196.

67. *ET Journal*, p. 172.

68. Unpublished letter from JMC to JHCN, [summer 1861], Kent County archive, U310 C75, #84.

69. Unpublished letter from JMC to JHCN, November 7, 1861, Kent County archive, U310 C75, #87.

70. Unpublished letter from CHC to JHCN, December 5, 1861, Kent County archive, U310 C76, #14.

71. Unpublished letter from JMC to JHCN, January 1, 1862, Kent County archive, U310, C75, #88.

72. O'Brien, vol. 3, p. 989.

73. Unpublished letter from JMC to JHCN, January 1, 1862, Kent County archive, U310, C75, #88. Original underlining.

74. Quoted in Fuller, *Three Freshwater Friends*, *op. cit.*, p. 14.

75. Wilfred Ward, *Men and Matters* (London: Longman, Green and Co., 1914): p. 254.

76. H. Taylor, vol. 2, p. 193. Original italics.

Chapter 6: **Domestic Arts**

1. Reprinted in Gernsheim, p. 180.

2. Lukitsh in Cox and Ford, p. 101.

3. Colin Ford, "Rediscovering Mrs. Cameron – and Her First Photograph," *Camera* 5 (May 1979): p. 24.

4. Mike Weaver was probably the first to insist, rightly, on Cameron's financial motives in taking up photography. See his introduction to Weaver, p. 21. Nonetheless, the impression persists that Cameron was a "lady amateur," or hobbyist. In the context of her time, Cameron defined herself as an amateur to differentiate herself from studio portraitists. This will come up again in later chapters.

5. For example, the April 7, 1868 letter from JMC to Henry Cole quoted in Mark Haworth-Booth, *Photography: An Independent Art* (Princeton: Princeton UP, 1997): p. 86. The original is in the National Art Library, Victoria and Albert Museum, Cole correspondence, box 8.

6. A photograph of Ewen in the Herschel Album (presented in November 1864 and updated in September 1867) is titled *My Son Ewen (now far away in Ceylon)*, Ford, p. 122. In the fall of 1865 Ewen left England, Charlie Hay and Henry Herschel Hay were at Charterhouse, and Hardinge had just started Oxford. Unpublished letter from JMC to JFWH, January 28, 1866, Royal Society, London, HS 5:162.

7. William C. Darrah, *Cartes de Visite in Nineteenth-Century Photography* (Gettysburg, VA: William C. Darrah Publishers, 1981): pp. 2–6.

8. Grace Seiberling, with Carolyn Bloore, *Amateurs, Photography, and the Mid-Victorian Imagination* (Chicago: U of Chicago Press, 1986): p. 2.

9. Helmut Gernsheim, *Lewis Carroll: Photographer*, revised edn. (NY: Dover Books, 1969): p. 51. See also Roger Taylor and Edward Wakeling, *Lewis Carroll, Photographer: The Princeton University Library Albums* (Princeton: Princeton UP, 2002): pp. 192, 252.

10. Edgar Yoxall Jones, *Father of Art Photography: O. G. Rejlander, 1813–1875* (Newton Abbot: David and Charles, Ltd., 1973): pp. 8–15.

11. *Ibid.*, pp. 18, 25.

12. *Ibid.*, pp. 31, 34.

13. There is a portrait of a half-clad toddler in both the Signor 1857 Album and the Mia Album, which was once attributed to Dodgson and dated 1859. It is now believed to be a portrait of Henry Herschel Hay Cameron taken in 1854, before Dodgson took up photography, so the photographer is considered unknown. See *Mia Album*, pp. 19, 61, and Lukitsh in Cox and Ford, p. 98.

14. April Watson, "A History from the Heart," in *Mia Album*, p. 21.

15. See, for example, Lukitsh in Cox and Ford, p. 103. April Watson, Colin Ford, and Mike Weaver have also suggested collaborations between Cameron and Rejlander at various points.

16. See Hopkinson, p. 95.

17. P. H. Emerson, "Mrs. Cameron," *Sun Artists* 5 (October 1890) (London: Kegan Paul): p. 35. Gernsheim quotes some of the same passage and dismisses the claim as "pure invention" in Gernsheim, p. 60. Incidentally, Emerson, who loved Cameron's portraits, did not admire this possibly collaborative portrait of Tennyson. Presumably it is the portrait included and reproduced in the Mia Album as cat. 64, *Mia Album*, p. 59.

18. Lukitsh in Cox and Ford, p. 105 and April Watson in *Mia Album*, p. 21.

19. Lindsay Smith, "The Politics of Focus: Feminism and Photography Theory," in Isobel Armstrong, ed., *New Feminist Discourses* (London: Routledge, 1992): pp. 242, 246–7.

20. Watson in *Mia Album*, p. 14.

21. Typescript of *My Precious Worthing Journal* by Margaret Hay Cameron, May 1845–May 1847. The current whereabouts of the original manuscript are not known.

22. Quentin Bell, *Virginia Woolf: A Biography* (NY: Quality Paperback Book Club, 1972): vol. 1, p. 17.

23. Noel Annan, *Leslie Stephen: The Godless Victorian* (NY: Random House, 1984): p. 128.

24. Bell, vol. 1, p. 59.

25. Holman Hunt and Woolner had a pattern of falling in love with the same women. They both proposed to Fanny Waugh, and Holman Hunt married her. Thomas Woolner married Fanny's sister Alice Waugh, and after Fanny's death Holman Hunt married their younger sister Edith. Anne Clark Amor, *William Holman Hunt: The True Pre-Raphaelite* (London: Constable, 1995): pp. 180–1.

26. Quoted in Annan, p. 365.

27. H. A. L. Fisher, *An Unfinished Autobiography* (London: Oxford UP, 1940): p. 12.

28. Joanne Lukitsh, "Album Photographs of Museum Walls: The Mia Album" in *Mia Album*, p. 30.

29. April Watson does suggest that the Mia Album is constructed to retain only "beautiful," happy memories; for example, there are no images of Julia Jackson after her bereavement, see her essay in *Mia Album*, p. 17.

30. Letter from Samuel Lawrence to JMC, August 22, 1863, excerpted in Cecil Y. Lang and Edgar F. Shannon, Jr., eds., *The Letters of Alfred Lord Tennyson* (Cambridge: Harvard UP, 1987): vol. 2, pp. 340–1. The original manuscript is in the Rosenbach Library, Philadelphia.

31. Lukitsh in Cox and Ford, pp. 101–2.

32. Mike Weaver, "Julia Margaret Cameron: The Stamp of Divinity," in Mike Weaver, ed., *British Photography in the Nineteenth Century* (Cambridge, UK: Cambridge UP, 1989): pp. 153–4. See also Lukitsh in Cox and Ford, p. 105.

33. Lukitsh in Cox and Ford, p. 101.

34. *Ibid.*, p. 101–2.

35. Lukitsh, "Album Photographs on Museum Walls: The Mia Album," *op. cit.*, p. 30.

36. In the appendix to his 1975 monograph Gernsheim describes several Cameron albums, including one given to Val Prinsep on his birthday in 1869 and another album given to Maria Jackson
on her birthday in 1872, that have since disappeared. Perhaps they were disassembled and sold
as individual prints, which is what happened to an album Gernsheim described as given to a
young woman named Beta Murray in 1870. Gernsheim, pp. 175–7.

37. Watson in *Mia Album,* p. 14.

38. Cox and Ford, Appendix C. My thanks to Julian Cox for making this appendix available to me
prior to publication.

39. *Ibid.*

40. Taylor and Wakeling, pp. xi, 123.

41. Winifred Gérin, *Anne Thackeray Ritchie* (Oxford: Oxford UP, 1981): p. 140.

42. Quoted in Gérin, p. 145.

43. Hester Ritchie, ed., *Thackeray and His Daughter: Letters and Journals of Anne Thackeray Ritchie*
(NY: Harper, 1924). My thanks to the archivists at Charterhouse and Oxford for helping me to
establish the dates of attendance of Cameron's sons.

44. Unpublished letter from JMC to JFWH, February 26, 1864, Royal Society, London, HS 5:159.

45. *Ibid.*

46. Unpublished letter from JMC to William Michael Rossetti, January 23, 1866, Gernsheim
Collection, Harry Ransom Humanities Research Center, University of Texas at Austin.

47. Joanne Lukitsh, "Julia Margaret Cameron and the 'Ennoblement' of Photographic Portraiture,"
in Kristine Ottesen Garrigan, ed., *Victorian Scandals* (Athens, OH: Ohio UP, 1992): pp. 211, 216.

48. See Juliet Hacking, *Princes of Victorian Bohemia: Photographs by David Wilkie Wynfield*
(London: National Portrait Gallery, 2000): pp. 9–11. Her excellent book also provides side-by-
side illustrations of Cameron's and Wynfield's portraits of Thoby Prinsep, showing the
remarkable similarities.

49. *Ibid.,* p. 29.

50. See unpublished letter from Philip Cunliffe Owen to JHCN, July 15, 1861, Kent County archive,
U310, C103. The women raised over £200.

51. Gernsheim, p. 181. The reference to the hens may be a sly joke too: the albumen that coated the
paper she printed on came from the whites of hen's eggs. See Grant B. Romer's appendix to
Joanne Lukitsh, *Cameron: Her Work and Career* (Rochester, NY: International Museum of
Photography at George Eastman House, 1986): p. 82.

52. Descriptions of Cameron's cameras and techniques come from Gernsheim, pp. 69–74. See
also a more recent and fuller discussion of Cameron's photographic process in Julian Cox's
essay in Cox and Ford. General information about photographic terms and techniques in the
1860s can be found in Gordon Baldwin's *Looking at Photographs: A Guide to Technical Terms*
(Malibu, CA: The J. Paul Getty Museum, 1991).

53. Gernsheim, p. 181.

54. Ford, p. 18. Ford also points out that the fact that Henry Herschel Hay was blind in one eye did
not deter him from becoming a photographer. But neither did it seem to result in photographs
as out-of-focus as his mother's.

55. Hacking, p. 16.

56. Gernsheim, p. 71.

57. Unpublished letter from JMC to JFWH, March 20, [1864], Royal Society, London, HS 5:158.

58. *Ibid.*

59. Lukitsh, *Cameron*, p. 12.

60. *Ibid.*

61. Cox and Ford, Appendix C. Original underlining.

62. Wilfred Blunt, *'England's Michelangelo': A Biography of G. F. Watts* (London: Hamish Hamilton, 1975): p. 104.

63. Quoted in Blunt, p. 105.

64. *Ibid.*

65. Both Ellen Terry quotations are reprinted in Blunt, pp. 105–6.

66. Nina Auerbach, *Ellen Terry: Player in Her Time* (New York: W. W. Norton, 1987): pp. 89–90.

67. Quoted in Blunt, p. 109.

68. Edith Nicholl Ellison, *A Child's Recollections of Tennyson* (NY: E. P. Dutton, 1906): pp. 72–3.

69. Fisher, p. 15.

70. Laura Troubridge, *Memories and Reflections* (London: William Heinemann, 1925): p. 34.

71. *Ibid.*, pp. 33–4.

72. Ann Thwaite, *Emily Tennyson: The Poet's Wife* (London: Faber and Faber, 1996): pp. 389–90. See also *ET Journal*, pp. 197–8.

73. Unpublished pamphlet by R. Derek Wood, "Julia Margaret Cameron's Copyrighted Photographs," May 1996. Available online at Midley's History of Early Photography (http://www.midleykent.fsnet.co.uk). Not all of the photographs that Cameron exhibited in May 1864 were already copyrighted. For example, Cameron did not register any portrait of Watts until June.

74. *Royal Photographic Society exhibit catalogues 1854–64* #10 (1864): pp. 6–10.

75. Hacking, p. 10.

76. These reviews are excerpted and summarized in Lukitsh, *Cameron*, pp. 41–4. For another discussion of Cameron's critical reception, see also Pam Roberts, "Julia Margaret Cameron: A Triumph over Criticism," in Graham Clarke, ed., *The Portrait in Photography* (London: Reaktion Books, 1982).

77. *Illustrated London News* 44 (June 11, 1864): p. 575.

78. *Photographic News* 8 (June 3, 1864): pp. 265–6.

79. *Photographic News* 8 (July 15, 1864): pp. 339–40.

80. Grace Seiberling with Carolyn Bloore, *Amateurs, Photography, and the Mid-Victorian Imagination* (Chicago: U of Chicago P, 1986): pp. 26–7. Newton later reversed his opinion on this subject.

81. *Photographic News* 8 (March 4, 1864): pp. 109–10. The *Reader* review (January 30, 1863) is quoted in the *Photographic News* article and also by Lukitsh in Garrigan.

82. Lukitsh in Garrigan, pp. 208–11.

83. *Ibid.*, pp. 221–5. Interestingly, the reviews single out Cameron's portraits for comment so exclusively that Lukitsh concluded that she only exhibited portraits at this show. However, it is clear from the Royal Photographic Society exhibition catalogue preserved at the National Art Library of the Victoria and Albert Museum that she in fact exhibited five photographs, including at least one allegorical study, *op. cit.*

84. *British Journal of Photography* (July 22, 1864): pp. 260–1.

85. The ways in which debates about photographic "focus" are gendered have been most influentially detailed by Smith, *op. cit.*, pp. 238–62.

86. Reprinted in Gernsheim, p. 181.

87. Information on Cameron's copyright registrations is drawn from R. D. Wood, *op. cit.*

88. See Smith, p. 249.

89. Letter from JMC to JFWH, December 31, 1864, Heinz Archive & Library, National Portrait Gallery, London. Reprinted in Ford, pp. 140–1. Original underlining.

90. Taylor and Wakeling, *Lewis Carroll Photographer* (Princeton: Princeton UP, 2002): pp. 82–3. Original italics.

91. *Ibid*. Original italics. See also Helmut Gernsheim, *Lewis Carroll, Photographer*, p. 60.

92. Una Taylor, *Guests and Memories* (London: Oxford UP, 1924): p. 312.

93. See Carol Armstrong, "From Clementina to Käsebier: The Photographic Attainment of the 'Lady Amateur,'" *October* 91 (Winter 2000): pp. 101–39 for more detail on Cameron and Carroll's photographic "dialogue" and an interesting discussion of gender and amateurism in Victorian photography.

94. Gernsheim, *Lewis Carroll, Photographer*, p. 60.

95. Smith makes the point that Gernsheim was the first important collector and historian of both Cameron and Carroll's work and that he compared the two in highly gendered ways, see pp. 250–3.

96. Ford, frontispiece.

97. *Ibid*., p. 116.

98. The letter is reprinted in Ford, pp. 140–1.

99. Reprinted in *Photographic Journal* 9 (December 15, 1864): pp. 167–8.

100. See, for example, unpublished letter from JFWH to JMC, February 5, 1866, Royal Society, London, HS 5:140.

101. These photograms are reproduced and discussed in Lukitsh in Cox and Ford, pp. 103–4 and also in Joanne Lukitsh, *Julia Margaret Cameron* (London: Phaidon, 2001): pp. 18–19.

102. See Keith I. P. Adamson, "Women in Photography," *Photographic Journal* (April 1985): pp. 156–61 for details about early women photographers.

103. Lukitsh in Cox and Ford, p. 101.

Chapter 7: Muses, Models, and Mothers

1. For an interesting and more detailed description of photography's relationship to the theater in Victorian England see Malcolm R. Daniel, "Darkroom Vs. Greenroom: Victorian Art Photography and Popular Theatrical Entertainment," *Image* 33:1–2, pp. 13–19.

2. Unpublished letter from HHC to CHC, n.d., Research Library, The Getty Research Institute, Los Angeles (850858), box 13, folder 14. The text I quote from is a typed transcript of the original, which Hardinge later speculated was from 1863 or 1864.

3. Blanche Warre Cornish, *Some Family Letters of W. M. Thackeray*, (NY: Houghton Mifflin, 1911): p. 57. Either Warre Cornish got the date wrong for this play or the Thackerays performed it often, because Mary Nassau Senior mentions seeing it performed by Minnie Thackeray and also Julia Hay Cameron in the 1850s. See M. C. M. Simpson, *Many Memories of Many People* (London: Edward Arnold, 1898): pp. 107–8.

4. See Carol MacKay, "'Only Connect': The Multiple Roles of Anne Thackeray Ritchie," *Library Chronicle of the University of Texas at Austin*, n.s. 30 (Austin: University of Texas, 1985): p. 86.

5. Juliet Hacking, *Princes of Victorian Bohemia* (London: National Portrait Gallery, 2000): p. 29. See also Chapter 3 of Caroline Dakers' *The Holland Park Circle: Artists and Victorian Society* (New Haven: Yale UP, 1999).

6. *ET Journal*, p. 257. For more detail about the plays that Cameron put on in Freshwater, including a reproduction of one of her playbills, see Ford's essay in Cox and Ford, pp. 32–5.

7. Unpublished letter from JMC to Hallam Tennyson, March 18, 1872, Tennyson Research Centre, Lincoln.

8. Edith Nicholl Ellison, *A Child's Recollections of Tennyson* (NY: E. P. Dutton, 1906): pp. 76–81.

9. Unpublished letter from JMC to Mrs. Isabel Bateman, December 3, Gernsheim Collection, Harry Ransom Humanities Research Library, University of Texas at Austin.

10. Nina Auerbach, *Ellen Terry: Player in Her Time* (NY: W. W. Norton, 1987): pp. 85–6 and Wilfred Blunt: *'England's Michelangelo': A Biography of G. F Watts* (London: Hamish Hamilton, 1975): pp. 104–5. The theatrical metaphor for the Terry sisters is also Auerbach's.

11. Ellen Terry, *The Story of My Life* (NY: Doubleday, 1907): p. 65.

12. Auerbach, *Ellen Terry*, p. 88.

13. *Ibid.*, p. 93.

14. A. M. W. Stirling, *Life's Little Day* (NY: Dodd, Mead, and Co., 1924): p. 220.

15. Terry, p. 64.

16. Blunt, p. 114.

17. Auerbach, *Ellen Terry*, p. 92.

18. See Cox and Ford, cat. 496–9.

19. Auerbach, *Ellen Terry*, p. 99.

20. *Ibid.*, pp. 116–17.

21. Terry, pp. 83–4.

22. Auerbach, *Ellen Terry*, pp. 140–1.

23. See Daniel, p. 13, and also Gernsheim's critique of Cameron's *Idylls of the King* photographs, pp. 80–1.

24. Daniel, p. 15.

25. Judith R. Walkowitz, *Prostitution and Victorian Society* (NY: Cambridge UP, 1980): p. 19. Walkowitz studied the Contagious Diseases Acts of the 1860s, which were being fought by feminists across the Solent from Cameron in the barracks town of Southampton. Feminists and working-class activists joined forces in protesting that forced physical examinations of prostitutes were likely to target respectable working-class women as well, pp. 109–10.

26. Stephanie Lipscomb, "Sitters' Biographies" in *JMC's Women*, p. 221.

27. Reprinted in Gernsheim, p. 182.

28. Quoted in Nicky Bird, *Tracing Echoes* (Leeds, UK: Wild Pansy Press, 2001): p. 64. Bird's lovely and interesting book revisits and reframes Cameron's work by photographing Dimbola during its renovation and using contemporary models to reconstruct some of Cameron's best-known images. She found and interviewed some of Hillier's descendants. I agree with Philippa Wright's quoted comment in the book that Cameron's work insists on more than usual recognition of her models, p. 62.

29. Hester Ritchie, ed., *Thackeray and His Daughter: Letters and Journals of Anne Thackeray Ritchie* (NY: Harper, 1924): pp. 138–40.

30. Marina Warner, *Alone of All Her Sex: The Myth and the Cult of the Virgin Mary* (NY: Alfred A. Knopf, 1976): p. 177.

31. In her book about the iconography of the Virgin Mary, Marina Warner points out the "muddle of Marys" and the confusion in the Scriptures about the number of women (and their identities) who witnessed parts of the Crucifixion and Resurrection, *op. cit.*, pp. 344–5. In Christian tradition the confusion encourages the identification of "Mary" with all women.

---

32. See Jeannene M. Przyblyski, "Julia Margaret Cameron's Women, Great Men, and Others," *Afterimage* 27:5 (March/April 2000): pp. 7–9.

33. Carol Mavor, *Pleasures Taken: Performances of Sexuality and Loss in Victorian Photographs* (Chapel Hill: Duke UP, 1995): p. 48. On the implications of touch in Cameron's technique, see also Julian Cox's essay in Cox and Ford, p. 53. Cox also points out that Charles Hay Cameron privileged touch as a primary mode of perception in his *Essay On the Sublime and the Beautiful*.

34. Mavor, pp. 24–5. Mavor makes this point specifically about Cameron's androgynous portraits of children but it is applicable to her whole oeuvre.

35. *Annals*, reprinted in Gernsheim, pp. 181, 183.

36. The power dynamic and erotics of the photographer/subject relationship are developed dramatically in Helen Humphrey's novel *Afterimage* (NY: St. Martin's, 2002), a fictionalized account of Cameron's work with maids.

37. Przyblyski, pp. 7–9.

38. See, for example, Nicole Cooley, "Ideology and the Portrait: Recovering the 'Silent Image of Woman' in the Work of Julia Margaret Cameron," *Women's Studies* 24 (1995): p. 370.

39. See Wolf in *JMC's Women*, p. 24.

40. Mavor, pp. 57, 60.

41. Przyblyski makes a similar argument, but only about Cameron and daughter figures, in her insightful review essay on Sylvia Wolf's exhibition of "Julia Margaret Cameron's Women," *op. cit.*

42. Unpublished letter from JMC to SLO, n.d., University of London Library, MS 804/1853.

43. In her discussion of Cameron's Madonna and child images Mavor cites Roland Barthes's use of the metaphor of an umbilical cord from his *Camera Lucida*. See Mavor, p. 54.

44. Przyblyski, pp. 7–9.

45. Alexander William Crawford, Lord Lindsay, *Sketches of the History of Christian Art*, 3 vols. (London: John Murray, 1847): p. xviii.

46. Weaver, p. 26.

47. *Ibid.*, pp. 26, 58.

48. Interestingly, Virginia Woolf wrote that her aunt Caroline Stephen thought that Florence Fisher was very like Cameron. Fisher was an accomplished musician who later married two academics: Leslie Stephen's biographer F. W. Maitland and then Francis Darwin. See Nigel Nicolson and Joanne Trautmann, eds., *The Letters of Virginia Woolf*, vol. 1 (1888–1912) (NY: Harcourt Brace Jovanovich, 1975): p. 34.

49. Weaver, pp. 30–1.

50. Mavor, p. 47.

51. For an interesting discussion of androgyny in Victorian theater see Nina Auerbach's analysis of the staging of *Peter Pan* in *Private Theatricals: The Lives of the Victorians* (Cambridge: Harvard UP, 1990): pp. 48–50.

52. Ann Thwaite, *Emily Tennyson: The Poet's Wife* (London: Faber and Faber, 1996): pp. 420–1.

53. *ET Letters*, pp. 187–8.

54. Blunt, p. 61.

55. Lindsay, pp. xi–xii.

56. Unpublished letter from GFW to JMC, June 21, 1865, Heinz Archive & Library, National Portrait Gallery, London, available online at http://www.npg.org.uk.

57. Unpublished and undated letter from GFW to JMC, Heinz Archive & Library, National Portrait Gallery, London, available online at http://www.npg.org.uk.

58. Julia Fagan King, "Cameron, Watts, Rossetti: The Influence of Photography on Painting," *History of Photography* 10:1 (January–March 1986): p. 21.

59. Reprinted in Gernsheim, p. 181.

60. *British Journal of Photography* 12 (May 19, 1865): pp. 267–8.

61. *Photographic Journal* 9 (February 15, 1865): p. 196.

62. *Photographic Journal* 9 (May 15, 1865): pp. 63–4.

63. *Reader* (March 18, 1865): pp. 320–1.

64. *Photographic News* (June 2, 1865): p. 255.

65. *Illustrated London News* 47 (July 15, 1865): p. 50.

66. *Photographic Journal* (August 15, 1865): p. 126.

67. For summaries of these reviews see Gernsheim, pp. 62–3.

68. Cole may also have been known to Charles Hay Cameron in the 1830s. Both men were friends with George Grote and associated with utilitarian societies then. The biographical information on Cole cited here is drawn from Sir Leslie Stephen and Sidney Lee, eds., *Dictionary of National Biography*, vol. 4 (1917): pp. 724–6, and Elizabeth Bonython, *King Cole: A Picture Portrait of Sir Henry Cole* (London: V & A Publications, 1982).

69. Mark Haworth-Booth, *Photography: An Independent Art – Photographs from the Victoria and Albert Museum* (London: V&A Publications, 1997): pp. 80–1. Haworth-Booth also paraphrases and quotes from Cameron's letters to Cole, which are at the National Art Library in the Victoria and Albert Museum.

70. *Ibid.*, pp. 81, 88.

71. *Ibid.*, p. 86.

72. Bonython, pp. 9–11.

73. Anne Thackeray Ritchie, "A Book of Photographs," originally published in *Pall Mall Gazette* (April 10, 1865): pp. 10–11. The quotations here come from *Toilers and Spinners* (London: Smith, Elder, & Co., 1874): pp. 225–7. Joanne Lukitsh also considers this article closely in her essay "The Thackeray Album: Looking at Julia Margaret Cameron's Gift to Her Friend Annie Thackeray" in Dave Oliphant, ed. and intro., *Gendered Territory: Photographs of Women by Julia Margaret Cameron* (Austin: Harry Ransom Humanities Research Center, University of Texas at Austin, 1996). Thackeray also offered a review of Cameron's work to *The Times* of London, which may or may not be this review that appeared in the *Pall Mall Gazette*; see Thackeray's bound and undated letters to J. Devane of *The Times* at the Gernsheim Collection, Harry Ransom Humanities Research Center, University of Texas at Austin.

74. Joanne Lukitsh, "The Thackeray Album," pp. 33–4. For convenience' sake, like Lukitsh, I will refer to Annie Thackeray by her maiden name; she did not marry Richmond Ritchie until 1877.

75. It is important to note, as Lukitsh does, that all of Cameron's presentation albums were altered after she gave them: most had images added after the original presentation date, but many also had images, or even whole pages, taken out as well. See Lukitsh, "Thackeray Album," p. 50.

76. Cox and Ford, Appendix C.

77. George Smith and Leslie Stephen, eds., *Dictionary of National Biography*, vol. 12 (1882): pp. 224–5.

78. The quotation as well as the figures come from D. P. O'Brien, ed., *The Correspondence of Lord Overstone* (Cambridge: Cambridge UP, 1971): vol. 3, pp. 1273–6.

79. *Ibid.*, vol. 3, pp. 1078–9.

80. Weaver, p. 15.

81. Letter dated May 5, 1865 and published in Roger W. Peattie, ed., *The Selected Letters of William Michael Rossetti* (University Park: Penn State UP, 1990): pp. 134–5.

82. William Allingham, *A Diary 1824–1889*, intro. John Julius Norwich (Middlesex: Penguin Books, 1985): p. 161. Cameron did bring Christina Rossetti examples of her work in June 1866 and invited her to Freshwater to meet Tennyson, but she only called at Little Holland House and later wrote to her brother William that she was "too shy" to meet the laureate. See Antony H. Harrison, ed., *The Letters of Christina Rossetti*, vol. 1: 1843–1873 (Charlottesville: UP of Virginia, 1997): pp. 274–5.

83. Unpublished letter from Dante Gabriel Rossetti to JMC, April 29, 1867, Gernsheim Collection, Harry Ransom Humanities Research Center, University of Texas at Austin.

84. This story is quoted variously in several sources. See, for example, Hopkinson, p. 82.

85. Unpublished letter from JMC to Jane Senior, June 29, 1865, National Museum of Photography, Film, and Television, Bradford, England.

86. Unpublished letters from CLN to SLO, September 2 and 9, 1866, University of London Library MS 804/1848–49.

87. Copyright information comes from R. D. Wood's unpublished essay "Julia Margaret Cameron's Copyrighted Photographs," May 1996. Available online at the Midley History of Early Photography (www.midleykent.fsnet.co.uk).

88. Charles and Frances Brookfield, *Mrs. Brookfield and Her Circle* (NY: Scribners and Sons, 1905): p. 514. Incidentally, Kate Perry got the name and age of the grandchild wrong: in November 1865 Cameron's eldest grandchild was Charlotte Mary Norman, aged five.

89. For more information about Cameron's relationship to Colnaghi's and other agents, see Cox and Ford, Appendix B.

90. Gernsheim, pp. 76–7. See also Sylvia Wolf, "'Mrs. Cameron's Photographs, Priced Catalogue': A Note on her Sales and Process" in *JMC's Women*, pp. 208–18 for more details.

91. The pamphlet survives as "Mrs. Cameron's Photographs," November 1865, in the National Art Library's collection at the Victoria and Albert Museum, #200.B.P.

92. *Illustrated London News* (November 11, 1865): p. 463 and (November 18, 1865): p. 486.

93. Thwaite, pp. 377–8.

94. [Coventry Patmore], "Mrs. Cameron's Photographs," *Macmillan's Magazine* 13 (January 1866): pp. 230–1.

95. Letter from JMC to William Michael Rossetti, January 23, 1866, reprinted in full in Gernsheim, pp. 34–5. Original underlining.

96. Unpublished letter from JMC to JFWH, January 28, 1866, Royal Society, London, HS 5:162. Original underlining.

97. Unpublished letter from JFWH to JMC, February 5, 1866, Royal Society, London, HS 5:163. The transcript of this letter is HS 5:140. Original underlining.

98. Herschel may have been describing *poses plastiques*, which were popular but mildly risqué because the performers were powdered and covered by flesh-colored stockings that gave the illusion of nudity.

99. Unpublished letter from JMC to JFWH, February 18, 1866, Royal Society, London, HS 5:164. Original underlining.

100. Unpublished letter from JMC to Henry Cole, February 21, 1866, National Art Library, Victoria and Albert Museum, Cole correspondence, box 8. Parts of this letter are quoted by Mark Haworth-Booth in *Photography: An Independent Art*, p. 84.

101. *Ibid.*

102. *Ibid*. Julian Cox points out that Cameron's talk of roundness may also refer to her practice of trimming her prints into tondos, see his essay in Cox and Ford, p. 65. Original underlining.
103. *Illustrated London News* (July 15, 1865): p. 50.
104. Emily Tennyson noted Worsley's burial at Freshwater in her diary on May 15 and added: "Mrs. Cameron who has suffered so from being so much in Mr. Worsley's room goes to Town." *ET Journal*, p. 247.
105. The photograph is reproduced in Joanne Lukitsh's *Julia Margaret Cameron* (London: Phaidon, 2001): pp. 52–3. Lukitsh uses the same quotation from Cameron's letter to Cole.
106. See the reproduced priced catalogue in Wolf's "'Mrs. Cameron's Photographs, Priced Catalogue': A Note on Her Sales and Processes" in *JMC's Women*, p. 211.
107. See Cox and Ford, Appendix C.
108. Letter from JFWH to JMC, September 25, 1866, reprinted in Ford, p. 142. Original underlining.
109. Audrey Linkman, *Photographic Portraits* (London: Tauris Parke Books, 1993): pp. 119–22.
110. *Photographic Journal* 9 (June 15, 1864): p. 56.
111. Mavor, pp. 55–7.
112. Orange and Beaumont, p. 16.
113. Quoted in Mavor, p. 35.
114. Quoted in Mavor, p. 28.
115. Auerbach, *Private Theatricals*, p. 100. Auerbach quotes the lines from Tennyson on page 55.
116. *Ibid*., pp. 31–2.
117. Unpublished letter from JMC to Anne Thackeray Ritchie, June 17, 1872, Eton College archive.
118. See the very interesting discussion of these photographs in Julian Cox's essay in Cox and Ford, p. 70.
119. Thomas Wentworth Higginson, *Cheerful Yesterdays* (NY: Houghton Mifflin, 1898): pp. 295–6.
120. Gernsheim, pp. 82–4.

Chapter 8: **Kings and Beggars, Heroes and Heroines**

1. My account of Mary Ryan's marriage is adapted from an earlier article I published entitled "Idylls of Real Life," *Victorian Poetry* (special issue on Word and Image) 33:3–4 (autumn–winter 1995): pp. 371–89.
2. Biographical information about Mary Ryan is scarce and contradictory. The most recent research into her life was done by Stephanie Lipscomb in *JMC's Women*, p. 226. Lipscomb discovered that Ryan was born on October 29, 1848 to Irish parents. She says that Cameron employed Mrs. Ryan until the move to the Isle of Wight. Cameron biographer Amanda Hopkinson suggests that Mrs. Ryan tried and failed to reclaim her daughter (Hopkinson, p. 67). See also Cameron's version of the story in footnote 15.

    Ryan's working-class origins remained problematic: in his autobiography Henry Cotton wrote that he married his wife in Freshwater, where she was "staying with" Cameron [Sir Henry Stedman Cotton, *Indian and Home Memories* (London: T. Fisher Unwin, 1911): pp. 54–5]. Their granddaughter, Juliana Hill, wrote to Helmut Gernsheim after the publication of his 1948 book on Cameron to dispute his version of the story. She corrected the name – Gernsheim had called her Kate Shepherd – and insisted that her grandmother was not a beggar girl but the Camerons' "adopted daughter." (Unpublished letters, May 30–November 9, 1951, Gernsheim Collection, Harry Ransom Humanities Research Center, University of Texas at Austin.)

Curiously, there is also some confusion over the identification of Henry Cotton. Ann Thwaite and Panthea Reid, for example, identify him as the son of Cameron's Isle of Wight neighbor, Benjamin Cotton, and brother of "Tiny" Cotton, who married the Captain Speedy who comes up later in the chapter. However, my research confirms that Henry Stedman Cotton was not from this family: he was the son of Joseph John Cotton [see John F. Riddick, *Who Was Who in India* (Westport, CT: Greenwood Press, 1998): p. 85].

3. Both quotes come from Henry Taylor, *Autobiography*, vol. 2 (London: Longmans, Green, and Co., 1885), pp. 186–7.

4. Interestingly, the exhibition catalogue for Cameron's Mia Album, which displays these early Cameron and/or Rejlander photographs, identifies the models as the aristocratic Alderson sisters who were merely posing as servants (*Mia Album,* p. 60). Nonetheless, Mary Ryan is clearly one of the models in plates 73 and 77.

5. The following quotations all come from Gernsheim, pp. 31–2. Gernsheim probably drew the story from the version in Henry Taylor's autobiography, although he may have had other sources that have since disappeared.

6. *ET Letters*, p. 214.

7. Wilfred Ward, *Men and Matters* (London: Longmans, Green & Co, 1914): p. 260.

8. *ET Letters*, p. 255.

9. Reprinted in Una Taylor, *Guests and Memories* (London: Oxford UP, 1924): pp. 215–16.

10. A. G. C. Liddell, *Notes from the Life of an Ordinary Mortal* (London: John Murray, 1911): p. 86.

11. *ET Journal*, p. 265.

12. Troubridge, *Memories and Reflections* (London: William Heinemann, 1925): p. 37.

13. It is not known how Ryan felt about modeling either. As mentioned, Mary Hillier did not particularly enjoy posing and Cyllene Wilson, who was taken into Cameron's household after she was orphaned, allegedly hated sitting for photographs so much that she ran away from the household in 1870 (Gernsheim, p. 193; Ford, pp. 130–1). However, Cameron photographs were often handed down through generations in her models' families.

14. H. Taylor, vol. 2, pp. 187–8.

15. M. D. Conway, "South-Coast Saunterings in England," *Harper's New Monthly Magazine* 40:238 (March 1870): p. 537. Curiously, the author of this article meets Cameron in 1870 and she again retells the story of Mary Ryan and her marriage. In this version, Ryan was an *orphaned* beggar whom Cameron adopted and intended to raise as a daughter. The family's circumstances changed, however, and Ryan was forced to become their maid instead (p. 540). Again, one can only speculate what Ryan herself thought of all this downward and upward mobility. The article's author ends the story by musing that Tennyson should base a poem on this story, though in a sense the story itself comes from a Tennyson poem . . .

16. *The Times* of Ceylon (April 1, 1879), quoted in G. Thomas, "Bogawantalawa, The Final Resting Place of Julia Margaret Cameron," *History of Photography* 5:2 (1981): pp. 103–4.

17. Reprinted in Gernsheim, p. 181.

18. There is some possibility that Cotton and Ryan may have modeled for this 1874 photograph of *King Cophetua and the Beggar Maid*, but I think it unlikely. First, the models don't look like Ryan and Cotton in the 1867 photographs. Second, Cotton and Ryan left England for India after their marriage in 1867 and it seems unlikely that they happened to pose for Cameron in England in 1874. Cotton's autobiography mentions no subsequent sittings for Cameron, and they are

identified as models for no other photographs after 1867. Charles W. Millard states that the models for *King Cophetua and the Beggar Maid* remain unidentified, but cites the possibility that the "beggar maid" was Kate Shepherd, adopted by Cameron as a child ["Julia Margaret Cameron and Tennyson's *Idylls of the King*," *Harvard University Bulletin* XXI, ii (1973): p. 194]. It is difficult to figure out the facts in these overlapping stories, but the confusion is at least partly owing to Cameron's close identification of models and characters.

19. *Percy's Reliques of Ancient Poetry* (Routledge, 1857): p. 93.

20. See Carol Armstrong, "Cupid's Pencil of Light: Julia Margaret Cameron and the Maternalization of Photography," *October* 76 (spring 1996): pp. 115–41 for an interesting discussion of this photograph. It was, of course, William Henry Fox Talbot, the inventor of English photography, who first described photographs as made by "pencils of light," thereby associating them both with nature (the sun) and art (drawing). The term "photograph," perhaps coined by Herschel, also literally means "light-writing."

21. Later on, it was very galling for Cameron that Henry Cotton earned more and rose further in the colonial civil service than her son Hardinge. See the unpublished letter from JMC to SLO, September 15, 1875, University of London Library, MS 804/1864.

22. In contrast to Charles Dodgson, who often used a low viewpoint to distort the bodies of his young female subjects, Cameron's low viewpoint seems sometimes to coincide with the viewpoint of the woman within the text and image. For example, here the camera mimics the beggar girl's view of the king standing above her in both the photograph and the poem.

23. Malcolm R. Daniel makes this point in his article on the influence of theater on Victorian photography, "Darkroom Vs. Greenroom: Victorian Art Photography and Popular Theatrical Entertainment," *Image* (33:1–2): pp. 16–18. See also Julian Cox's description of the photograph in *In Focus: Julia Margaret Cameron* (Los Angeles: The J. Paul Getty Museum, 1996): p. 98.

24. A much more detailed account of Cullwick's role-playing can be found in Chapter 3 of Anne McClintock's *Imperial Leather: Race, Gender, and Sexuality in the Colonial Contest* (NY: Routledge, 1995).

25. Quoted in Gernsheim, p. 36. This may be a garbled version of a story Julia Stephen tells in her entry for Cameron in the *Dictionary of National Biography,* reprinted in Diane F. Gillespie and Elizabeth Steele, eds., *Julia Duckworth Stephen: Stories for Children, Essays for Adults* (NY: Syracuse UP, 1987): pp. 214–15. In Stephen's version, the retort is in response to a valentine from Cameron.

26. Reprinted in Alan and Mary McQueen Simpson, eds. and intro., *I Too Am Here: Selections from the Letters of Jane Welsh Carlyle* (NY: Cambridge UP, 1977): p. 81. Original italics.

27. Clyde Ryals and Kenneth J. Fielding, eds., *The Collected Letters of Thomas and Jane Welsh Carlyle*, vol. 26: 1851 (Durham, NC: Duke UP, 1998): p. 230. Original italics.

28. Thomas Carlyle, "Shooting Niagara – And After?," *Macmillan's Magazine* vol. XVI (August 1867).

29. Thomas Carlyle, *Sartor Resartus and On Heroes and Hero Worship*, intro. W. H. Hudson (London: Everyman's Library, 1965): p. 385.

30. *Ibid.*, p. 239.

31. Quoted in Ford, p. 116.

32. Herschel's diary is on microfilm from the Royal Society, London. N.S. 10744, reel 28.

33. Reprinted in Gernsheim, pp. 182–3.

34. Unpublished letter from JMC to JFWH, April 20, 1867, Royal Society, London, HS 5:166.

35. Quoted in Gernsheim, pp. 190–1.
36. Unpublished letter from JMC to JFWH, March 3, 1868, Royal Society, London, HS 5:168.
37. William Allingham, *A Diary, 1824–1889*, intro. John Julius Norwich (NY: Penguin Books, 1985): pp. 152–3. Original italics.
38. See R. D. Wood, "Julia Margaret Cameron's Copyrighted Photographs," unpublished booklet, May 1996, available online at the Midley History of Early Photography (www.midleykent.fsnet.co.uk).
39. Reprinted in Gernsheim, p. 182.
40. *Ibid.*, p. 189.
41. Lytton Strachey, *Biographical Essays* (NY: Harcourt, Brace & World, n.d.): p. 251.
42. "Fine-Art Gossip," *Athenaeum* (June 22, 1867): p. 827.
43. Phyllis Rose makes this argument in *Parallel Lives: Five Victorian Marriages* (NY: Knopf, 1983): pp. 244–5.
44. One review is quoted at length in Gernsheim, pp. 63–4.
45. This anecdote is mentioned in Sarah Angelina Acland's unpublished autobiography, "Memories in my 81st Year," Bodleian Library, Oxford University, MS. Eng. Misc. d. 14, fol. 46r. My thanks to Julian Cox for forwarding this reference to me.
46. Unpublished letter from John Ruskin to JMC, February 23, 1868, Wilson Centre for Photography. Quoted by Cox in Cox and Ford, p. 75, note 56. Original italics.
47. Gordon S. Haight, ed., *The George Eliot Letters*, vol. V: 1869–73. (New Haven: Yale UP, 1955): p. 133.
48. See a reproduction of "Madame Reiné" in Lukitsh, p. 20. Interestingly, William Makepeace Thackeray wrote in 1846 that his nine-year-old daughter would grow up to be a "man of genius," quoted in Lillian F. Shankman, ed., *Anne Thackeray Ritchie: Journals and Letters* (Columbus: Ohio UP, 1994): pp. ix–x. Virginia Woolf described Anne Thackeray Ritchie as "a writer of genius" in the obituary she wrote; see Winifred Gérin, *Anne Thackeray Ritchie: A Biography* (Oxford: Oxford UP, 1981): p. 276.
49. My account of the Jamaican uprising draws on Bernard Semmel's fascinating *Jamaican Blood and Victorian Conscience* (Boston: Houghton Mifflin & Company, 1962), especially the first two chapters.
50. *Ibid.*, p. 104.
51. Carlyle, *Sartor*, pp. 422–3.
52. Semmel, pp. 122–3. Also quoted in Rose, p. 264.
53. Semmel, p. 114.
54. H. Taylor, vol. 2, pp. 265, 268.
55. Unpublished letter from JMC to JFWH, February 18, 1866, Royal Society, London, HS 5:164.
56. Vincent Quinn and John Prest, eds., *Dear Miss Nightingale: A Selection of Benjamin Jowett's Letters to Florence Nightingale, 1860–1893* (Oxford: Clarendon Press, 1987): p. 138.
57. However, the feminist *Englishwoman's Magazine* advocated the expansion of employment opportunities for women and mentioned Cameron as a role model in an 1867 article recommending that women go into the field of photography. Cited by Pamela Gerrish Nunn in Nicky Bird, *Tracing Echoes* (Leeds, UK: Wild Pansy Press, 2001): p. 10.
58. Rose, p. 265. Leslie Stephen, she notes interestingly, was an exception to this rule. He was more liberal in politics than he was as a husband and father. Stephen was ardently opposed to both Eyre and the Abyssinian War; see Panthea Reid, "Virginia Woolf, Leslie Stephen, Julia Margaret Cameron, and the Prince of Abyssinia: An Inquiry into Certain Colonialist Representations," *Biography* 22:3 (summer 1999): pp. 334–5.

---

59. Quoted in Barbara Charlesworth Gelpi, "King Cophetua and Coventry Patmore," *Victorian Poetry* 34:4 (winter 1996): p. 485. My thanks to Barbara Gelpi for sharing her article with me.

60. Ann Thwaite, *Emily Tennyson: The Poet's Wife* (London: Faber and Faber, 1996): epigraph and p. 1.

61. Unpublished letter from Charles Darwin to Joseph Hooker, August 17, 1868, Cambridge University Library.

62. Allingham, pp. 184–5.

63. The Amharic names of Alámayou, his attendant, and his father are variously transcribed into English, so for convenience' sake I have followed Cameron's spellings.

64. Reid, pp. 324–32.

65. *ET Journal*, pp. 278–9.

66. The Abyssinian attendant has been called Báshá Félika, but Jeff Rosen was the first to point out that that is the Amharic name for Captain Speedy; see "Cameron's Photographic Double Takes," in Julie F. Codell and Dianne Sachko Macleod, eds., *Orientalism Transposed: The Impact of the Colonies on British Culture* (London: Ashgate, 1998): p. 179. The name of the Abyssinian attendant is unclear, but he has sometimes been called Casa, so I have followed Rosen in using that name.

67. Joanne Lukitsh makes a similar point about sales in her book *Julia Margaret Cameron*, pp. 98–9. R. D. Wood's comprehensive list of Cameron's copyrighted works includes thirteen images of the threesome registered between July 23–29, 1868, yet William Allingham notes in his diary that Cameron photographed Alámayou on August 21 as well, though no additional photographs were copyrighted. This demonstrates how difficult it is to come to general conclusions about Cameron's work solely from her copyrighted photographs, though it is often necessary to speculate. See Allingham, p. 185, *ET Journal*, p. 276, and R. D. Wood, *op. cit.*

68. Rosen, p. 173.

69. Reid reproduces and examines many contemporary illustrations in her article, pp. 323–55.

70. *ET Journal*, p. 278.

71. Reid, p. 336 and Allingham, pp. 184–5.

72. Allingham, pp. 185–6.

73. Reid, pp. 337–8.

74. Unpublished letter from JMC to SLO, n.d., University of London Library MS 804/1853.

75. D. P. O'Brien, *The Correspondence of Lord Overstone*, vol. 3 (Cambridge: Cambridge UP, 1971): p. 1133.

76. Unpublished letter from JMC to SLO, n.d., University of London Library MS 804/1853.

77. Unpublished letter from CHC Jr. to SLO, November 6, 1867, University of London Library, MS 804/1854.

78. Unpublished letter from HHC to SLO, December 30, 1867, University of London Library, MS 804/1855.

79. Allingham, p. 171. Jeff Rosen notes that Allingham puts "I blew the trumpet for it in the Pall Mall" in quotation marks and concludes that it is Annie Thackeray who said it and wrote the article. Thackeray's known review of Cameron's work in the *Pall Mall Gazette* appeared much earlier, in April 1865, so it remains to be determined if she wrote the one that appeared January 29, 1868, but it is possible; see Rosen, p. 177.

80. The reviews are quoted at length in Gernsheim, pp. 65–7.

81. Sylvia Wolf, "'Mrs. Cameron's Photographs, Priced Catalogue': A Note of Her Sales and Process," in *JMC's Women,* pp. 208–18.

82. Curiously, this Daniel Gurney had married Lady Harriet Hay, a relative of Charles Hay Cameron's mother, Lady Margaret Hay. So Cameron had several personal ties to this patron. The Gurneys were a wealthy Quaker family from Norfolk who fell on hard times when the Gurney Bank failed. The family liquidated all of its assets and Alice Prinsep Gurney's daughters, Laura and Rachel, were sent to live with their grandparents, the Prinseps. See Troubridge, p. 5 and *passim.*

83. Unpublished letter from JMC to Henry Cole, April 7, 1868, National Art Library, Victoria and Albert Museum, Cole correspondence, box 8. Marie Spartali was one of the few female artists Cameron is known to have had contact with. Spartali modeled for several Pre-Raphaelite artists but also studied painting with Ford Madox Brown and exhibited her own work in London throughout her life.

84. Cox and Ford, Appendix C.

85. Wolf in *JMC's Women,* pp. 209–11 and footnote 8.

86. Unpublished letter from JMC to Henry Cole, June 12, 1869, National Art Library, Victoria and Albert Museum, Cole correspondence, box 8. In a later letter to Herschel on this subject, Cameron complained of losing the negative of one of her portraits of him and one of *Christabel.* See unpublished letter from JMC to JFWH, February 6, 1870, Royal Society, London, HS 5:170.

87. *Photographic Journal* 14 (May 15, 1869): p. 34.

88. Unpublished letter from JMC to JFWH, February 6, 1870, Royal Society, London, HS 5:170.

89. Transcript of an unpublished letter from JMC to HHC, October 19, 1871, Research Library, The Getty Research Institute, Los Angeles (850858), box 1, folder 9.

90. Christof Wegelin, ed., *Tales of Henry James* (NY: W. W. Norton and Co., 1984): p. 249.

91. "Gossip: Photographic Society of Scotland," *Photographic Notes* (15 March 1864): p. 80. Also quoted by Daniel, p. 18. Original italics.

Chapter 9: **The Fall of Camelot**

1. Unpublished letter from JMC, enclosed with correspondence to Sir John Simeon, January 16, 1870, Syracuse University Library, New York.

2. Laura Troubridge, *Memories and Reflections* (London: William Heinemann, 1925): p. 32.

3. Hester Thackeray Fuller and Violet Hammersley, eds., *Thackeray's Daughter: Some Recollections of Anne Thackeray Ritchie* (Dublin: Euphorion Books, 1951): pp. 111, 115.

4. Unpublished letter from JMC to JFWH, February 6, 1870, Royal Society, London, HS 5:170.

5. *Ibid.*

6. Reprinted in Gernsheim, p. 182.

7. Unpublished letter from JMC to Sir William Gregory, October 3, 1872, Special Collections, Robert W. Woodruff Library, Emory University.

8. Sylvia Wolf, "'Mrs. Cameron's Photographs, Priced Catalogue': A Note of Her Sales and Process," in *JMC's Women,* p. 216.

9. Anne Thackeray Ritchie, *From Friend to Friend* (NY: E. P. Dutton, 1920): p. 27.

10. Unpublished letter from JMC to JFWH, February 6, 1870, Royal Society, London, HS 5:170.

11. Transcript of an unpublished letter from JFWH to HHHC, February 16, 1870, Royal Society, London, HS 5:298. The original manuscript is HS 5:317.

12. The last two quotes come from unpublished letters by HHHC to JFWH, the first dated February 18, 1870 and the second undated, Royal Society, London, HS 5:318–19.

13. Ann Thwaite, *Emily Tennyson: The Poet's Wife* (London: Faber and Faber, 1996): p. 495.

14. Quoted in Diane F. Gillespie and Elizabeth Steele, *Julia Duckworth Stephen: Stories for Children, Essays for Adults* (Syracuse, NY: Syracuse UP, 1987): p. 7.

15. See, for example, Cameron's unpublished letter to her sister Maria Jackson, February 6, 1878, Berg Collection, New York Public Library.

16. According to R. D. Wood's study of Cameron's copyright lists and output, Cameron registered between fifty-eight and 109 photographs for copyright annually during the productive years 1864 to 1868. In 1869 her annual registrations drop off dramatically to just sixteen photographs and they remain under thirty per year through 1875; see R. D. Wood, *op. cit.*

17. *ET Letters*, p. 265.

18. *Ibid.*, p. 251.

19. See Emily Tennyson's letter on February 21, 1871 to Hallam praising the renovations in *ET Letters*, p. 268. Cameron's letter to Hardinge, with the enclosed accounts, is reprinted in Weaver, pp. 63–7. The originals are in the Getty Research Institute.

20. Unpublished letter from JMC to Jane Senior, March 10, 1874, National Museum of Photography, Film, and Television, Bradford, England.

21. See letter reprinted in Weaver, p. 66.

22. Transcript of an unpublished letter from JMC to HHC, April 3, 1873, Research Library, The Getty Research Institute, Los Angeles (850858), box 1, folder 9.

23. Reprinted in Weaver, p. 67. Original italics.

24. *Ibid.*, p. 66.

25. Unpublished letter from JMC to "Pinkie" Ritchie, November 21, 1871, Gernsheim Collection, Harry Ransom Humanities Research Center, University of Texas at Austin. Excerpted in Gernsheim, p. 39. Original underlining.

26. The train station at Brockenhurst, New Forest, still contains reproductions of nine Cameron portraits with an inscription that reads: "This gallery of the great men of our age is given for this room by Mrs. Cameron in grateful memory of this being the spot where she first met one of her sons after a long absence of four years in Ceylon," dated November 11, 1871. It was stumbling on this display that Helmut Gernsheim credited with sparking his interest in Cameron and her work. When he first saw them before the Second World War, there were eleven originals still hanging in the waiting room; see Gernsheim, p. 15.

27. Unpublished letter from JMC to James T. and Annie Fields, September 2, 1872, Huntington Library, San Marino.

28. Hopkinson, pp. 151–2.

29. Philippa Wright, "Little Pictures: Julia Margaret Cameron and Small-Format Photography," in Cox and Ford, pp. 81–93 *passim*.

30. Ritchie, p. 27.

31. Presumably the city now called Anuradhapura in northcentral Sri Lanka.

32. Unpublished letter from JMC to Sir William Gregory, October 3, 1872, Special Collections, Robert W. Woodruff Library, Emory University. Original underlining.

33. *Ibid.*

34. Thwaite, p. 495.

35. Unpublished letter from JMC to Sir William Gregory, May 14?, 1873, Special Collections, Robert W. Woodruff Library, Emory University.

36. Unpublished letter from HHHC to CHC Jr., March 10, Research Library, The Getty Research Institute, Los Angeles (850858), box 13, folder 10.

37. Thwaite, p. 495.

38. Unpublished letter from JMC to Sir William Gregory, October 3, 1872, Special Collections, Robert W. Woodruff Library, Emory University.

39. *ET Letters*, p. 300.

40. Transcript of unpublished letter from JMC to HHC, April 3, 1873, Research Library, The Getty Research Institute, Los Angeles (850858), box 1, folder 9.

41. *Ibid*. Original underlining.

42. Unpublished letter from JMC to Sir William Gregory, May 14?, 1873, Special Collections, Robert W. Woodruff Library, Emory University.

43. *Ibid*.

44. Unpublished letter from JMC to Sir William Gregory, January 8, 1873 [1874], Special Collections, Robert W. Woodruff Library, Emory University. This letter includes one of Cameron's four known poems.

45. These visits were chronicled in Julia Norman's surviving appointment diaries, twelve volumes of which were recently discovered at the Centre for Kentish Studies, Kent County archive, U310 F14 (1859–62 and 1864–71). These diaries were unfortunately discovered when this biography was already in production. John Beaumont is the only scholar who has yet read them and I am grateful for his generosity in sharing his findings with me.

46. Unpublished letter from Maria Jackson to Julia Jackson Duckworth, November 17, [1873], University of Sussex Library, Special Collections: Charleston Papers (SxMs 56) Addition 1. Original underlining. My thanks to Panthea Reid and Joy Eldridge for finding this letter and sharing it with me.

47. Quoted in Thwaite, p. 495.

48. Reprinted in Gernsheim, p. 183.

49. My discussion of Cameron's illustrations for the *Idylls of the King* are a revision and expansion on an earlier article: see Victoria C. Olsen, "Idylls of Real Life," *Victorian Poetry* 33:3–4 (autumn–winter 1995): pp. 371–89.

50. Alfred Tennyson, *Idylls of the King*, ed. J. M. Gray (London: Penguin Books, 1983): p. 11. All references to the poem are to this edition.

51. Transcript of unpublished letter from JMC to Sir Edward Ryan, November 29, 1874, Gilman Paper Company archive. Original underlining. Quoted in Gernsheim, p. 42, and reprinted pp. 45–6.

52. *Ibid*.

53. The poem is printed in full in Gernsheim, p. 48.

54. Robert Bernard Martin, *Tennyson: The Unquiet Heart* (Oxford: Oxford UP, 1980): p. 415.

55. Wilfred Blunt, '*England's Michelangelo': A Biography of George Frederic Watts* (London: Hamish Hamilton, 1975): p. 79.

56. Gernsheim, p. 48. Ann Thwaite suggests otherwise in her biography of Emily Tennyson, p. 507.

57. Transcript of an unpublished letter from JMC to Edward Ryan, December 12, 1874. Gilman Paper Company archive. Reprinted in Gernsheim, pp. 47–8.

58. Transcript of an unpublished letter from JMC to Edward Ryan, December 4, 1874, Gilman Paper Company archive, quoted in Gernsheim, p. 43. Tennyson's comment reflects the lines he wrote

into Arthur's scene with Guinevere: "To reverence the King, as if he were/their conscience, and their conscience as their King" ("Guinevere," ll. 465–6).

59. Transcripts of unpublished letters from JMC to Sir Edward Ryan, November 29, December 4, and December 6, 1874, Gilman Paper Company archive.

60. Cameron asks Ryan coyly if he can guess the character Charles Hay plays in her *Idylls*: "you ought to know his tendency!" Unpublished letter from JMC to Edward Ryan, November 29, 1874, Gilman Paper Company archive. There were such rumors about Tennyson as well, which Woolf drew on in her play *Freshwater*.

61. Unless otherwise specified, most of the factual details about Cameron's *Idylls of the King* come from Charles W. Millard's careful comparative study of the extant volumes in "Julia Margaret Cameron and Tennyson's *Idylls of the King*," *Harvard Library Bulletin*, 21:2 (April 1973): pp. 187–201.

62. This story is retold in Gernsheim, p. 45, among other places.

63. Transcript of an unpublished letter from JMC to Edward Ryan, December 4, 1874, Gilman Paper Company archive. Quoted in Gernsheim, p. 45. Debra N. Mancoff follows Gernsheim in referring to Lord Lindsay, but based on the transcript of the manuscript I believe Cameron was referring to Colonel Loyd Lindsay instead. See Debra N. Mancoff, "Legend 'From Life': Cameron's Illustrations to Tennyson's 'Idylls of the King'" in *JMC's Women*, p. 99. However, Loyd Lindsay's widow wrote that Cameron believed her husband to be the ideal type of King Arthur, see Harriet S. Wantage, *Lord Wantage: A Memoir* (London: Smith Elder, 1907): p. 132.

64. The identifications of models in copyright registration come from R. D. Wood's unpublished catalogue of Cameron's copyrighted photographs, *op. cit.*

65. The identifications of Lancelot, Vivien, and Guinevere are drawn from Stephanie Lipscomb's research, "Sitters' Biographies," in *JMC's Women*, p. 219. Henry Taylor's daughter mentions in a memoir that the village carpenter modeled for Lancelot; see Una Taylor, *Guests and Memories* (London: Oxford UP, 1924): p. 215. Carol Armstrong argues that the Pale Nun and the third image of Guinevere with the Little Novice are both modeled by Mary Hillier. While Hillier did pose as the Pale Nun, I do not believe that she modeled for the third Guinevere. Although it is not specifically confirmed in the copyright registration records, I believe that "Mrs. Hardinge" modeled for all the Guinevere photographs in the *Idylls*. See Carol Armstrong, *Scenes in a Library: Reading the Photograph in the Book, 1843–1875* (Cambridge: The MIT Press, 1998): p. 407.

66. The identification and biographical information about Agnes Mangles are found in Stephanie Lipscomb's essay in *JMC's Women*, p. 224. This Agnes Mangles was probably the much-younger sister of Tennyson's neighbor and friend at Aldworth, James Henry Mangles [Earl A. Knies, ed. and intro., *Tennyson at Aldworth: The Diary of James Henry Mangles* (Athens: Ohio UP, 1984): p. 33]. James Henry and Agnes Mangles seem also to have been nephew and niece of Ross Donnelly Mangles, a member of the Bengal judiciary when the Camerons lived in Calcutta and later a director of the East India Company. Charles Norman married Emily Mangles, probably a daughter of Ross Donnelly, as his second wife in 1878.

67. "A Reminiscence by a Lady Amateur," *Photographic News* (January 1, 1886): p. 3.

68. *Ibid.*, p. 2.

69. Jerome Hamilton Buckley, *Tennyson: The Growth of a Poet* (Cambridge: Harvard UP, 1960): pp. 172–3.

70. Armstrong, p. 371. I am greatly indebted to Armstrong's reading of Cameron's *Idylls*, though my evidence for supporting some of her arguments tends to be more biographical and I am also elaborating an argument I made earlier in "Idylls of Real Life," *op. cit.*

71. Armstrong, pp. 373, 382. Jennifer Pearson Yamashiro makes a similar argument in "Idylls in Conflict: Victorian Representations of Gender in Julia Margaret Cameron's Illustrations of Tennyson's 'Idylls of the King'," in Dave Oliphant, ed., *Gendered Territory: Photographs of Women by Julia Margaret Cameron* (Austin: Harry Ransom Humanities Research Center, University of Texas at Austin, 1996): p. 99 and *passim.*

72. *Ibid.*, p. 392. See also pages 365–9 for Armstrong's argument about Cameron's use of hand-writing, signature, and excerpt to take over Tennyson's text.

73. Mancoff in *JMC's Women, op. cit.*, p. 96 and footnote 29.

74. Armstrong also makes the point that Vivien is identified with Cameron but uses different evi-dence – the stillness cast by Vivien's spell resembles the stillness enforced by Victorian posing, *op. cit.*, pp. 392–3. I agree but find the "moving hands" also evocative of Cameron's "blurry" pho-tographic style and also her artist's "handiwork."

75. Armstrong, pp. 395–400. Armstrong also aptly notes the sexual connotations of the empty shield cover.

76. Quoted in Millard, p. 192. The original anecdote is in V. C. Scott O'Connor, "Mrs. Cameron, Her Friends, and Her Photographs," *Century Magazine* 55:1 (November 1897): p. 9.

77. This point is also made by Joanne Lukitsh in "Julia Margaret Cameron's Photographic Illustrations to Alfred Tennyson's *The Idylls of the King*" in Thelma S. Fenster, ed. and intro., *Arthurian Women: A Casebook* (NY: Garland Publishing, 1996): p. 258.

78. Unpublished letter from JMC to Sir William Gregory, January 8, 1873 [1874], Special Collections, Robert W. Woodruff Library, Emory University. Original underlining.

79. Transcript of an unpublished letter from JMC to Sir Edward Ryan, December 6, 1874, Gilman Paper Company archive. Original underlining.

80. Unpublished letter from CHC Jr. to SLO, December 18, 1874, University of London Library, MS 804/1860.

81. Unpublished letters and telegram between HHHC and CLN, May–July, 1876, Centre for Kentish Studies, Kent County archive, U310 C64A.

82. See unpublished letters from CHC Jr. and HHHC to SLO, January 22 and 28, 1876, University of London Library, MS 804/1867–68. Charles Norman reported the mortgage repaid in full in a letter of May 21, 1878, University of London Library, MS 804/1872.

83. Thwaite, p. 547.

84. In fact, in Malory's version of the story Mordred is King Arthur's illegitimate son. Tennyson rewrote the story to make Guinevere alone the source of the contagious sin that spreads through the knights. See Mark Girouard, *The Return to Camelot: Chivalry and the English Gentleman* (New Haven: Yale UP, 1981): p. 184.

85. See for example, Debra N. Mancoff's essay in *JMC's Women*, p. 40 and *passim.*

86. Girouard, pp. 151–2.

87. Quoted in Girouard, pp. 172–3. See all of his Chapter 11 for more details on the role of chivalry in the public schools.

88. *Ibid.*, pp. 208–9.

89. Robert Buchanan, *The Fleshly School of Poetry and Other Phenomena of the Day* (London: Strahan, 1872): p. 32.

90. Thwaite, p. 538.

91. *Ibid.*, p. 513 and *passim.*

92. It has always been assumed that the photographs for volume two were not made during the same sittings as volume one in the fall of 1874, but rather in the spring of 1875 right before publication in May. Millard notes this, for example, based on the fact that some *Idylls* prints from volume two are dated 1875 (p. 194). But Gernsheim also quotes an October 1874 letter that mentions the portrait of *Maud* that closes volume two (p. 44), so perhaps at least some of the photographs from volume two were among the 200-odd photographs Cameron made and rejected in the fall. Also, it seems difficult to imagine that she could have reconvened all of the earlier models several months later, including some she may have hired and some who may only have visited the Isle of Wight briefly.

93. See Lukitsh, "Julia Margaret Cameron's Photographic Illustrations to Alfred Tennyson's *The Idylls of the King,*" *op. cit.*, p. 258.

94. Quoted in Gernsheim, p. 49, original italics.

95. Gernsheim, p. 44.

96. Transcript of an unpublished letter from JMC to Edward Ryan, December 6, 1874, Gilman Paper Company archive. Interestingly, Cameron also described her model as "lissome," a term closely associated with Vivien in the poem.

97. There is some disagreement about whether the books made money or not; see Mancoff in *JMC's Women*, p. 105, n. 5. I believe that it is unlikely that the project was profitable – for the reasons I suggest – but not impossible.

98. Cameron may have considered other book-illustration projects at this time, because she produced photographs after George Eliot's *Adam Bede*. See Hopkinson, p. 152.

99. Beaumont Newhall, *A History of Photography*, revised edn. (NY: Museum of Modern Art, 1988): p. 251.

100. Helmut Gernsheim, *Incunabula of British Photographic Literature* (London: Solar Press, 1984): p. 7.

101. Gernsheim, pp. 45–7.

102. Transcript of an unpublished letter from JMC to Edward Ryan, November 29, 1874, Gilman Paper Company archive, reprinted in Gernsheim, p. 46.

103. See Armstrong on Cameron's *Idylls* in the context of the Victorian illustrated book market, p. 364. See also my "Idylls of Real Life" article, *op. cit.*

104. Gernsheim, p. 77.

105. Weaver, p. 26.

106. Gernsheim, p. 81; original italics. Curiously, this quotation paraphrases a passage in Coventry Patmore's 1866 review of Cameron's photographs: "We are not sure, indeed, that the singular art with which Mrs. Cameron has often arranged the draperies of her figures does not increase the effect of the 'realistic' air which most of her groups persist in maintaining for themselves, after all has been done to bring them into the pure region of ideality," *Macmillan's* (January 1866): p. 231. I discuss this in more detail in my article "Idylls of Real Life," *op. cit.*

107. Juliet Hacking, *Princes of Victorian Bohemia* (London: National Portrait Gallery, 2000): p. 28. Hacking points out that Wynfield only photographed English artists in costume: Manet, Legros, and American sitters were photographed as themselves; see p. 26. Perhaps foreigners were thought to be always in costume.

108. Malcolm R. Daniel, "Darkroom Vs. Greenroom: Victorian Art Photography and Popular Theatrical Entertainment," *Image* 33:1–2, p. 13.

109. Charles Hay Cameron, *Two Essays On the Sublime and Beautiful and On Duelling* (London: private printing, 1835): p. 31.

110. Quoted in Christopher Ricks, *Tennyson* (NY: Macmillan and Co, 1972): p. 272. Original italics.

111. Something of a trend can perhaps be seen in a recent exhibition of Lewis Carroll's photographs, which brackets the vexed question of his intentions toward his child sitters and concentrates instead on the theatricality of his costume dramas. See Douglas Nickel's catalogue *Dreaming in Pictures* (San Francisco: San Francisco Museum of Modern Art, 2002).

112. Millard, p. 200.

Chapter 10: Eden

1. This account of the departure comes from Anne Thackeray Ritchie, *From Friend to Friend* (NY: E. P. Dutton, 1920): pp. 30–1.

2. Hester Thackeray Fuller and Violet Hammersley, eds., *Thackeray's Daughter* (Dublin: Euphorion Books, 1951): p. 116.

3. Unpublished letter from JMC to JFWH, February 6, 1870, Royal Society, London, HS 5:170.

4. The correspondence between the Cameron family and its lawyers and trustees during the summer of 1875 is in the Isle of Wight County Record Office, JER/CAM. Hardinge Hay Cameron also obtained a mortgage of £2,000 from Julia Duckworth at 6 per cent interest, though it is unclear why he needed capital at this time. Before they left England the Camerons made appointments to their wills dividing their estate between their three youngest sons (since Eugene and Ewen received separate appointments of £3,000 each upon their marriages). Since the Freshwater property appears as a security to Hardinge's loan it seems that the Camerons transferred its deed to Hardinge, who then mortgaged it to Julia Duckworth for some ready cash.

5. Unpublished letter from Ewen Hay Cameron to A. Harbottle Estcourt, June 11, 1875, Isle of Wight County Record Office, JER/CAM.

6. The Tennyson family libraries own several copies of books given by Julia Margaret Cameron or inscribed with her name or her husband's. A copy of Carl von Wotteck's four-volume *General History of the World* (1842) is inscribed "Charles Hay Cameron. Feb. 11th, '44" with a message "A Birthday gift for my loved Papa from his fond little Ewen. Feb. 11th '44." Underneath this on volume 1 is written "A. Tennyson, bought at Cameron's sale." See Nancie Campbell, *Tennyson in Lincoln: A Catalogue of the Collections in the Research Centre* (Lincoln: Tennyson Society, 1971): vol. 1, p. 89.

7. Winifred Gérin, *Anne Thackeray Ritchie* (Oxford: Oxford UP, 1981): p. 266.

8. Unpublished letter from JMC to SLO, September 15, 1875, University of London Library, MS 804/1864.

9. Unpublished letter from JMC to an unnamed recipient, September 6, 1875, Isle of Wight County Record Office, JER/CAM.

10. Laura Troubridge, *Memories and Reflections* (London: William Heinemann, 1925): p. 39.

11. D. P. O'Brien, ed., *The Correspondence of Lord Overstone* (Cambridge, UK: Cambridge UP, 1971): vol. 3, p. 1283.

12. Unpublished letter from JMC to SLO, September 15, 1875, University of London Library, MS 804/1864.

13. Unpublished letter from CHC to SLO, September 17, 1875, University of London Library, MS 804/1865.

14. Sylvia Wolf also makes this point in *JMC's Women,* p. 48.

15. See R. D. Wood's unpublished pamphlet, "Julia Margaret Cameron's Copyrighted Photographs," May 1996, available online at the Midley History of Early Photography (www.midleykent.fsnet.co.uk).

16. Gernsheim, pp. 52–4.

17. Cameron refers to autotypes in letters to Henry Taylor (May 21, 1876, Bodleian Library, Oxford University, MS d. 13, f. 70–87) and to her son Hardinge [August 3, 1876, Research Library, The Getty Research Institute, Los Angeles (850858), box 1, folder 9]. The information on the Autotype Company records comes from Gernsheim, p. 187, n. 75.

18. Gérin, p. 164.

19. Quoted in Gernsheim, p. 51. The original manuscript is in the Tennyson Research Centre, Lincoln.

20. V. C. Scott O'Connor, "Mrs. Cameron's Photographs," *The Century Magazine* 55:1 (November 1897): p. 10. This anecdote may relate to a later stop in Malta.

21. Letter from JMC to Annie Thackeray Ritchie, November 10, [1875], Gernsheim Collection, Harry Ransom Humanities Research Center, University of Texas at Austin, reprinted in Gernsheim, p. 51.

22. *Ibid.*, p. 52.

23. See the unpublished letters from CHC Jr. and HHHC to SLO, January 22 and 28, 1876, University of London Library, MS 804/1867–68.

24. See Leonard Huxley, ed., *The Life and Letters of Sir Joseph Dalton Hooker,* reprint, 2 vols. (NY: Arno Press, 1978): vol. 2, pp. 1–7. Hooker was enthusiastic about what he called "Economic Botany," the cultivation of commercial crops in new locations, and he apparently advised Ceylonese planters to go into rubber as early as 1875.

25. Unpublished letter from JMC to Henry Taylor, May 21, 1876, Bodleian Library, Oxford University, MS d. 13, f. 70–87.

26. Cameron's surviving letters from Ceylon are addressed from St. Regulus, Lindula in 1876 and Kalutara or Cameron's land in 1877.

27. Unpublished letter from JMC to Sir William Gregory, January 8, 1873 [1874], Special Collections, Robert W. Woodruff Library, Emory University.

28. Unpublished letter from JMC to Sir William Gregory, November 22, 1877, Special Collections, Robert W. Woodruff Library, Emory University.

29. See, for example, her unpublished letter to Gregory, February 9, 1876, Special Collections, Robert W. Woodruff Library, Emory University. Gregory also nicknamed Sara Prinsep "the Hen."

30. Quoted in Una Taylor, *Guests and Memories* (London: Oxford UP, 1924): p. 227.

31. Manuscript by JMC, November 20, 1876, Research Library, The Getty Research Institute, Los Angeles (850858), reprinted in Weaver, p. 68.

32. The poem is reprinted in full in Gernsheim, p. 185.

33. See Sylvia Wolf's essay in *JMC's Women,* p. 75.

34. See Nicole Cooley, "Ideology and the Portrait: Recovering the 'Silent Image of Woman' in the Work of Julia Margaret Cameron," *Women's Studies* 24 (1995): p. 380. While I don't agree with Cooley's point about Cameron's passivity in the poem, hers is one of the only critical discussions of Cameron's poetry and it is thought-provoking.

35. Quoted in Una Taylor, p. 228. Interestingly, this comment is made in the context of Cameron's reaction to Henry Taylor's autobiography. It is his friends, and her own, that she is specifically describing.

36. Undated manuscript by JMC, Research Library, The Getty Research Institute, Los Angeles (850858), reprinted in Weaver, p. 68.

37. Unpublished letter from JMC to Sir William Gregory, April 13, 1876, Special Collections, Robert W. Woodruff Library, Emory University.

38. Unpublished letter from JMC to Henry Taylor, May 21, 1876, Bodleian Library, Oxford University, MS d. 13, f. 70–87.

39. See unpublished letter from JMC to Henry Taylor, March 8, 1875, Bodleian Library, Oxford University, MS d. 12, f. 396–9, and Una Taylor, pp. 227–8.

40. Marianne North, *Recollections of a Happy Life*, ed. Mrs. John Addington Symonds, 2 vols. (London: Macmillan, 1892): vol. 1, pp. 314–15.

41. Unpublished letter from JMC to Sir William Gregory, November 26, 1877, Special Collections, Robert W. Woodruff Library, Emory University. In this letter Cameron also notes that she was "not at this time photographing" or else she would have made a portrait of another civil servant friend, James Martin, to send to his mother. Since Cameron spent most of 1878 in England, this suggests that her Ceylonese photographs were most likely made from 1876 to mid-1877.

42. North, p. 315.

43. *Ibid.*, pp. 315–16, 322.

44. The exceptions among art historians studying Cameron's Ceylonese photographs are Marie Czach, Lori Cavagnaro, and especially Joanne Lukitsh. The exhibit called "Julia Margaret Cameron's Women," curated by the Art Institute of Chicago, which toured the Museum of Modern Art in New York and the San Francisco Museum of Modern Art in 1998–99, did not display any of Cameron's Ceylonese photographs.

45. See Cox and Ford, Chapter 8, for a complete list. The Ceylonese landscape photograph that Cameron sent to Gustave Doré with two of her own photographs, mentioned by Gernsheim, was not taken by her as she had not yet moved to Ceylon at the time.

46. Lori Cavagnaro, "Julia Margaret Cameron: Focusing on the Orient," in Dave Oliphant, ed., *Gendered Territory: Photographs of Women by Julia Margaret Cameron* (Austin: Harry Ransom Humanities Research Center, University of Texas at Austin, 1996): p. 140.

47. Cameron exhibited some of her *Idylls of the King* photographs in Philadelphia. One American reviewer, who admittedly did not believe in photography as an art form, condemned them. See "Characteristics of the International Fair," *Atlantic Monthly* 39:231 (January 1877): p. 94.

48. Ray Desmond, *Victorian India in Focus: A Selection of Early Photographs from the Collection in the India Office Library and Records* (London: Her Majesty's Stationery Office, 1982): p. 37 and plate 39, p. 51. When Cameron attended a Photographic Society meeting in person in London on May 15, 1869 to ask for help with her damaged negatives, the meeting concluded with a showing and discussion of a recent album of Indian photographs, probably one of those published by the India Office. *Photographic Journal* 14 (May 15, 1869): pp. 34–5.

49. Cavagnaro, p. 139.

50. For another comparison of Cameron's Ceylonese images to her English work and to colonial photography see Joanne Lukitsh, "'Simply Pictures of Peasants': Artistry, Authorship, and Ideology in Julia Margaret Cameron's Photography in Sri Lanka, 1875–1879," *Yale Journal of Criticism* 9:2 (1996): pp. 290–1.

51. Quoted in Desmond, p. 38.

52. I put these racial terms in quotation marks because I mean them to refer to black-and-white photography and because they are historically contingent terms. I do not know that the

unnamed model in the Ceylonese photograph was considered "black" within her own community or even within Cameron's Anglo-colonial community. Similarly, I can assume that Hillier was "white," but Victorian definitions of race were different to ours: in mid-century English rhetoric the Irish (like Mary Ryan) were considered a different "race." Joanne Lukitsh sketches some of this ambiguous ground too in her comparison of a photograph of Mary Ryan called *The Irish Immigrant* to *Cingalese Girl*. See her article, "'Simply Pictures of Peasants'," pp. 300–5.

53. Lori Cavagnaro also notes that Cameron's Ceylonese photographs break down established categories for understanding her art, especially gender categories, but she concludes that Cameron was forced to abandon or modify her artistic practice in order to accommodate a more ethnographic practice, *op. cit.*, p. 142.

54. Unpublished letter from JMC to William Gregory, April 13, 1876, Special Collections, Robert W. Woodruff Library, Emory University.

55. Unpublished letter from JMC to William Gregory, November 26, 1877, Special Collections, Robert W. Woodruff Library, Emory University. Original underlining.

56. *Ibid.*

57. Ann Thwaite, *Emily Tennyson: The Poet's Wife* (London: Faber and Faber, 1996): p. 521.

58. Unpublished letter from JMC to William Gregory, November 26, 1877, Special Collections, Robert W. Woodruff Library, Emory University. Original underlining.

59. Thwaite, p. 528.

60. Letter from JMC to Emily "Pinkie" Ritchie, April 18, 1878, Gernsheim Collection, Harry Ransom Humanities Research Center, University of Texas at Austin. Reprinted in Gernsheim, pp. 54–5.

61. Troubridge, p. 43.

62. Gérin, pp. 186–7 and Thwaite, p. 521.

63. Gérin, pp. 214–15 and Thwaite, p. 565.

64. Unpublished letter from JMC to Sir William Gregory, May 14, 1873, Special Collections, Robert W. Woodruff Library, Emory University.

65. Unpublished letter from JMC to Maria Jackson, February 6, 1878, Berg Collection, New York Public Library. The letters to Julia Duckworth and Leslie Stephen are in the same collection.

66. Undated letter from JMC to Annie Thackeray Ritchie, Gernsheim Collection, Harry Ransom Humanities Research Center, University of Texas at Austin.

67. Quoted in Fuller and Hammersley, p. 155.

68. See Campbell, vol. 1, p. 138 and William Plomer, ed. and intro., *Kilvert's Diary: Selections from the Diary of Reverend Francis Kilvert* (London: Jonathan Cape, Ltd., 1940): vol. 3, p. 402.

69. *ET Letters,* p. 316, and unpublished letter from JMC to Alfred Tennyson, October 15, 1878, Tennyson Research Centre, Lincoln.

70. The earliest version of this anecdote that I have found is in Ritchie, p. 37.

71. See Gernsheim's excerpts from the *Ceylon Times* and the *Liverpool Mercury*, pp. 56–7.

72. *Photographic News* (March 7, 1879): p. 109.

73. O'Connor, p. 10. In fact, Eugene and Charlie Hay were not present. Hardinge's wife wrote an account to her mother in England of Charles Hay's death on May 12 and she refers only to Hardinge, Henry, Ewen, Topsy, and the maid Ellen Ottingham at the deathbed. She also roughly confirms his last statement, though without the reference to Priam. I also use her dating for the death: Gernsheim states May 4, but Hardinge's wife stated he died four days

before her letter – thus, May 8. See the transcript of an unpublished letter from Catherine McLeod Cameron to her mother, May 12, 1880, Research Library, The Getty Research Institute, Los Angeles (850858), box 14, folder 1.

74. Ismeth Raheem and Percy Colin Thomè, *Images of British Ceylon: Nineteenth Century Photography of Sri Lanka* (Singapore: Times Editions, 2000): p. 38.

75. *ET Letters,* p. 316.

76. Unpublished letter from Emily Tennyson to the Cameron family, March 5, 1879, Rosenbach Library, Philadelphia, EL3/.T312/MS2.

77. See O'Brien, vol. 3, pp. 1308–9 and an unpublished letter from Eugene Hay Cameron to SLO, February 14, 1878, University of London Library, MS 804/1871.

78. Hill, pp. 173–4.

79. Unpublished letter from CHC Jr. to SLO, October 1, 1880, University of London Library, MS 804/1873.

80. Wolf's essay in *JMC's Women,* p. 47. See also cat. nos. 1058 and 1059 in Cox and Ford.

81. See R. D. Wood's unpublished list of Henry Herschel Hay Cameron's copyrighted photographs, available online at the Midley History of Early Photography (www.midleykent.fsnet.co.uk).

82. Helmut Gernsheim, *Lewis Carroll, Photographer* (NY: Dover Books, 1969): p. 82. Woolf suggests going to "Cousin Henry" for a portrait of her sister Vanessa in 1898. See Nigel Nicolson and Joanne Trautman, eds., *The Letters of Virginia Woolf, Vol. 1 1888–1912* (NY: Harcourt Brace Jovanovich, 1975): p. 18.

83. Thwaite, p. 579.

84. Ford in Cox and Ford, p. 32.

85. Troubridge, p. 38.

86. *Ibid.,* p. 35.

Epilogue: "Life Stand Still Here"

1. An early version of this epilogue was given as a talk entitled "Family Fictions: Julia Margaret Cameron and Virginia Woolf." It was part of an exhibit and symposium hosted by Scripps College in October 1996. My thanks to Mary McNaughton for inviting my participation.

2. Virginia Woolf, *Freshwater: A Comedy* (San Diego: Harcourt Brace Jovanovich, 1976): p. 69. All quotations from the play will come from this edition. Unless otherwise stated, the information about the first and only performance of the play by the Bloomsbury group comes from Lucio P. Ruotolo's introduction, pp. v–ix.

3. Natasha Aleksiuk makes this point in "'A Thousand Angles': Photographic Irony in the Work of Julia Margaret Cameron and Virginia Woolf," *Mosaic: A Journal for the Interdisciplinary Study of Literature* 33:2 (June 2000): pp. 125–42.

4. Woolf and Fry, p. 24.

5. Orange and Beaumont, p. 49.

6. Both quotes from Woolf come from Nigel Nicolson and Joanne Trautman, eds., *The Letters of Virginia Woolf, Vol. 1 1888–1912* (NY: Harcourt Brace Jovanovich, 1977): pp. 44, 234.

7. See Noel Annan, "The Intellectual Aristocracy" in J. H. Plumb, ed., *Studies in Social History: A Tribute to George Trevelyan* (London: Longmans, Green and Co., 1955).

8. Val Williams, "Only Connect: Julia Margaret Cameron and Bloomsbury," *Photographic Collector* 4:1 (Spring 1983): p. 42.

9. Angelica Garnett, *Deceived With Kindness: A Bloomsbury Childhood* (San Diego: Harcourt Brace Jovanovich, 1985): p. 12.

10. See Diane F. Gillespie, "'Her Kodak Pointed at His Head': Virginia Woolf and Photography" in Diane F. Gillespie, ed., *The Multiple Muses of Virginia Woolf* (Columbia: U of Missouri P, 1993): p. 114. This letter is also quoted by Williams, p. 40.

11. Woolf and Fry, p. 26.

12. Regina Marler, ed., *Selected Letters of Vanessa Bell* (NY: Pantheon Books, 1993): p. 254.

13. Virginia Woolf, *To the Lighthouse* (San Diego: Harcourt Brace Jovanovich, 1955): p. 241.